Bootstrap French Grammar

Learn French grammar step-by-step with 224 topics and over 4,000 examples

First Edition

Peter Vujanovic

Declan Software Ltd.

Copyright © 2022 by Peter Vujanovic. All rights reserved

Published by Declan Software Ltd., London, United Kingdom.

No part of this publication may be reproduced, stored in a retrieval system, or transmitted in any form or by any means, electronic, mechanical, photocopying, recording, scanning, or otherwise, except as permitted under Section 107 or 108 of the 1976 United States Copyright Act, without either the prior written permission of the Publisher, or authorization through payment of the appropriate per-copy fee. Requests to the Publisher for permission should be addressed to the Permissions Department, Declan Software https://www.declansoftware.com/go/permissions.

Limit of Liability/Disclaimer of Warranty: While the publisher and the author have used their best efforts in preparing this book, they make no representations or warranties with respect to the accuracy or completeness of the contents of this book and specifically disclaim any implied warranties of merchantability or fitness for a particular purpose. No warranty may be created or extended by sales representatives or written sales materials. The advice and strategies contained herein may not be suitable for your situation. You should consult with a professional where appropriate. Neither the publisher nor the author shall be liable for any loss of profit or any other commercial damages, including but not limited to special, incidental, consequential, or other damages.

Declan Software also publishes its books in a variety of electronic formats. Some content that appears in print may not be available in electronic books. For more information about Declan Software products, visit our web site at www.declansoftware.com.

ISBN 978-0-6455314-9-7 (paper)

For my girls

Table of Contents

1. Subject Pronouns and 'to be' - the verb **être** — 1
2. Plural Personal Pronouns - **nous, vous, ils** & **elles** — 3
3. Politeness in French - the pronouns **vous** and **tu** — 5
4. Asking questions using inversion — 7
5. It is, that is, they are - **c'est** & **ce sont** — 9
6. Genders and the definite articles - **le** & **la** — 11
7. In and on - the prepositions **dans** & **sur** — 14
8. Negation, not - **ne pas** — 16
9. Adjectives and gender - masculine and feminine — 18
10. Feminine adjectives - some rules — 21
11. Feminine adjectives - doubling the final consonant — 24
12. The position of adjectives — 26
13. Indefinite articles - **un** & **une** — 30
14. The verb 'to have' - **avoir** — 32
15. Idiomatic expressions with **avoir** — 35
16. Plural nouns — 37
17. The plural definite article - **les** — 39
18. Plural nouns - exceptions — 41
19. Plural adjectives — 44
20. **Vous** and agreement of adjectives — 46
21. **C'est** with adjectives — 48
22. There is & there are - **Il y a** — 50
23. The plural indefinite article - **des** — 52
24. The plural indefinite article **des** with adjectives — 54
25. Using **ce** as a personal pronoun — 56
26. Possession - the particle **de** — 58
27. Contents - **de** — 61
28. To go - the verb **aller** — 64
29. Location and destination ('in' or 'at' and 'to') - the preposition **à** — 66
30. To come - the verb **venir** — 68
31. Provenance (from) - the preposition **de** — 70
32. Questions with nouns - repeating the subject — 72
33. Questions with **est-ce que** — 74
34. Irregular Adjectives — 76
35. Special adjectives - **vieil, bel, nouvel** & **fol** — 79
36. To want - the verb **vouloir** — 81
37. Demonstrative Adjectives - **ce, cet, cette** and **ces** — 83
38. This one here and those ones there - the particles **-ci** and **-là** — 85

Table of contents - continued

39.	Demonstrative Pronouns - this one, that one - **celui, celle, ceux & celles**	87
40.	Who and that - the subject relative pronoun **qui**	89
41.	Who and that - the object relative pronoun **que**	91
42.	Indefinite Relative Pronouns - **ce qui & ce que**	93
43.	To do, to make - the verb **faire**	95
44.	What? - questions with **qu'est-ce que**	98
45.	To see - the verb **voir**	100
46.	Dual-verb constructions - conjugated + infinitive	103
47.	To be able to - the verb **pouvoir**	105
48.	Which - **quel, quelle, quels & quelles**	107
49.	Which one - **lequel, laquelle, lesquels & laquelles**	110
50.	The Possessive Adjectives	112
51.	The Possessive Pronouns	115
52.	The partitive articles - **du, de la & des**	117
53.	Negative partitive - **pas de**	120
54.	Using **pas** without **ne**	123
55.	There is not - **il n'y a pas**	125
56.	Lots of, a little of - **beaucoup de & un peu de**	127
57.	-ER verbs like **aimer**	130
58.	-ER verbs exceptions	133
59.	Verbs with prepositions - **parler à & parler de**	135
60.	The Subject Pronoun **on**	137
61.	The definite article - concepts, topics and issues	139
62.	Object pronouns	142
63.	Negation with object pronouns	145
64.	Reflexive personal pronouns	147
65.	Reflexive verbs	149
66.	Negating reflexive verbs	153
67.	To find and to be located - the verbs **trouver & se trouver**	155
68.	Parts of the body and reflexive verbs	158
69.	Dual-verb sentences with reflexive verbs	160
70.	Indirect object pronouns - 'to' or 'for' someone	162
71.	Another person's body parts	165
72.	Order of pronouns	167
73.	This here and that there - **cela** and **ceci**	169
74.	The demonstrative pronoun **ça**	171
75.	Subject repetition	173
76.	-IR Verbs	175

Table of contents - continued

77.	Irregular **-IR** verbs - Part I	177
78.	Irregular **-IR** verbs - Part II	180
79.	Irregular **-IR** verbs - Part III	183
80.	Irregular **-IR** verbs - Part IV	186
81.	The strange case of **asseoir** & **s'asseoir**	190
82.	To have to or must - the verb **devoir**	193
83.	It is necessary - the impersonal verb **falloir**	195
84.	More impersonal verbs - **rester** & **manquer**	197
85.	Because - **parse que**, **car**, **puisque** & **comme**	199
86.	It turns out - **s'avérer**	201
87.	Regular **-RE** Verbs	202
88.	The many uses of the verb **rendre**	205
89.	The conjunction **que**	208
90.	To say - the irregular verb **dire**	210
91.	Negative pronouns - **rien** & **personne**	213
92.	Negative adverbs - **jamais** & **plus**	216
93.	Negative adjectives - **aucun** & **nul**	219
94.	Neither nor - **ne..ni..ni..**	222
95.	Double negatives	225
96.	Only - the restrictive **ne.. que**	227
97.	Causative construction with **faire**	231
98.	Getting someone to do something	234
99.	Past tense - **Le passé composé**	236
100.	Past participles for regular **-IR** & **-RE** verbs	239
101.	Irregular past participles	243
102.	Must, have to - the verb **devoir**	247
103.	Past participles of **avoir** & **être**	251
104.	Past tense and negation - **le passé composé** with **ne..pas**	253
105.	**Passé composé** - agreement of the past participle	256
106.	**Passé composé**, negation and word order	260
107.	**Passé composé** with **être**	263
108.	**Passé composé** with **être** verbs used transitively	267
109.	**Passé composé** with reflexive verbs	271
110.	The Reflexive Causative - **se faire**	275
111.	To miss -**manquer**	277
112.	Almost - **avoir failli**	279
113.	Past participles as adjectives	281
114.	If, so and yes - **si**	284

Table of contents - continued

115.	Passive voice	286
116.	What is your job? - **Quel est votre travail ?**	290
117.	Present participles as adjectives	292
118.	Immediate past, continuous present and immediate future	295
119.	The two ways to know - **savoir** and **connataire**	298
120.	The various uses of the verb **arriver**	301
121.	The verb **se passer**	304
122.	To take place - **avoir lieu**	306
123.	Verbs + preposition **à** + infinitive	308
124.	Negating the infinitive	311
125.	The verb infinitive as a noun	313
126.	Verb infinitives after certain prepositions	316
127.	Verbs + preposition **de** + infinitive	318
128.	Stressed pronouns - with prepositions and conjunctions	321
129.	Stressed pronouns - for emphasis and abbreviation	325
130.	Stressed pronouns - with **à** and **même**	327
131.	Stressed pronouns - agreement and disagreement	329
132.	Using **pas** without **ne**	331
133.	The position of adverbs	334
134.	Comparison of quantities of nouns - **plus**, **moins** & **autant**	337
135.	Comparison of adjectives and adverbs - **plus**, **moins** & **aussi**	339
136.	Comparisons of 'good' - **meilleur** & **pire**	342
137.	Comparisons of 'well' - **meiux** & **mal**	344
138.	Superlatives	346
139.	The infinitive following adjectives or nouns - using **de** or **à**	348
140.	Idiomatic expressions with **avoir..de**	351
141.	The future tense - **le futur proche**	354
142.	Verbs of perception and the infinitive	356
143.	Verbs of perception and agreement	359
144.	Some, any and a few - **quelques**	361
145.	Common uses of **quelque**	363
146.	Indefinite pronouns with an adjective require **de**	365
147.	Any or unspecified - **n'importe**	367
148.	All of or every - **tout** as an adjective	370
149.	Everything and all of them - **tout** as a noun or pronoun	372
150.	Very or extremely - **tout** as an adverb	375
151.	Own and clean - **propre**	377
152.	The past continuous - **L'imparfait**	379

Table of contents - continued

153.	The irregular **imparfait** of **être**	382
154.	A few irregular **imparfait** conjugations	384
155.	Was going to - **aller** from the **futur proche** in the **imparfait**	386
156.	Talking about the weather	388
157.	The pluperfect - **Le plus-que-parfait**	390
158.	**Concordance des temps - le passé composé**	392
159.	Present participles as adverbal gerunds	395
160.	Present participles of **avoir**, **être** and **savoir**	398
161.	Present participles as adjectives - modifying a noun	400
162.	The days of the week - **Quel jour est-ce ?**	401
163.	Telling the time - **Quelle heure est-il ?**	403
164.	For how long? - durations with **pendant**, **depuis** & **pour**	406
165.	How long does it take?	409
166.	Time ago - **il y a**	411
167.	How long since? - **ça fait combien de temps?**	412
168.	Dates	414
169.	Intervals of time - **du..au** & **de..à**	417
170.	Time with **dans** and **en**	419
171.	**Matin** & **matinée**, **soir** & **soirée**, **jour** & **journée** and **an** & **année**	420
172.	How old are you? - talking about age	423
173.	**Le futur simple**	425
174.	**Le futur simple** - **avoir** and **être**	428
175.	**Le futur simple** - other irregulars	431
176.	**Si** with **le futur simple**	434
177.	When **où** means 'when'	436
178.	More time-related prepositions	438
179.	As soon as and since - **dès que** and **depuis que**	440
180.	The pronoun **y**	442
181.	Expressions using **y**	445
182.	The pronoun **en**	446
183.	Expressions using **en**	450
184.	Of which, about which - the relative pronoun **dont**	452
185.	What - **quoi**	455
186.	Relative pronouns after propositions with **de** - **duquel, de laquelle, desquels** & **desquelles**	457
187.	Relative pronouns after prepositions without **de** - **lequel, laquelle, lesquels** & **lesquelles**	460
188.	Relative pronouns **auquel, auxquels** & **auxquelles**	463
189.	In what way? - **de quelle manière** & **de quelle façon**	466
190.	In the style of or in the manner of - **à la**	468

Table of contents - continued

191.	Because of - **grâce à** & **à cause de**	470
192.	It is about - **il s'agit de**	473
193.	The Imperative	475
194.	The Negative Imperative	479
195.	Irregular Imperatives - **avoir**, **être** & **savoir**	481
196.	The future perfect - **Le futur antérieur**	483
197.	If... then - **Le conditionnel présent**	486
198.	Polite requests and wishes - **Le conditionnel présent** of **vouloir** & **aimer**	488
199.	Could - the conditional **pouvoir**	490
200.	Would have - **Le conditionnel passé**	492
201.	Should, should have - the conditional **devoir**	494
202.	The verb **tenir** and it's many uses	496
203.	The subjunctive mood - **Le subjonctif**	499
204.	Irregular subjunctives - **être** & **avoir**	503
205.	The past subjunctive - **Le passé du subjonctif**	506
206.	More irregular subjunctives - **faire**, **aller** & **pouvoir**	509
207.	Two more irregular subjunctives - **savoir** & **vouloir**	511
208.	So that - the subjunctive conjunctions **pour que** & **afin que**	513
209.	Although - the subjunctive conjunction **bien que** & **quoique**	515
210.	Until - the subjunctive conjunction **jusqu'à ce que**	517
211.	The subjunctive with negated verbs expressing doubt or uncertainty	519
212.	Subjunctive with Negative Pronouns and Indefinite Pronouns	521
213.	To see to it that - the subjunctive with **faire en sorte que**	523
214.	Impersonal subjunctives - **falloir**, **pleuvoir** & **valoir**	524
215.	Whatever, whoever, whenever - the subjunctive with **quoi que**, **qui que** & **où que**	525
216.	Whichever - the subjunctive and indefinite pronoun **quel que**	527
217.	Inverted subjunctive conjunctions	528
218.	Superlative and the subjunctive	529
219.	The subjunctive and the **ne explétif**	531
220.	Subjunctive conjunctions with and without the **ne explétif**	533
221.	Before and after - **avant que** & **après que**	535
222.	To have to - **avoir à**	538
223.	Direct and indirect speech - **il dit que...**	539
224.	Common French Idioms	542

Acknowledgments

I wish to thank a few people for advising on aspects of the book:

- **Aude Vial**, **Aurore Baudin** and **Constance de Crayencour** for proofreading the French and the English translations, as well as for invaluable advice on aspect of the grammar.
- **Alma Chomel** for doing a superb job recording the 4000 French examples for the companion mobile application.

Any errors are, of course, entirely the responsibility of the author.

The book is dedicated to my girls, Tatiana, Ella, and Nelly, who bore with me throughout the many of hours that went into composing this grammar.

Preface

Bootstrap French Grammar is a new way to learn French grammar that focuses heavily on examples. Starting from the very beginning, the idea is progress in small self-contained steps (called 'topics'). Each topic includes a brief explanation of a grammar pattern and then provides lots of examples that illustrate the grammar. Each example includes its English translation, as well as notes highlighting how the example illustrates that topic's grammar. New vocabulary is also explained in the example notes as it is encountered.

And of course, when used in tandem with the mobile application, the audio pronunciation is available for every example.

The *Bootstrap French Grammar* is for English-speaking pupils and students of French at the introductory stage. It assumes zero knowledge of French grammar or vocabulary.

How to use this book with the companion mobile app

This is the companion book to the ***Bootstrap French Grammar*** mobile application. The iOS and Android apps can be downloaded from the app stores using the following QR code links:

The application contains all the same content as this book but with the addition of high-quality native speaker recordings of all examples. So, if you prefer to have the grammar set out in book form but would also like to be able to listen to the example sentences, then the book/app combination is perfect for you.

The book and app are easy to coordinate using QR codes. Just use the app to scan the QR code in the title bar of any topic in the book and the app takes you straight to the app topic where you will find high-quality audio examples matching the examples in that topic of the book.

❖ Subject Pronouns and 'to be' - the verb *être*

The French verb **être** means 'to be'.

Être is its infinitive (or dictionary) form of the verb. But when used in a sentence its form changes — it conjugates. How it conjugates depends who or what is "being" - this is to say, it depends on who or what is the subject of the verb.

Below are the present tense conjugations of **être** with the singular subject pronouns: **je** - 'I', **tu** - 'you', **il** - 'he' and **elle** - 'she'.

- **je suis** - 'I am'
- **tu es** - 'you are'
- **il est** - 'he is'
- **elle est** - 'she is'

So **suis** is the **je** conjugation of the verb **être**. Likewise, **es** is the **tu** conjugation, **est** is the **il** or **elle** conjugation.

The examples below illustrate how the conjugations of the verb **être** are used. And new vocabulary is also introduced.

EXAMPLES:

je suis
I am
💡 être ⇒ (je) suis - 'I am'

tu es
you are
💡 être ⇒ (tu) es - 'you are'

il est
he is
💡 être ⇒ (il) est - 'he is'

elle est
she is
💡 être ⇒ (elle) est - 'she is'

Je suis ici.
I am here.
📖 ici (adv) means 'here'

TOPIC 1 ❖ Subject Pronouns and 'to be' - the verb *être*

Tu es à l'heure.
You are on time.

- à l'heure (adj) means 'on time'

Il est en retard.
He is late.

- en retard (adj) means 'late'

Elle est en avance.
She is early.

- en avance (adj) means 'early'

Je suis loin.
I am far away.

- loin (adj) means 'far away'

Il est proche.
He is close.

- proche (adj) means 'close'

Elle est là-bas.
She is over there.

- là-bas (adv) means 'over there'

Tu es en retard.
You are late.

Je suis d'accord.
I agree. *OR* I am in agreement.

- d'accord means 'agree' or 'in agreement'

Tu es d'accord ?
You are in agreement? *OR* Do you agree?

- We can ask a question in French by just raising the tone at the end of a sentence. This is called a 'declarative question'

Il est où ?
Where is he?

- où means 'where'
- Note that in French there is a space before the question mark

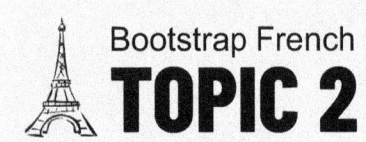 

Bootstrap French
TOPIC 2

❖ Plural Personal Pronouns - *nous, vous, ils & elles*

The plural pronouns ('we', 'you' and 'they') and their **être** conjugations are as follows:
- **nous sommes** - 'we are'
- **vous êtes** - 'you (plural) are'
- **ils sont** - 'they are'
- **elles sont** - 'they (females) are'

Note that French has a special plural 'you' form - **vous** - as in 'y'all', 'you guys'.

And French has both male and female forms of 'they' - **ils** & **elles**.
- When there is a mix of males and females in a group, they are referred to using the male pronoun **ils**.

The examples below illustrate uses of these ponouns and conjugations and introduce new vocabulary.

EXAMPLES:

nous sommes
we are
💡 être ⇒ (nous) sommes - 'we are'

vous êtes
you (plural) are *OR* 'you guys' are
💡 être ⇒ (vous) êtes - 'you (plural) are'

ils sont
they are
💡 être ⇒ (ils) sont - 'they are'

elles sont
they (females) are
💡 être ⇒ (elles) sont - 'they (females) are'

Nous sommes ici.
We are here.

Vous êtes en retard.
You (plural) are late.
💡 Note the sound change vou[s] ⇒ vou[z]. Certain ending consonants are sounded (and may change) if followed by a vowel. This is called **liaison**

TOPIC 2 ❖ Plural Personal Pronouns - *nous, vous, ils & elles*

Ils sont à l'heure.
They are on time.

Elles sont en avance.
They (females) are early.

Nous sommes loin.
We are far away.

Ils sont là-bas.
They are over there.

Elles sont où maintenant ?
Where are they (females) now?

✎ **maintenant** (adv) means 'now'

Maintenant elles sont loin.
Now they (females) are far away.

Vous êtes toujours ici.
You (plural) are always here.

✎ **toujours** (adv) means 'always'

Ils sont souvent en retard.
They are often late.

✎ **souvent** (adv) means 'often'

Bootstrap French
TOPIC 3

❖ Politeness in French - the pronouns *vous* and *tu*

In addition to **vous** being the second person **plural** pronoun ('y'all', 'you guys'), it is also used when addressing someone **politely** or **formally** - someone you have just met, your teacher or your boss etc.

On the other hand, the other singular 'you' pronoun **tu** is used when talking to someone you are **familiar** with - to friends and family etc.

Whether **vous** refers (formally) to a single person or to multiple people ('you guys') can sometimes be ambiguous and the meaning needs to be understood from context.

- Henceforth in the examples 'you' in the English translation will be marked (**formal**) when the singular **vous** in being used, (**plural**) for the plural **vous** and (**familiar**) for **tu**.

EXAMPLES:

Tu es en retard.
You (familiar) are late.
💡 Here is one of many exceptions we will encounter in French - there is no liaison after the **es**.

Tu es où ?
Where are you (familiar)?

Salut Jacques, tu es en avance.
Hi Jacques, you (familiar) are early.
💡 **salut** is a common informal greeting. And farewell.

Bonjour Madame, vous êtes en avance.
Hello Madam, you (formal) are early.
📖 **madam** (f) means 'Mrs' or 'madame'
💡 **madame** is capitalised when addressing her directly

Vous êtes français, Monsieur ?
Are you (formal) French, sir?
📖 **français** (m) means 'French (male)'
📖 **monsieur** (m) means 'Mr' or 'sir'
💡 **monsieur** is capitalised when addressing him directly

Vous êtes où ?
Where are you (formal)?

TOPIC 3 ❖ Politeness in French - the pronouns *vous* and *tu*

Pourquoi vous êtes ici ?
Why are you (formal) here?

🎓 pourquoi (adv) means 'why'

Bon, vous êtes d'accord.
Good, you (formal) agree.

🎓 bon (adj) means 'good'

❖ Asking questions using inversion

Asking questions in French can be straightforward - just use a normal declarative statement with a rising intonation at the end to make it a question.

But when the subject is a pronoun it is more common to form a question by **inversion** - that is by inverting the subject pronoun and verb and joining them with a hyphen.

With inversion question words like **où** ('where') and **pourquoi** ('why') should be moved to the beginning of the sentence.

Note that **suis-je** ('am I') is rarely used.

Note also that liaison is forbidden for inverted pairs. For example **êtes-vous ici** - there is NO liaison **vou[z]** even though the following word **ici** begins with a vowel.

EXAMPLES:

Es-tu proche ?
Are you (familiar) close by?
- tu es ⇒ es-tu - 'are you?'

Où êtes-vous ?
Where are you (formal)?
- vous êtes ⇒ êtes-vous - 'are you?'

Pourquoi est-elle ici ?
Why is she here?
- elle est ⇒ est-elle - 'is she?'

Sont-elles ici maintenant ?
Are they (females) here now?
- elles sont ⇒ sont-elles - 'are they (females)?'

Sommes-nous en retard ?
Are we late?
- nous sommes ⇒ sommes-nous - 'are we?'

Est-elle française ?
Is she French?
- elle est ⇒ est-elle - 'is she?'
- française means 'French (female)'

TOPIC 4 ❖ Asking questions using inversion

Est-il anglais ?
Is he English?
- il est ⇒ est-il - 'is he?'
- anglais (m) means 'English (male)'

Juliette, est-elle vraiment ici ?
Juliette - is she really here?
- elle est ⇒ est-elle - 'is she?'
- vraiment means 'really'

Êtes-vous souvent ici ?
Are you (formal) often here?
- vous êtes ⇒ êtes-vous - 'are you?'

Sont-ils en vacances ?
Are they (males) on holidays?
- ils sont ⇒ sont-ils - 'are they?'
- en vacances means 'on holidays'

Êtes-vous d'accord, Monsieur ?
Do you (formal) agree, Sir? *OR* Are you in agreement, Sir?
- vous êtes ⇒ êtes-vous - 'are you?'

Bootstrap French
TOPIC 5

❖ It is, that is, they are - *c'est* & *ce sont*

The word **ce** means 'that' or 'it'. It can refer to anything - animals, objects or concepts. And can be both singular and plural.

- In short, **ce** is a very general, very useful and very common word in French. There is no exact English equivalent.

Combined with the verb **être** ('to be') we have the very common phrase **c'est** - 'it is' or 'that is'.

- The **est** is the **il** or **elle** conjugation of the verb **être** ('to be').
- And we have the contraction **ce**+**est** ⇒ **c'est**.

- In French, when we have a word ending in a vowel and another starting with a vowel side-by-side, to avoid having two vowel sounds together, we often drop the first vowel and replace it with an apostrophe and join the words together. So **ce**+**est** ⇒ **c'est**.

The plural form of **c'est** is **ce sont** ('these are' or 'those are') which uses the **ils** or **elles** conjugation of **être**.

- However, you will commonly hear people say **c'est** even in situations where the plural **ce sont** should be used.

The inverted question form of **c'est** is **est-ce ?**.

- And while the plural question form **sont-ce ?** is grammatically correct, it is never used.

EXAMPLES:

C'est loin d'ici.
It is far from here.

d'ici means 'from here'
d'ici is a contraction of **de** (from) and **ici** (here)

Non, c'est près d'ici.
No, it is close by.

près means 'close'
près d'ici means 'close by' or 'close from here'

C'est qui ?
It is who? *OR* Who is it?

qui means 'who'

TOPIC 5 ❖ It is, that is, they are - *c'est* & *ce sont*

Qui est-ce ?
Who is it?

Inverted question form: **c'est** ⇒ **est-ce ?** - 'is it?'

C'est Juliette.
It is Juliette.

Est-ce Jacques ?
Is it (that) Jacques?

Oui, c'est Jacques.
Yes, it's Jacques.

oui means 'yes'

Où est-ce ?
Where is it?

C'est là-bas.
It is over there.

C'est ici.
It is here.

C'est magnifique !
It is magnificent!

magnifique (adj) means 'magnificent' or 'wonderful'

Ce sont Jacques et Juliette.
They are Jacques and Juliette.

et means 'and'

Ce sont monsieur et madame Dupont.
This is Mr and Mrs Dupont.

monsieur and **madame** are not capitalized if not directly addressing the person

Bootstrap French
TOPIC 6

❖ Genders and the definite articles - *le* & *la*

All nouns (things and concepts) in French have a gender - either masculine or feminine.

And like the English 'the' - French also uses the **definite article**. But unlike English, the definite article in French depends on gender (and number).

- The definite article **le** is used for masculine nouns.
- And the definite article **la** is used for feminine nouns.

When the noun starts with a vowel, both **le** and **la** contract with an apostrophe to **l'** and the contracted **l'** is attached to the noun.

Note that there are no hard and fast rules governing which nouns are masculine and which are feminine. They just need to be remembered.

EXAMPLES:

Le chien est ici.
The dog is here.
📖 **chien** (m) means 'dog'
💡 **le chien** is masculine

La vache est là-bas.
The cow is over there.
📖 **vache** (f) means 'cow'
💡 **la vache** is feminine

Où est le chat ?
Where is the cat?
📖 **chat** (m) means 'cat'
💡 **le chat** is masculine

La gare est loin d'ici ?
The (train) station far from here?
📖 **gare** (f) means 'station'
💡 **la gare** is feminine

Le bureau est près d'ici.
The office is close to here.
📖 **bureau** (m) means 'office' or 'desk'
💡 **le bureau** is masculine

TOPIC 6 ❖ Genders and the definite articles - *le* & *la*

La poste est assez proche.
The post office is quite close.
- poste (f) means 'post office'
- la poste is feminine
- assez (adv) means 'quite' or 'enough'

Le restaurant est magnifique.
The restaurant is magnificent.
- restaurant (m) means 'restaurant'
- le restaurant is masculine

Le garçon est en retard.
The boy is late.
- garçon (m) means 'boy'
- le garçon is masculine

La fille est à l'heure.
The girl is on time.
- fille (f) means 'girl'
- la fille is feminine

D'où est le monsieur ?
From where is the gentleman?
- monsieur (m) means 'gentleman'
- le monsieur is masculine
- d'où means 'from where'

La madame est d'ici ?
The lady is from here?
- madame (f) means 'lady'
- la madame is feminine

L'oiseau est là-bas.
The bird is over there.
- oiseau (m) means 'bird'
- l'oiseau is masculine
- Contraction when there are two opposing vowels: **le** + **oiseau** ⇒ **l'oiseau**

French Grammar

TOPIC 6 ❖ Genders and the definite articles - *le* & *la*

Est-ce l'université là-bas ?
Is that the university over there?
- **université** (f) means 'university'
- **l'université** is feminine
- Contraction: **la** + **université** ⇒ **l'université**

Non, l'université est ici.
No, the university is here.
- **non** means 'no'

Bootstrap French
TOPIC 7

❖ In and on - the prepositions *dans* & *sur*

Prepositions are words that indicate position or location.

Two of the most useful French prepositions are **dans** and **sur**.
- The preposition **dans** means 'in'.
- The preposition **sur** means 'on'.

Like in English, French propositions appear before the noun (and its article).

EXAMPLES:

Le chien est dans le jardin.
The dog is in the garden.
- jardin (m) means 'garden'
- dans before the noun le jardin

Es-tu dans la maison ?
Are you (familiar) in the house?
- maison (f) means 'house'

Qui est dans la chambre ?
Who is in the room?
- chambre (f) means 'room' or 'bedroom'

Philippe et Jacques sont dans le parc.
Phillippe and Jacques are in the park.
- parc (m) means 'park'

L'oiseau est dans l'arbre.
The bird is in the tree.
- arbre (m) means 'tree'

La vache est dans le champ.
The cow is in the field.
- champ (m) means 'field'

La billetterie - est-elle dans la gare ?
The ticket office - is it in the station?
- billetterie (f) means 'ticket office'

TOPIC 7 ❖ In and on - the prepositions *dans* & *sur*

Est-elle dans le bus ?
Is she is on (in) the bus ?
- bus (m) means 'bus'

Le tablier est sur le crochet.
The apron is on the hook.
- tablier (m) means 'apron'
- crochet (m) means 'hook'
- sur before the noun le crochet

La chaussure est sur la table.
The shoe is on the table.
- chaussure (f) means 'shoe'
- table (f) means 'table'

Sont-ils sur le bateau ?
Are they on the boat?
- bateau (m) means 'boat'

La bougie est sur le gâteau.
The candle is on the cake.
- bougie (f) means 'candle'
- gâteau (m) means 'cake'

La voiture est sur le boulevard.
The car is on the boulevard.
- voiture (f) means 'car'
- boulevard (m) means 'boulevard'

Le vélo est dans la rue.
The bike is on the street.
- vélo (m) means 'bicycle'
- rue (f) means 'street'

Bookstrap

❖ Negation, not - *ne pas*

To negate a statement in French we put **ne** and **pas** either side of the verb.

- As previously, if the word after **ne** begins with a vowel then **ne** contracts to **n'** and is attached to that word.

Note that inverted question forms like **est-ce** remain attached when negated. So we have **n'est-ce pas** - 'isn't it?' with the contraction **n'** and the inverted hyphenated attachment **est-ce**.

EXAMPLES:

Je ne suis pas là.
I am not here/there.
- Negation by putting **ne** & **pas** either side of the verb **suis**
- **là** means 'in some (expected) location'

Le chien n'est pas dans le jardin.
The dog is not in the garden.
- Contraction: **ne** + **est** ⇒ **n'est**

Tu n'es pas proche ?
Are you (familiar) not close by?
- Contraction: **ne** + **es** ⇒ **n'es**

Le monsieur n'est pas en retard.
The gentleman is not late.

N'est-ce pas Jacques là-bas ?
Is that not Jacques over there?
- Hyphenated question forms like **est-ce** remain attached when negated

Vous n'êtes pas d'accord ?
You (formal) are not in agreement?
- Contraction: **ne** + **êtes** ⇒ **n'êtes**

Nous ne sommes pas à l'heure.
We are not on time.

La billetterie n'est pas dans la gare.
The ticket office is not in the station.

TOPIC 8 ❖ Negation, not - *ne pas*

Nous ne sommes pas à la plage.
We are not at the beach.
- plage (f) means 'beach'
- à la plage means 'to the beach'

Pourquoi n'est-elle pas ici ?
Why is she not here?
- Hyphenated question forms like **est-elle** remain attached when negated

Ils ne sont pas encore en vacances ?
They (males) are not yet on holidays?
- encore means 'yet' or 'more' or 'still'

Pourquoi ne sont-elles pas encore là ?
Why aren't they (females) here yet?
- Hyphenated question forms like **sont-elles** remain attached when negated

Juliette et Jacques ne sont pas ici.
Juliette and Jacques are not here.
- et means 'and'

Ce n'est pas l'université.
This is not the university.
- c'est back to its uncontracted form **ce est** before negation ⇒ **ce n'est pas**

Ce n'est pas Romain.
That is not Romain.

La voiture n'est pas sur le boulevard.
The car is not on the boulevard.

Le vélo n'est pas dans la rue.
The bike is not on the street.

Bootstrap French
TOPIC 9

❖ Adjectives and gender - masculine and feminine

Adjectives are words that describe a noun. For example 'big' and 'strong'.

In French adjectives should agree with the noun in both gender and number.

This means that an adjective may change depending on whether the noun it is describing is masculine or feminine, and singular or plural.

- In general singular masculine adjectives end with a consonant.
- And the general rule is to get the singular feminine form we append an **-e** to the masculine form of the adjective.

Note however that there are lots of exceptions to this rule. We will cover these exceptions in the next couple of topics.

EXAMPLES:

Il est grand.
He is big.
  grand (adj) means 'big'

Elle est grande aussi.
She is big also.
  grand (adj.m) ⇒ *grande* (adj.f)
  aussi (adj) means 'also' (also used as a comparative)

Marc est fort.
Marc is strong.
  fort (adj) means 'strong"

Camille est forte.
Camille is strong.
  fort (adj.m) ⇒ *forte* (adj.f)

Jacques est-il français ?
Jacques, is he French?
  français (adj) means 'French"

Juliette est-elle vraiment française ?
Juliette, is she really French?
  français (adj.m) ⇒ *française* (adj.f)

French Grammar

TOPIC 9 ❖ Adjectives and gender - masculine and feminine

Es-tu prêt ?
Are you (familiar) (male) ready?
- prêt (adj) means 'ready"

Elle n'est pas encore prête.
She is not yet ready.
- prêt (adj.m) ⇒ prête (adj.f)

Le café est noir.
The coffee is black.
- noir (adj & noun.m) means 'black"

La voiture n'est pas noire.
The car is not black.
- noir (adj.m) ⇒ noire (adj.f)

Je ne suis pas encore fatigué.
I (male) am not tired yet.
- fatigué (adj) means 'tired"

Pourquoi es-tu déjà fatiguée ?
Why are you (familiar) (female) already tired?
- fatigué (adj.m) ⇒ fatiguée (adj.f)

La maison est assez petite.
The house is quite small.
- petit (adj) means 'small'
- petit (adj.m) ⇒ petite (adj.f)

La piscine est vraiment froide.
The pool is really cold.
- froid (adj) means 'cold'
- froid (adj.m) ⇒ froide (adj.f)

Le lait est froid et l'eau est froide.
The milk is cold and the water is cold.
- eau (f) means 'water'
- lait (m) means 'milk"
- froid (adj.m) ⇒ froide (adj.f)

TOPIC 9 ❖ Adjectives and gender - masculine and feminine

La chambre est bien chaude.
The room is quite warm.
- chaud (adj) means 'warm' or 'hot'
- chaud (adj.m) ⇒ chaude (adj.f)
- bien (adv) means 'quite' or 'well'

Le café est chaud et l'eau est chaude.
The coffee is hot and the water is hot.
- café (m) means 'coffee' or 'café"

Bootstrap French
TOPIC 10

❖ Feminine adjectives - some rules

As we saw previously, getting the feminine form of an adjective can be as simple as appending an **-e** to the masculine form.

There are however several rule-based expectations that depend on the ending of the masculine form. Three such rules are:

- An **-f** masculine ending becomes **-ve** for the feminine adjective.
- An **-er** masculine ending becomes **-ère** for the feminine adjective.
- An **-eux** masculine ending becomes **-euse** for the feminine adjective.

EXAMPLES:

Le chapeau est neuf et la cravate est neuve aussi.
The hat is new and the tie is also new.
- **neuf** (adj) means 'new'
- **neuf** (m) ⇒ **neuve** (f) - An -f ending becomes -ve
- **chapeau** (m) means 'hat'
- **cravate** (f) means 'tie' or 'necktie'

La femme est sportive mais le mari n'est pas du tout sportif.
The wife is sporty but the husband is not at all sporty.
- **sportif** (adj) means 'sporty'
- **sportif** (m) ⇒ **sportive** (f) - An -f ending becomes -ve
- **femme** (f) means 'wife' or 'woman'
- **mari** (m) means 'husband'
- **ne...pas du tout** means 'not at all'

Le garçon est vif et la fille est vive aussi.
The boy is lively and the girl is also lively.
- **vif** (adj) means 'lively' or 'alert'
- **vif** (m) ⇒ **vive** (f) - An -f ending becomes -ve

La chemise est chère. Mais le pull n'est pas cher.
The shirt is expensive. But the jumper is not expensive.
- **cher** (adj) means 'expensive' or 'dear'
- **cher** (m) ⇒ **chère** (f) - An -er ending becomes -ère
- **chemise** (f) means 'shirt'
- **pull** (m) means 'sweater' or 'jumper' or 'pullover'

TOPIC 10 ❖ Feminine adjectives - some rules

La valise est légère mais le sac n'est pas léger.
The suitcase is light but the bag is not light.
- léger (adj) means 'light (weight)'
- léger (m) ⇒ légère (f) - An -er ending becomes -ère
- valise (f) means 'suitcase'
- sac (m) means 'bag'

Le vin n'est pas étranger - il est français - mais la bière est étrangère.
The wine is not foreign - it's French - but the beer is foreign.
- étranger (adj) means 'foreign'
- étranger (m) ⇒ étrangère (f) - An -er ending becomes -ère
- bière (f) means 'beer'

La femelle est dangereuse, mais le mâle n'est pas dangereux.
The female is dangerous, but the male is not dangerous.
- dangereux (adj) means 'dangerous'
- dangereux (m) ⇒ dangereuse (f) - An -eux ending becomes -euse
- femelle (f) means 'female'
- mâle (m) means 'male'

L'artichaut est délicieux. Et la pomme de terre est délicieuse aussi.
The artichoke is delicious. And the potato is delicious too.
- délicieux (adj) means 'delicious'
- délicieux (m) ⇒ délicieuse (f) - An -eux ending becomes -euse
- artichaut (m) means 'artichoke'
- pomme de terre (f) means

Pourquoi est-elle malheureuse ?
Why is she unhappy?
- malheureux (adj) means 'unhappy'
- malheureux (m) ⇒ malheureuse (f)

La musique de Noël est festive.
Christmas music is festive.
- festif (adj) means 'festive'
- festif (m) ⇒ festive (f)
- la musique de Noël (f) means 'Christmas misuc'

Le repas est délicieux et la tarte est aussi délicieuse.
The meal is delicious and the pie is also delicious.
- délicieux (m) ⇒ délicieuse (f) - An -eux ending becomes -euse
- repas (m) means 'meal'
- tarte (f) means 'tarte'

TOPIC 10 ❖ Feminine adjectives - some rules

La fille est première de la classe.
The girl is first in the class.

- **premièr** (adj) means 'first'
- **premièr** (m) ⇒ **première** (f)
- **classe** (f) means 'classroom'
- **de la classe** means 'of the class'

Bootstrap French
TOPIC 11

❖ Feminine adjectives - doubling the final consonant

As we saw, the general rule is to add **-e** to make a feminine adjective.

But if the masculine adjective ends with an **-n**, **-s**, or **-l** then we double that final consonant before adding **-e** to make it feminine.

For example:
- **bon ⇒ bonne** - 'good' — double the **-n** and add an **-e**.
- **gros ⇒ grosse** - 'fat' or 'big' — double the **-s** and add an **-e**.
- **gentil ⇒ gentille** - 'nice' or 'kind' — double the **-l** and add an **-e**.

EXAMPLES:

Le pain est très bon mais la tarte n'est pas bonne.
The bread is very good but the pie is not good.
- **bon** (m) means 'good'
- **bon** (m) ⇒ **bonne** (f)
- **pain** (m) means 'bread'
- **tarte** (f) means 'pie (usually sweet)'

Est-elle gentille ?
Is she nice?
- **gentil** (m) means 'nice' or 'kind'
- **gentil** (m) ⇒ **gentille** (f)

L'enseignant est gentil et la directrice est aussi gentille.
The teacher is nice and the directress is also nice.
- **enseignant** (m) means 'teacher'
- **directrice** (f) means 'headmistress'

Le bâtiment dans le jardin est ancien.
The building in the garden is old.
- **ancien** (adj) means 'old' or 'ancient'

La rue est ancienne.
The street is old.
- **ancien** (m) ⇒ **ancienne** (f)

French Grammar

TOPIC 11 ❖ Feminine adjectives - doubling the final consonant

La music est trop basse.
The music is too low.
- bas (adj) means 'low'
- bas (m) ⇒ basse (f)

La vie est cruelle.
Life is cruel.
- cruel (adj) means 'cruel'
- cruel (m) ⇒ cruelle (f)

Le chat est gros mais heureux.
The cat is fat but happy.
- gros (adj) means 'fat' or 'big'

La chatte n'est pas grosse mais est aussi heureuse.
The cat (female) is not fat but is also happy.
- gros (m) ⇒ grosse (f)
- chatte (f) means 'female cat'

Le bébé est mignon et la fille est aussi mignonne.
The baby is cute and the girl is also cute.
- mignon (adj) means 'cute'
- mignon (m) ⇒ mignonne (f)

Julien n'est pas européen mais Veronica est européenne.
Julien is not European but Veronica is European.
- européen (m) means 'European'
- européen (m) ⇒ européenne (f)

Juliette, est-elle vraiment australienne ? Non, mais David est australien.
Juliette, is she really Australian? No, but David is Australian.
- australien (adj) means 'Australian'
- australien (m) ⇒ australienne (f)

Bootstrap French
TOPIC 12

❖ The position of adjectives

In French adjectives that directly modify a noun ('the angry dog' rather than 'the dog is angry') mostly come after the noun - not before like in English.

But there is a class of adjectives that precede the noun.

Adjectives that relate to beauty, age, number, goodness and size tend to precede the noun.

- Beauty includes adjectives like **beau** ('handsome' or 'beautiful') and **joli** ('pretty').
- Age includes **jaune** ('young') and **vieux** ('old') and **nouveau** ('new").
- Number includes **autre** ('other'), **chaque** ('each' or 'every') and **dernier** ('last').
- Goodness includes **bon** ('good'), **gentil** ('kind'), **mauvais** ('bad') and **meilleur** ('better').
- Size includes **grand** ('large'), **petit** ('small'), **court** ('short'), **long** ('long'), **gros** ('fat' or 'big'), **haut** ('high').

This group includes many adjectives that have irregular feminine and plural forms.

EXAMPLES:

Le beau jardin privé
The beautiful private garden

- beau is a 'beauty' adjective so comes before the noun
- beau (m) means 'beautiful' or 'handsome'
- privé (m) means 'private'

La belle femme exotique
The beautiful exotic woman

- belle is a 'beauty' adjective so comes before the noun
- belle (f) means 'beautiful'
- exotique (m,f) means 'exotic'

La jolie fleur rouge
The pretty red flower

- jolie is a 'beauty' adjective so comes before the noun
- jolie (f) means 'pretty'
- fleur (f) means 'flower'
- rouge means 'red'

TOPIC 12 ❖ The position of adjectives

La jeune fille blonde
The blonde girl
- jeune is an 'age' adjective so comes before the noun
- jeune fille means 'girl' (not 'young girl')
- blonde (f) means 'blonde'

Le jeune homme brun
The young brunette man
- jeune is a 'age' adjective so comes before the noun
- jeune homme (m) means 'young man'

Le vieux monsieur fatigué
The old tired gentleman
- vieux is a 'age' adjective so comes before the noun
- vieux (m) means 'old'
- fatigué (m) means 'tired'

La vieille dame fatiguée
The old tired lady
- vieille is a 'age' adjective so comes before the noun
- dame (f) means 'lady' or 'women'

La nouvelle voiture blanche
The new white car
- nouvelle is a 'age' adjective so comes before the noun
- nouvelle (f) means 'new'

Le nouveau voisin anglais
The new English neighbor
- nouveau is a 'age' adjective so comes before the noun
- nouveau (m) means 'new'
- voisin (m) means 'neighbour'
- anglais (m) means 'English'

L'autre chose étrange
The other strange thing
- autre is a 'number' adjective so comes before the noun
- autre (m,f) means 'other'
- chose (m) means 'thing'
- étrange (m) means 'strange'

TOPIC 12 ❖ The position of adjectives

Chaque jour chaud et chaque nuit chaude
Every hot day and every hot night
- **chaque** is a 'number' adjective so comes before the noun
- **jour** (m) means 'day'
- **nuit** (f) means 'night'

La première fois
The first time
- **première** is a 'number' adjective so comes before the noun
- **fois** (m) means 'time'

Le dernier étage
The last floor
- **dernier** is a 'number' adjective so comes before the noun
- **etage** (m) means 'floor' or 'story'

Le petit jeu amusant
The short fun game
- **petit** is a 'size' adjective so comes before the noun
- **jeux** (m) means 'game'
- **amusant** means 'fun' or 'amusing'

Le gentil prof américain
The nice American teacher
- **gentil** is a 'goodness' adjective so comes before the noun
- **prof** (m) means 'teacher' (abbreviation of **professor**)
- **américain** (m) means 'American (male)'

Le mauvais film allemand
The bad German film
- **mauvais** is a 'goodness' adjective so comes before the noun
- **mauvais** (m) means 'bad'
- **allemand** (m) means 'German (male)'

Le petit problème courant
The little common problem
- **petit** is a 'size' adjective so comes before the noun
- **problème** (f) means 'problem'
- **courant** (m) means 'common' or 'not rare'

TOPIC 12 ❖ The position of adjectives

Le grand homme poilu
The big hairy man
- grand is a 'size' adjective so comes before the noun
- poilu (m) means 'hairy' (f. poilue)

Le gros chat roux
The big ginger cat
- gros is a 'size' adjective so comes before the noun
- roux (adj) means 'red' or 'ginger' (hair color)

La grosse poule grise
The big grey hen
- grosse is a 'size' adjective so comes before the noun
- poule (f) means 'hen'
- grise (f) means 'grey' (m. gris)

La longue rue droite
The long straight street
- longue is a 'size' adjective so comes before the noun
- droite (f) means 'straight' or 'right'

Le grand bâtiment étroit
The tall narrow building
- grand is a 'size' adjective so comes before the noun
- baitement (m) means 'building'
- étroit (adj) means 'thin' or norrow (for structures)

Bootstrap French
TOPIC 13

❖ Indefinite articles - *un* & *une*

The singular indefinite article in English is 'a' (or 'an'). It marks a single previously unspecified object.

In French the definite article serves the same purpose but there are two - depending on gender: **un** is the masculine and **une** is the feminine.

EXAMPLES:

Un petit problème
A little problem

Un grand homme
A great man

Une histoire drôle
A funny story

 drôle (m,f) means 'funny'

Un film super
A great movie

 film (m) means 'movie' or 'film'

Une première fois
A first time

Une jeune fille
A girl

Un jeune homme
A young man

Une grave erreur
A big mistake

Un beau jardin
A beautiful garden

Une école publique
A public school

 publique (m,f) means 'public'

TOPIC 13 ❖ Indefinite articles - *un* & *une*

Un train en retard
A late train

Une bibliothèque près d'ici
A library near here
  📖 **bibliothèque** (f) means 'library'

Ce n'est pas un grave problème.
It's not a serious problem.

Ce n'est pas une université.
That is not a university.

❖ The verb 'to have' - *avoir*

The French verb **avoir** means 'to have'.

- **avoir** is the infinitive or dictionary form.

The verb **avoir** has the following present tense conjugations:

- **j'ai** - 'I have'
- **tu as** - 'you (singular familiar) have'
- **il a** & **elle a** - 'he has' & 'she has'
- **nous avons** - 'we have'
- **vous avez** - 'you (plural & singular formal) have'
- **ils ont** & **elles ont** - 'they (males and mixed) have' & 'they (females) have'

EXAMPLES:

J'ai une nouvelle voiture.
I have a new car.
💡 Note the contraction **je** + **ai** becomes **j'ai**

Tu as le pain.
You (familiar) have the bread.

Il a un petit problème.
He has a little problem.

Elle n'a pas la clé.
She doesn't have the key.
✏ **clé** (f) means 'key'

Nous avons un gros chat.
We have a big cat.

Vous avez le livre vert.
You (formal) have the green book.
✏ **vert** (m) means 'green'

Ils ont une grande maison blanche.
They have a big white house.

TOPIC 14 ❖ The verb 'to have' - *avoir*

Ont-elles un ordinateur puissant ?
Do they (females) have a powerful computer?
- **ordinateur** (m) means 'computer'
- **puissant** (m) means 'powerful' or 'strong'

Tu as un grand vélo, n'est-ce pas ?
You (familiar) have a big bike, don't you?
- **n'est-ce pas ?** means 'is it not?'
- But in this context 'don't you?' is better

Ai-je vraiment la clé ?
Do I really have the key?

As-tu une petite amie ?
Do you (familiar) have a girlfriend?
- **petite amie** (f) means 'girlfriend'

A-t-elle un petit ami ?
Does she have a boyfriend?
- Note the injection of a **t** to separate the two vowels in **a-t-elle**
- **petit ami** (m) means 'boyfriend'

N'a-t-il pas un nouveau voisin ?
Doesn't he have a new neighbor?
- Note that the hyphenated verb-pronoun question is not split when negating

Avez-vous le billet ?
Do you (formal) have the ticket?

Ont-ils un enfant ?
Do they have a child?
- **enfant** (m) means 'child'

N'ont-elles pas un frère ?
Don't they (females) have a brother?
- **frère** (m) means 'brother'

Ont-ils une table dans la pièce ?
Do they have a table in the room?
- **pièce** (f) means 'room' or 'play' or 'part'

TOPIC 14 ❖ The verb 'to have' - *avoir*

Vous avez raison.

You (formal) are right.

- This is the most common way to say 'You are right' in French
- Literally 'You have reason'
- **raison** (f) means 'reason'

Bootstrap French
TOPIC 15

❖ Idiomatic expressions with *avoir*

There are many idiomatic expressions that use the verb **avoir**.

Take note - many of these expressions are quite different to how these ideas are expressed in English.

EXAMPLES:

J'ai chaud.
I am hot.
- **avoir chaud** means 'to be hot'
- In French 'I HAVE hot' rather than 'I AM hot' but only when talking about people

As-tu froid ?
Are you (familiar) cold?
- **avoir froid** means 'to be cold'
- In French 'I HAVE cold' rather than 'I AM cold' but only when talking about people

Pourquoi tu as peur ?
Why are you (familiar) afraid?
- **avoir peur** means 'to be afraid'
- In French 'I HAVE fear' rather than 'I AM afraid'

Vous avez raison - la réponse est correcte.
You (formal) are right - the answer is correct.
- **avoir raison** means 'to be right'
- In French 'I HAVE right' rather than 'I AM right'

Vous avez tort - la réponse est incorrecte.
You (formal) are wrong - the answer is incorrect.
- **avoir tort** means 'to be wrong'
- In French 'I HAVE wrong' rather than 'I AM wrong'

Les enfants ont faim.
The children are hungry.
- **avoir faim** means 'to be hungry'
- In French 'I HAVE hunger' rather than 'I AM hungry'

TOPIC 15 ❖ Idiomatic expressions with *avoir*

Le chien a soif.
The dog is thirsty.
- **avoir soif** means 'to be thirsty'
- In French 'I HAVE thirst' rather than 'I AM thirsty'

Elle a sommeil.
She is sleepy.
- **avoir sommeil** means 'to be sleepy'
- In French 'I HAVE sleepiness' rather than 'I AM sleepy'

Il a honte.
He's ashamed.
- **avoir honte** means 'to be ashamed'
- In French 'I HAVE shame' rather than 'I AM ashamed'

Tu as de la chance.
You (familiar) are lucky.
- **avoir de la chance** means 'to be lucky'
- In French 'I HAVE SOME luck' rather than 'I AM lucky'
- The **de** here means 'some'

Bootstrap French
TOPIC 16

❖ Plural nouns

Most nouns in French form the plural by adding an **-s**.

There are of course expectations which are covered in a coming topic.

- More often than not this **-s** is unpronounced unless there is liaison due to a following vowel.

EXAMPLES:

J'ai deux bouteilles.
I have two bottles.
- **une bouteille ⇒ deux bouteilles**
- **bouteille** (f) means 'bottle'
- **deux** (num) means 'two'

As-tu trois sœurs ?
Do you (familiar) have three sisters?
- **une sœur ⇒ trois sœurs**
- **sœur** (f) means 'sister'
- **trois** (num) means 'three'

Pourquoi avez-vous quatre voitures ?
Why do you (formal) have four cars?
- **une voiture ⇒ quatre voitures**
- **quartre** (num) means 'four'

Ils ont cinq chiens.
They have five dogs.
- **un chien ⇒ cinq chiens**
- **cinq** (num) means 'five'

Elle a six chats.
She has six cats.
- **un chat ⇒ six chats**
- **six** (num) means 'six'

TOPIC 16 ❖ Plural nouns

Sept pommes - c'est beaucoup !
Seven apples - that is a lot!
- une pomme ⇒ sept pommes
- pomme (f) means 'apple'
- sept (num) means 'seven'

Huit cerises sont dans la boîte.
Eight cherries are in the box.
- une cerise ⇒ huit cerises
- cerise (f) means 'cherry'
- boîte (f) means 'box'
- huit (num) means 'eight'

Pourquoi avons-nous neuf chaises ?
Why do we have nine chairs?
- une chaise ⇒ neuf chaises
- chaise (f) means 'chair'
- neuf (num) means 'nine'

Est-ce possible - dix personnes dans une voiture ?
Is it possible - ten people in a car?
- une personne ⇒ dix personnes
- personne (f) means 'person'
- dix (num) means 'ten'

Bootstrap French
TOPIC 17

❖ The plural definite article - *les*

The French plural definite article is **les** and does not vary with gender.
- In English we use 'the' regardless of whether it is singular or plural.

EXAMPLES:

Où sont les clés ?
Where are the keys?
- la clé ⇒ les clés

Les lunettes sont dans la cuisine.
The (eye) glasses are in the kitchen.
- les lunettes are always plural
- lunettes (pl) means '(eye) glasses'

Les enfants sont là.
The children are there.
- l'enfant ⇒ les enfants

Pourquoi n'avez-vous pas les réponses ?
Why don't you (formal) have the answers?
- la réponse ⇒ les réponses
- réponse (f) means 'answer'

Jacques a les fiches.
Jacques has the documents.
- la fiche ⇒ les fiches
- fiche (f) means 'form'

Les chaises ne sont pas dans la salle.
The chairs are not in the room.
- la chaise ⇒ les chaises
- salle (f) means 'room'

Le chat est avec les chiens.
The cat is with the dogs.
- le chien ⇒ les chiens
- avec means 'with'

TOPIC 17 ❖ The plural definite article - *les*

Les arbres ne sont pas loin d'ici.
The trees are not far from here.

💡 l'arbre ⇒ les arbres

Les garçons ont le ballon.
The boys have the ball.

💡 le garçon ⇒ les garçons
📝 **ballon** (m) means '(inflated) ball' or 'ballon'

Bootstrap French
TOPIC 18

❖ Plural nouns - exceptions

While adding an **s** to a noun to form the plural is the general rule, there are several exceptions:

- words ending in **-eu**, **-au**, and **-eau** - add an **-x** instead of an **-s**.
- words ending in **-al** and many ending in **-ail** - remove the **l** (and the **-i-** if there is one) and add **-ux**.
- many words ending in **-ou** - add an **-x** instead of an **-s**.
- words that end in **-s**, **-z**, or **-x** do not change at all – the singular and plural forms are the same.
- the plural of **œil** (eye) is **yeux** (eyes), which is the only highly irregular plural noun in French.

EXAMPLES:

Les jeux dans les cartons.
The games in the (cardboard) boxes.
- le jeu ⇒ les jeux : -eu ending ⇒ add -x
- jeu (m) means 'game'
- carton (m) means 'cardboard box'

Les oiseaux dans les arbres.
The birds in the trees.
- l'oiseau ⇒ les oiseaux : -eau ending ⇒ add -x
- oiseau (m) means 'bird'

Les gâteaux dans la boulangerie.
The cakes in the bakery.
- le gâteau ⇒ les gâteaux : -eau ending ⇒ add -x
- boulangerie (f) means 'bakery'

Les morceaux sur la table.
The pieces on the table.
- le morceau ⇒ les morceaux : -eau ending ⇒ add -x
- morceau (m) means 'piece' or 'bit'

TOPIC 18 ❖ Plural nouns - exceptions

Les bateaux dans le port.
The boats in the harbor.
- le bateau ⇒ les bateaux : -eau ending ⇒ add -x
- bateau (m) means 'boat'
- port (m) means 'port' or 'harbour'

Les chapeaux sur le banc.
The hats on the bench.
- le chapeau ⇒ les chapeaux : -eau ending ⇒ add -x
- chapeau (m) means 'hat'
- banc (m) means 'bench'

Les cadeaux dans le sac.
The gifts in the bag.
- le cadeau ⇒ les cadeaux : -eau ending ⇒ add -x
- cadeau (m) means 'gift' or 'present'

Les manteaux dans l'armoire.
The coats in the wardrobe.
- le manteau ⇒ les manteaux : -eau ending ⇒ add -x
- manteau (m) means 'coat'
- armoire (f) means 'wardrobe'

Les chevaux dans le pré.
The horses in the field.
- le cheval ⇒ les chevaux : -al ending ⇒ -aux
- cheval (m) means 'horse'
- pré (m) means 'field' or 'meadow'

Les journaux sur l'étagère.
The newspapers on the shelf.
- le journal ⇒ les journaux : -al ending ⇒ -aux
- journal (m) means newspaper
- étagère (f) means 'shelf'

Les animaux dans le zoo.
The animals in the zoo.
- l'animal ⇒ les animaux : -al ending ⇒ -aux
- animal (m) means 'animal'
- zoo (m) means 'zoo'

TOPIC 18 ❖ Plural nouns - exceptions

Les travaux dans la rue.
The works on the road.

- le travail ⇒ les travaux : -ail ending ⇒ -aux
- travail (m) means 'work' or 'job'

Les bijoux sur le plateau.
The jewels on the tray.

- le bijou ⇒ les bijoux : -ou ending ⇒ add -x
- bijou (m) means 'jewel'
- plateau (m) means 'tray' or 'platter' or 'plateau'

La douleur dans les genoux.
The pain in the knees.

- le genou ⇒ les genoux : -ou ending ⇒ add -x
- genou (m) means 'knee'
- douleur (f) means 'pain'

Les croix dans l'église.
The crosses in the church.

- la croix ⇒ les croix : -x ending doesn't change
- croix (f) means 'cross'
- église (f) means 'church'

Les nez sur les visages.
The noses on the faces.

- le nez ⇒ les nez : -z ending doesn't change
- nez (m) means 'nose'
- visage (f) means 'face'

Les œufs dans la boîte.
The eggs in the box.

- l'œuf ⇒ les œufs : the f becomes silent
- eggs
- the f becomes silent
- œuf (m) means 'egg'

Tout le monde a deux yeux.
Everyone has two eyes.

- l'œil ⇒ les yeux : the only highly irregular plural in French
- œil (m) means 'eye'
- tout le monde means 'everyone' (Literally 'all the world')

❖ Plural adjectives

The general rule for forming a plural adjective is to add an **-s** to the singular adjective. So the plural feminine form would generally end in **-es**.

The exceptions are:
- For adjectives that end in **-s** or **-x** we don't need (another) **-s**.
- For masculine adjectives that end in **-eau** or **-al**, the plural form usually changes it to **-eaux** or **-aux**.

EXAMPLES:

J'ai deux très bonnes amies françaises.
I have two very good French friends (females).
- une bonne amie (f) ⇒ bonnes amies (pl.f)
- ami (m) means 'friend'

Les histoires intéressantes sont terminées.
The interesting stories are over.
- une histoire intéressante (f) ⇒ histoires intéressantes (pl.f)
- histoire (f) means 'story'
- terminé (m) means 'finished' or 'over' or 'ended'

Les deux grands hôtels sont ici.
The two big hotels are here.
- un grand hôtel (m) ⇒ grands hôtels (pl.m)

Elle a deux chats noirs.
She has two black cats.
- un chat noir (m) ⇒ chats noirs (pl.m)

Les lourdes valises sont dans la voiture.
The heavy suitcases are in the car.
- une lourde valise (f) ⇒ lourdes valises (pl.f)
- lourd (m) means 'heavy'

Les anciens élèves sont déjà là.
The former students are already there.
- un ancien élève (m) ⇒ anciens élèves (pl.m)
- ancien (m) means 'former'
- élève (m) means 'student' or 'pupil'

TOPIC 19 ❖ Plural adjectives

Les visiteurs français sont-ils déjà dans la salle ?
Are French visitors already in the room?
- un visiteur français (m) ⇒ visiteurs français (pl.m)
- français ends in -s so is unchanged in the plural
- visiteur (m) means 'visitor'

Les virages dangereux sur la route.
Dangerous bends on the road.
- virage dangereux (f) ⇒ virages dangereux (pl.f)
- dangereux ends in -x so is unchanged in the plural
- virage (f) means 'bend' or 'curve'

Les élèves sont très heureux.
The students are very happy.
- heureux (m) ⇒ heureux (pl.m)
- heureux ends in -x so is unchanged in the plural
- heureux (m) means 'happy'

La maison et le jardin sont beaux.
The house and the garden are beautiful.
- beau (m) ⇒ beaux (pl.m)

J'ai quelques nouveaux professeurs.
I have some new teachers.
- nouveau professeur (m) ⇒ nouveaux professeurs (pl.m)

Êtes-vous très occupés ?
Are you (plural) busy?
- occupé (m) ⇒ occupés (pl.m)

Les trains spéciaux sont rapides.
Special trains are fast.
- un train spécial (m) ⇒ trains spéciaux (pl.m)
- spécial (m) means 'special'
- rapide (m) means 'quick' or 'fast'

Les sports nationaux sont le foot et le rugby.
The national sports are football/soccer and rugby.
- un sport national (m) ⇒ sports nationaux (pl.m)
- national (m) means 'national'

❖ *Vous* and agreement of adjectives

As we saw previously, the pronoun **vous** can refer (formally) to one person, or multiple (plural) people. And these people can be male or female or a mix.

Adjectives that modify the pronoun **vous** need to agree in number and gender with the intention of the pronoun.

EXAMPLES:

Êtes-vous fatigué, Monsieur ?
Are you tired, sir?

Êtes-vous fatiguée, Madame ?
Are you tired, madame?

Êtes-vous fatigués, Messieurs ?
Are you tired, gentlemen?
> **messieurs** is the plural form of **monsieur**

Êtes-vous fatiguées, Mesdames ?
Are you tired, ladies?
> **mesdames** is the plural form of **madame**

Êtes-vous fatigués, Mesdames et Messieurs ?
Are you tired, ladies and gentlemen?
> Recall that when groups of people are mixed with use the masculine plural

Monsieur, vous êtes mouillé !
Sir, you are wet!
> **mouillé** (adj) means 'wet'

Madame, vous êtes mouillée !
Madam, you are wet!

Messieurs, vous êtes mouillés !
Gentlemen, you are wet!

Mesdames, vous êtes mouillées !
Ladies, you are wet!

TOPIC 20 ❖ *Vous* and agreement of adjectives

Mesdames et messieurs, vous êtes mouillés !
Ladies and gentlemen, you are wet!

❖ *C'est* with adjectives

We previously introduced **c'est** which means 'it is' or 'that is'.

- Recall that **c'est** is constructed from **ce** + **est**. The pronoun **ce** is masculine.

So if **c'est** is used with just an (isolated) adjective, then the adjective should always be masculine, even if the pronoun **ce** refers back to a feminine noun.

So **c'est belle** is NOT possible in French, even if you are talking about something feminine.

EXAMPLES:

La France est belle. Oui, c'est beau.
France is beautiful. Yes, it is beautiful.
- Even though **la France** is feminine

La rue n'est pas étroite. Non, ce n'est pas étroit.
The street is not narrow. No, it is not narrow.
- **étroit** (adj) means 'narrow'

L'eau est chaude. Non, ce n'est pas chaud.
The water is hot. No, it is not hot.

La tarte est trop sucrée. Oui, c'est très sucré.
The tart is too sweet. Yes, it is very sweet.
- **sucré** (adj) means 'sweet' or 'sugary'

La musique, c'est bon.
The music, it is good.

C'est intéressant, la mathématique, n'est-ce pas?
It is interesting, mathematics, isn't it?

C'est génial, cette chanson !
It is awesome, that song!
- **génial** (adj) means 'awesome' or 'great'

Les asperges sont chères. Oui, c'est cher.
Asparagus is expensive. Yes, it is expensive.
- Even though **asperges** is feminine
- Also recall that colloquially **c'est** can refer to plurals
- **asperge** (f) means 'asparagus'

TOPIC 21 ❖ *C'est* with adjectives

Les montagnes, c'est beau !
The mountains, they are beautiful!

- Even though **montagnes** is feminine
- **montagne** (f) means 'mountain'

Bootstrap French
TOPIC 22

❖ There is & there are - *Il y a*

The construction **il y a** is used to express existence in French.

In English we use 'there is' or 'there are'.

- The **il** is 'it', the **y** is 'there' and the **a** is the **il** conjugation of the verb **avoir** ('to have').

The form does not change whether we are referring to the existence of one thing (singular) or of multiple of things (plural).

A common question form is by inversion: **Y a-t-il..?**

EXAMPLES:

Il y a un élève dans la classe.
There is a student in the classroom.

Il y a deux élèves dans la classe.
There are two students in the classroom.

Il y a un nuage blanc dans le ciel.
There is one white cloud in the sky.
     nuage (f) means 'cloud'

Il y a trois cuillères et deux fourchettes sur la table.
There are three spoon and two forks on the table.
     cuillère (f) means 'spoon'
     fourchette (f) means 'fork'

Il y a douze œufs dans chaque boîte.
There are twelve eggs in each box.

Il y a une tache sur la moquette.
There is a stain on the carpet.
     tache (f) means 'stain'
     moquette (f) means 'carpet'

Il y a un pommier dans le jardin.
There's an apple tree in the garden.
     pommier (m) means 'apple tree'

TOPIC 22 ❖ There is & there are - *Il y a*

Y a-t-il un taxi dans la rue ?
Is there a taxi in the street?

📎 **taxi** (m) means 'taxi' or 'cab'

Pourquoi y a-t-il une souris dans la maison ?
Why is there a mouse in the house?

📎 **souris** (m) means 'mouse'

Où y a-t-il un policier ?
Where is there a policeman?

📎 **policier** (m) means 'policeman'

Pourquoi y a-t-il une chaussure dans le lit ?
Why is there a shoe in the bed?

📎 **lit** (m) means 'bed'

Y a-t-il un problème ?
Is there are problem?

Il y a plusieurs solutions possibles.
There are several possible solutions.

📎 **plusieurs** means 'several'
📎 **solution** (f) means 'solution'
📎 **possible** (m) means 'possible'

Qu'est-ce qu'il y a ?
What is the matter?

💡 A common way to ask 'What is the matter?' or 'What is wrong" Literally 'what is there?'

Bootstrap French
TOPIC 23

❖ The plural indefinite article - *des*

Unlike English, French has a plural indefinite article - **des**.

The particle **des** refers to more than one countable object (like 'eggs' or 'bottles of milk') but **not** uncountable objects (like 'milk' or 'air').

Like the plural definite article **les**, **des** is the same for masculine and feminine nouns.

EXAMPLES:

As-tu des amis ?
Do you (familiar) have friends?
💡 The **des** is necessary in the French.

Oui, j'ai des amis.
Yes, I have friends.
💡 The **des** is necessary in the French.
📖 oui means 'yes'

Elle a des fleurs dans les cheveux.
She has flowers in her hair.
📖 fleur (m) means 'flower'

Il y a des élèves dans la classe.
There are students in the classroom.

Il y a des nuages dans le ciel.
There are clouds in the sky.

Il y a des cuillères et des fourchettes sur la table.
There are spoons and forks on the table.

Il y a des œufs dans le réfrigérateur.
There are eggs in the refrigerator.
📖 réfrigérateur (m) means refrigerator

Il y a des taches sur la moquette.
There are stains on the carpet.

Nous avons des pommiers dans le jardin.
We have apple trees in the garden.

TOPIC 23 ❖ The plural indefinite article - *des*

Y a-t-il des taxis dans la rue ?
Are there taxis in the street?

Pourquoi y a-t-il des souris dans la maison ?
Why are there mice in the house?

Où y a-t-il des policiers ?
Where is there policemen?

Pourquoi y a-t-il des chaussures dans le lit ?
Why are there shoes in the bed?

Y a-t-il des problèmes ?
Are there are problems?

Il y a des solutions possibles.
There are possible solutions.

❖ The plural indefinite article *des* with adjectives

If the plural indefinite article **des** is immediately followed by an adjective, it becomes **de**.

And if the adjective relates to quantity - like **plusieurs** ('several') or **quelques** ('a few', 'or some') - the **des** is removed completely.

- Except **beaucoup** which is always **beaucoup de**

Note also the standard contraction - if **de** is followed by a noun that starts with a vowel **de** becomes **d'** and is attached to the noun.

EXAMPLES:

Avez-vous de jeunes amis ?
Do you (formal) have young friends?
💡 **des** ⇒ **de** before the adjective **jeunes**

J'ai des amis américains.
I have American friends.
💡 **des** remains as the adjective is after the noun

Elle a de grandes fleurs dans les cheveux.
She has big flowers in her hair.
💡 **des** ⇒ **de** before the adjective **grandes**

Elle a des fleurs blanches dans les cheveux.
She has white flowers in her hair.
💡 **des** remains as the adjective is after the noun

Il y a de beaux nuages dans le ciel.
There are beautiful clouds in the sky.
💡 **des** ⇒ **de** before the adjective **beaux**

Il y a des nuages blancs dans le ciel.
There are white clouds in the sky.
💡 **des** remains as the adjective is after the noun

Nous avons de vieux pommiers dans le jardin.
We have old apple trees in the garden.
💡 **des** ⇒ **de** before the adjective **vieux**

TOPIC 24 ❖ The plural indefinite article *des* with adjectives

Pourquoi y a-t-il de grosses souris dans la maison ?
Why are there large mice in the house?
💡 **des** ⇒ **de** before the adjective **grosses**

Pourquoi y a-t-il des chaussures sales dans le lit ?
Why are there dirty shoes in the bed?
💡 **des** remains as the adjective is after the noun

Y a-t-il des problèmes sérieux ?
Are there are serious problems?
💡 **des** remains as the adjective is after the noun

Il existe des solutions possibles.
There are possible solutions.
💡 **des** remains as the adjective is after the noun

Il y a plusieurs nuages dans le ciel.
There are several clouds in the sky.
💡 **plusieurs** replaces **des**

Il y a quelques œufs dans le réfrigérateur.
There are a few eggs in the refrigerator.
💡 **quelques** replaces **des**

Il y a beaucoup de livres sur l'étagère.
There are many books on the shelf.
💡 **beaucoup de** is an invariant phrase

Tu as beaucoup d'amis.
You (familiar) have many friends.
💡 **de + amis** ⇒ **d'amis**

❖ Using *ce* as a personal pronoun

We previously saw the particle **ce** used in the pattern **c'est** where it means 'this' or 'that'.

In additional to referring to inanimate objects **ce** can also be used like a personal pronoun - just like **il** (he) and **elle** (she).

- But it can be used in this way only before an indefinite article: **un**, **une** and **des**.

The plural form **ce sont** ('they are') is also used and should be followed by **des** (or **de** if immediately followed by an adjective as per the previous topic).

EXAMPLES:

C'est une jolie femme.
She is a pretty woman.

C'est un beau garçon.
He is a beautiful boy.

C'est un boulanger.
He is a baker.

C'est une bonne élève.
She is a good pupil.
  élève (m.f) means 'pupil' or 'student'

Ce sont des hommes courageux.
They are brave men.
  courageux (m) means 'brave' or 'courageous'

Ce sont des Français.
They are French.
  Français (m) means 'French person' (not capitalized for a noun)

Ce sont de nouveaux enseignants.
They are new teachers.
  enseignant (m) means 'teacher'
  des ⇒ **de** because it is followed by an adjective

Ce sont de bons amis.
They are good friends.
  des ⇒ **de** because it is followed by an adjective

TOPIC 25 ❖ Using *ce* as a personal pronoun

C'est une chanteuse exceptionnelle.
She is an exceptional singer.
- chanteur (m) means 'singer'
- exceptionnel (m) means 'exceptional'

C'est une journaliste célèbre.
She is a famous journalist.
- journaliste (m.f) means 'journalist'
- célèbre (m.f) means 'famous'

C'est un grand écrivain.
He is a great writer.
- écrivain (m) means 'writer'

❖ Possession - the particle *de*

The word **de** is very common in French and has several uses - one of which we have already seen (as a contraction of **des**).

One of the main uses of **de** is as a particle that expresses belonging or possession - like 'of' or apostrophe 's' in English.

It may or may not be followed by an article. If the 'owner' includes a definite article then we have:

- feminine: **de** + **la** ⇒ **de la**
- masculine: **de** + **le** ⇒ **du**
- plural: **de** + **les** ⇒ **des**

EXAMPLES:

C'est le livre de Jean_Paul.
It is Jean-Paul's book.

La voiture de Nicole n'est pas petite.
Nicole's car is not small.

La poste de Brest est ouverte aujourd'hui.
The Brest post office is open today.
- **ouvert** (m) means 'open'
- **aujourd'hui** (adv) means 'today'

Qui est la reine d'Angleterre ?
Who is the queen of England?
- **reine** (f) means 'queen'
- **Angleterre** (f) means 'England'

La poignée de la porte est cassée.
The door handle is broken.
- **poignée** (f) means 'handle' or 'knob'
- **cassé** (m) means 'broken'

La hauteur de l'échelle est bonne.
The height of the ladder is fine.
- **hauteur** (f) means 'height'
- **échelle** (f) means 'ladder'

TOPIC 26 ❖ Possession - the particle *de*

La bibliothèque de l'université est fermée demain.
The library of the university is closed tomorrow.
- *fermé* (m) means 'closed' or 'shut'
- *demain* (adv) means 'tomorrow'

Avez-vous la clé de la moto ?
Do you (formal) have the motorbike key?
- *moto* (f) means 'motorbike'

Il est le président de la République.
He is the president of the Republic.
- *président* (m) means 'president'
- *république* (f) means 'republic'

Qui a le mot de passe de l'ordinateur ?
Who has the password for the computer?
- *mot de passe* (m) means 'password'

C'est la résidence du président.
That is the residence of the president.
- *résidence* (f) means 'residence'

Où est le parking du bureau ?
Where is the office parking?
- *parking* (m) means 'parking lot' or 'car park'

Le tableau du saint est dans l'église.
The painting of the saint is in the church.
- *tableau* (m) means 'painting'
- *saint* (m) means 'saint'

Elle est la mère du professeur.
She is the mother of the teacher.
- *mère* (f) means 'mother'

Les fenêtres des chambres sont verrouillées.
The windows of the bedrooms are locked.
- *fenêtre* (f) means 'window'
- *verrouillé* (m) means 'locked'

La couleur des chaussures est étrange.
The color of the shoes is strange.
- *couleur* (f) means 'color'

TOPIC 26 ❖ Possession - the particle *de*

La taille des chaussettes est parfaite.
The size of the socks is perfect.
- taille (f) means 'size'
- chaussette (f) means 'sock'
- parfait (m) means 'perfect'

La fin de la paix et le début d'une guerre.
The end of peace and the start of a war.
- fin (f) means 'end' or 'finish'
- paix (f) means 'peace'
- début (m) means 'start' or 'beginning'
- guerre (f) means 'war'

Il est le capitaine d'une équipe.
He is the captain of a team.
- capitaine (m) means 'captain'
- équipe (f) means 'team'

C'est un oncle de Paul.
He is an uncle of Paul.
- oncle (m) means 'uncle'

C'est le chien d'Hélène et de Marine.
It is the dog of Hélène and Marine.
- Note that the particle *de* should be applied each instance of an 'owner'.

Bootstrap French
TOPIC 27

❖ Contents - *de*

The particle **de** can be used to specify contents or collective quantities.

- In this way it can be used to specify the 'content' of volumes or weights.

Note that after **de** the object is singular if it is uncountable (eg. liquids, like "water") or a concept (like 'war' and 'love'). And it should be plural if the object is countable (like 'artichokes' and 'radishes').

EXAMPLES:

une tasse de thé vert
a cup of green tea
- tasse (f) means 'cup'
- thé (m) means 'tea'
- thé is uncountable so after **de** is should be singular

un verre de vin rouge
a glass of red wine
- verre (m) means 'glass'
- vin (m) means 'wine'

une bouteille de champagne
a bottle of champagne
- bouteille (f) means 'bottle'

une tranche de pâté
a slice of pâté
- tranche (f) means 'slice'
- pâté means 'pâté'

une tranche de fromage suisse
a slice of Swiss cheese
- fomage (m) means 'cheese'
- suisse means 'Swiss'
- Suisse (f) means 'Switzerland'

une boîte de camembert
a box of camembert
- boîte (f) means 'box'

TOPIC 27 ❖ Contents - *de*

une boîte d'artichauts
a box of artichokes

💡 **artichaut** is countable so after **de** is should be plural ⇒ **artichauts**

une botte de radis
a bundle of radishes

📚 **botte** (f) means 'bundle' or 'bunch'
📚 **radis** (m) means 'radis'
💡 **les radis** is the plural of **le radis**

un plateau de pêches jaunes
a platter of yellow peaches

📚 **pêche** (f) means 'peach'
📚 **jaune** (m) means 'yellow'

une barquette de fraises
a punnet of strawberries

📚 **barquette** (f) means 'punnet'
📚 **fraise** (f) means 'strawberry'

un bouquet d'iris
a bunch of irises

📚 **bouquet** (m) means 'bouquet' or 'bunch'
📚 **iris** (m) means 'iris (flower)'

un morceau de pizza
a piece of pizza

un paquet de biscuits
a packet of cookies

📚 **paquet** (m) means 'packet'
📚 **biscuit** (m) means 'cookie' or 'biscuit'

un film de guerre
war movie

💡 In this case **guerre** is an uncountable concept so is in the singular after **de**

un roman d'amour
a romance novel

📚 **roman** (m) means 'novel'
📚 **amour** (f) means 'love'
💡 **amour** is an uncountable concept so is in the singular after **de**.

TOPIC 27 ❖ Contents - *de*

un kilo de pommes
one kilo of apples
- **kilo** (m) means 'kilogramme'

un demi-kilo de carottes
half a kilo of carrots
- **demi** means 'half'
- **carotte** (f) means 'carrot'

un litre de lait
a liter of milk

cinq cents grammes de farine
five hundred grams of flour
- **cent** (number) means 'hundred'
- **gramme** (m) means 'gramme'
- **farine** (f) means 'flour'

une pinte de bière
a pint of beer
- **pinte** (f) means 'pint' or 'half a litre'

un demi de bière
half a beer
- **demi** (m) means 'half'
- in the case of beer **un demi** is half **une pinte** or a quarter of a litre

une carafe d'eau
a jug of water
- carafe (f) is a 'jug'
- **eau** (f) means 'water'

❖ To go - the verb *aller*

The verb **aller** means 'to go'. It is classified as an **-ER**-type verb due to its **-er** ending. Its present tense conjugations are as follows:

- **je vais** - 'I go'
- **tu vas** - 'you (familiar) go'
- **il & elle va** - 'he goes' or 'she goes'
- **nous allons** - 'we go'
- **vous allez** - 'you (plural)' or 'you (formal) go'
- **ils & elles vont** - 'they go'

Note that the present tense in French could mean the simple present (eg. 'I go everyday') or the present continuous (eg, 'I am going at the moment').

EXAMPLES:

je vais
I go / I am going

tu vas
you (familiar) go / you are going

il va
he goes / he is going

elle va
she goes / she is going

nous allons
we go / we are going

nous n'allons pas
we do not go / we are not going

vous allez
you (plural) go / you are going

ils vont
they go / they are going

French Grammar

TOPIC 28 ❖ To go - the verb *aller*

elles vont
they (females) go / they are going

Jacques va.
Jacques goes/is going.

Jean et Alexandre vont.
Jean and Alexandre go/are going.

Ça va ?
How goes it? *OR* How are you?
- A very common greeting - literally 'it goes?'
- **ça** means 'it' or 'this'

Ça va bien ?
It is going well?
- Literally 'it goes well?'
- **bien** means 'well' or 'fine'

Oui, ça va.
Yes, it goes fine. *OR* Yes, I am well.

Non, ça ne va pas.
No, it is not going well.

Où allez-vous ?
Where are you (formal) going?
- **où** means both 'where' (location) and 'to where' (destination)

Où vont-elles ?
Where are they (females) going?

Pourquoi vas-tu ?
Why are you (familiar) going?

Je vais avec Alec.
I'm going with Alec.

❖ Location and destination ('in' or 'at' and 'to') - the preposition *à*

The preposition **à** can mean either 'at' or 'to'
- Used with a verb of motion (like **aller**) it means 'to' a destination.
- Used with a static verb (like **être**) means 'at' a location.

When **à** is followed by a definite article we have the contractions:
- **à** + **le** ⇒ **au**
- **à** + **les** ⇒ **aux**

But **à la** and **a l'** are unchanged.

EXAMPLES:

Il est à Paris.
He is in Paris.

Les enfants sont à l'école aujourd'hui.
The children are at school today.

Il est au bureau.
He is at the office.

Ils sont au parc ou à l'église.
They are at the parc or at church.

Nous sommes à la piscine.
We are at the swimming pool.

Êtes-vous au petit restaurant chinois ?
Are you (formal) at the small Chinese restaurant?
- *chinois* (m) means 'Chinese'
- *la Chine* means 'China'

Le restaurant est au premier étage.
The restaurant is on the first floor.

Ils vont à Nantes.
They are going to Nantes.

Demain, nous allons à Nice.
Tomorrow we are going to Nice.

TOPIC 29 ❖ Location and destination ('in' or 'at' and 'to')

Allez-vous souvent à Londres ?
Do you (formal) go to London often?

Pourquoi va-t-elle au magasin ?
Why is she going to the shop?

   magasin (m) means 'shop'

Pourquoi vas-tu au bureau maintenant ?
Why are you (familiar) going to the office now?

Le bus va au centre de la ville.
The bus is going to the center of the city.

   centre (m) means 'center' or 'centre'
   ville (f) means 'city' or 'town'

Nous allons aux États_Unis.
We are going to the United States.

   Les États Unis means 'the United States'

Bootstrap French
TOPIC 30

❖ **To come - the verb *venir***

The verb **venir** means 'to come'. It is an **-IR**-type verb.
Its present tense conjugations are as follows:
- **je viens** - 'I come'
- **tu viens** - 'you (familiar) come'
- **il & elle vient** - 'he comes' or 'she comes'
- **nous venons** - 'we come'
- **vous venez** - 'you (plural) come' or 'you (formal) come'
- **ils & elles viennent** - 'they come'

Recall that the present tense in French could mean the simple present (eg. 'I come everyday') or the present continuous (eg, 'I am coming at the moment').

EXAMPLES:

je viens
I come / I am coming

tu viens
you (familiar) come / you are coming

il vient
he comes / he is coming

elle ne vient pas
she does not come / she is not coming

nous venons
we come / we are coming

vous venez
you (plural) come / you are coming

ils ne viennent pas
they don't come / they are not coming

elles viennent
they (females) come / they are coming

TOPIC 30 ❖ To come - the verb *venir*

Qui vient avec Pierre ?
Who is coming with Pierre?

Louis vient avec Pierre.
Louis is coming with Pierre.

Pourquoi viennent-ils ?
Why are they coming?

Ils viennent pour une tasse de thé.
They are coming for a cup of tea.

Bootstrap French
TOPIC 31

❖ Provenance (from) - the preposition *de*

Another use of the preposition **de** is to mean 'from'.

When **de** is followed by a definite article we have the contractions:

- de + le ⇒ du
- de + les ⇒ des

But **de la** and **de l'** are unchanged.

This topic's examples also introduce the verb **revenir** ('to return') which conjugates in exactly the same way as **venir**.

EXAMPLES:

Je viens de Paris.
I come from Paris.

Il vient du Royaume_Uni.
He comes from the UK.

Elle vient des États_Unis.
She comes from the United States.

Qui vient des Pays_Bas ?
Who is from the Netherlands?

Pourquoi viens-tu ?
Why are you (familiar) coming?

Je reviens de la bibliothèque.
I'm back from the library.

  revenir means 'to return'
  revenir conjugates in exactly the same way as **venir**.

Tante Margot revient de l'hôpital aujourd'hui.
Aunt Margot is coming back from the hospital today.

Nous revenons bientôt.
We're coming back soon.

Les soldats reviennent de la guerre.
The soldiers return from the war.

TOPIC 31 ❖ Provenance (from) - the preposition *de*

Sacha et Julia ne reviennent pas.
Sasha and Julia do not return.

Pourquoi revient-elle si tard ?
Why does she come back so late?

- **tard** means 'late'

D'où venez-vous ?
Where do you (formal) come from?

- Note the contraction **de** + **où** ⇒ **d'où**

Il est de retour du travail.
He's back from work.

- **etre de retour** means 'to be back'

Bootstrap French
TOPIC 32

❖ Questions with nouns - repeating the subject

We previous saw the questions in French can used the inverted-hyphenated pronoun-verb pattern.

When the subject of a question is a noun (and not just a pronoun) we can still use the inverted form but the subject needs to be repeated.

Such a question is formed by first stating the noun and then asking the question using the inverted-hyphenated form with the pronoun that matches the subject noun.

EXAMPLES:

Pierre vient-il aujourd'hui ?
Is Pierre coming today?

Sophie vient-elle maintenant ?
Is Sophie coming now?

L'hôtel est-il dans le centre-ville ?
Is the hotel in the city center?

Gabriel a-t-il une copine ?
Does Gabriel have a girlfriend?
   copine (f) means 'friend' or 'girlfriend' (when the genders are the opposite)

La porte est-elle encore fermée ?
Is the door still closed?

Quand Monique revient-elle ?
When is Monique coming back?
   quand means 'when'

La fille est-elle étudiante ?
Is the girl a student?

Les Dupont vivent-ils à Londres ?
Do the Duponts live in London?
   les Dupont here is 'the Duponts' or the Dupont family

Le médecin a-t-il une voiture rouge ?
Does the doctor have a red car?
   médecin (m) means 'doctor'

French Grammar

TOPIC 32 ❖ Questions with nouns - repeating the subject

Le chat est-il dans l'arbre ?
Is the cat in the tree?

Tante Margot revient-elle de l'hôpital aujourd'hui ?
Aunt Margot, is she coming back from the hospital today?

Sacha et Julia ne reviennent-ils pas ?
Sacha and Julia, aren't they coming back?

La patronne vient-elle de Paris ?
Does the boss (female) come from Paris?

📖 **patron** (m) means 'boss' or 'owner of the business'

Louis vient-il avec Pierre ?
Is Louis coming with Pierre?

❖ Questions with *est-ce que*

Another way to ask questions in French is to start the question with 'est-ce que...'
Literally **est-ce que** means 'is it that'.
- In fact **est-ce que** is the inversion of **c'est que** ('it is that').

Note that the **que** contacts when it is followed by a vowel. So for example **est-ce que + il ⇒ est-ce qu'il** ('is it that he...')

EXAMPLES:

Est-ce que tu es fatigué ?
Are you (familiar) tired?

Est-ce qu'elles sont à l'heure ?
Are they on time?

Est-ce que nous sommes en retard ?
Are we late?

Est-ce que vous êtes française ?
Are you (formal) (female) French?

Est-ce que Pierre vient aujourd'hui ?
Is Pierre coming today?

Est-ce que Sophie vient-elle maintenant ?
Is Sophie coming now?

Est-ce que l'hôtel est dans le centre-ville ?
Is the hotel in the city center?

Est-ce que Gabriela a un copain ?
Does Gabriel have a boyfriend?

   🖉 **copain** (m) means 'friend' or 'boyfriend'

Est-ce qu'il vient avec Pierre ?
Does he come with Pierre?

Est-ce que la porte est encore fermée ?
Is the door still closed?

TOPIC 33 ❖ Questions with *est-ce que*

Est-ce que les Dupont vivent à Londres ?
Do the Duponts live in London?

Est-ce que le médecin a une voiture rouge ?
Does the doctor have a red car?

Est-ce que tante Margot revient de l'hôpital aujourd'hui ?
Is Aunt Margot coming back from the hospital today?

Est-ce que Sacha et Julia ne reviennent pas ?
Aren't Sacha and Julia coming back?

Est-ce que la patronne vient de Paris ?
Does the boss come from Paris?

Est-ce qu'il y a un bus au centre-ville ?
Is there a bus to the center of town?

Est-ce qu'il y a une douzaine d'œufs dans la boîte ?
Are there a dozen eggs in the box?

 douzaine (f) means 'dozen'

Quand est-ce que Monique revient du bureau ?
When is Monique coming back from the office?

Bootstrap French
TOPIC 34

❖ Irregular Adjectives

There are several very common French adjectives that are irregular and should just be memorized.

This topics' examples illustrate the following important but irregular adjectives.

- **vieux** (m) ⇒ **vieille** (f) - 'old'
- **beau** (m) ⇒ **belle** (f) – 'handsome' or 'beautiful'
- **nouveau** (m) ⇒ **nouvelle** (f) – 'new'
- **faux** (m) ⇒ **fausse** (f) – 'false'
- **doux** (m) ⇒ **douce** (f) – 'sweet' (including figuratively)
- **fou** (m) ⇒ **folle** (f) – 'crazy'
- **long** (m) ⇒ **longue** (f) – 'long'
- **frais** (m) ⇒ **fraîche** (f) – 'fresh'
- **gentil** (m) ⇒ **gentille** (f) – 'kind'
- **nul** (m) ⇒ **nulle** (f) – (slang) 'rubbish' or 'not good'
- **sec** (m) ⇒ **sèche** (f) – 'dry'
- **favori** (m) ⇒ **favorite** (f) – 'favorite'

EXAMPLES:

La boutique n'est pas vieille mais le quartier est très vieux.
The shop is not old but the neighborhood is very old.
   vieux (m) ⇒ vieille (f)
   quartier (f) means 'neighborhood' or 'area'

Tu viens d'une très belle ville.
You (familiar) come from a very nice town.
   beau (m) ⇒ belle (f)
   ville (f) means 'town' or 'city'

En plus, là-bas, le temps est toujours très beau.
In addition, there, the weather is always very beautiful.
   temps means 'the weather' or 'time'
   en plus means 'in addition' or 'more'

TOPIC 34 ❖ Irregular Adjectives

Le nouveau président a-t-il une nouvelle stratégie ?
Does the new president have a new strategy?
- nouveau (m) ⇒ nouvelle (f)
- stratégie (f) means 'strategy'

Le résultat est clairement faux.
The result is clearly wrong.
- résultat (m) means 'result' or 'outcome'

La rumeur d'une guerre est-elle fausse ?
Is the rumor of a war false?
- faux (m) ⇒ fausse (f)
- rumeur (f) means 'rumour'

Il y a une bouteille de cidre doux dans le frigo.
There's a bottle of sweet cider in the fridge.
- cidre (m) means 'cider'
- frigo (m.slang) means 'fridge'

C'est une petite fille très douce.
She is a very sweet girl.
- doux (m) ⇒ douce (f)
- Note that ce can be used as a pronoun ('he' or 'she') to directly refer to people

Je ne suis pas fou. Et elle non plus n'est pas folle.
I am not crazy. And neither is she crazy.
- fou (m) ⇒ folle (f)
- non plus (adv) means 'neither' or 'also'

Le livre n'est pas long mais la pièce est très longue.
The book is not long but the play is very long.
- long (m) ⇒ longue (f)

La pomme verte est fraîche mais l'avocat n'est pas frais.
The green apple is fresh but the avocado is not fresh.
- frais (m) ⇒ fraîche (f)

Le professeur n'est pas gentil mais la directrice est très gentille.
The professor is not nice but the director is very nice.
- gentil (m) ⇒ gentille (f)
- gentil (m) means 'kind' or 'nice'

TOPIC 34 ❖ Irregular Adjectives

Le livre est nul et la pièce est aussi nulle.
The book sucks and the play sucks too.

- nul (m) ⇒ nulle (f)
- nul (m) means 'rubbish' or 'useless' or 'bad'

Est-ce que le jean est sec ?
Are the jeans dry?

- jean (m) means 'jeans'

La chemise est déjà sèche.
The shirt is already dry.

- sec (m) ⇒ sèche (f)

C'est le plat favori de la famille.
It's the family's favorite dish.

- famille (f) means 'family'

C'est la musique favorite de Sonia.
It's Sonia's favorite music.

- favori (m) ⇒ favorite (f)
- music (f) means 'music'

Bootstrap French
TOPIC 35

❖ Special adjectives - *vieil, bel, nouvel* & *fol*

The singular masculine adjectives: **beau**, **vieux**, **nouveau** and **fou** take special forms when they are followed by a noun that begins with a vowel or a silent **h**.

- beau ⇒ bel
- vieux ⇒ vieil
- nouveau ⇒ nouvel
- fou ⇒ fol

EXAMPLES:

C'est un vieil homme.
He's an old man.

Il y a un bel arbre dans le jardin.
There is a beautiful tree in the garden.

Il y a un nouvel hôtel au centre de la ville.
There is a new hotel in the center of town.

C'est un vieil oncle.
He's an old uncle.

Le nouvel épisode est ce soir.
The new episode is tonight.

Il a un fol appétit !
He has a huge (crazy) appetite!

Henri est un vieil ami.
Henry is an old friend.

C'est un vieil ami d'enfance.
He's an old childhood friend.

Ils ont un bel appartement à Paris.
They have a nice apartment in Paris.

Le nouvel ordinateur est cher
The new computer is expensive

TOPIC 35 ❖ Special adjectives - *vieil, bel, nouvel* & *fol*

Le vieil hôpital est très beau.
The old hospital is very beautiful.

Y a-t-il un nouvel élève dans la classe ?
Is there a new student in the class?

Ce bel enfant est orphelin.
This beautiful child is an orphan.

Les nouveaux hôtels sont dans un bel endroit.
The new hotels are in a beautiful location.

❖ To want - the verb *vouloir*

The verb **vouloir** means 'to want'.

Its present tense conjugations are as follows:
- **je veux** - 'I want'
- **tu veux** - 'you (familiar) want'
- **il & elle veut** - 'he/she wants'
- **nous voulons** - 'we want'
- **vous voulez** - 'you (plural) want' or 'you (formal) want'
- **ils & elles veulent** - 'they want'

Caution should be exercised when using **vouloir** in the first person - **je veux** can sound abrupt and rude. There are better options for expressing 'I want' or 'I would like' which will be covered in an upcoming topic.

EXAMPLES:

je veux
I want

tu veux
you (familiar) want

il veut
he wants

nous voulons
we want

vous voulez
you (formal) want

ils ne veulent pas
they (males) do not want

elles veulent
they (females) want

Je veux un bel homme et un homme riche.
I want a handsome man and a rich man.

✎ **riche** (m) means 'rich' or 'well-off'

TOPIC 36 ❖ To want - the verb *vouloir*

Est-ce que tu veux le riz ?
Do you (familiar) want the rice?

   riz (m) means 'rice'

Qui veut une part de pizza ?
Who wants a piece of pizza?

   part (f) means 'piece' or 'share'

Pierre veut-il un demi de bière ?
Pierre - does he want a half (25 cl) of beer?

Pourquoi voulez-vous un nouvel ordinateur aussi cher ?
Why do you (formal) want such an expensive new computer?

Elles veulent quelque chose.
They (females) want something.

Ne veulent-elles pas une carafe d'eau ?
Don't they (females) want a jug of water?

Voulez-vous un café, Monsieur ?
Would you (formal) like (do you want) a coffee, Sir?

Oui, je veux bien, merci.
Yes, I would like (that), thank you.

   vouloir bien has the sense of enthusiastically wanting something

❖ Demonstrative Adjectives - *ce*, *cet*, *cette* and *ces*

The French demonstrative adjectives ('this' or 'that' or 'these' or 'those') are
- **ce** (singular, male)
  - **ce** becomes **cet** when followed by a vowel or mute **h**
- **cette** (singular, female)
- **ces** (plural, male & female) - 'these'

These demonstrative adjectives do not distinguish between 'this' (close by) and 'that' (further away) or 'these' and 'those'. This is addressed in the next topic.

EXAMPLES:

Ce garçon est intelligent.
This boy is smart.
📖 **intelligent** (m) means 'smart' or 'intelligent'

Cet homme est beau.
This man is handsome.

Cet arbre est très effrayant.
This tree is very scary.
📖 **effrayant** (m) means 'scary'

Cette fille est belle.
This girl is beautiful.

Ces hommes sont méchants.
These men are nasty.
📖 **méchant** (m) means 'nasty, or 'wicked' or 'mean' or 'badly behaved'

Ce gâteau est délicieux.
This cake is delicious.

Cet homme est beau mais il n'est pas très gentil.
This man is handsome but he is not very nice.

Je veux cette fleur rouge, s'il vous plaît.
I want this red flower, please.
📖 **s'il vous plait** means 'please' or (literally) 'if it pleases you'

TOPIC 37 ❖ Demonstrative Adjectives - *ce*, *cet*, *cette* and *ces*

Qui veut cette grande part de pizza ?
Who wants that big slice of pizza?

Il y a un homme curieux dans cette histoire.
There is a curious man in this story.

🍃 **curieux** (m) means 'curious' or 'strange'

Le chat va dans cette chambre.
The cat goes into that room.

Ces enfants sont insupportables.
These kids are insufferable.

🍃 **insupportable** (m) means 'insufferable' or 'unbearable' or 'can't stand'

La couleur de ces chaussures est étrange.
The color of these shoes is strange.

Cette boutique est neuve, mais ce quartier est très ancien.
This shop is new (just opened) but this neighborhood is very old.

🍃 **neuf** (m) means 'brand new'

Cette fille est-elle étudiante ?
Is this girl a student?

Ce train va-t-il à Paris ?
Does this train go to Paris?

Elle veut un grand et bel appartement à Paris.
She wants a big and nice apartment in Paris.

Cette maison est l'ancienne demeure du grand écrivain Honoré de Balzac.
This house is the former home of the great writer Honoré de Balzac.

🍃 **demeure** (f) means 'residence' or 'home'

Bootstrap French
TOPIC 38

❖ **This one here and those ones there - the particles *-ci* and *-là***

The particles **-ci** and **-là** can be partnered with the demonstrative adjectives (**ce, cette** & **ces**) to specify exactly which object is being referred to.
- **-ci** refers to an object close by or close at hand.
- **-là** refers to an object further away or beyond reach.

The particles are attached to the demonstrative adjectives with a dash.

EXAMPLES:

Cette chemise-ci est trop grande.
This shirt (here) is too big.
📖 **trop** means 'too' or 'too much' or 'excessively'

Cette valise-ci est assez lourde.
This suitcase (here) is quite heavy.
📖 **assez** means 'quite' or 'enough'

Mais cette valise-là n'est pas lourde.
But that suitcase (there) is not heavy.

Voulez-vous ces livres-ci ou ces livres-là ?
Do you (formal) want these books (here) or those books (there)?
📖 **ou** means 'or'

Ces livres-là sont très bon marché.
Those books (there) are very cheap.
📖 **bon marché** means 'cheap'

Allons-nous dans ce restaurant-ci ou dans ce restaurant-là ?
Are we going to this restaurant or that restaurant?

Ce restaurant-ci est trop cher.
This restaurant is overpriced.
📖 **cher** means 'expensive' or 'overpriced'

Ces femmes-là sont fascinantes.
Those women are fascinating.
📖 **fascinant** (m) means 'fascinating'

TOPIC 38 ❖ This one here and those ones there

Ces tomates-ci sont fraîches.
These tomatoes are fresh.

tomate (f) means 'tomato'

Cette chaise-là est cassée.
This chair is broken.

Ce tableau-ci est très connu.
This painting is very well known.

connu (m) means 'well known'

Ces demoiselles-là sont très impatientes.
Those ladies are very impatient.

demoiselle (f) means 'young lady'
impatient (m) means 'impatient'

Ces fraises-ci ne sont pas bon marché.
These strawberries are not cheap.

Bootstrap French
TOPIC 39

❖ **Demonstrative Pronouns - this one, that one -** *celui, celle, ceux & celles*

The demonstrative pronouns **celui**, **celle**, **ceux** & **celles** replace a specific noun that was previously mentioned or alluded to.

- The equivalent in English is 'one' or 'the one' - as in 'I want this one' or 'The one that I want'.

In French, these pronouns must agree with in number and gender with the noun they refer to.

Like the demonstrative adjectives, the particles **-ci** and **-là** can be used to better specify which 'one'.

EXAMPLES:

Il veut celui-ci.
He wants this one.

J'ai deux cafés ; celui-ci est décaféiné.
I have two coffees; this one is decaffeinated.

C'est une bonne idée, et j'aime aussi celle de Paul.
It's a good idea, and I like Paul's one too.

C'est le livre d'histoire, mais où est celui de chimie ?
That is the history book, but where is the chemistry one?

Il y a deux livres ; celui-ci est d'Hugo, celui-là est de Balzac.
There are two books; this one is by Hugo, that one by Balzac.

Celui-ci ou celui-là ?
This one or that one?

> When the gender is not clear or not previously specified, French always defaults to the masculine. Hence **celui** in this example.

Cette voiture est celle du médecin.
This car is the doctor's one.

Ce roman est trop court, et celui-là est trop long.
This novel is too short, and this one is too long.

TOPIC 39 ❖ Demonstrative Pronouns

Entre ces deux robes, je veux celle-ci.
Between these two dresses, I want this one.

✏ entre means 'between' or 'among'

Tu veux celles-ci ou celles-là ?
Do you (familiar) want these (ones here) or those (ones there)?

J'ai deux pommes. Qui veut celle-ci ?
I have two apples. Who wants this one?

J'aime les deux. Quel est le prix de celui-ci ?
I like both. What is the price of this one?

✏ les deux means 'both'

Vous ne voulez pas celui-là ? Qu'en est-il de celui-ci ?
You (formal) don't want this one? What about this one?

✏ qu'en est-il de means 'what about (something)'

Ceux-ci sont chers et ceux-là sont bon marché.
These are expensive and these are cheap.

✏ bon marché (adj) means 'cheap'

Bootstrap French
TOPIC 40

❖ Who and that - the subject relative pronoun *qui*

The indefinite pronoun **qui** means 'who' and refers to people.

But **qui** can also be used as a subject relative pronoun that refers to the subject of a sentence or clause. In this case, it can mean either 'who' or 'that'.

- This is equivalent to the 'that' in the sentence 'The apple that is green'. The 'that' is the subject (pronoun) of the verb 'to be'.

People, animals and objects can all be referred to using the relative pronoun **qui**.

And the relative pronoun can refer to singular and plural subjects.

Also note that **qui** NEVER becomes **qu'** in front of a vowel or mute **h-**.

EXAMPLES:

Qui est-ce ?
Who is this?
> The indefinite pronoun **qui** is the subject

Qui est à la porte ?
Who is at the door?

Qui est cet homme ?
Who is that man?

La pomme qui est verte.
The apple that is green.
> As a relative pronoun **qui** is the subject of the second clause - **qui est verte**

Les pommes qui sont vertes.
The apples that are green.
> The relative pronoun **qui** refers to a plural subject

J'ai un fils qui est étudiant à l'université.
I have a son who is a university student.
> **qui** can refer to both people and things

J'ai des enfants qui sont étudiants à l'université.
I have children who are university students.

TOPIC 40 ❖ Who and that - the subject relative pronoun *qui*

Je veux une maison qui est petite.
I want a house that is small.

qui est does NOT contract to *qu'est*

Le musée qui est célèbre n'est pas ouvert.
The museum which is famous is not open.

L'homme qui est dans le coin, c'est mon oncle.
The man who is in the corner, he is my uncle.

coin (m) means 'corner'

Ce sont les trains qui sont vraiment rapides.
Those are the trains that are really fast.

Celui-ci est le train rapide qui va directement à Marseille.
This one (here) is the fast train that goes directly to Marseille.

directement means 'directly'

Le chien qui est là-bas est perdu.
The dog that is over there is lost.

perdu (adj) means 'lost'

Ce sont les gens qui veulent du café.
These are the people who want coffee.

gens (m.pl) means 'people' (only ever used in the plural)

C'est la dame qui a cinq fils.
That is the lady who has five sons.

Est-ce qu'il y a un bus qui va au centre-ville ?
Is there a bus that goes to the center of the city?

Oui, il y a plusieurs bus qui vont au centre-ville.
Yes, there are several buses that go downtown.

C'est qui le gars qui est dans le journal aujourd'hui ?
Who's the guy who in the newspaper today?

French Grammar

❖ Who and that - the object relative pronoun *que*

The object pronoun **que** means 'what' or 'that' and refers to a direct object. Unlike the subject relative pronoun **qui**, it cannot be the subject of a verb.

- In English it is like the 'what' in 'You want what?' and **not** 'What is making that noise?'.

As an object pronoun **que** can only refer to things and not people. We use **qui** to refer to people.

Que can also serve as the object **relative** pronoun that refers to a direct object in a sentence or clause.

- This is equivalent to the 'that' in the sentence 'The apple that I want'. The 'that' is the subject of the verb 'to want' — a pronoun referring to 'the apple'.

As an object relative pronoun **que** can refer to both people or things - singular or plural.

Unlike **qui**, **que** does not contract to **qu'** if it proceeds a vowel or mute **h**.

EXAMPLES:

Que veux-tu ?
What do you (familiar) want?
- The indefinite pronoun **que** is the object

Qu'avez-vous dans le sac ?
What do you (formal) have in the bag?

La pomme que je veux.
The apple that I want.
- As a relative pronoun **que** is the object of the second clause - **que je veux**

Les pommes vertes que je veux.
The green apples that I want.
- The relative pronoun **que** refers to a plural object

Voici la glace que vous voulez.
Here is the ice cream that you (formal) want.

Le livre que vous voulez est intéressant.
The book that you (formal) want is interesting.

Les fruits qu'ils ont - ils sont délicieux.
The fruits that they have - they are delicious.

TOPIC 41 ❖ Who and that - the object relative pronoun *que*

Les pommes que j'ai à la maison sont très aigres.
The apples that I have at home are very sour.

Il y a un trou dans le papier que vous avez dans votre sac.
There is a hole in the paper that you (formal) have in your bag.

Voici les papiers que vous voulez.
Here are the papers that you (formal) want.

Il y a des documents dans le bureau qu'ils veulent.
There are some documents in the office that they want.

Y a-t-il des livres dans cette boîte que vous voulez ?
Are there any books in this box that you (formal) want?

Sont-ce les clés qu'ils veulent ?
Are these the keys that they want?

Les timbres qu'elle a dans ce livre sont rares.
The stamps she has in that book are rare.

- **timbre** (m) means 'postage stamp'
- **rare** (adj) means 'rare'

❖ Indefinite Relative Pronouns - *ce qui* & *ce que*

When the subject or object is missing in a relative clause, we can use the pronoun **ce** in its place.

And in combination with the subject and object relative pronouns we have **ce que** and **ce qui**.

- **ce qui** serves as the indefinite **subject** in a relative clause.
- **ce que** serves as the indefinite (direct) **object** in a relative clause.

In English these might be 'the thing that' or 'that which' or simply 'what'.

Unlike **qui** and **que** themselves, **ce qui** and **ce que** cannot refer to people.

If we have sufficient information about **ce** we can use **ceux qui** for plurals, and **celle qui** if it is feminine etc.

EXAMPLES:

Je veux ce qu'elle a dans le sac.
I want what she has in the bag.
- 💡 **ce** is an unmentioned object that **elle a dans le sac**

J'ai ce qu'elle veut dans ce sac.
I have what she wants in this bag.
- 💡 **ce** is an unmentioned object **dans ce sac** that **elle veut**

Pourquoi veux-tu ce qu'elle a dans ce sac ?
Why do you (familiar) want what she has in that bag?

Voici ce que tu veux, n'est-ce pas ?
Here is what you (familiar) want, right?
- 📖 **voici** means 'this is' or 'here is'

Ce que j'ai dans ce sac est précieux.
That which I have in this bag is precious.
- 📖 **précieux** (adj) means 'precious'

Ce qu'il veut, c'est celui-ci.
What he wants, it is this one (here).
- 💡 This is a common formulation that adds suspense

Ce qu'ils veulent, ce sont ceux qui sont sur la table.
What they want, it is those that are on the table.

TOPIC 42 ❖ Indefinite Relative Pronouns - *ce qui* & *ce que*

J'ai celui que tu veux.
I have the one (masculine) that you (familiar) want.
- celui is the object of tu veux
- Perhaps referring to (masculine) le livre

Voilà celle qu'ils veulent.
This is the one (feminine) they want.
- voilà means 'there is' or 'this is'
- Perhaps referring to (feminine) la bouteille du vin

Je veux ceux qui sont dans le placard.
I want those ones that are in the cupboard.
- placard (m) means 'cupboard' or 'closet'

Je veux ce qu'elle a.
I want what she has.

Elle veut vraiment celle qui est dans la vitrine.
She really wants the one that is in the shop window.
- Perhaps talking about (feminine) la chemise
- vitrine (f) means 'shop window'

Qu'est-ce que c'est ?
What is 'that which' it is? *OR* What is that?
- The ce que in this common phrase is in fact the indefinite relative pronoun

Bootstrap French
TOPIC 43

❖ To do, to make - the verb *faire*

The verb **faire** means 'to do' or 'to make'. It is an **-RE** verb but is irregular.
Its present tense conjugations are as follows:
- **je fais** - 'I do'
- **tu fais** - 'you (familiar) do'
- **il & elle fait** - 'he/she does'
- **nous faisons** - 'we do'
- **vous faites** - 'you (plural) do' & 'you (formal) do'
- **ils & elles font** - 'they do'

There are many idiomatic uses of **faire** a few of which are introduced in this topic's examples.

EXAMPLES:

je fais
I do / I am doing

tu fais
you (familiar) do / you are doing

il fait
he does / he is doing

elle ne fait pas
she does not do / she is not doing

nous faisons
we do / we are doing

vous faites
you (formal) do / you are doing

ils ne font pas
they (males) do not do / they are not doing

elles font
they (females) do / they are doing

TOPIC 43 ❖ To do, to make - the verb *faire*

Je fais un gâteau pour la fête.
I am making a cake for the party.

- *fête* (f) means 'party'

Il fait des projets pour les vacances d'été.
He is making plans for the summer holidays.

- *faire des projets* (verb) means 'to make plans'
- *été* (m) means 'summer'

Qui fait la cuisine dans la famille ?
Who cooks in the family?

- *faire la cuisine* (verb) means 'to cook' or 'to do the cooking'

Ce soir, nous faisons la fête avec des amis.
Tonight we are having a party with friends.

- *faire la fête* (verb) means 'to have a party'

Les parents font attention avec les enfants dans l'eau.
Parents are careful with the children in the water.

- *faire attention* (verb) means 'to take care' or 'to be careful'

La femme fait le ménage chaque matin.
The wife does the housework every morning.

- *ménage* (m) means 'household'
- *faire le ménage* (verb) means 'to do housework'

Mais le mari fait la grasse matinée chaque matin.
But the husband sleeps in every morning.

- *faire la grasse matinée* (verb) means 'to sleep in'

Pourquoi vous faites la tête tous les deux aujourd'hui ?
Why are you (plural) both sulking today?

- *faire la tête* (verb) means 'to sulk' or 'to be in a bad mood'
- *tous les deux* means 'both'

Après la Covid, nous ne faisons pas la bise.
After COVID we don't greet with kisses.

- *faire la bise* (verb) means 'to greet by kissing cheeks'

Ce que je fais n'est pas difficile.
What I do is not difficult.

L'homme qui fait la cuisine est un chef.
The man who is cooking is a chef.

French Grammar

TOPIC 43 ❖ To do, to make - the verb *faire*

Ce qui fait du bruit est inconnu.
What is making the noise is unknown.
- **fait du bruit** (verb) means 'to make noise'
- **inconnu** (adj) means 'unknown'

❖ What? - questions with *qu'est-ce que*

We have already encountered **que** as the relative pronoun when it is the subject of the sentence.

Que itself can also be used to ask the question 'what' when referring to the subject of a verb. Such questions usually take the inverted-hyphenated form.

We also saw how **est-ce que** is used to ask a question when the subject is included.

We can combine **que** and **est-ce que** into the very common question pattern **qu'est-ce que** which simply means 'what?'.

- **qu'est-ce que** literally translates as 'what is it that...'

Note that like **est-ce que**, **qu'est-ce que** is already an inversion so nothing else in the question should be inverted.

EXAMPLES:

Que fait-il ?
What is he doing?
  💡 Asking a question with **que** and inversion

Qu'est-ce que c'est ?
What is that?

Qu'est-ce que tu veux ?
What do you (familiar) want?

Qu'est-ce que tu fais ?
What are you (familiar) doing?

Qu'est-ce que vous faites à Paris ?
What are you (formal) doing in Paris?

Qu'est-ce qu'il y a dans la boîte bleue ?
What's in the blue box?
  🔖 **bleu** (m) means 'blue'

Qu'est-ce que vous avez dans cette poche ?
What do you (formal) have in that pocket?
  🔖 **poche** (f) means 'pocket'

TOPIC 44 ❖ What? - questions with *qu'est-ce que*

Qu'est-ce qu'il y a dans ce petit trou ?
What is there in that little hole?

📖 **trou** (m) means 'hole'

Qu'y a-t-il dans ce portefeuille ?
What is there in that wallet?

💡 Asking a question with **que** and inversion

📖 **portefeuille** (m) means 'wallet'

❖ To see - the verb *voir*

The verb **voir** means 'to see'.

It is a very common but irregular **-IR** verb. Its conjugations should be memorized.

Its present tense conjugations are as follows:

- **je vois** - 'I see'
- **tu vois** - 'you (familiar) see'
- **il & elle voit** - 'he/she sees'
- **nous voyons** - 'we see'
- **vous voyez** - 'you (plural) see' & 'you (formal) see'
- **ils & elles voient** - 'they see'

The verb **voir** can also mean 'to understand' just like 'to see' can in English.

Note that also like in English there is a distinction in French between **voir** ('to see') and **regarder** ('to look' or 'to watch').

EXAMPLES:

je vois
I see

tu vois
you (familiar) see

il voit
he sees

elle ne voit pas
she does not see

nous voyons
we see

vous voyez
you (formal) see

ils ne voient pas
they (males) do not see / they are not seeing

TOPIC 45 ❖ To see - the verb *voir*

elles voient
they (females) see / they are seeing

Je vois un tigre là-bas.
I see a tiger over there.

Je vois deux personnes au loin.
I am seeing two people in the distance.

    au loin means 'in the distance'

Est-ce que tu vois les clés ?
Do you (familiar) see the keys?

Voyez-vous la différence ?
Do you (formal) see the difference?

    différence (f) means 'difference'

Avec ces lunettes, elle voit clairement maintenant.
With these glasses, she sees clearly now.

    clairement means 'clearly'

aujourd'hui, nous voyons très bien le mont Blanc.
Today, we can see Mont Blanc very well.

Qu'est-ce qu'il voit dans ce trou ?
What does he see in this hole?

Est-ce que vous voyez le navire à l'horizon ?
Do you (formal) see the ship on the horizon?

    navire (m) means 'ship'
    horizon (m) means 'horizon'

Ah oui, je vois maintenant.
Ah yes, I see (understand) now.

Je vois maintenant pourquoi vous voulez une réponse immédiatement.
I see (understand) now why you (formal) want an answer immediately.

    immédiatement means 'immediately'

TOPIC 45 ❖ To see - the verb *voir*

Nous voyons des étoiles brillantes avec le télescope.
We see bright stars with the telescope.

- étoile (f) means 'star'
- brillant (m) means 'bright'
- télescope (m) means 'telescope'

Je ne vois pas ce que tu vois.
I don't see what you (familiar) see.

❖ Dual-verb constructions - conjugated + infinitive

In French, certain verbs can be followed by second verb in its infinitive (for dictionary) form.

One such **auxiliary** verb is **vouloir** ('to want to'). So for example:

- **vouloir faire** - 'to want to do'
- **vouloir voir** - 'to want to see'
- **vouloir être** - 'to want to be'
- **vouloir avoir** - 'to want to have'

When negating the **ne..pas** only goes either side of the auxiliary verb - for example **ne vouloir pas faire** ('to not want to do').

EXAMPLES:

Elle veut aller à la boulangerie.
She wants to go to the bakery.

Nicole veut voir ce film.
Nicole wants to see this movie.

Qu'est-ce que tu veux faire aujourd'hui ?
What do you (familiar) want to do today?

Je veux faire un gâteau pour la soirée.
I want to make a cake for the evening.
   soirée (f) means 'evening party'

Est-ce que vous voulez aller à l'opéra ce soir ?
Do you (formal) want to go to the opera tonight?
   opéra (f) means 'opera'

Qui veut faire le ménage ?
Who wants to do the housework?

Je veux avoir trois enfants.
I want to have three children.

Il veut être seul.
He wants to be alone.
   seul means 'alone'

TOPIC 46 ❖ Dual-verb constructions - conjugated + infinitive

Ils veulent faire la grasse matinée ce week-end.
They want to sleep in this weekend.

Voulez-vous faire une fête ?
Do you (formal) want to have a party?

Pourquoi ne veux-tu pas aller à l'école ?
Why don't you (familiar) want to go to school?

Il ne veut pas venir à la réunion.
He doesn't want to come at the meeting.

💡 **ne..pas** only on the first (auxiliary) verb
✏️ **réunion** (f) means 'meeting'

Elle ne veut pas être en retard.
She does not want to be late.

Bien sûr, nous ne voulons pas avoir la grippe.
Of course we do not want to have the flu.

✏️ **grippe** (f) means 'flu'

Voulez-vous avoir celui-ci ?
Do you (formal) want to have this one (here)?

Pourquoi veux-tu voir ce qu'elle a dans ce sac ?
Why do you (familiar) want to see what she has in that bag?

Je veux avoir ceux qui sont dans le placard.
I want to have the ones that are in the closet.

Sacha et Julia, ne veulent-ils pas revenir aujourd'hui ?
Sacha and Julia, don't they want to come back today?

Je ne veux pas acheter un seul de ces livres.
I don't want to buy a single one of these books.

✏️ **un(e) seul(e) de** means 'a single one of'

Je veux faire exactement ce que tu fais.
I want to do exactly what you (familiar) are doing.

✏️ **exactement** (adv) means 'exactly'

❖ To be able to - the verb *pouvoir*

The verb **pouvoir** means 'to be able to'.

The meaning is both 'to be capable of' and also 'to have permission to' or 'to be allowed to'.

It is a highly irregular verb. Its present tense conjugations are as follows:

- **je peux** - 'I can'
- **tu peux** - 'you (familiar) can'
- **il & elle peut** - 'he/she can'
- **nous pouvons** - 'we can'
- **vous pouvez** - 'you (plural) can' & 'you (formal) can'
- **ils & elles peuvent** - 'they can'

Pouvoir is another French verb that can be an auxiliary followed by a second verb in its infinitive.

EXAMPLES:

je peux
I can

tu peux
you (familiar) can

il peut
he can

elle ne peut pas
she can not

nous pouvons
we can

vous pouvez
you (formal) can

ils ne peuvent pas
they (males) can not

elles peuvent
they (females) can

TOPIC 47 ❖ To be able to - the verb *pouvoir*

Il peut aller à l'école.
He can go to school.

Je peux voir un oiseau vert sur le toit.
I can see a green bird on the roof.
  toit (m) means 'roof'

Où pouvons-nous aller cet après-midi ?
Where can we go this afternoon?

Pouvez-vous voir le cerf-volant dans l'arbre ?
Can you (formal) see the kite in the tree?
  cerf-volant (f) means 'kite'

Peut-elle faire le lit ?
Can she make the bed?

Qu'est-ce que nous pouvons faire à la maison ?
What can we do at home?

Que pouvez-vous voir dans le trou ?
What can you (formal) see in the hole?

Je peux voir une grosse araignée noire dans le trou.
I can see a big black spider in the hole.

Ne pouvez-vous pas voir l'horloge d'ici ?
Can you (formal) not see the clock from here?

Pouvons-nous avoir ceux-là dans la vitrine ?
Can we have those ones in the shop window?

Pouvez-vous être à la maison ce soir ?
Can you (formal) be at home this evening?

Qui peut venir à la fête demain soir ?
Who can come to the party tomorrow evening?

Peuvent-ils revenir ?
Can they come again?

Je ne peux pas voir les journaux sur l'étagère.
I cannot see the newspapers on the shelf.

Bootstrap French
TOPIC 48

❖ Which - *quel, quelle, quels* & *quelles*

The Interrogative adjectives **quel**, **quelle**, **quels** and **quelles** mean 'which'.

And in French these must agree in gender and number with the object being referred to:

- **quel** - masculine singular
- **quelle** - feminine singular
- **quels** - masculine plural
- **quelles** - feminine plural

Normally as question words, these should come at the start of the phrase. But colloquially, they can go anywhere.

When used with the verb **être** ('to be'), **quel** etc. can simply mean 'what'.

EXAMPLES:

Quel film veux-tu voir ?
What movie do you (familiar) want to see?

Quelle jupe veux-tu ?
What skirt do you (familiar) want?

Quelle ville est la plus jolie : Annecy ou Nancy ?
Which city is the prettiest: Annecy or Nancy?
  ✏ **le** (or **la**) **plus** means 'the most'
  💡 **la plus jolie** therefore is 'the most pretty' or 'the prettiest'

Quels livres veut-elle ?
What books does she want?
  💡 **livres** is masculine plural so use **quels**

Quel plat veux-tu ?
What dish do you (familiar) want?

À quel théâtre allez-vous demain ?
Which theatre are you (formal) going to tomorrow?
  ✏ **théâtre** (m) means 'theatre'

TOPIC 48 ❖ Which - *quel, quelle, quels & quelles*

Quels pays d'Europe sont montagneux ?
Which countries in Europe are mountainous?

- **pays** is masculine but the number is ambiguous, but **sont** implies plural so use **quels**
- **pays** (m) means 'country'
- **montagneux** (m) means 'mountainous'

Dans quelle boîte est la récompense ?
In which box is the reward (prize)?

- **recompense** (f) means 'reward'

Sur quelles montagnes est-ce qu'il y a des chèvres de montagne ?
On which mountains are there mountain goats?

- **montagnes** is feminine plural so we use **quelles**
- **montagne** (f) means 'mountain'
- **chèvre** (f) means 'goat'

Quels types de bagues y a-t-il dans la bijouterie ?
What types of rings are there in the jewelry store?

- **bague** (f) means 'ring' (jewelry)

Quel jour es-tu libre ?
What day are you (familiar) free?

- **libre** (m) means 'free'

Quelle est la solution ?
What is the solution?

- Here **quelle** with the verb **être** is 'what is' rather than 'which is'

Quels sont les cours les plus intéressants ?
What are the most interesting courses?

- **cours** (m) means 'course' or 'subject' or 'lesson'

Quelle est la plus belle princesse du royaume ?
Who is the most beautiful princess in the kingdom?

- **princesse** (f) means 'princess'
- **royaume** (m) means 'kingdom'

Quel jour sommes-nous ?
What day of the week is it?

- This is a standard to ask what day of the week it is.

Quelle heure est-il ?
What time is it?

- This is one standard to ask the time of day.

TOPIC 48 ❖ Which - *quel, quelle, quels & quelles*

Quelle est l'adresse du bureau ?
What is the address of the office?
- Here **quelle** with the verb **être** is 'what is' rather than 'which is'

Quelle est la capitale de l'Allemagne ?
What is the capital of German?
- Here **quelle** with the verb **être** is 'what is' rather than 'which is'
- **allemand** (f) means 'German'
- **capitale** (f) means 'capital city'

Quels sont les pays francophones ?
What are the French-speaking countries?
- Here **quels** with the verb **être** is 'what are' rather than 'which are'
- **francophone** (m) means 'French speaking'

❖ Which one - *lequel*, *laquelle*, *lesquels* & *laquelles*

The Interrogative pronouns **lequel**, **laquelle**, **lesquels** and **lesquelles** mean 'which one' or 'which ones'.

They are the pronominal counterparts of the adjectives **quel**, **quelle**, **quels** and **quelles**.

And in French these must also agree in gender and number with the object being referred to:

- **lequel** - masculine singular
- **laquelle** - feminine singular
- **lesquels** - masculine plural
- **lesquelles** - feminine plural

When used with a preposition (like **à** and **de**) these pronouns simply mean 'to which' or 'in which'.

Also with certain prepositions we see the same contractions as with prepositions and the definite articles. For example **à** + **lequel** ⇒ **auquel** ('to which' - masculine).

EXAMPLES:

Lequel voulez-vous, celui-ci ou celui-là ?
Which one do you (formal) want, this one or that one?

Je veux un fruit. Lequel veux-tu ?
I want (a piece of) fruit. Which one do you (familiar) want?

  fruit (m) means 'fruit' or 'a piece of fruit'

Je veux voir le film. Lequel voulez-vous voir ?
I want to see the film. Which one do you (formal) want to see?

Je veux la pomme là-bas. Laquelle ?
I want the apple over there. Which one?

Lequel de ces deux médecins veux-tu voir ?
Which one of these two doctors do you (familiar) want to see?

Avez-vous les clés ? Lesquelles ?
Do you (formal) have the keys? Which ones?

TOPIC 49 ❖ Which one - *lequel, laquelle, lesquels & laquelles*

Avez-vous le marteau ? Lequel ? Le grand ?
Do you (formal) have the hammer? Which one? The big one?

- *marteau* (m) means 'hammer'
- Note the use of an adjective (*grand*) as a specifying noun - *le grand ?*

La ville dans laquelle il y a une grande tour, c'est Paris !
The city in which there is a big tower, that is Paris!

Il y a deux options sur la carte. Laquelle voulez-vous ?
There are two options on the menu. Which one do you (formal) want?

- *option* (f) means 'option'
- *carte* (f) means 'menu' or 'map'

Laquelle de ces deux voitures est la plus rapide ?
Which one of these two cars is the fastest?

Voici deux femmes. Laquelle des deux est la plus belle ?
Here are two women. Which of the two is more beautiful?

Cinq maisons sont disponibles. Lesquelles voulez-vous voir ?
Five houses are available. Which ones do you (formal) want to see?

- *disponible* (m) means 'available'

Nous allons à la plage. À laquelle allons-nous ?
We are going to the beach. To which one are we going?

- à + laquelle ⇒ à laquelle (to which)

Nous pouvons aller dans plusieurs pays de l'Europe. Auxquels voulez-vous aller ?
We can go to several countries in Europe. Which ones do you (formal) want to go to?

- à + lesquels ⇒ auxquels (to which ones)

La ville dans laquelle je vais demain, c'est Avignon.
The city I'm going to tomorrow is Avignon.

- à + laquelle ⇒ à laquelle (to which)

Le cinéma près duquel il y a un grand parc.
The cinema near which there is a large park.

- près de + lequal ⇒ près duquel (close from which)

C'est la robe dans laquelle elle est la plus belle.
This is the dress in which she is most beautiful.

- dans + laquelle (in which)

❖ The Possessive Adjectives

The French possessive adjectives ('my', your', 'his' etc.) depend on gender and number:
- **je** ⇒ **mon** (masc), **ma** (fem) & **mes** (plural) – 'my'
- **tu** ⇒ **ton** (masc), **ta** (fem) & **tes** (plural) – 'your'
- **il** & **elle** ⇒ **son** (masc), **sa** (fem) & **ses** (plural) – 'his' or 'her'
- **nous** ⇒ **notre** (masc and fem) & **nos** (plural) – 'our'
- **vous** ⇒ **votre** (masc and fem) & **vos** (plural) – 'your'
- **ils** & **elles** ⇒ **leur** (masc and fem) & **leurs** (plural) – 'their'

Note that if a feminine noun begins with a vowel or mute **h**, to avoid contiguous vowels, the masculine possessive pronoun is used.

EXAMPLES:

Où est mon frère ?
Where is my brother?
　le frère is singular masculine ⇒ mon frère

Ma tasse est vide.
My cup is empty.
　la tasse is feminine ⇒ ma tasse
　vide (m) means 'empty'

Mes parents sont actuellement à Toulouse.
My parents are currently in Toulouse.
　les parents is plural ⇒ mes parents
　actuellement means 'currently' or 'at present'

Je ne vois pas ton frère mais ta sœur est là-bas.
I can't see your (familiar) brother but your sister is over there.
　la sœur is singular feminine ⇒ ta sœur

Dans ta ville, est-ce qu'il y a une piscine ?
In your (familiar) town, is there a swimming pool?
　la ville is singular feminine ⇒ ta ville

Quelles sont tes couleurs préférées ?
What are your (familiar) favorite colors?
　les couleurs is plural ⇒ tes couleurs

TOPIC 50 ❖ The Possessive Adjectives

Sa grand-mère et son grand-père viennent aujourd'hui.
His/her grandmother and grandfather are coming today.

- la grand-mère is singular feminine ⇒ sa grand-mère
- le grand-père is singular masculine ⇒ son grand-père
- grand-mère (f) means 'grandmother'
- grand-père (m) means 'grandfather'

Voilà votre billet.
Here is your (formal) ticket.

- le billet in singular ⇒ votre billet

Où sont vos amis ?
Where are your (formal) friends?

- les amis is plural ⇒ vos amis

Quelle est votre adresse ?
What is your (formal) address?

- l'adresse is singular ⇒ votre adresse

Leur chien est malade.
Their dog is sick.

- le chien is singular ⇒ leur chien

Leurs chats sont très mignons.
Their cats are very cute.

- les chats is plural ⇒ leurs chats

Est-ce que nos voisins ont des enfants ?
Do our neighbors have children?

- les voisins is plural ⇒ nos voisins

Voici mon amie Marie.
This is my friend Marie.

- The feminine amie (f) starts with a vowel so mon rather than ma is used

Je vais à ton école.
I am going to your (familiar) school.

- The feminine école (f) starts with a vowel so ton rather than ta is used.

C'est son idée.
It is his/her idea.

- The feminine idée (f) starts with a vowel so son rather than sa is used.

TOPIC 50 ❖ The Possessive Adjectives

Mon horloge est cassée.

My clock is broken.

💡 The feminine horloge (f) starts with mute **h** so **mon** rather than **ma** is used.

Bienvenue Mesdames et Messieurs !

Welcome ladies and gentlemen!

💡 The change from **madame** (singular) ⇒ **mesdames** (plural)

💡 The adjective changes from **Monsieur** (singular) ⇒ **Messieurs** (plural)

Mesdemoiselles, voulez-vous une coupe de champagne ?

Young ladies, would you (plural) like a glass of champagne?

💡 The change from **mademoiselle** (singular) ⇒ **mesdemoiselles** (plural)

✏ **coupe** (f) means 'goblet' or 'champagne glass' or '(fruit) bowl' or '(prize) cup'

❖ The Possessive Pronouns

Possessive pronouns ('mine', 'yours', 'his', 'hers' etc.) are used in place of nouns to indicate to whom or to what those nouns belong.

The 21 French possessive pronouns depend on gender and number:

- **je** ⇒ **le mien** (sing.masc), **la mienne** (sing.fem), **les miens** (pl.masc) & **les miennes** (pl.fem)
- **tu** ⇒ **le tien** (sing.mac) etc. as above.
- **il** & **elle** ⇒ **le sien** (sing.mac) etc. as above.
- **nous** ⇒ **le** & **la nôtre** (sing masc & fem) & **les nôtres** (plural)
- **vous** ⇒ **le** & **la vôtre** (sing masc & fem) & **les vôtres** (plural)
- **ils** & **elles** ⇒ **le** & **la leur** (masc and fem) & **les leurs** (plural)

Note that the gender and number of the possessive pronoun must agree with the gender and number of the noun possessed, not (like in English) that of the possessor.

Note also the any prepositions (like **à** and **de**) that precede the possessive pronouns will contract as per normal with the definite articles (**le**, **la** & **les**).

EXAMPLES:

Voilà ton cahier. Mais où est le mien ?
Here is your (familiar) notebook. But where is mine?
💡 **le cahier** is masciline singular ⇒ **le mien**
📖 **cahier** (m) means 'exercise book'

Ce sont mes clés. Où sont les tiennes ?
These are my keys. Where are yours (familiar)?
💡 **les clés** is plural feminine ⇒ **les teinnes**

Est-ce que c'est son stylo ? Oui, c'est le sien.
Is that his pen? Yes, it's his.
💡 **le stylo** is singular masculine ⇒ **le sien**

Notre valise est noire et la leur est rose.
Our suitcase is black. Theirs is pink.
💡 **la valise** is singular feminine ⇒ **la leur**

Il y a un chapeau dans le placard, mais ce n'est pas le vôtre.
There's a hat in the closet, but it's not yours (formal).

TOPIC 51 ❖ The Possessive Pronouns

Il y a deux pains au chocolat - celui-ci c'est le mien et celui-là c'est le tien.
There are two pain au chocolates - this one (here) is mine and that one (there) is yours (familiar).

Il y a des chaussures dans la machine à laver, mais ce ne sont pas les vôtres.
There are shoes in the washing machine, but they're not yours (formal).

🖋 machine à laver (f) means 'washing machine'

La chaise bleue est la mienne, la rouge est la tienne.
The blue chair is mine, the red is yours (familiar).

Mes cheveux sont plus longs que les tiens.
My hair is longer than yours (familiar).

Ses idées et les miennes sont vraiment différentes.
His ideas and mine are really different.

Notre père est âgé, mais le vôtre est plus jeune.
Our father is old but yours (formal) is younger.

Oui, ces trois enfants sont les nôtres.
Yes, these three children are ours.

Je vois plusieurs voitures, mais je ne vois pas la mienne.
I see several cars, but I don't see mine.

Tes stylos sont dans ta chambre, les miens sont sur la table.
Your (familiar) pens are in your room, mine are on the table.

Leur chien est rapide, le vôtre est lent.
Their dog is fast, yours (formal) is slow.

Mes parents sont américains. Les leurs aussi.
My parents are American. Theirs too.

Notre vieille voiture fait encore des siennes.
Our old car is still acting up.

🖋 faire des siennes (verb) means 'to be up to its old tricks' or 'to act up'

Je vais dehors avec des amis ce soir. Tu es des nôtres ?
I am going out with some friends this evening. Will you (familiar) join us?

🖋 être des nôtres (verb) means 'to be one of us' or 'to join us'

Bootstrap French
TOPIC 52

❖ **The partitive articles -** *du, de la* **&** *des*

Another common use of the word **de** is as a partitive. This is like the words 'some' or 'any' in English.

- The singular partitive article refers to an unspecified quantity of an **uncountable** noun - like liquids, powders and grains.
  - The singular forms are **de la** (feminine) and **du** (masculine) with the contraction **de l'** if the noun starts with a vowel or a mute **h**.
- A plural partitive article **des** is used with undefined qualities of **countable** items - like people, machines, buildings etc.
  - The plural form is **des** regardless of gender.

The partitive article should agree with the noun in gender and number.

EXAMPLES:

Je veux de l'eau.
I want (some) water.
💡 **l'eau** is uncountable

Avez-vous du pain à la maison ?
Do you (formal) have (any) bread at home?
💡 **le pain** is uncountable when we mean 'any bread'

Voulez-vous du café ?
Do you (formal) want (some) coffee?
💡 **le café** is uncountable when we mean 'some coffee'

Tu peux avoir de la viande.
You (familiar) can have (some) meat.
📖 **viande** (f) means 'meat'

As-tu de l'huile d'olive ?
Do you (familiar) have (any) olive oil?
📖 **huile d'olive** (f) means 'olive oil'

Les enfants veulent du lait ce matin.
The children want (some) milk this morning.

TOPIC 52 ❖ The partitive articles - *du, de la* & *des*

Je veux de la salade et des pâtes.
I want (some) salad and (some) pasta.
- salade (f) means 'salade'
- pâtes (pl.f) means 'pasta'
- les pâtes is always plural when meaning 'pasta' and it is countable.

Vous voulez du vin blanc, n'est-ce pas ?
You (formal) want (some) white wine, don't you?

As-tu de l'argent ?
Do you (familiar) have any money?
- argent (m) means 'money' or 'silver'

Elle veut du beurre sur sa baguette.
She wants (some) butter on her baguette.
- beurre (f) means 'butter'

Voici du gâteau. C'est un petit morceau du gâteau.
Here's some cake. It's a small piece of the cake.
- Some cake - not the whole cake
- entier (m) means 'whole'
- l'entier (m) means 'the whole thing'

Il y a de la glace sur ta chemise.
There is some ice-cream on your (familiar) shirt.
- glace (f) means 'ice cream' or 'ice' or 'mirror'

Vous voulez des légumes ?
Do you (formal) want (some) vegetables?
- légume (m) means 'vegetable'

Dans la vitrine il y a des gâteaux qui sont très beaux.
In the window there are (some) cakes which are very beautiful.

Y a-t-il des lettres dans la boîte à lettres ?
Are there (any) letters in the mailbox?
- la boîte à lettres means 'mailbox'

Elle a des amies formidables.
She has wonderful friends.
- formidable (m) means 'great' or 'tremendous'

Avez-vous des livres dans votre valise ?
Do you (formal) have (any) books in your suitcase?

TOPIC 52 ❖ The partitive articles - *du, de la* & *des*

Le professeur a de la patience.
The teacher has (some) patience.
- Not specifying how much patience he has
- **patience** (f) means 'patience'

Tu as de la chance.
You (familiar) are lucky. *OR* You are having some luck.
- Not specifying how much luck you have
- **chance** (f) means 'luck' or 'chance'

Bootstrap French
TOPIC 53

❖ Negative partitive - *pas de*

In negative sentences, the partitive articles (**du**, **de la**, **de l'** and **des**) all change to **de**.

- **de** is used whether the noun is singular or plural, countable or non-countable.

The exception is that after the verb **être** (and other verbs of state) we should use the normal partitives (**de la** or **du**).

EXAMPLES:

Je ne veux pas d'eau.
I don't want water.

As-tu de l'eau ? Non, je n'ai pas d'eau.
Do you (familiar) have water? No, I don't have water.
  💡 de l'eau ⇒ d'eau in the negative

Je ne veux pas de lait dans mon café.
I don't want milk in my coffee.
  💡 du lait ⇒ de lait in the negative

Il n'a pas d'amis.
He has no friends.
  💡 des amis ⇒ d'amis in the negative

N'avez-vous pas de pain à la maison ?
Don't you (formal) have bread at home?
  💡 le pain is uncountable when we mean 'some bread'

Heureusement, nous n'avons pas de souris dans notre maison.
Luckily we don't have mice in our house.
  💡 des souris ⇒ de souris in the negative
  ✏ heureusement means 'luckily' or 'happily'

Je suis vraiment désolé, nous n'avons pas de pain au chocolat aujourd'hui.
I'm really sorry, we don't have pain au chocolate today.
  ✏ désolé (m) means 'sorry'

Elle ne veut pas de beurre sur sa baguette.
She does not want any butter on her baguette.

TOPIC 53 ❖ Negative partitive - *pas de*

Voulez-vous de la viande ? Non, je ne veux pas de viande.
Do you (formal) want meat? No, I don't want meat.

Malheureusement je n'ai pas d'argent en ce moment.
Unfortunately I don't have any money right now.

🕮 **en ce moment** means 'at the moment' or 'right now'

C'est du sel ? Non, ce n'est pas du sel - c'est du sucre.
Is it (some) salt? No, it's not (some) salt - it's s (some) sugar.

💡 Use the positive partitive (**de la** or **du**) after **être** even in a negative (**ne pas**) sentence.

Ce n'est pas du jus d'orange. C'est de l'eau.
It is not (some) orange juice. It is (some) water.

💡 Use the positive partitive (**de la** or **du**) after **être** even in a negative (**ne pas**) sentence.

Je n'ai pas de pêches blanches.
I don't have (any) white peaches.

Le professeur n'a pas de patience.
The teacher has (some) patience.

💡 de la patience ⇒ de patience

Le zoo n'a pas d'animaux.
The zoo has no animals.

Cet étudiant ne fait pas d'économies.
This student doesn't save money.

🕮 **faire des économies** (verb) means 'to save money'

Elle n'a pas de stylo dans son cartable.
She has no pens in her school bag.

🕮 **cartable** (m) means 'school bag'

Ce n'est pas du jus d'orange. C'est du jus de pomme.
It isn't orange juice. It's apple juice.

💡 Normal partitive **du** with **être**

Ce ne sont pas des crayons.
Those are not pencils.

💡 Normal partitive **des** with **être**

TOPIC 53 ❖ Negative partitive - *pas de*

Ce n'est pas de la crème fraîche.
That is not fresh cream.
- Normal partitive **de la** with **être**
- **crème fraîche** (f) means 'crème fraîche' or 'sour cream'

❖ Using *pas* without *ne*

There are many negative colloquial phrases that drop **ne** and use just **pas**.

Using **pas** alone is somewhat familiar and in most cases it is contraction of a complete sentence that uses **ne...pas**.

EXAMPLES:

Pas possible !
Not possible!
> A contraction of **Ce n'est pas possible.**

Ça va ? Pas mal.
How are you? Not bad.
> A contraction of **Ça ne va pas mal.**

C'est un homme pas sympathique.
He's an unfriendly man.
> A contraction of **C'est un homme qui n'est pas sympathique.**

Pas gentil, ça.
Not nice, that.
> A contraction of **Ça, ce n'est pas gentil.**

Je veux de la bière, mais pas beaucoup.
I want beer, but not much.
> A contraction of **...mais je n'en veux pas beaucoup.** ('...but I don't want much of it'). More about that **en** ('of it') in a later topic.

Pourquoi pas ?
Why not?
> Perhaps answering **Voulez-vous une bière ?** ('Do you want a beer?')

Pas comme ça !
Not like this! *OR* Not in that way!
> Perhaps answering **Est-ce que je peux le faire comme ça ?** ('Can I do it like this?')

Pas si vite !
Not so fast!
> Perhaps answering **Puis-je aller très vite ?** ('Can I go very fast?')

TOPIC 54 ❖ Using *pas* without *ne*

Il est ravi ? Pas ravi, mais content.
Is he delighted? Not delighted, but happy.

💡 A contraction of **Il n'est pas ravi.**

Est-il là ? Non, pas encore.
Is he there? No, not yet.

💡 A contraction of **Non, il n'est pas encore là.**

Aimez-vous le chocolat ? Ben oui, mais pas trop.
Do you (formal) like chocolate? Well yes, but not too much.

💡 A contraction of **Je n'aime pas le chocolate trop.'** ('I don't like chocolate too much')

🏷 **ben** (exclamation) means 'well'

Tu fais la cuisine ? Oui mais pas souvent.
Do you (familiar) cook? Yes, but not often.

💡 A contraction of **Je ne fait pas la cuisine souvant.**

Tu as faim ? Pas du tout !
You (familiar) are hungry? Not at all!

💡 A contraction of **Je n'ai pas du tout faim.**

Ah non, pas encore ça !
Oh no, not that again!

💡 A contraction of **Ce n'est pas ça encore !** ('It is not that again!')

Tu viens, ou pas ?
Are you (familiar) coming or not?

💡 A contraction of **...ou ti ne viens pas ?**

Pas vrai ?
Not true?

💡 A contraction of **N'est-ce pas vrai.** ('That is not true')

❖ There is not - *il n'y a pas*

The pattern **il y a..** ('there is' or 'there are') is negated as **il n'y a pas..** ('this is not' or 'there are not').

It is very common to see the negative partitive **pas de** used in this context - that is **il n'y a pas de..** - 'there is not any' OR 'there are not any..'

EXAMPLES:

Est-ce qu'il y a du riz ? Non, il n'y a pas de riz.
Is there rice? No, there is no rice.
- du riz ⇒ de riz in the negative

Il n'y a pas de confiture sur ma tartine.
There's no jam on my toast.
- **confiture** (f) means 'jam'
- **tartine** (f) means 'slice of bread' (often a slice from a baguette)

Il n'y a pas de chiens dans ce parc.
There are no dogs in this park.

Il n'y a pas d'oiseaux dans la forêt.
There are no birds in the forest.

Pourquoi n'y a-t-il pas de piles dans cette torche ?
Why aren't there any batteries in this torch?
- **pile** (f) means 'battery'
- **torche** (f) means 'torch'

Il n'y a pas de nuages dans le ciel.
There are no clouds in the sky.

Il n'y a pas de dessin sur ta chemise.
There is no drawing on your (familiar) shirt.
- **dessin** (f) means 'drawing' or 'design'

Dans la vitrine, il n'y a pas de gâteaux qui sont très beaux.
In the shop window there are no cakes which are very beautiful.

TOPIC 55 ❖ There is not - *il n'y a pas*

N'y a-t-il pas de lettres dans la boîte à lettres ?
Aren't there any letters in the mailbox?

- **la boîte à lettres** means 'mailbox'

Est-ce qu'il n'y a pas au moins un médecin ici ?
Isn't there at least one doctor here?

- **au moins** means 'at least'
- Instead of the partitive **de** the indefinite article **un** is used to emphasize **at least one**.

Pas de problème !
No problem!

- A contraction of **Il n'y a pas de problème !**

Pas de problème sur la route ?
No problem on the road?

- The **il n'y a** can be (and commonly is) omitted.

❖ Lots of, a little of - *beaucoup de* & *un peu de*

The word **beaucoup** means 'a lot' or 'many' and when it is used to quantify a noun it needs **de**.

Whether we use **de** or **des** depends on whether we need a definite article to talk about something that has already been specified. If so then we use **des** ('of the'). Recall that **des** comes from **de + les**.

There are many other quantifiers like **beaucoup de**. These include:

- **un peu de** = 'not much of'
- **un petit peu de** is very common - 'a little bit of'
- **trop de** = 'too much of'
- **assez de** = 'enough of'
- **plus de** = 'more of'
- **peu de** = 'few of' or 'not much of' with a nuance of 'a lack of' or 'insufficient'

EXAMPLES:

Il y a beaucoup d'eau dans la carafe.
There is a lot of water in the carafe.

J'ai beaucoup de temps.
I have plenty of time.

Il y a trop de personnes dans le bus, n'est-ce pas ?
There are too many people on the bus, aren't there?

Il n'y a pas beaucoup de grands arbres dans le parc.
There are not many tall trees in the park.
💡 Negative so require the partitive **de**

Tu as assez d'amis.
You (familiar) have enough friends.

Je n'ai pas assez d'argent.
I do not have enough money.

Est-ce qu'il y a encore de cidre dans cette bouteille ?
Is there more cider in this bottle?

TOPIC 56 ❖ Lots of, a little of - *beaucoup de* & *un peu de*

Oui, il y a un peu de cidre dans la bouteille.
Yes, there is a little cider in the bottle.

Y a-t-il trop de sucre dans votre thé ?
Is there is too much sugar in your (formal) tea?

Je veux plus de cette bière.
I want more of that beer.

J'ai peu d'argent.
I have little (insufficient) money.

Elle veut juste un petit peu de lait dans son café.
She wants just a little bit of milk in her coffee.

- **un petit peu** is very common - 'a little bit'
- **juste** means 'just' or 'only' or 'fair' or 'justified'

Elle a peu de lait dans son café.
She has little (not enough) milk in her coffee.

- **content** (m) means 'glad' or 'pleased' or 'satisfied'

Malheureusement, j'ai peu d'argent en ce moment.
Unfortunately I have little (insufficient) money at the moment.

- **malheureusement** means 'unfortunately'

Peu des gens qui sont ici sont suédois.
(Too) few of the people who are here are Swedish.

- **les gens** have been specified so use **des** (of the)
- **suédois** (m) means 'Swedish'

Trop des gens qui sont dans la boîte de nuit sont jeunes.
Too many of the people in the nightclub are young.

- **des gens** because 'the people who are in the night club' has ben specified

Beaucoup des plats qui sont sur la table sont épicés.
Many of the dishes on the table are spicy.

- **des plats** because 'the dishes' have been specified - those on the table.

Beaucoup des poissons qui sont dans le filet sont petits.
Many of the fish in the net are small.

- **filet** (f) means 'net'
- **les poissons** have been specified so use **des** (of the)

TOPIC 56 ❖ Lots of, a little of - *beaucoup de* & *un peu de*

Beaucoup des idées de Jean_Luc sont intéressantes.
Many of Jean-Luc's ideas are interesting.
💡 **les idées** have been specified so use **des** (of the)

Bootstrap French
TOPIC 57

❖ **-ER** verbs like *aimer*

The verb **aimer** ('to like' or 'to love') is what is called an **-ER** type verb.
- There are several groupings of French verbs that depend on the ending of the infinitive form. And that determines how they conjugate.

Most **-ER** type verbs conjugate in the same way. They drop the **-er** ending and add the following endings:

- For **je**: drop the **-er** and add **-e** so **aimer** ⇒ **j'aime**
- For **tu**: drop the **-er** and add **-es** so **aimer** ⇒ **tu aimes**
- For **il** & **elle**: a drop the **-er** and dd **-e** so **aimer** ⇒ **il aime**
- For **nous**: drop the **-er** and add **-ons** so **aimer** ⇒ **nous aimons**
- For **vous**: drop the **-er** and add **-ez** so **aimer** ⇒ **vous aimez**
- For **ils** & **elles**: drop the **-er** and add **-ent** so **aimer** ⇒ **ils aiment**

Other **-ER** verbs include **préfèrer** ('to prefer'), **porter** ('to carry' or 'to wear') and **regarder** ('to watch'). And many many other common verbs.

Beware of verbs ending in **-ger** and **-cer** which conjugate slightly differently. This is covered in the next topic.

Also note that just because the infinitive of a verb ends in **-er** does not necessarily mean it conjugates according to this pattern — there are exceptions. Recall the verb **aller** (to go) which conjugates very irregularly (eg. **je vais**).

EXAMPLES:

J'aime seulement ce type de chocolat.
I only like this type of chocolate.
💡 aimer ⇒ j'aime

Quelle variété de pomme aimez-vous ?
What variety of apple do you (formal) like?
💡 aimer ⇒ vous aimez
📖 variété (f) means 'variety'

Nos enfants aiment aller au parc aquatique.
Our children like to go to the water park.
💡 aimer ⇒ ils aiment
📖 parc aquatique (m) means 'water park'

TOPIC 57 ❖ -ER verbs like aimer

Entre ces deux robes, elle préfère celle-là sur ce mannequin.
Between these two dresses, she prefers this one on this mannequin.

💡 préférer ⇒ elle préfère

📖 robe (f) means 'dress'

Qu'est-ce que vous aimez à Paris ?
What do you (formal) like in (about) Paris?

💡 aimer ⇒ vous aimez

Même s'il y a beaucoup de bons gâteaux, je préfère celui-ci.
Although there are many good cakes, I prefer this one.

💡 préférer ⇒ je préfère

Nous aimons nos vacances à la plage.
We love our holidays at the beach.

💡 aimer ⇒ nous aimons

Mais il préfère les vacances d'été à la montagne.
But he prefers summer holidays in the mountains.

💡 préférer ⇒ il préfère

Préfèrent-ils aller à Rome cet été ?
Do they prefer to go to Rome this summer?

💡 préférer ⇒ ils préfèrent

Il y a beaucoup de belles voitures, mais je préfère la mienne.
There are a lot of nice cars, but I prefer mine.

💡 préférer ⇒ je préfère

Qu'est-ce que tu portes sur la tête ?!
What is that you (familiar) are wearing on your head?!

💡 porter ⇒ tu porte

💡 Note we don't say sur ta tête

Qui porte la grosse valise lourde ?
Who is carrying the big heavy suitcase?

💡 porter ⇒ il porte

Ils portent des manteaux chauds.
They are wearing warm coats.

💡 porter ⇒ ils portent

TOPIC 57 ❖ -ER verbs like *aimer*

Elle n'aime pas porter de chaussures. Elle préfère porter des sandales.
She does not like to wear shoes. She prefers to wear sandals.
- aimer ⇒ elle aime
- préférer ⇒ elle préfère
- sandale (f) means 'sandal'

N'aimez-vous pas quand il y a beaucoup de beurre dans votre nourriture ?
Don't you (formal) like when there is a lot of butter in your food?
- aimer ⇒ vous aimez
- nourriture (f) means 'food'

Qui préfère avoir du sel dans sa glace ?
Who prefers to have salt in their ice cream?
- préférer ⇒ il préfère

Ce sont des hommes qui préfèrent être seuls.
They are men who prefer to be alone.
- préférer ⇒ ils préfèrent

Elle porte toujours des bottes rouges et porte un parapluie rouge.
She always wears red boots and carries a red umbrella.
- porter ⇒ elle porte
- parapluie (m) means 'umbrella'

Regardez-vous un film français ce soir ?
Are you (formal) watching a French film tonight?
- regarder ⇒ vous regardez

Nous regardons le coucher de soleil du haut de la montagne.
We are watching the sunset from the top of the mountain.
- regarder ⇒ nous regardons
- coucher de soleil (m) means 'sunset'
- haut (m) means 'top'

Bootstrap French
TOPIC 58

❖ **-ER verbs exceptions**

-ER verbs that end in **-ger** and **-cer** have irregular **nous** conjugations.
Verbs that end in **-ger** conjugate to **-geons** for **nous**. So for example:
- **manger** ('to eat') ⇒ **nous mangeons**
- **nager** ('to swim') ⇒ **nous nageons**
- **partager** ('to share') ⇒ **noun partageons**

Verbs that end in **-cer** conjugate to **-çons** for **nous**. For example:
- **commencer** ('to start') ⇒ **nous commençons**
- **prononcer** ('to pronounce') ⇒ **nous prononçons**

EXAMPLES:

Nous mangeons des œufs tous les matins.
We eat eggs every morning.
- **tous** means 'every' or 'all'
- **tous les matins** means 'every morning'

Nous nageons dans la mer tous les après-midis.
We swim every afternoon.
- **mer** (f) means 'sea'
- **après-midi** (m) means 'afternoon'
- **les après-midi** is also acceptable for the plural

Nous partageons notre nourriture avec les voisins.
We share our food with the neighbors.

Nous voyageons chaque hiver.
We travel every winter.
- **hiver** (m) means 'winter'

Nous changeons les pneus de notre voiture.
We are changing the tires on our car.
- **pneu** (m) means 'tire' or 'tyre'

Nous déménageons de Paris à Nantes.
We are moving from Paris to Nantes.

TOPIC 58 ❖ -ER verbs exceptions

Nous mélangeons de la farine avec du lait.
We are mixing flour with milk.

🍃 farine (f) means 'flour'

Nous commençons l'année scolaire demain.
We start the school year tomorrow.

🍃 année scolaire (f) means 'school year'

Nous ne prononçons pas correctement les mots français.
We are not pronouncing the French words correctly.

🍃 correctement means 'correctly'
🍃 mot (m) means 'word'

Nous annonçons nos fiançailles.
We are announcing our engagement.

🍃 fiançailles (pl.f) means 'engagement' (always plural)

Nous remplaçons les freins de nos vélos.
We are replacing the brakes of our bicycles.

🍃 frein (m) means 'brake'

❖ Verbs with prepositions - *parler à* & *parler de*

Many French verbs can be followed by a preposition which changes its meaning.
One such verb is **parler** which means 'to speak' or 'to talk'.
 - **parler** conjugates like a standard **-ER** verb.
The propositions that follow **parler** modify its meaning. For instance:
* **parler à** means 'to talk to'
* **parler avec** means 'to speak with'
* **parler de** means 'to speak about'
* **parler en** means 'to speak in (a language)'

Note that all these permutations take a noun after the preposition.

In later topics we will see many other verbs that, like **parler**, modify with many different prepositions.

EXAMPLES:

Je parle français.
I speak French *OR* I am speaking French.

Elle parle assez bien le français.
She speaks French quite well.

Il ne parle pas la langue russe.
He does not speak the Russian language.
  langue (f) means 'tongue' or 'language'
  russe (m.f) means 'Russia' or 'Russian'

Que parle-t-il exactement ?
What is he saying exactly?

À qui parlez-vous ?
Who are you (formal) talking to?

Il veut parler au patron.
He wants to talk to the boss.

De quoi parlez-vous ?
What are you (formal) talking about?
  quoi means 'what' - should be used with a preposition

TOPIC 59 ❖ Verbs with prepositions - *parler à* & *parler de*

Nous parlons des projets de la famille pour les vacances d'été.
We talk about the family's plans for the summer vacation.

De quoi parles-tu avec ma sœur ?
What are you (familiar) talking about with my sister?

Nous parlons de la météo.
We are talking about the weather.

🎓 **météo** (f) means 'weather' or 'weather forecast'

De quel type de travail parlez-vous ?
What type of work are you (formal) talking about?

Le directeur parle aux lycéens.
The principal talks to the high school students.

🎓 **lycéen** (m) means 'high school student'

Ils parlent toujours de jeux informatiques.
They always talk about computer games.

🎓 **jeux** (m) means 'game' (plural is **les jeux**)
🎓 **informatique** (f) means 'computing'
🎓 **jeux informatique** (m) means 'computer game'

Parle-t-il en espagnol avec sa mère ?
Does he speak in Spanish with his mother?

🎓 **espagnol** (m) means 'Spanish'

❖ The Subject Pronoun *on*

The pronoun **on** is widely used in colloquial French.

Nowadays **on** is very often used instead of **nous**. Indeed to some extent it has replaced **nous** in colloquial spoken French.

But it also retains the somewhat broader meaning of the collective 'one', 'you', 'people' or 'someone' or even 'they'.

- **On** behaves like **il** & **elle** when conjugating verbs.

EXAMPLES:

On parle en français à l'école.
We (everyone) speak French at school.

Olivier et moi, on est mariés.
Olivier and I, we are married.
- marié (m) means 'married'

On est à côté de la mer, c'est chouette !
We are by to the sea, it's great!
- à côté de means 'next to' or 'by'
- chouette (m) means 'cool'

On voit souvent notre famille.
We often see our family.
- chouette (adj) means 'great' or 'cool' or 'brilliant'

On voyage souvent : on a de la chance !
We travel often: we are lucky!

On a une vie simple et on est heureux.
We have a simple life and we are happy.

En France, on mange son hamburger avec une fourchette et un couteau.
In general in France, one (people) eats his∆her hamburger with a fork and a knife.
- en France means 'in France'

Ici, on parle anglais.
We (people) speak English here.

TOPIC 60 ❖ The Subject Pronoun *on*

On est fous !
People are crazy!

Qu'est-ce qu'on fait ?
What are we doing?

Va-t-on à la plage ?
Are we going to the beach?

On ne peut pas tout savoir.
One (people) cannot know everything.

- *tout* (pronoun) means 'everything'
- *savoir* (verb) means 'to know'

Que fait-on ici après le travail ?
What does one (people) do here after work?

- *après* means 'after'

On peut regarder le lever du soleil sur la plage.
You (one) can watch the sunrise on the beach.

- *lever du soleil* (m) means 'sunrise'

On ne peut pas manger dans le métro.
You (one) cannoteat on the subway.

- *métro* (m) means 'subway' or 'metro'

❖ The definite article - concepts, topics and issues

The definite article in French is a little different than in English:
- General concepts - Definite articles are used to talk about a noun or group of nouns in a general sense or as a concept or notion.
  - In English we sometimes use the plural to do this. For example 'Green beans are good' or 'I like dogs'.
- Topics and Issues - Abstractions, politics, school subjects, and languages all need a definite article in French.

EXAMPLES:

Les haricots verts sont bons.
Green beans are good.
- Referring to **haricots verts** in a generic sense
- **haricot vert** (m) means 'green beans' (singular in French)

L'or est cher.
Gold is expensive.
- **l'or** refers to 'gold' in general and not 'the gold'
- **or** (m) means 'gold'

J'aime bien faire de l'auto-stop.
I quite like hitchhiking.
- **auto-stop** (m) means 'hitchhiking'
- **faire de l'auto-stop** means 'to hitchhike'

Il parle très bien le français.
He speaks French very well.
- He is not speaking French now, but he speaks French in a general sense.

Je parle mal l'italien.
I speak Italian badly.
- I am not speaking Italian badly now, but I speak Italian badly in a general sense
- **mal** (adj) means 'badly' or 'incorrectly'

Il aime les mathématiques.
He loves mathematics.
- **mathématiques** (pl.m) means 'mathematics'

TOPIC 61 ❖ The definite article - concepts, topics and issues

Il parle de la loi.
He is speaking about the law.
- In English we use 'the law' much like in French **la loi**
- **loi** (f) means 'law'

J'aime regarder le rugby et le football.
I like to watch rugby and football.
- **regarder** (verb) means 'to watch'

L'eau est bonne pour la santé.
Water is good for (one's) health.
- Here both definite articles serve the general concept function
- **santé** (f) means 'health'

Je n'aime pas le fromage de chèvre.
I don't like goat's cheese.
- **fromage** (m) means 'cheese'

Ils aiment les oignons, mais pas l'ail.
They like onions but not garlic.
- **oignon** (m) means 'onion'
- **ail** (m) means 'garlic'

En général, les Français sont sympathiques.
The French are friendly.
- **en général** means 'in general'
- **sympathique** (m) means 'nice' or 'friendly'

La patience est une qualité utile.
Patience is a useful quality.
- **qualité** (f) means 'quality' or 'trait'
- **utile** (m.f) means 'useful'

Elle n'aime pas du tout le froid.
She doesn't like the cold at all.
- **froid** (m) means 'cold' (noun and adjective)

J'aime le théâtre, mais je préfère le cinéma.
I like the theater but I prefer the cinema.
- **théâtre** (m) means 'theatre'

La vie est difficile sans argent.
Life is difficult without money.
- **sans** means 'without'

TOPIC 61 ❖ The definite article - concepts, topics and issues

La France fait partie de l'Europe.
France is part of Europe.

📖 **faire partie** (verb) means 'to be part of'

C'est la vie.
That's life.

❖ Object pronouns

We saw that the personal adjectives (**je**, **tu**, **il** etc.) refer to the a person or people who are the subject of a sentence.

When referring to a person, animal or thing that is the **object** of a sentence, we use a (direct) object pronoun.

The French direct object pronouns are:

- **je** ⇒ **me**: 'me'
- **tu** ⇒ **te** : 'you' (familiar)
- **il** & **on** ⇒ **le** : 'him' or 'it'
- **elle** ⇒ **la** : 'her' or 'it'
- **nous** ⇒ **nous** : 'us'
- **vous** ⇒ **vous** : 'you' (formal & plural)
- **ils** & **elle** ⇒ **les** : 'them'

Those that end in a vowel all contract with an apostrophe when followed by a word beginning with a vowel. So **me** ⇒ **m'** etc.

For inanimate things ('it'), whether we use **le** or **la** depends on the gender of said object.

The object pronoun comes immediately before the verb that acts upon it.

 - This is unlike in English where the pronoun comes after the verb.

EXAMPLES:

Je vous aime bien.
I like you (formal).
aimer bien means 'to like'

Tu m'aimes ?
Do you (familiar) love me?
Used in this way *aimer* implies 'love'

Pouvez-vous nous voir ?
Can you (formal) see us?

Oui, je vous vois.
Yes, I see you (plural).

TOPIC 62 ❖ Object pronouns

Où est Christine ? Qui peut la voir ?
Where is Christine? Who can see her?

> The object pronoun **la** comes before the verb that acts upon it (**voir**) and not the auxiliary verb (**pouvoir**)

Je la vois.
I see her.

Où sont les clés ? Qui les voit ?
Where are the keys? Who sees them?

Je les vois là-bas.
I see them over there.

Maman, papa, vous nous regardez ?
Mom, Dad, are you (formal) watching us?

Oui, nous vous regardons.
Yes, we are watching you (plural).

Les Français sont sympathiques. Je les aime bien.
The French are friendly. I like them.

C'est un raisin. Je peux le manger ?
It's a grape. Can I eat it?

> The object pronoun **le** comes before the verb that acts upon it (**manger**) and not the auxiliary verb (**pouvoir**)

Ce croissant - je peux le manger ?
That croissant - can I eat it?

Tu veux le manger ?
Do you (familiar) want to eat it?

Désolé, je le mange.
Sorry - I am eating it.

Qui porte la valise lourde ? Il la porte.
Who is carrying the heavy suitcase? He is carrying it.

Est-ce qu'il la porte ?
Is he carrying it (female)?

Pourquoi le portez-vous ?
Why are you (formal) carrying it?

TOPIC 62 ❖ Object pronouns

Son numéro de téléphone - l'avez-vous ?
His telephone number - do you (formal) have it?

🖉 numéro de téléphone (m) means 'telephone number'

Je l'écris dans le cahier.
I write it in the notebook.

Il l'invite à la fête.
He is inviting her to the party.

🖉 inviter (verb) means 'to invite'

Ces chaussures - je les achète.
These shoes - I am buying them.

🖉 acheter (verb) means 'to buy'

Je regarde ce film. Bénédicte le regarde aussi.
I am watching this movie. Bénédicte is watching it too.

❖ Negation with object pronouns

To negate a sentence with a direct object pronoun, wrap **ne...pas** around both the object pronoun and the verb.

If there are dual verbs (auxiliary + infinitive) then the **ne... pas** wraps around just the auxiliary verb. And the object pronoun remains immediately before the verb that acts upon it – that is the infinitive.

EXAMPLES:

Je ne le mange pas.
I don't eat it.

Qui porte la valise lourde ? Elle ne la porte pas.
Who is carrying the heavy suitcase? She is not carrying it.

Je ne vous aime pas.
I do not love you (formal).

Tu ne m'aimes pas ?
Don't you (familiar) love me?

Je ne l'écris pas dans le cahier.
I don't write it in the notebook.

Il ne les voit pas.
He does not see them.

Nous ne vous regardons pas.
We are not looking at you (formal).

Il ne l'invite pas à la fête.
He is not inviting her to the party.

Ces chaussures sont trop grandes - je ne les achète pas.
These shoes are too big - I am not buying them.

Je regarde le film. Bénédicte ne le regarde pas.
I am watching the movie. Bénédicte is not watching it.

J'aime la langue italienne, mais je ne la parle pas.
I like the Italian language but I don't speak it.

TOPIC 63 ❖ Negation with object pronouns

Aimes-tu les dessins animés ? Non, je ne les regarde pas.
Do you (familiar) like cartoons? No, I don't watch them.

Ce croissant - je ne peux pas le manger ?
This croissant - can't I eat it?

💡 **ne... pas** around the auxiliary verb only

Tu ne veux pas le manger ?
Don't you (familiar) want to eat it?

💡 **ne... pas** around the auxiliary verb only

Les clés - je ne sais pas où elles sont.
The keys - I don't know where they are.

💡 **ne... pas** around the auxiliary verb only

❖ Reflexive personal pronouns

Reflexive pronouns indicates that the subject of the verb is performing that action on itself.

- In English the reflexive pronouns are 'myself', 'yourself' etc. and are used in the same way - for example 'I wash myself'.

The French reflexive pronouns are as follows:

- **je ⇒ me** : 'myself'
- **tu ⇒ te** : 'yourself' (familiar)
- **il, elle, on ⇒ se** : 'himself', 'herself', 'itself', 'oneself'
- **nous ⇒ nous** : 'ourselves'
- **vous ⇒ vous** : 'yourself '(formal), 'yourselves'
- **ils & elle ⇒ se** : 'themselves'

The pronouns **me**, **te** and **se** contract with an apostrophe when followed by a word that begins with a vowel or mute **h**.

EXAMPLES:

Je me regarde dans le miroir.
I look at myself in the mirror.

📖 **miroir** (m) means 'mirror'

Ils se voient souvent.
They see each other often.

Elles se parlent.
They (females) talk to each other.

Vous vous voyez.
You (formal) see yourself.

Je me demande.
I wonder. *OR* I ask myself.

💡 This is how to say 'I wonder' in French.

Elle se lave.
She washes herself.

📖 **laver** (verb) means 'to wash'

💡 **laver** is an **-ER** verb

TOPIC 64 ❖ Reflexive personal pronouns

Nous nous parlons de la météo.
We talk to each other about the weather.

Mon père se rase chaque matin.
My dad shaves himself every morning.

L'enfant s'habille tout seul.
The child dresses him∆herself.

On s'amuse.
We are amusing ourselves. *OR* We are having fun.

Est-ce que vous vous lavez ?
Do you (formal) wash yourself?

Ils s'habillent dans la cabine d'essayage.
They are dressing (themselves) in the fitting room.

 ✎ **cabine d'essayage** (f) means 'fitting room' or 'dressing room'

Pouvez-vous vous voir sur cette photo ?
Can you (formal) see yourself in this photo?

Non, je ne me vois pas sur la photo.
No, I don't see myself in the photo.

La mère et le fils se voient tous les week-ends.
The mother and son see each other every weekend.

 ✎ **week-end** (m) means 'weekend'
 ✎ **tous les week-ends** means 'every weekend'

❖ Reflexive verbs

Reflexive (or prenominal) verbs are verbs that incorporate a reflexive pronoun and imply that the subject of the verb is performing that action on itself.

The dictionary form of reflexive verbs use the **se** reflexive pronoun. But in general use the pronoun that matches the subject should be substituted.

Some common reflexive (-ER) verbs are:

- **se lever** - 'to wash oneself' (**lever** means 'to wash')
- **se coucher** - 'to go to bed' (**coucher** means 'to lay down')
- **se cacher** - 'to hide (oneself)' (**cacher** means 'to hide')
- **se brûler** - 'to burn oneself' (**brûler** means 'to burn')
- **se baigner** - 'to bathe oneself', to swim (**baigner** means 'to bathe')
- **s'excuser** - 'to apologize' or 'to excuse oneself' (**excuser** means 'to excuse' or 'to forgive')
- **se fâcher** - 'to be angry' or 'to be mad'
- **se fatiguer** - 'to get tired'
- **s'habiller** - 'to get dressed' or 'to dress up' (**habiller** means 'to dress' or 'to clothe')
- **se préparer** - 'to get prepared' or 'to prepare oneself' (**préparer** means 'to prepare')
- **se tromper** - 'to make a mistake' or 'to be wrong' (**tromper** means 'to trick' or 'to deceive')
- **s'appeler** - 'to call oneself' or 'to be called' (**appeler** means 'to call')
- In French 'my name is X' is expressed as 'I call myself X' (**je m'appelle X**)

Note that with the negative **ne..pas**, the reflexive pronoun stays attached to the verb.

EXAMPLES:

Elle se lave dans le bain.
She washes (herself) in the bath.
 🍥 **bain** (m) means 'bath'

Elle lave le chien.
She washes the dog.
 💡 Not reflexive

Il se couche très tard.
He goes to bed very late.

TOPIC 65 ❖ Reflexive verbs

Il couche les enfants pour la nuit.
He puts the children to bed for the night.
💡 Not reflexive
📖 **pour** means 'for'

Nous nous cachons dans l'armoire.
We are hiding in the wardrobe.

Nous cachons les cadeaux.
We are hiding the gifts.
📖 **cadeau** (m) means 'gift' or 'present'

Souvent, je me brûle sur la cuisinière.
Often I burn myself on the stove.
📖 **cuisinière** (f) means 'stove' or 'cooker'

Je brûle les ordures.
I burn garbage.
💡 Not reflexive
📖 **ordures** (pl.m) means 'garbage' or 'rubbish'

Est-ce que vous vous baignez à la plage ?
Do you (formal) swim at the beach?

Vous ne vous baignez pas à la plage ?
Don't you (formal) swim at the beach?
💡 Note that with the negative **ne..pas** the reflexive pronoun stays attached to the verb

Baignez-vous le bébé chaque soir ?
Do you (formal) bathe the baby every evening?
💡 Not reflexive
📖 **bébé** (m) means 'baby'

Ils sont en retard - ils s'excusent.
They are late - they apologize.

Ils vous excusent d'être en retard.
They excuse you (formal) for being late.
💡 Not reflexive

Pourquoi tu te fâches contre ta fille ?
Why are you (familiar) mad at your daughter?
💡 In French 'one gets angry **against** someone' (**on se fâche contre quelqu'un**)
📖 **contre** means 'against'

TOPIC 65 ❖ Reflexive verbs

Les élèves fatiguent le professeur avec leurs interminables questions.
The students tire the teacher with their endless questions.
- 💡 Not reflexive
- 📖 **interminable** means 'endless' or 'never-ending' or 'interminable'

Les étudiants se fatiguent après une longue journée.
Students get tired after a long day.
- 📖 **journée** (f) means 'day'

Ils s'habillent pour la soirée déguisée.
They dress up for the fancy dress party.
- 📖 **la soirée déguisée** means 'fancy dress party'

Ils habillent bien leurs enfants pour le froid.
They dress their children well for the cold.
- 💡 Not reflexive

Elles ne se préparent pas pour l'examen.
They are not preparing themselves for the exam.
- 💡 In the negative **se** & **préparent** stay together
- 📖 **examen** (m) means 'exam' or 'test'

Elles préparent tout pour la fête d'anniversaire.
They (females) are preparing everything for the birthday party.
- 💡 Not reflexive
- 📖 **anniversaire** (m) means 'birthday'

Le voleur trompe le vieil homme.
The thief tricks the old man.
- 📖 **voleur** (m) means 'thief'

Le vieil homme se trompe sur le voleur.
The old man is mistaken about the thief.
- 💡 Not reflexive
- 💡 In French 'one is mistaken **on** something or someone' (**on se trompe sur quelque chose ou sur quelqu'un**)

La dame appelle ses enfants pour le dîner.
The lady is calling her children for dinner.
- 💡 Not reflexive

Je m'appelle Jean_Luc.
My name is Jean-Luc.

TOPIC 65 ❖ Reflexive verbs

La dame s'appelle madame Dupont.
The lady is called Madame Dupont. *OR* The lady's name is Madame Duport.

- In French 'her name is X' is expressed as 'she calls herself X' (**elle s'appelle X**)

Comment s'appelle-t-elle ?
What is her name?

- Literally 'How does she call herself?'
- **comment** means 'how'

Elle s'appelle Jeanne d'Arc.
Her name is Joan of Arc.

- Literally 'She calls herself Joan of Arc'

Comment vous appelez-vous ?
What is your (formal) name?

- The first **vous** is the reflexive pronoun
- Literally 'How do you call youself?'

Bootstrap French
TOPIC 66

❖ Negating reflexive verbs

Negating a reflexive verb is straight forward - simply the wrap the complete verb (including the reflexive pronoun) in **ne..pas**.

EXAMPLES:

Elle ne se lave pas.
She doesn't wash.

Elle ne se maquille pas.
She doesn't wear make-up.

    📖 **se maquiller** (verb) means 'to put on makeup' or 'to wear makeup'

Il ne se couche pas trop tard.
He doesn't go to bed too late.

Je ne me lève pas tôt.
I don't get up early.

Cette dame ne s'appelle pas madame Dupont.
This lady is not called Madame Dupont.

Pourquoi tu ne te fâches pas contre ta fille ?
Why don't you (familiar) get mad at your daughter?

Il ne s'appelle pas Julien. Il s'appelle Jacques.
His name is not Julien. His name is Jacques.

Les enfants ne se cachent pas dans l'armoire.
Children don't hide in the closet.

Il ne s'amuse pas beaucoup.
He's not having much fun.

Pourquoi vous ne vous lavez pas tous les matins ?
Why don't you (formal) bathe every morning?

Je ne veux pas me raser.
I don't want to shave.

    💡 The auxiliary verb should be negated when dual verbs are used.

TOPIC 66 ❖ Negating reflexive verbs

Il n'aime pas se tromper.
He doesn't like to be wrong.

💡 The auxiliary verb should be negated when dual verbs are used.

❖ To find and to be located - the verbs *trouver* & *se trouver*

The verb **trouver** and its reflexive counterpart **se trouver** are both very common.
- The verb **trouver** means 'to find' or 'to be able to find'.
  - It's meaning can also be figurative (like in English) to give one's impression of something - as in 'I find that strange'.
  - **trouver** does not means 'to look for' - that is the verb **chercher**.
- The reflexive form **se trouver** means 'to find oneself' or 'to be located'
  - The form is commonly used to talk about the location of something.
  - It is also be used to talk about one's state of being.

Both **trouver** and **se trouver** are regular **-ER** verbs.

EXAMPLES:

Je ne trouve pas mes lunettes.
I can't find my glasses.

> In the present tense **trouver** in the sense of 'to find' is only used in the negative - 'to be unable to find'. **Je trouve mes lunettes.** doesn't really make sense.

Je cherche mes clés, mais je ne les trouve pas.
I'm looking for my keys but I can't find them.

> **chercher** (verb) means 'to look for'

Je trouve ça très bizarre.
I find that very odd.

> **bizarre** (m) means 'odd' or 'strange'

Je trouve ses parents très cool.
I find his parents very cool.

> **cool** (m) means 'cool' (Very common in young colloquial French)

Je les trouve trop cool.
I find them so cool.

> **trop** colloquially can also mean 'so' or 'really'

Je ne le trouve pas du tout intéressant.
I don't find him interesting at all.

L'escalade - trouvez-vous cela dangereux ?
Climbing - do you (formal) find it dangerous?

TOPIC 67 ❖ To find and to be located - the verbs *trouver* & *se trouver*

Je trouve ça extrêmement dangereux !
I find that extremely dangerous!
- *extrêmement* (adverb) means 'extremely'

Où se trouve la poste ?
Where is the post office?
- The reflexive *se trouver* talking about location

La poste se trouve au bout de cette rue.
The post office is at the end of this street.
- *bout* (m) means 'end'

Où se trouve la tour Eiffel ?
Where is the Eiffel Tower?

La tour Eiffel se trouve à Paris.
The Eiffel Tower is located in Paris.

Nice se trouve dans le sud de la France.
Nice is in the South of France.

Les Champs_Élysées, ils ne se trouvent pas à Lille ?
The Champs Elysées, aren't they (isn't it) in Lille?

Vous vous trouvez devant une maison très ancienne.
You (formal) are in front of a very old house.
- Or 'We find ourselves in front of...'

Nous nous trouvons d'accord avec le président.
We agree with the president.
- Or 'We find ourselves in agreement with the president'

Je me trouve bien.
I am well.
- The reflexive *se trouver* talking personal state of being

Je ne me trouve pas bien.
I don't feel well.

Je me trouve mal.
I fainted. *OR* I passed out.
- The past tense must be implied

On se trouve belles.
We find ourselves beautiful.

TOPIC 67 ❖ To find and to be located - the verbs *trouver* & *se trouver*

Elles te trouvent sympa.
They (females) find you nice.

Et maintenant, nous nous trouvons dans une situation difficile.
And now we find ourselves in a difficult situation.

❖ Parts of the body and reflexive verbs

When referring to a part of the body in French we don't use the possessive adjective ('my leg' or 'his back').

Instead in French the definite article is used ('la jambe' or 'le dos')

And often whose body part it is conveyed by which reflexive pronoun is used.

- We could also of course use the possessive **de** to specify who the body part belongs to - for example **la jambe de Jacques**.

EXAMPLES:

Je me brosse les dents.
I brush my teeth.
- se brosser means 'to brush oneself'
- dent (f) means 'tooth'

Elles se brossent les dents.
They (females) are brushing their teeth.

Pourquoi ne te brosses-tu pas les dents ?
Why don't you (familiar) brush your teeth?

Vous brossez-vous les cheveux ?
Do you (formal) brush your hair?
- With inverted questions the pronoun stays attached to the verb.

Ils se lavent le visage.
They wash their faces.
- visage (f) means 'face'

Est-ce qu'elle se lave les mains ?
Does she wash her hands?
- main (f) means 'hand'

Se lave-t-elle les mains ?
Does she wash her hands?
- With inverted questions the pronoun stays attached to the verb.

TOPIC 68 ❖ Parts of the body and reflexive verbs

Se rase-t-il le visage ?
Does he shave his face?
- With inverted questions the pronoun stays attached to the verb
- se raser means 'to shave oneself'

Il se coupe toujours un doigt avec ce couteau.
He always cuts a finger with this knife.
- doigt (m) means 'finger'
- couteau (m) means 'knife'

Dans cette scène, elle se casse la jambe.
In this scene she breaks her leg.
- scène (f) means 'scene'
- casser (verb) means 'to break'
- jambe (f) means 'leg'

Elle se coupe les ongles.
She is cutting her fingernails.
- ongle (m) means 'fingernail'

Bootstrap French
TOPIC 69

❖ **Dual-verb sentences with reflexive verbs**

When a reflexive verb is used in the infinitive after another verb, the reflexive pronoun should agree with the subject of the sentence.

EXAMPLES:

Est-ce que je peux m'allonger un peu ?
Can I lay down a bit?
- me agrees with je
- s'allonger means 'to lie down'

Bien sûr, tu peux t'allonger un peu si tu le souhaites.
Of course, you (familiar) can lie down a bit if you want.
- te agrees with tu
- souhaiter (verb) means 'to wish' or 'to hope for'

Ils veulent se marier cet été.
They want to get married this summer.
- se agrees with ils

Je n'aime pas me lever tôt.
I don't like getting up early.
- me agrees with je

Il n'aime pas se lever tôt.
He doesn't like to get up early.
- se agrees with il

Elle veut se brosser les cheveux.
She wants to brush her horses.
- se agrees with elle

Il aime se vanter beaucoup tout le temps.
He likes to brag a lot all the time.
- se agrees with il
- se vanter (verb) means 'to brag'

French Grammar

TOPIC 69 ❖ Dual-verb sentences with reflexive verbs

Comment pouvons-nous nous sauver de ce cauchemar ?
How can we save ourselves from this nightmare?

- nous agrees with nous
- se sauver (verb) means 'to save oneself'
- cauchemar (m) means 'nightmare'

Les enfants, pouvez-vous aller vous amuser et ne pas me déranger ?
Children - can you (plural) amuse yourselves and not bother me?

- vous agrees with vous
- s'amuser' means 'to amuse oneself' or 'to enjoy oneself'

Ils veulent s'excuser pour leur mauvais comportement.
They want to apologize for their bad behavior.

- se agrees with ils
- comportement (m) means 'behavior'

Pourquoi tu ne veux pas te coucher trop tard ?
Why don't you (familiar) want to go to bed too late?

- te agrees with tu

Nous ne voulons pas nous trouver dans une situation difficile.
We don't want to find ourselves in a difficult situation.

- nous agrees with nous

❖ Indirect object pronouns - 'to' or 'for' someone

Many verbs imply that the action is directed 'to' someone or is being done 'for' someone.

Such verbs can include the preposition **à** or **pour** after the verb.

- We previously saw the example of **parler à** ('to speak **to**').

In place of a regular noun, such verbs can take an **indirect object pronoun**.

The indirect object pronouns are:

- **je ⇒ me** : 'to me' or 'for me'
- **tu ⇒ te** : 'to you' or 'for you' (familiar)
- **il, elle, on ⇒ lui** : 'to him/her' or 'for him/her'
- **nous ⇒ nous** : 'to us' or 'for us'
- **vous ⇒ vous** : 'to you' or 'for you' (formal & plural)
- **ils & elle ⇒ leur** : 'to them' or 'for them'

If we use one of these Indirect object pronouns with a verb that includes a preposition, the preposition is dropped because the pronoun itself already includes the (dative) sense of 'to' or 'for'.

Note that Indirect object pronouns can only refer to a person or other animate nouns.

EXAMPLES:

L'homme vous donne le pain. Et je vous donne le lait.
I a giving (formal) the bread to you. And I am giving you some milk.
💡 The verb is **donner à** ('to give to') and **vous** ('to you') is the indirect object

Tu parles à Louis. Et je lui parle aussi.
You (familiar) speak to Louis. And I speak to him too.
💡 The verb is **parler à** ('to speak to') and **lui** ('to him') is the indirect object.

Vous achetez des livres pour Jacques et Jean. Leur père leur achète aussi des livres.
You (formal) buy books for Jacques and Jean. Their father buys them books too.
💡 The verb is **acheter pour** ('to buy for') and **leur** ('for them') is the indirect object

Tu donnes un crayon à Philippe. Je lui donne aussi un stylo.
You (familiar) are giving a pencil to Philippe. I am also giving him a pen.
💡 The verb is **donner à** ('to give to') and **lui** ('to him') is the indirect object
✏ **crayon** (m) means 'pencil'

TOPIC 70 ❖ Indirect object pronouns - 'to' or 'for' someone

Nous vous posons une question.
We are asking you (formal) a question.
- The verb is **poser à** ('to ask (a question) give to') and **vous** ('to you') is the indirect object
- **poser** (verb) means 'to pose (a question)' or 'to lay down'

Vous ne nous répondez pas.
You (formal) are not answering (responding to) us.
- The verb is **répondre à** ('to respond to (someone)') and **nous** ('to us') is the indirect object

Pourquoi vous ne nous répondez pas ?
Why don't you (formal) answer us?
- The verb is **répondre à** ('to respond to (someone)') and **nous** ('to us') is the indirect object

Je t'achète une chemise.
I am buying you (familiar) a shirt.
- The verb is **acheter pour** ('to buy for') and **te** ('for you') is the indirect object

Il lui donne des fleurs chaque semaine.
He is giving him∆her flowers every week.
- The verb is **donner à** ('to give to') and **lui** ('to him/her') is the indirect object
- **semaine** (f) means 'week'

Peux-tu me prêter un peu d'argent ?
Can you (familiar) lend me a little money?
- The verb is **prêter à** ('to lend (to)') and **me** ('to me') is the indirect object

Pourquoi tu ne peux pas lui prêter cent euros ?
Why can't you (familiar) lend him∆her a hundred euros?
- The verb is **prêter à** ('to lend (to)') and **te** ('to you') is the indirect object

L'école leur annonce sa fermeture.
The school announces to them its closure.
- The verb is **annoncer à** ('to announce (to)') and **leur** ('to them') is the indirect object

Je lui téléphone dès que j'ai des nouvelles.
I call him∆her as soon as I have news.
- The verb is **téléphoner à** ('to telephone (to)') and **leur** ('to him/her') is the indirect object
- **dès que** means 'as soon as'

Jean_Paul parle à sa mère. Marie veut aussi lui parler.
Jean-Paul talks to his mother. Marie also wants to talk to her.
- The verb is **parler à** ('to speak to') and **lui** ('to her') is the indirect object.

TOPIC 70 ❖ Indirect object pronouns - 'to' or 'for' someone

Pouvez-vous nous faire le ménage ?
Can you (formal) clean for us?

💡 The verb is **faire pour** ('to do (something) for') and **nous** ('for us') is the indirect object.

Tu lui fais un gâteau ?
Are you (familiar) baking him∆her a cake?

💡 The verb is **faire pour** ('to do (something) for') and **lui** ('for him/her') is the indirect object.

Est-ce que je peux te demander conseil ?
Can I ask you (familiar) for advice?

📖 The verb is **demander à** ('to ask (to someone)') and **te** ('to you') is the indirect object. conseil (m) means 'advice'

📖 **demander conseil** (verb) means 'to ask for advice'

Mon père brosse les dents de ma sœur.
My father brushes my sister's teeth.

💡 CAUTION: In the case where a pronoun is not used, another structure is required - in this case the possessive **de**

Brosse-t-elle les cheveux de Brigitte ?
Does she brush Brigitte's hair?

💡 CAUTION: In the case where a pronoun is not used, another structure is required - in this case the possessive **de**

Pourquoi ne lave-t-il pas les mains de son fils ?
Why is he not washing his son's hands?

💡 CAUTION: In the case where a pronoun is not used, another structure is required - in this case the possessive **de**

Où sont les enfants ? Les parents les appellent.
Where are the children? The parents call them.

💡 CAUTION: The verb is **appeler** ('to call to') takes the **direct** object so **les** here

Le dîner de Jean_Luc est prêt. Pouvez-vous, s'il vous plaît, l'appeler ?
Jean-Luc's dinner is ready. Can you (formal) please call him?

💡 CAUTION: The verb is **appeler** ('to call to') takes the **direct** object so **le** here

Bootstrap French
TOPIC 71

❖ Another person's body parts

As discussed earlier, when referring to a part of the body in French we don't use the possessive adjective ('my leg' or 'his back') but instead we use the definite article (**la jambe** or **le dos**).

This includes when referring to other people's body parts.

This means that we need some other device to specify whose body part we are referring to.

The **indirect object pronouns** can be used for this purpose.

- Recall that indirect object pronouns imply that something is being done 'for someone' or 'to someone'.

Or we can simply use the possessive **de** to say 'the body part **of** someone'.

EXAMPLES:

Mon père me brosse les dents.
My father brushes my teeth (for me).
  💡 **mon pere** is the subject, **les dents** is the object and **me** is the indirect object

Paul est jeune. Je lui brosse encore les dents.
Paul is young. I still brush his teeth (for him).
  💡 **je** is the subject, **les dents** is the object and **lui** is the indirect object

Lui brosse-t-elle les cheveux ?
Does she brush his∆her hair (for him∆her)?
  💡 **elle** is the subject, **les cheveux** is the object and **lui** is the indirect object

Je leur lave le visage.
I wash their faces (for them).
  💡 **je** is the subject, **le visage** is the object and **leur** is the indiect object

Est-ce qu'elle te lave les mains ?
Does she wash your (familiar) hands (for you)?
  💡 **elle** is the subject, **les mains** is the object and **te** is the indiect object

Est-ce que la nounou te lave les mains ?
Does the nanny wash your hands (for you)?
  📖 **nounou** (f) means 'nanny'

TOPIC 71 ❖ Another person's body parts

Pouvez-vous nous laver les mains ?
Can you (formal) wash our hands (for us)?

Elle lui coupe les cheveux.
She cuts his hair (for him).

Pourquoi lui ne brossez-vous pas les dents ?
Why don't you brush his∆her teeth (for him∆her)?

> With the negative **ne..pas** the indirect object pronoun stays attached to the verb

Je ne leur lave pas le visage.
I don't wash their faces (for them).

Est-ce qu'elle coupe les ongles d'Éléa ?
Is she is cutting Elea's fingernails?

> Here we use the possessive **de** to specify whose fingernails

Oui, elle lui coupe les ongles.
Yes, she is cutting her fingernails (for her).

Bootstrap French
TOPIC 72

❖ Order of pronouns

In the case where we have both a direct object pronoun **and** an indirect object pronoun the order in which they appear in a sentence is an issue.

- For instance do we say **je le lui fais** or **je lui le fais** ('I do it for him/her') ?

We know that both the object pronoun and the indirect object pronoun should come before the verb - but which one first?

The rule is pretty straight forward:

- The indirect pronouns **me**, **te**, **se**, **nous** and **vous** come before the direct object pronouns.
- The indirect pronouns **lui** and **leur** always come after the direct object pronouns.

In general with negation the **ne.. pas** encompasses both pronouns and (present tense) verb. There are exceptions.

EXAMPLES:

Je le lui donne.
I am giving it to him∆her.
  lui after the direct object pronoun le

Tu me le demandes.
You (familiar) are asking me.

Il les leur apporte.
He is bringing them (plural) to them.
  leur after the direct object pronoun les

Je vous donne cette carte. Je vous la donne.
I am giving you (formal) this card. I am giving it to you.

Ils le leur demandent.
They ask them that.
  leur after the direct object pronoun le

Nous vous le demandons.
We are asking you (plural) that.

Nicolas t'achète ce café ? Oui, il me l'achète.
Is Nicolas buying you (familiar) that coffee? Yes, he is buying it for me.

TOPIC 72 ❖ Order of pronouns

Nicolas achète du thé pour Perrine. Il le lui achète.
Nicolas is buying some tea for Perrine. He is buying it for her.

Tu ne le lui donnes pas.
You (familiar) are not giving it to him.
  💡 **lui** after the direct object pronoun **le**

Ne le lui donnez-vous pas ?
Aren't you (formal) giving it to him?
  💡 **lui** after the direct object pronoun **le**

Pouvez-vous nous le faire ?
Can you (formal) do it for us?

Pourquoi ne pouvez-vous pas nous le donner ?
Why can't you (formal) give it to us?
  💡 **lui** after the direct object pronoun **le**

Je ne veux pas le lui donner.
I don't want to give it to him.
  💡 With **vouloir** the **ne.. pas** typically encompasses only it
  💡 **lui** after the direct object pronoun **le**

Où est mon mouchoir ? Je vous le cherche.
Where's my handkerchief? I'm looking for it for you (formal).
  ☛ **chercher** (verb) means 'to look for'

French Grammar 168

Bootstrap French
TOPIC 73

❖ This here and that there - *cela* and *ceci*

We have previously seen **ce** - the impersonal indefinite demonstrative pronoun.

Two common derivatives of **ce** are **ceci** and **cela**.

- **ceci** is the contraction of **ce** + **ici** and means 'this'.
- **cela** is the contraction of **ce** + **là** and means 'that'.

Note however that **ceci** is rare in spoken French except when is used for contrast alongside **cela**.

Colloquially **cela** is used to mean both 'this' and 'that'.

Ça is the informal replacement for both **cela** and **ceci** - see the next topic.

EXAMPLES:

Je ne veux pas ceci, je veux cela.
I don't want this, I want that.

Qui fait cela ?
Who is doing that?

Ceci peut nous aider.
This can help us.

Cela va dans la cuisine.
That goes in the kitchen.

Cela ne m'intéresse pas.
I do not care. *OR* That does not interest me.

Pourquoi tu brûles cela ?
Why are you (familiar) burning that?

C'est délicieux. Qu'est-ce que cela ?
This is delicious. What is that?

Cela dépend.
It depends.

TOPIC 73 ❖ This here and that there - *cela* and *ceci*

Cela dit, il est quand même un très bon ami.
That said, he is still a very good friend.

- **cela dit** means 'that said' or 'having said that'
- **quand même** means 'even so' or 'still'

❖ The demonstrative pronoun *ça*

The word **ça** means 'it', 'this' or 'that'.
It is actually a contraction of **cela**, which means 'that' or 'that there'.
It is familiar but very commonly used colloquially, especially in idiomatic expressions.
And it can be used both as a subject and object.

EXAMPLES:

Comment ça va ?
How is it going? *OR* How are you?

Ça va ? Oui, ça va bien.
Is it going (OK)? Yes, it is going fine.

Ça dépend.
It depends.
  ✎ **dépendre** (verb) means 'to depend'

C'est ça.
That's it.

Ça alors !
Wow! *OR* So that is how it is!
  ✎ **alors** means 'so' (Used widely and has in fact many different and subtle meanings)

Qu'est-ce que c'est que ça ?
What is that?

Ça marche !
That works!
  ✎ **marcher** (verb) means 'to work' or 'to walk'

Qu'est-ce que ça veut dire ?
What does it mean?
  ○ literally 'What does it want to say?'
  ✎ **vouloir dire** means (literally) 'to want to say' but also 'to mean'

Ça m'aide beaucoup.
It helps me a lot.
  ✎ **aider** (verb) means 'to help'

TOPIC 74 ❖ The demonstrative pronoun *ça*

Est-ce que vous pouvez me donner un peu de ça ?
Can you (formal) give me some of that?

La grammaire française ? Je trouve ça trop difficile !
French grammar? I find it too difficult!

📖 **trouver** (verb) means 'to find'

Les escargots ? J'adore ça !
Snails? I love that!

💡 Can even be used as a plural pronoun

📖 **escargot** (m) means 'snail'

Ça ne m'intéresse pas.
It does not interest me.

📖 **intéresser** (verb) means 'to interest'

Ça se passe comment ?
How does it happen?

📖 **se passer** (reflexive verb) means 'to happen' or 'to take place'

Bravo, ça commence bien.
Well done, it's off to a good start.

On peut dire ça.
You could say that.

📖 **dire** (verb) means 'to say'

Comme ça !
Like that!

📖 **comme** means 'like' or 'in (that/this) way'

C'est comme ça.
It's like that. *OR* That is the way it is.

La vie, c'est comme ça.
Life - it is like that.

📖 **vie** (f) means 'life'

Voyez-vous ce monsieur ? – Qui ça ?
Do you (formal) see this gentleman? - Who is that?

❖ Subject repetition

A common feature of spoken French is **subject repetition**.

The pattern is to state the subject of a sentence and then follow it with a subject pronoun that refers back to the stated subject.

While technically incorrect it is a very common informal way to put emphasis on the subject.

The same idea can also formulated using **qui** although with less emphasis.

This kind of repetition can also be used in questions.

EXAMPLES:

Lillie, elle est très gentille.
Lillie, she's very nice.

Mon père, il n'est pas patient.
My father, he is not patient.
  patient (adj) means 'patient'

Ça, c'est très bien.
That, it is very good.

Mathieu, il adore jouer au tennis.
Mathieu, he loves playing tennis.

La France, elle est belle.
France, she is beautiful.

La France, c'est beau.
France, it is beautiful.
  Recall that **c'est** allows take a masculine adjective

C'est Jean qui n'arrête pas d'appeler.
It is Jean who keeps calling.

Quant à Jean_Paul, il n'est pas encore là.
As for Jean-Paul, he isn't here yet.
  quant à means 'as for' or 'regarding'

TOPIC 75 ❖ Subject repetition

C'est Paul qui paie les factures.
It is Paul who pays the bills.
- payer (verb) means 'to pay'
- facture (f) means 'bill'

C'est ton chien qui aboie.
It is your (familiar) dog who is barking.

Qui est-ce qui n'arrête pas d'appeler ?
Who is it that keeps calling?

Pourquoi ton frère ne vient-il pas ?
Why isn't your (familiar) brother coming?

Comment son chien s'est-il échappé ?
How did his dog escape?
- échapper (verb) means 'to escape'

Cécile, ne mange-t-elle pas des pommes ?
Cécile, doesn't she eat apples?

❖ -IR Verbs

The second type of regular French verbs are those ending in **-IR**.

These include **finir** ('to finish'), **réussir** ('to succeed'), **choisir** ('to choose'), **agir** ('to take action'), **agrandir** ('to make larger' or 'to extend'), **guérir** ('to get better' or 'to heal') & **remplir** ('to fill').

Taking **finir** as an example, this verb type conjugates in the present tense as follows.

- **je finis** - 'I finish'
- **tu finis** - 'you (familiar) finish'
- **il** & **elle finit** - 'he/she finishes'
- **nous finissons** - 'we finish'
- **vous finissez** - 'you (plural) & you (formal) finish'
- **ils** & **elles finissent** - 'they finish'

EXAMPLES:

Je finis mon dîner.
I am finishing my dinner.
  🔖 **finir** (verb) means 'to finish'

Finis-tu tes devoirs ?
Are you (familiar) finishing your homework?
  🔖 **devoir** (m) means 'an item of homework'
  💡 Homework generally is **les devoirs** (plural)

Il finit le travail.
He is finishing the job.

Elle finit la cuisine.
She is finishing the cooking.

Nous le finissons maintenant.
We are finishing it now.

Finissez-vous la peinture aujourd'hui ?
Are you (formal) finishing the painting today?

Ils le finissent pour vous maintenant.
They are finishing it for you (formal) now.

TOPIC 76 ❖ -IR Verbs

Nous finissons nos études cette semaine.
We finish our studies this week.

✎ étude (f) means 'study' or 'studying'

Je réussis ma formation.
I am succeeding in my training.

✎ réussir (verb) means 'to succeed'
✎ formation (f) means 'training'

Est-ce qu'il réussit à parler français ?
Is he succeeding at speaking French?

✎ réussir à (verb) means 'to succeed at (something) or (doing something)'

Ils réussissent à arriver au Grand Palais à l'heure.
They manage to arrive at the Grand Palais on time.

✎ arriver (verb) means 'to arrive' or 'to happen' or 'to manage to'

Je choisis des légumes au marché.
I am choosing vegetables at the market.

✎ choisir (verb) means 'to choose'

Choisissez-vous celui-ci ?
Do you (formal) choose this one?

Nous agrandissons notre jardin.
We are making our garden larger.

✎ agrandir (verbs) means 'to make larger' or 'to extend'

Votre blessure guérit-elle ?
Is your (formal) injury healing?

✎ guérir (means) means 'to get better' or 'to heal'
✎ blessure (f) means 'injury'

Pourquoi remplis-tu le vase ?
What are you (familiar) filling the vase?

✎ remplir (verb) means 'to fill'

Ils remplissent leurs verres d'eau.
They are filling their glasses with water.

✎ remplir de (verb) means 'to fill with (something)'

Bootstrap French
TOPIC 77

❖ Irregular *-IR* verbs - Part I

There are many important **-IR** verbs that are irregular.
The next few topics will go through these in groups that are irregular in a similar way.
This first group are verbs that end in **-MIR**, **-TIR** or **-VIR**.
- For **je**, **tu** and **il & elle** we drop the three-letter endings and add **s**, **s** and **t**.
- For **nous**, **vous** and **ils & elles** we drop the **-IR** and add **-ons**, **-ez** and **-ent**.

Examples of this irregular group are:
- **dormir** - 'to sleep' (-MIR ending)
- **mentir** - 'to lie' (-TIR ending)
- **partir** - 'to leave' (-TIR ending)
- **sortir** - 'to go out' (-MIR ending)
- **sentir** - 'to feel' (-TIR ending)
- **servir** - 'to serve' (-MIR ending)

EXAMPLES:

je dors
I sleep
- dormir (verb) means 'to sleep'
- dormir: drop -mir and add -s ⇒ je dors

Tu dors très longtemps.
You (familiar) sleep a very long time.
- dormir: drop -mir and add -s ⇒ tu dors

Le chien - il dort généralement dans la voiture.
The dog - he usually sleeps in the car.
- dormir: drop -mir and add -t ⇒ il dort

Nous dormons sur le lit.
We sleep on the bed.
- dormir: drop -ir and add -ons ⇒ nous dormons

Dormez-vous toujours seul ?
Do you (formal) always sleep alone?
- dormir: drop -ir and add -ez ⇒ vous dormez

TOPIC 77 ❖ Irregular -IR verbs - Part I

Elles dorment sous la tente.
They sleep in the tent.
- dormir: drop -ir and add -ent ⇒ elles dorment
- tente (f) means 'tent'

je mens
I lie
- mentir (verb) means 'to lie'
- drop -tir and add -s ⇒ je mens

Pourquoi mens-tu souvent ?
Why do you (familiar) often lie?

Chaque fois qu'il parle, il ment.
Whenever he speaks, he lies.
- chaque fois que means 'each time that' or 'whenever'

Nous ne mentons pas sur l'accident.
We don't lie about the accident.
- mentir sur (verb) means 'to lie about (something)'

Vous nous mentez.
You (formal) are lying to us.

Ils mentent à leurs parents et à leurs professeurs.
They are lying to their parents and teachers.

je sers
I serve
- servir (verb) means 'to serve' or 'to be of use' or 'to serve (a purpose)'
- drop -vir and add -s ⇒ je sers

Tu sers de très gros repas !
You (familiar) serve very big meals!

Quand sert-on le thé ?
When do 'they' serve tea? *OR* When is tea served?

Nous servons le thé après le repas.
We serve tea after the meal.

Servez-vous les invités bientôt ?
Are you (formal) serving the guests soon?
- invité (m) means 'guest'

TOPIC 77 ❖ Irregular -*IR* verbs - Part I

Mes parents ne servent pas d'alcool aux repas.
My parents do not serve alcohol at meals.

📖 **alcool** (m) means 'alcohol'

Ça peut encore servir.
It can still be used. *OR* It still might be useful.

💡 Recall that **ça** is a common way to say 'it' or 'that'

❖ Irregular *-IR* verbs - Part II

The second group of irregular **-IR** verbs are those that end in **-LLIR**, **-FRIR** or **-VRIR**.

The present tense conjugations are as follows:

- Drop the **-IR** and add **-e** for **je**, add **-es** for **tu**, add **-e** for **il** & **elle**, add **-ons** for **nous**, add **-ez** for **vous** and add **-ent** for **ils** & **elles**.

Examples of this irregular group are:

- **ouvrir** - 'to open' (-VRIR ending)
- **couvrir** - 'to cover' (-VRIR ending)
- **cueillir** - 'to pick' or 'to gather' (-LLIR ending)
- **offrir** - 'to offer' or 'to give' or 'to treat' (-FRIR ending)
- **souffrir** - 'to suffer' (-FRIR ending)

EXAMPLES:

J'ouvre la porte.
I open the door.
- *ouvrir* (verb) means 'to open'
- *ouvrir*: drop *-ir* and add *-e* ⇒ je ouvre

Tu ouvres grand la bouche.
You (familiar) open your mouth wide (big).
- *ouvrir*: drop *-ir* and add *-es* ⇒ tu ouvres
- *bouche* (f) means 'mouth'

Il ouvre la porte pour la vieille dame.
He opens the door for the old lady.
- *ouvrir*: drop *-ir* and add *-e* ⇒ il ouvre

Nous ouvrons le paquet de biscuits.
We open the package of cookies.
- *ouvrir*: drop *-ir* and add *-ons* ⇒ nous ouvrons

Quand ouvrez-vous la boutique ?
When do you (formal) open the store?
- *ouvrir*: drop *-ir* and add *-ez* ⇒ vous ouvrez

TOPIC 78 ❖ Irregular -IR verbs - Part II

Pourquoi ne l'ouvrent-ils pas maintenant ?
Why don't they open it now?

💡 ouvrir: drop -ir and add -ent ⇒ ils ouvrent

Pouvez-vous ouvrir le livre à la page cent un ?
Can you (formal) open the book to page one hundred and one?

📖 page (f) means 'page'

Je la couvre d'une couverture.
I am covering her with a blanket.

📖 couvrir (verb) means 'to cover'
📖 couverture (f) means 'blanket'
💡 CAUTION: Note that it is NOT couvrir avec une couverture but couvrir de

Est-ce que tu couvres la nourriture ?
Are you (familiar) covering the food?

Le parc couvre la moitié de l'État.
The park covers half the state.

📖 moitié (f) means 'half'
📖 état means 'state (political)' or 'state (condition)'

Nous le couvrons avec de l'eau.
We cover it with water.

Couvrez-vous les fissures avec de la peinture ?
Do you (formal) cover the cracks with paint?

📖 fissure (f) means 'crack'
📖 peinture (f) means 'paint'

Ils se couvrent de crème solaire.
They cover themselves with sunscreen.

📖 crème solaire (f) means 'sun cream'

Je cueille des baies dans la forêt.
I pick berries in the forest.

📖 cueillir (verb) means 'to pick' or 'to gather'
📖 baie (f) means 'berry'
📖 forêt (f) means 'forest'

Tu cueilles les raisins le matin, n'est-ce pas ?
You (familiar) pick the grapes in the morning, don't (you)?

📖 raisin (f) means 'grape'

TOPIC 78 ❖ Irregular -IR verbs - Part II

Elle cueille des fraises des bois.
She picks wild strawberries.

Nous cueillons les mûres à l'automne.
We pick blackberries in the fall/autumn.
- mûre (f) means 'blackberry'
- automne (m) means 'fall' or 'autumn'

Cueillez-vous déjà des pommes ?
Do you (formal) already pick apples?

Ils cueillent les légumes et les servent immédiatement.
They pick the vegetables and serve them immediately.

J'offre un repas à vos amis.
I'm buying your (formal) friends a meal.
- offrir (verb) means 'to offer' or 'to give' or 'to treat'

Tu m'offres un café ?
Are you (familiar) buying (treating) me a coffee?

Il lui offre des roses.
He gives her roses.

Nous souffrons de la grippe.
We are suffering from the flu.
- souffrir (verb) means 'to suffer'

Souffrez-vous des dents ?
Do you (formal) suffer from teeth (pain)?

Les animaux souffrent beaucoup du froid.
The animals suffer a lot from the cold.

❖ Irregular -IR verbs - Part II I

The third group of irregular -IR verbs are those that end in -ENIR.

The present tense conjugations are as follows:

- Drop the -ENIR and add -iens for je, add -iens for tu, add -ient for il &elle, add -enons for nous, add -enez for vous and add -iennent for ils & elles.

Examples of this irregular group are:

- **venir** - 'to come'
- **devenir** - 'to become'
- **provenir** - 'to come from' or 'to originate from'
- **se souvenir** - 'to remember'
- **soutenir** - 'to support' or 'to maintain'
- **obtenir** - 'to get' or 'to achieve' or 'to obtain'

EXAMPLES:

Je viens toujours dans ce parc après le travail.
I always come to this park after work.
  venir (verb) means 'to come'
  venir: drop -enir and add -iens ⇒ je viens

D'où viens-tu ?
Where do you (familiar) come from?
  venir: drop -enir and add -iens ⇒ tu viens

Elle vient de Pologne.
She comes from Poland.
  venir: drop -enir and add -ient ⇒ elle vient
  Pologne (f) means 'Poland'

Nous venons voir notre amie Charlotte.
We are coming to see our friend Charlotte.
  venir: drop -enir and add -enons ⇒ nous venons
  venir voir means 'to come to see'

Vous venez souvent ici ?
Do you (formal) come here often?
  venir: drop -enir and add -enez ⇒ vous venez

TOPIC 79 ❖ Irregular -IR verbs - Part III

Ils viennent parfois dans notre restaurant.
They sometimes come to our restaurant.
- venir: drop -enir and add -iennent ⇒ ils viennent
- parfois means 'sometimes'

Je te soutiens de tout cœur.
I support you (familiar) whole-heartedly.
- soutenir (verb) means 'to support' or 'to maintain'
- de tout cœur means 'whole-heartedly'

Quand je suis triste, tu me soutiens.
When I'm sad, you (familiar) support me.

Elle soutient son frère dans ses études.
She supports her brother in his studies.

Nous soutenons l'avis du patron.
We support the opinion of the boss.
- avis (m) means 'opinion' or 'notice' or 'advice' or 'opinion'

Vous soutenez le président ?
Do you (formal) support the president?

Ces arcs - ils soutiennent la façade de l'église.
These arches - they support the facade of the church.
- arc (m) means 'arch' or 'bow'
- façade (f) means 'façade' or 'front (of a building)'

Il soutient qu'il a raison.
He maintains that he is right.
- soutenir que means 'to maintain that'
- avoir raison means 'to be right'

Il devient adolescent.
He is becoming a teenager.
- devenir (verb) means 'to become'
- adolescent (m) means 'teenager'

Je ne me souviens pas.
I do not remember.
- se souvenir (verb) means 'to remember'

TOPIC 79 ❖ Irregular -IR verbs - Part II I

Te souviens-tu des paroles de cette chanson ?
Do you (familiar) remember the words of this song?
- **se souvenir de** (verb) means 'to remember (something)'
- **parole** (f) means 'word' or 'speech'
- **chanson(f)** means 'song'

Il obtient un prêt auprès d'une banque.
He gets a loan from a bank.
- **obtenir** (verb) means 'to get' or 'to achieve' or 'to obtain'
- **prêt** (m) means 'loan'
- **banque** (f) means 'bank'

❖ Irregular *-IR* verbs - Part IV

The final group of irregular **-IR** verb are completely or truly irregular - each conjugates in its own unique way.

This group includes **voir** ('to see') and **avoir** ('to have') which we already covered in earlier topics.

Other common verbs in the group include:

- **courir** - 'to run' or 'to race'
- **recevoir** - 'to receive' or 'to receive (guests or people in meetings)'
- **mourir** - 'to die'
- **valoir** - 'to be worth'

There are several more important verbs of this type - they will be discussed separately in coming topics.

EXAMPLES:

Je cours au travail le matin.
I run to work in the morning.
- courir ⇒ je cours
- courir (verb) means 'to run' or 'to race'

Pourquoi cours-tu partout ?
Why do you (familiar) run everywhere?
- courir ⇒ tu cours

Il court pour Peugeot.
He races for Peugeot.
- courir ⇒ il court

Nous sommes en retard - nous courons vers l'arrêt de bus.
We are late - we are running to the bus stop.
- courir ⇒ nous courons

Courez-vous régulièrement ?
Do you (formal) run regularly?
- courir ⇒ vous courez
- régulièrement (adv) means 'regularly'

TOPIC 80 ❖ Irregular -IR verbs - Part IV

Les chevaux - ils courent très vite.
The horses - they run very fast.
- courir ⇒ ils courent

Je reçois une pension du gouvernement.
I receive a pension from the government.
- recevoir ⇒ je reçois
- recevoir (verb) means 'to receive' or 'to receive (guests or people in meetings)'
- pension (f) means 'pension'

Recevez-vous maintenant du courrier à votre nouvelle adresse ?
Are you (formal) now receiving mail at your new address?
- recevoir ⇒ tu reçois
- courrier (m) means 'mail'

Il reçoit souvent des lettres de la mairie.
He often receives letters from the town hall.
- recevoir ⇒ il reçoit
- mairie (f) means 'town hall'

Dans cette partie du pays, nous recevons beaucoup de pluie au printemps.
In this part of the country we receive a lot of rain in spring.
- recevoir ⇒ nous recevons
- pluie (f) means 'rain'
- printemps (m) means 'spring'

En France, recevez-vous des contraventions par courrier ?
In France do you (formal) receive parking tickets by mail?
- recevoir ⇒ vous recevez
- contravention (f) means 'parking ticket'

Ils reçoivent des invités dans la grande salle.
They receive guests in the grand hall.
- recevoir ⇒ ils reçoivent

Je meurs de faim !
I'm starving! *OR* I am dying of hunger!
- mourir ⇒ je meurs
- mourir (verb) means 'to die'
- faim (f) means 'hunger'

TOPIC 80 ❖ Irregular -IR verbs - Part IV

Dans le nord, si tu ne t'habilles pas bien, tu meurs.
In the north, if you (familiar) don't dress well, you die.

- 💡 mourir ⇒ tu meurs

Elle meurt de soif.
She is dying of thirst.

- 💡 mourir ⇒ il meurt
- 📖 soif (f) means 'thirst'

Nous mourons de froid !
We are dying of cold!

- 💡 mourir ⇒ nous mourons

Si vous ne mangez pas, vous mourez.
If you (formal) don't eat, you die.

- 💡 mourir ⇒ vous mourez

Les enfants meurent d'ennui.
The children are dying of boredom.

- 💡 mourir ⇒ ils meurent
- 📖 mourir de means 'to die of (something)'l ennui (m) means 'boredom' or 'problem'

Je meurs d'envie d'un café.
I'm dying for a coffee.

- 📖 mourir d'envie de means 'to die to have (something)'

Je vaux un million d'euros.
I am worth one million euros.

- 💡 valoir ⇒ je vaux
- 📖 valoir (verb) means 'to be worth'
- 📖 million (m) means 'million'

Tu vaux mieux que ça.
You (familiar) are better than that.

- 💡 valoir ⇒ tu vaux
- 💡 This is an expression

Ça vaut combien ?
How much is it worth?

- 💡 valoir ⇒ il vaut
- 📖 combien means 'how much'

Cette voiture vaut très cher.
This car is worth a lot.

TOPIC 80 ❖ Irregular -IR verbs - Part IV

Ça vaut mieux.
It's better. *OR* That would be better.

📖 **mieux** means 'better'

Il vaut mieux que je parte.
It is better that I leave.

Nous valons tous pareil.
We are all worth the same. /

💡 Or 'We are all worth the same.' **valoir** ⇒ **nous valons**

📖 **pareil** (m) means 'the same'

💡 The feminine of **pareil** is **pareille**)

Vous valez beaucoup pour notre entreprise.
You (formal) are worth a lot to our company.

💡 **valoir** ⇒ **vous valez**

📖 **entreprise** (f) means 'company' or 'business'

Les timbres - ils valent plus ensemble.
The stamps - they are worth more together.

💡 **valoir** ⇒ **ils valent**

📖 **ensemble** means 'together'

Bootstrap French
TOPIC 81

❖ The strange case of *asseoir* & *s'asseoir*

The verb **asseoir** means 'to seat (someone)'. And it's reflexive counterpart **s'asseoir** means 'to perform the action of sitting oneself down'.

Technically these are **-IR** verbs but they are truly irregular.

This verb (and many other words) were 'reformed' in the 1990s. So **asseoir** became **assoir**.

However, despite the official change, the modernized forms have not really taken hold with the French public, particularly the plural conjugations.

- In particular, the modernized **nous assoyons** and **vous assoyez** are strenuously avoided.

Here are the old & new conjugations - you are likely to encounter both forms:

- **j'assieds** & **j'assois**
- **t'assieds** & **t'assois**
- **il assied** & **il assoit**
- **nous asseyons** & **nous assoyons** [avoid]
- **vous asseyez** & **vous assoyez** [avoid]
- **ils asseyent** & **ils assoient**

If you are using the companion app, you will hear in the examples that the pronunciations are also different. But both are acceptable.

EXAMPLES:

Je m'assieds sur ce fauteuil.
I sit on this armchair.
💡 Old form
💡 s'asseoir (means) 'to sit (oneself) down'
🔖 fauteuil (m) means 'armchair'

Tu t'assieds sur le tabouret.
You (familiar) sit down on the stool.
💡 Old form
🔖 tabouret (m) means 'stool'.

Il s'assied sur cette chaise.
He sits down on that chair.
💡 Old form

TOPIC 81 ❖ The strange case of *asseoir* & *s'asseoir*

Nous nous asseyons sur la table basse.
We sit down on the coffee table.
💡 Old form
📖 **table basse** (f) means 'coffee table'

Vous vous asseyez sur le canapé.
You (formal) sit down on the sofa.
💡 Old form
📖 **canapé** (m) means 'sofa' or 'couch'

Ils s'asseyent sur le repose-pied.
They sit down on the footstool.
💡 Old form
📖 **repose-pied** (m) means 'foot stool'

Je m'assois sur le banc.
I am sitting on the bench.
💡 Modernized form
📖 **banc** (m) means 'bench'

Tu t'assois sur la chaise longue.
You (familiar) sit on the lounge chair.
💡 Modernized form
📖 **chaise longue** (f) means 'lounge chair' or 'deck chair'

Elle s'assoit sur la pelouse.
She is sitting on the lawn.
💡 Modernized form
📖 **pelouse** (f) means 'lawn'

Nous nous asseyons sur le mur du jardin.
We sit on the garden wall.
💡 Old form
💡 Modernized form **asseyons** is the modern form should be avoided
📖 **mur** (m) means 'wall'

Vous vous asseyez sur la couverture de pique-nique.
Are you (formal) sitting on the picnic blanket.
💡 Old form
💡 Modernized form **assoyez** is the modern form should be avoided
📖 **pique-nique** (m) means 'picnic'

TOPIC 81 ❖ The strange case of *asseoir* & *s'asseoir*

Ils s'assoient par terre.
They are sitting on the ground.
💡 Modernized form
✍ **par terre** means 'on the ground' or 'on the floor'

J'assieds le bébé sur la chaise pour le repas.
I seat the baby on the chair for the meal.
💡 Old form
✍ **asseoir** (verb) means 'to seat (someone)'

Pourquoi asseyez-vous les élèves par terre ?
Why are you (formal) seating the students on the ground?
💡 Old form
✍ **par terre** means 'on the ground' or 'on the floor'

Les gens qui s'asseyent à cette table sont mes amis.
The people who are sitting at the table are my friends.
💡 Old form

❖ To have to or must - the verb *devoir*

The verb **devoir** means 'to have to' or 'must be'. It is a very common auxiliary.

Devoir has three meanings: (i) requirement as in 'to be required to do'; (ii) supposition as in 'to probably be doing' or 'must be doing'; and (iii) debt or obligation as in 'to owe' someone something.

- The first two are very similar to the word 'must' in English. For example 'He must work' (requirement) and 'He must be working late' (supposition).

It is an irregular **-IR** verb that conjugates in the present tense as follows:

- **je dois**
- **tu dois**
- **il** & **elle doit**
- **nous devons**
- **vous devez**
- **ils** & **elle doivent**

EXAMPLES:

Je dois aller à l'école.
I have to go to school.

Tu dois manger ton dîner.
You (familiar) have to eat your dinner.

Il doit travailler tard le soir.
He must work late at night.

Ta chambre doit toujours être en ordre.
Your (familiar) room should always be in order.
   ✎ **en ordre** means 'in order'

Nous devons faire le ménage.
We have to do the housework.

Devez-vous payer cette amende cette semaine ?
Do you (formal) have to pay that fine this week?

Ils doivent faire leurs devoirs maintenant.
They have to do their homework now.

TOPIC 82 ❖ To have to or must - the verb *devoir*

Tu dois être fatigué.
You (familiar) must be tired.

Il doit travailler tard.
He must be working late.

Le nouveau bureau doit ouvrir bientôt.
The new office must be opening soon.

Ça doit être le facteur.
Must be the postman.
  ☞ **facteur** (m) means 'postman'

Je dois huit euros à mon ami.
I owe my friend eight euros.
  ☞ **devoir à** means 'to owe to (someone)'

Pourquoi lui dois-tu de l'argent ?
Why do you (familiar) owe him money?

Vous me devez une explication !
You (formal) owe me an explanation!
  ☞ **explication** (f) means 'explanation'

Je me dois des vacances après tout ça.
I owe myself a vacation after all that.

Ils te doivent bien ça.
They (certainly) owe you (familiar) that.

❖ It is necessary - the impersonal verb *falloir*

The verb **falloir** means 'to need', 'to be necessary' or 'to be lacking'.

It is stronger and more formal than **devoir** and can have the advantage of being indirect.

- It's indirectness is virtue being an impersonal verb meaning - that is its subject is only ever the third person singular pronoun 'il'.
- In the present tense we have **il faut...** - 'it is necessary...'
- One would NEVER say **je faux** or **nous fallons** etc.

It can be used either with a second (infinitive) verb or with a noun.

Beware though - if it is followed by **que** and a complete clause then the second verb will need to be in the subjective mood. This will be covered in a later topic.

The pattern **il faut** can also take the indirect object pronoun such as 'il me faut..' meaning 'it is necessary for me...'.

In the negative (**il ne faut pas...**) it is a negative command ('one must not') rather than expressing that something is optionally not a requirement ('one doesn't have to').

EXAMPLES:

Il faut faire attention !
(You) have to be careful!

   faire attention (verb) means 'to be careful'

Il faut vendre la voiture.
(We) have to sell the car.

Il faut commencer.
(We) must start.

Il te faut faire attention !
You (familiar) have to be careful!

Il nous faut vendre la voiture.
We need to sell the car.

Il faut un visa pour voyager dans certains pays.
(You) need a visa to travel to some countries.

Il me faut de l'aide.
I need help.

TOPIC 83 ❖ It is necessary - the impersonal verb *falloir*

Il faut enlever les chaussures.
(You) have to take (your) shoes off.

Qu'est-ce qu'il te faut ?
What do you (familiar) need?

Il me faut un stylo noir.
I need a black pen.

Il faut faire tes devoirs maintenant.
(You) have to do your (familiar) homework now.

💡 Speaking to someone specifically so 'tes devoirs'

Il faut faire ses devoirs avant l'école.
One must do one's homework before school.

💡 Speaking genereally so 'ses devoirs'

Il faut bien maîtriser la grammaire française.
On must master well French grammar.

✏ **maîtriser** (verb) means 'to master' or 'to control'

Il ne faut pas marcher sur la pelouse.
Do not walk on the lawn.

Il ne faut pas laisser la porte ouverte.
Do not leave the door open.

✏ **laisser** (verb) means 'to leave' or 'to let' or 'to allow'

Il ne faut pas réveiller un chat qui dort.
One must not wake a sleeping cat.

💡 Or 'Let sleeping dogs lie'

Il ne faut pas oublier ce fait.
This fact should not be forgotten.

✏ **fait** (m) means 'fact'

Il ne faut pas faire ça !
(You) must not do that!

💡 Or 'You shouldn't do that!'

Bootstrap French
TOPIC 84

❖ More impersonal verbs - *rester* & *manquer*

Two more very useful impersonal verbs are **rester** and **manquer**.
Both are regular **-ER** verbs.

- **rester** means 'to remain' or 'to have (something) left'
- **manquer** means 'to miss' or 'to lack' or 'to be short of'

Both of these verbs can take both a direct and indirect object.

- So we can say 'someone (indirect) lacks something (direct)' or 'something (direct) remains for someone (indirect)'.

Note that both of these verbs can also be used normally - conjugated for the first, second and third person - though the meanings are different.

- The many permutations of the verb **manquer** will be covered in a later topic.
- The verb **rester** means 'to stay' or 'to remain' when not used impersonally. For example **Je reste à la maison ce week-end.**

EXAMPLES:

Il reste deux tomates.
There are two tomatoes left.
💡 Or 'There remain two tomatoes'

Il me reste dix euros.
I have ten euros left.
💡 Or 'There remain for me ten euros'

Reste-t-il des pommes ?
Are there any apples left?

Il ne reste pas de pain.
There is no bread left.

Il me reste assez de temps.
I have enough time left.

Il reste trente minutes avant le décollage d'avion.
There are thirty minutes left before the takeoff of the plane.
📖 **décollage** (f) means 'take off'
📖 **avion** (m) means 'aeroplane' or 'airplane'

TOPIC 84 ❖ More impersonal verbs - *rester* & *manquer*

Il manque un cinquième couvert à la table.
A fifth place setting is missing at the table.

- *cinqième* means 'fifth'
- *couvert* (m) means '(table) place setting'

Il manque des pages dans ce livre.
There are pages missing from this book.

Il manque encore dix euros.
There are still ten euros missing.

Il nous manque de la farine.
We are short of flour.

C'est tout ce qui reste.
That's all that is left.

Voilà tout ce qui me reste.
Here is all I have left.

Il ne manque pas d'un certain charme.
It does not lack a certain charm.

- *charme* (m) means 'charm'

Il ne manque pas un bouton de guêtre.
An idiom meaning 'Everything is where it belongs.'

- Literally 'A gaiter button is not lacking.'

❖ Because - *parse que, car, puisque* & *comme*

There are three common ways to say 'because' in French:
- **parse que**
- **car**
- **puisque**

While there are grammatical differences between the three, they are in fact used interchangeably.

 - The only wrinkle is that **car** cannot start a sentence.

The word **comme** is a little different and is best translated as 'given that', 'as' or 'since'.

Comme typically begins a sentence and sets up a reason for some result.

EXAMPLES:

J'achète cette bouteille d'eau parce que j'ai soif.
I buy this bottle of water because I'm thirsty.

Pourquoi allez-vous à la plage ? Parce qu'il fait beau.
Why are you (formal) going to the beach? Because it's beautiful outside.

Parce qu'il n'a pas d'argent, il ne peut pas venir.
Because he has no money, he can't come.

Pourquoi es-tu en retard ? Parce qu'il y a des embouteillages.
Why are you (familiar) late? Because there are traffic jams.

J'apprends le français car j'aime la France.
I am learning French because I love France.

Je suis en retard car il y a des embouteillages.
I am late because there are traffic jams.

Ils ne partent pas en vacances car ils n'ont pas d'argent.
They do not go on vacation because they have no money.

La réunion est annulée car le président est malade.
The meeting is canceled because the president is ill.

TOPIC 85 ❖ Because - *parse que*, *car*, *puisque* & *comme*

David ne peut pas venir car il est à l'université.
David can't come because he's at university.

Tu peux partir puisque tu es malade.
You can leave since you (familiar) are sick.

Puisque c'est son erreur, il m'aide.
Since it's his mistake, he helps me.

Comme il est faible, il ne peut pas le soulever.
Since he is weak, he cannot lift it.

soulever (verb) means 'to lift' or 'to raise'

Comme ta sœur a actuellement le ballon, tu ne peux pas jouer avec.
As your (familiar) sister currently has the ball, you cannot play with it.

Comme il n'est pas là, je dois le faire.
Since he's not here, I have to do it.

Comme d'habitude, son histoire est fausse.
As usual, his∆her story is wrong.

comme d'habitude means 'as usual'

Bootstrap French
TOPIC 86

❖ It turns out - *s'avérer*

The verb **s'avérer** used impersonally is a very common way to say that something turned out in a particular way.

EXAMPLES:

La petite hache s'avère très utile.
The small ax turns out to be very useful.

Il s'avère que tout le monde dépend de nous.
It turns out that everyone depends on us.

Il s'avère qu'il reste seulement trois pommes sur le pommier.
It turns out that there are only three apples left on the apple tree.

Ce qu'il a dit à propos d'une guerre s'avère complètement faux.
What he said about a war turns out to be completely wrong.
   📖 **s'avérer faux** (verb) means 'to turn out to be wrong' or 'to turn out to be false'

Comme d'habitude, son histoire s'est avérée fausse.
As usual, his story turned out to be wrong.

Notre voyage en Grèce s'est avéré coûteux.
Our trip to Greece turned out to be expensive.
   📖 **s'avérer coûteux** (verb) means 'to turn out to be expensive'
   📖 **coûteux** (adj) means 'expensive' or 'costly'

Cette solution s'avère très coûteuse.
This solution is very expensive.

Son état s'est avéré extrêmement grave.
His condition turned out to be extremely serious.
   📖 **état** (m) means 'state' or 'condition'

Il peut s'avérer nécessaire si le temps est mauvais.
It may be necessary if the weather is bad.

Regular -RE Verbs

The third French verb type are those ending in **-RE**.

The present tense conjugations are as follows:

- Drop the **-RE** and add **-s** for **je**, add **-s** for **tu**, add nothing for **il &elle**, add **-ons** for **nous**, add **-ez** for **vous** and add **-ent** for **ils & elles**.

Common examples of this regular group are:

- **attendre** - 'to wait (for)'
- **défendre** - 'to defend'
- **descendre** - 'to descend'
- **entendre** - 'to hear'
- **étendre** - 'to stretch' or 'to lay out'
- **fondre** - 'to melt'
- **pendre** - 'to hang' or 'to suspend'
- **perdre** - 'to lose'
- **prétendre** - 'to claim'
- **répondre** - 'to answer'
- **vendre** - 'to sell'

EXAMPLES:

J'attends ma copine.
I'm waiting for my girlfriend.
attendre (verb) means 'to wait (for)'

Tu attends qui ?
Whom are you (familiar) waiting for?

Il défend son frère des grands garçons à l'école.
He defends his brother from the big boys at school.

Nous nous défendons contre l'attaque.
We are defending ourselves against attack.
défendre (verb) means 'to defend'

Descendez-vous avec l'ascenseur ou les escaliers ?
Do you (formal) go down with the elevator or the stairs?
descendre (verb) means 'to descend'

TOPIC 87 ❖ Regular -RE Verbs

Vous croyez tout ce que vous entendez.
You (formal) believe everything that you hear.

- entendre (verb) means 'to hear'
- croire (verb) means 'to believe'

Ils entendent les oiseaux dans la forêt.
They hear the birds in the forest.

Le chat s'étend sur le matelas.
The cat stretches out on the mattress.

- s'étendre (verb) means 'to stretch (oneself)' or 'to lay out (oneself)'
- matelas (m) means 'mattress'

La neige fond sous le soleil brûlant.
The snow is melting under the scorching sun.

- fondre (verb) means 'to melt'
- brûlant (m) means 'blazing' or 'scorching'

La lampe pend du plafond.
The lamp hangs from the ceiling.

- pendre (verb) means 'to hang' or 'to suspend'
- plafond (le) means 'ceiling'

Je perds patience.
I'm losing patience.

- perdre (verb) means 'to lose'

Tu te perds ?
Are you (familiar) lost?

Nous perdons notre temps ici.
We are wasting our time here.

Il prétend être un médecin.
He claims to be a doctor.

- prétendre (verb) means 'to claim'

Je ne prétends pas comprendre les femmes.
I don't claim to understand women.

- comprendre (verb) means 'to understand'

Pourquoi ne me répondez-vous pas ?
Why don't you (formal) answer me?

- répondre (verb) means 'to answer'

TOPIC 87 ❖ Regular -RE Verbs

Elle pose des questions en français, mais il répond en anglais.
She asks questions in French but he answers in English.

Nous ne le vendons pas.
We are not selling it.

✐ **vendre** (verb) means 'to sell'

Ils ne vendent pas d'œufs au supermarché.
They don't sell eggs in the supermarket.

Les chaussures se vendent par paires.
Shoes are sold in pairs.

✐ **par paires** means 'in pairs'

Bootstrap French
TOPIC 88

❖ The many uses of the verb *rendre*

The verb **rendre** is a regular **-RE** verb.
It has several widely used meanings:
- **rendre à** - 'to give back' or 'to return (something to someone)'
- **rendre** + adjective - 'to make' or 'to cause something to be' or 'to render' -
- **rendre** - 'to vomit'
- **rendre visit** - 'to visit' or 'to pay a visit'

And reflexively:
- **se rendre** - 'to go somewhere regularly'
- **se rendre compte de** - 'to realize (something)' or 'to notice (something)'
- 'To realize **that**...' requires the conjunction **que** which is covered in the next topic.

EXAMPLES:

Je rends ce livre à mon ami.
I am returning the book to my friend.

Rendez-vous ces livres à la bibliothèque ?
Are you (formal) returning these books to the library?

Nous vous rendons vos vélos.
We return your (formal) bikes to you.

Il me faut lui rendre la clé de sa voiture.
I have to give him back the key to his car.

Il me rend la clé de ma voiture.
He gives me back the key to my car.

Je dois vous rendre la monnaie.
I have to give you (formal) change.

    ✎ **monnaie** (f) means 'change' or 'coin'

aujourd'hui, nous rendons visite à papi.
Today we are visiting Grandpa.

    💡 You cannot use **visiter** + person. **Visiter** as a verb is used with places, for example 'Je visite Paris'

    ✎ **papi** (slang) means 'granddad'

TOPIC 88 ❖ The many uses of the verb *rendre*

Ce week-end, nous rendons visite à mes parents.
This weekend we are visiting my parents.

Ils nous rendent visite.
They are visiting us.

Ça me rend malade.
That makes me sick.

Elle rend sa mère heureuse.
She makes her mother happy.

Ces crimes racistes nous rendent malades.
These racist crimes make us sick.

Cet ordinateur me rend chèvre.
This computer is driving me nuts.

> *se rendre chèvre* means 'to drive one crazy'. This is an exception to the **se rendre** + adjective pattern.

Ces multiples mots de passe me rendent dingue.
These multiple passwords are driving me nuts.

> *dingue* (m.f) means 'crazy'

Les enfants me rendent folle aujourd'hui !
The kids are driving me (female) crazy today!

Vous voulez me rendre responsable de l'accident.
You (formal) want to make me responsible (blame) me for the accident.

Tu te rends ridicule.
You (familiar) make yourself (look) ridiculous.

> *ridicule* (m) means 'ridiculous'

Je veux me rendre utile.
I want to make myself useful.

Il se rend à Londres tous les week-ends.
He goes to London every weekend.

Comment est-ce que tu te rends au travail ?
How do you (familiar) get to work?

Je me rends compte de mon erreur.
I realize my mistake.

TOPIC 88 ❖ The many uses of the verb *rendre*

Vous rendez-vous compte de la gravité de la situation ?
Do you (formal) realize the gravity of the situation?

- **gravité** (f) means 'gravity'
- **situation** (f) means 'situation'

❖ The conjunction *que*

We previously saw **que** as an object relative pronoun (for example: **La glace que tu veux.**).

It can also function as a conjunction to join two parts (clauses) of a sentence.

- In the same way as the English conjunction 'that' (for example: 'I think that I like it').

Que typically follows a verb and the second clause (with another verb) immediately follows it.

Unlike in English, the **que** cannot (casually) be dropped between joined clauses.

CAUTION: many **verb + que** pairs require the next clause be in the subjunctive mood. This will be covered in a later topic.

- For example **il faut que...** & **je veux que...** both require the next clause to be in the subjunctive.

Verbs expressing thoughts and speech + **que** do not require a following subjunctive clause.

EXAMPLES:

Je pense que tu as raison.
I think you (familiar) are right.
- **penser** (verb) means 'to think'
- **penser que** means 'to think that'

Il pense qu'il m'aime.
He thinks he loves me.

Elle sait que vous êtes là.
She knows you (formal) are there.
- **savoir** (verb) means 'to know'
- **savoir que** means 'to know that'

J'espère que tu vas mieux.
I hope you (familiar) are feeling better.
- **espèrer** means 'to hope'
- **espérer que** means 'to hope that'

Je pense que finalement, c'est fini.
I think it's finally over.

TOPIC 89 ❖ The conjunction *que*

Elle se rend compte qu'elle fait un erreur.
She realizes that she is making an error.

📖 *se rendre compte que* means 'to realise that'

Je me rends compte qu'il n'y a pas d'essence dans la voiture.
I realize that there is no gas in the car.

📖 *essence* (f) means 'gas' or 'petrol'

Est-ce que tu te rends compte que tu n'as plus d'argent ?
Do you realize that you (familiar) have no more money?

Je crois qu'il vient demain.
I believe he is coming tomorrow.

Il prétend qu'il est astronaute.
He claims he is an astronaut.

📖 *astronaute* (m) means 'astronaut'

J'entends que le président prend sa retraite.
I hear the president is retiring.

📖 *prend sa retraite* (verb) means 'to retire'

Quand je lui demande, il me répond qu'il ne comprend pas.
When I ask him, he replies that he does not understand.

💡 MORE

Elle ment quand elle dit qu'elle ne sait pas où il est.
She lies when she says she doesn't know where he is.

Je vois que tu parles bien français.
I see that you (familiar) speak French well.

Sentez-vous que la tâche est trop difficile ?
Do you (formal) feel that the task is too difficult?

📖 *tâche* (f) means 'task' or 'stain'

Vous souvenez-vous qu'ils viennent de Grèce ?
Do you (formal) remember that they come from Greece?

📖 *Grèce* (f) means 'Greece'

Bootstrap French
TOPIC 90

❖ To say - the irregular verb *dire*

The important verb **dire** means 'to say' or 'to tell' and is a uniquely irregular **-RE** verb. It conjugates in the present tense as follows:
- **je dis** - 'I say'
- **tu dis** - 'you (familiar) say'
- **il** & **elle dit** - 'he/she says'
- **nous disons** - 'we say'
- **vous dites** (highly irregular) - 'you (formal) say' and 'you (plural) say'
- **ils & elle disent** - 'they (male and female) say'

To say 'to talk about (something)' use **dire de (quelque chose)**.

And for 'to say that' use **dire que**. The subjunctive is not required.

EXAMPLES:

Je dis que je ne peux pas venir ce soir.
I am saying I can't come tonight.

Il te dit « bonjour » - tu ne peux pas l'entendre ?
He is saying 'hello' to you (familiar) - can't you hear him?

Qu'est-ce que tu dis de ce sujet ?
What do you (familiar) say about this subject?

✎ sujet (m) means 'subject' or 'toipc'

Il dit que la route est bloquée.
He says the road is blocked.

✎ bloqué (m) means 'blocked'

Nous lui disons tous les jours qu'il doit travailler dur à l'école.
We tell him every day that he has to study hard at school.

✎ dur (adj.adv) means 'hard'

Pourquoi dites-vous ça ?
Why do you (formal) say that?

Ils disent qu'il y a des embouteillages sur le périphérique.
They say there are traffic jams on the ring road.

✎ embouteillage (m) means 'traffic jam'

TOPIC 90 ❖ To say - the irregular verb *dire*

Il dit qu'il se rend compte de son erreur.
He says he realizes his mistake.

Qui leur dit qu'ils peuvent aller sur cette île ?
Who is telling them they can go to this island?
- *île* (f) means 'island'

Il veut dire quelque chose à propos du vol.
He wants to say something about the theft.
- *vol* (m) means 'theft' or 'flight'

Elle dit que nous pouvons commencer.
She says we can start.

Que dites-vous de cette proposition ?
What do you (formal) say to this offer?
- *proposition* (f) means 'offer' or 'proposal' or 'proposition'

Qu'est-ce que tu dis de ma cravate ?
What do you (familiar) say about my tie?

Je me dis souvent que ça va.
I often tell myself that it's okay.

Ça veut dire quoi ?
What does it mean?
- A very common why to ask about meaning
- *vouloir dire* means 'to mean'

Il ne faut pas lui dire ça, d'accord ?
Do not tell him that, OK?

Qu'est-ce que voulez-vous dire ?
What do you (formal) mean?

Que veux-tu dire ?
What do you (familiar) mean?

Je veux dire, comment pouvons-nous connaître la vérité ?
I mean, how can we know the truth?
- *vérité* (f) means 'truth'

Ce n'est pas bon - c'est-à-dire, ce ne me va pas.
It's not good - that is to say, it doesn't suit me.
- *c'est-à-dire* means 'that is to say'

TOPIC 90 ❖ To say - the irregular verb *dire*

Comme on dit - c'est la vie !
As they say - c'est la vie!

- Or 'As one says...'

Comment dit-on « strange » en français ?
How do you say 'strange' in French?

- Or 'How does one say...?' - a common why to ask how to say something.

J'entends dire que les résultats de l'élection sont faux.
I hear that the election results are fake.

- **entendre dire que** means 'to hear that'
- **élection** (f) means 'election'

On entend dire qu'il trompe sa femme.
Rumor has it that he is cheating on (tricking) his wife.

- **on entend dire que** means 'one hears that' or 'the rumor is that'

Bootstrap French
TOPIC 91

❖ Negative pronouns - *rien* & *personne*

We previously saw how to use **ne..pas** to negate a verb in French.

There are many negative pronouns that can replace **pas** in the **ne..pas** negative construction to further detail the negation.

Rein and **personne** are two such pronouns:

- **ne..rien** means 'nothing' or 'not any'
- **ne..personne** means 'nobody' or 'no one' or 'not anyone'

Both of these are **subject** pronouns and are therefore always the subject of the (negated) sentence.

And as such, like any other subject noun, they can begin a sentence. But the **ne** should always precede the verb.

EXAMPLES:

Je ne mange rien.
I eat nothing.

Ça ne vaut rien.
It is worth nothing.

Ils n'ont rien dans leurs sacs.
They have nothing in their bags.

Il ne pense à rien.
He's not thinking about anything.
> Recall **penser à** is to 'think about' so **penser à rien** is 'to think about nothing'

Il ne veut rien dire.
He doesn't mean anything. *OR* He doesn't want to say anything.
> Recall that **vouloir dire** is used for 'to mean'

Il n'y a rien dans cette boîte.
There is nothing in this box.

Je ne vois personne.
I do not see anyone.

Il n'y a toujours personne dans le resto.
There is still no one in the restaurant.

TOPIC 91 ❖ Negative pronouns - *rien* & *personne*

Il ne reste rien.
Nothing is left.

Il ne reste personne.
There is no one left.

Rien ne me dérange.
Nothing bothers me.

   🖉 déranger (verb) means 'to bother'

Rien ne se passe.
Nothing is happening.

   🖉 se passer (verb) means 'to happen' or 'to take place'

Personne ne joue dans le parc.
Nobody plays in the park.

   🖉 jouer (verb) means 'to play'

Personne ne mange dans ce bistrot.
No one eats in this bistro.

   🖉 bistrot (m) means 'bistro'

Pourquoi tu ne dis rien à propos de ma cravate ?
Why don't you (familiar) say anything about my tie?

   🖉 à propos de means 'about' or 'on the subject of'

Ils n'ont rien dans leurs sacs à dos.
They have nothing in their backpacks.

   🖉 sac à dos (m) means 'backpack'

Je pense qu'il n'aime personne.
I think that he doesn't love anyone.

Rien ne m'énerve.
Nothing bothers me.

   🖉 s'énerver means 'to be bother by (something)' or 'to get worked up'

Personne n'est en retard.
Nobody is late.

Rien n'est plus facile.
Nothing is easier.

   💡 Here **plus** has the meaning 'more' so **plus facile** = 'easier'

TOPIC 91 ❖ Negative pronouns - *rien* & *personne*

Ça ne fait rien.
It does not matter.
- A very common colloquialism - literally 'That makes nothing'

❖ Negative adverbs - *jamais* & *plus*

A couple of negative pronouns that infer 'time' act like adverbs. The most common are:

- **ne..jamais** means 'never' or 'not ever'
- **ne..plus** means 'no longer', 'not again' or 'no more'
- **ne..nullement** means 'by no means' or 'not at all'
- **ne..guère** means 'hardly' or 'scarcely'

EXAMPLES:

Elle ne voyage jamais.
She never travels.

Tu n'es jamais à l'heure.
You (familiar) are never in time.

Je ne peux jamais faire la grasse matinée.
I can never sleep in.

Elle ne l'aime plus.
She doesn't love him anymore.

Pourquoi vous ne dites plus que vous êtes fatigué ?
Why don't you say anymore that you (formal male singular) are tired?

Ce n'est nullement vulgaire.
It is by no means vulgar.

  vulgaire (adj) means 'vulgar'

Je ne veux jamais grandir.
I never want to grow up.

Mes parents ne savent jamais où je suis.
My parents never know where I am.

Il ne se rend jamais compte que sa chemise est à l'envers.
He never realizes that his shirt is inside out.

French Grammar

TOPIC 92 ❖ Negative adverbs - *jamais* & *plus*

Je ne suis nullement le seul avec cette opinion.
I am by no means the only one with this opinion.

- *opinion* (f) means 'opinion'
- *le seul* is an abbreviation of **la seule personne**

Elle ne veut plus lui parler.
She doesn't want to talk to him anymore.

Elle ne s'ennuie jamais.
She is never bored.

- *s'ennuyer* means 'to be bored'

Elle ne sort guère.
She hardly goes out.

Il ne mange guère.
He hardly eats.

Il n'y a guère d'espoir.
There is hardly any hope.

- *espoir* (m) means 'hope'

Ce n'est guère mieux.
It's scarcely any better.

Il n'y a jamais de sucre dans la maison.
There is never any sugar in the house.

aujourd'hui, il n'y a plus de trains pour la Bretagne.
Today there are no more trains for Brittany.

Le prix de l'or ne monte jamais beaucoup.
The price of gold never goes up very much.

Il ne reste plus.
There is no more. *OR* No more remains.

- *rester* (verb) means 'to remain'
- *rester* can be used as an impersonal verb - **il reste...** for 'there remains...'

Les artichauts ne sont jamais bons sur ce marché.
Artichokes are never good in this market.

Il ne travaille guère, mais il gagne beaucoup d'argent.
He hardly works but he earns a lot of money.

- *gagner* (verb) means 'to earn' or 'to win'

TOPIC 92 ❖ Negative adverbs - *jamais* & *plus*

Ils n'ont jamais de réponse quand on leur demande.
They never have an answer when we ask.

Il n'est guère patient.
He is not very (hardly) patient.

Pourquoi n'y a-t-il jamais de serviettes propres dans la salle de bain ?
Why are there never any clean towels in the bathroom?
- serviette (f) means 'towel'
- propre (m.f) means 'clean'

Ils ne pensent jamais aux conséquences de leurs paroles.
They (females) never think about the consequences of their words.
- conséquence (f) means 'consequence'
- parole (f) means 'speech' or '(a) spoken word'

Ils ne dépensent jamais un centime !
They never spend a penny!
- dépenser (verb) means 'to spend'
- centime (m) means 'cent (euros)'

Il ne faut jamais s'asseoir sur cette table.
One must never sit down on this table.

Léa n'habite plus à Strasbourg.
Lea no longer lives in Strasbourg.
- habiter (verb) means 'to live (in)'

Les travaux routiers ne sont nullement finis.
The roadworks are by no means complete.
- travaux routiers (m.pl) means 'roadworks'
- complet (m) means 'complete'

Ce n'est nullement la solution à ce problème difficile.
This is by no means the solution to this difficult problem.

❖ Negative adjectives - *aucun* & *nul*

Many negative pronouns behave like adjectives.

These therefore require a noun to qualify.

Common ones include:

- **ne..aucun(e)** means 'none' or 'not one'
- **aucun(e) de** is also commonly used to plural nouns at the start of a sentence.
- **ne..nul(le)** means 'not any'
- **nul(le)** can only be used with collective or uncountable nouns, like liquids and emotions.
- **ne..guère de** means 'hardly any (of something)'

Like all French adjectives these pronouns need to agree with the gender of the noun.

And like regular French adjectives, these pronouns should always come before the noun, even if they start a sentence.

EXAMPLES:

Nous n'avons aucune idée.
We have no idea.
- **aucune** agrees with **idée** (f)

Il n'a aucune amie.
He doesn't have any (female/girl) friends.
- Or 'any (female) friends'
- **aucune** agrees with **amie** (f)

Je n'ai aucun ami.
I don't have a friend.
- Or 'any friends'
- **aucun** agrees with **ami** (m)

Je n'ai aucun talent.
I have no talent.
- **aucun** agrees with **talent** (m)

Nous n'allons nulle part pour le Nouvel An.
We're not going anywhere for New Years.
- **nulle** agrees with **part** (f)

TOPIC 93 ❖ Negative adjectives - *aucun* & *nul*

Nous n'avons aucune solution à ce problème.
We have no solution to this problem.

- *aucune* agrees with *solution* (f)

Je ne trouve nulle eau.
I can't find any water.

Nulle part on ne peut voir un arbre dans le désert.
Nowhere can one see a tree in the desert.

- *nul(le)* with the noun and *ne* with the verb
- *nulle part* (f) means 'nowhere'
- *nulle* agrees with the feminine noun *part*

On ne peut voir un arbre nulle part dans le désert.
One cannot see a tree anywhere in the desert.

- *nul(le)* with the noun and *ne* with the verb

Elle ne fait aucune faute.
She does not make any mistakes.

- *faute* (f) means 'mistake'

Je ne lis aucun de ces livres.
I am not reading any of these books.

Je ne reçois aucun appel - mon téléphone est en panne.
I don't receive any phone calls - my phone is broken.

- *être en panne* (verb) means 'to be broken' or 'to be not working'

Je ne bois guère de café.
I drink hardly any coffee.

Il ne reste guère de nourriture dans le frigo.
There remains hardly any food in the fridge.

Il n'y a guère de gens qui peuvent parler la langue celtique.
There are hardly any people who can speak the Celtic language.

Guère de gens ne restent dans la salle de conférence.
Not many people remain in the room.

- *conférence* (f) means 'conference'

Nous n'avons guère d'argent sur notre compte bancaire.
We have hardly any money remaining in our bank account.

- *compte bancaire* (f) means 'bank account'

TOPIC 93 ❖ Negative adjectives - *aucun* & *nul*

Aucune idée.
(I have) no idea.
💡 Common abbreviation of **Je n'ai aucune idée.**

Ils ne voient nul mal.
They don't see any harm.
📖 **mal** (m) means 'harm' or 'evil' or 'ache' or 'sickness'

Aucun étudiant n'étudie l'allemand cette année.
No student is studying German this year.
💡 **aucun** qualifies a noun so can start a sentence.

Aucun de mes amis n'habite en France.
None of my friends live in France.
💡 **aucun de** qualifies a noun so can start a sentence.

De toutes ses paroles, aucune n'est crédible.
Of all his/her words, none is credible.
💡 A reordering of **Aucune de toutes ses paroles n'est crédible.**
📖 **crédible** (m.f) means 'credible'

❖ Neither nor - *ne..ni..ni..*

The emphatic coordinating conjunction **ne..ni..ni..** allows us to negate a sequence.

Ni..ni.. can be used with both nouns, pronouns, verbs.

When used with nouns, any indefinite articles (**un**, **une** and **des**) or partitive articles (**de**) disappear altogether. The definite article (**le**, **la** or **les**) remains.

But when used with a list of verbs, each verb needs to be individually negated with a **ne**.

With this negation only the definite articles can be used. And then only when referring to specific objects.

More familiarly, you may hear **ne..pas..ni** with **pas** replacing the first **ni**. The meaning is not changed.

EXAMPLES:

Il n'a ni frères ni sœurs.
He has no brothers or sisters.

Il ne veut ni les chaussettes rouges ni les chaussettes bleues.
He doesn't want the red socks or the blue socks.

Je ne vois ni la lune ni les étoiles.
I see neither the moon nor the stars.

Elle ne prend ni lait ni sucre avec son café.
She takes neither milk nor sugar with her coffee.
  ♡ The partitive **de** disappears

On ne voit ni route ni chemin.
You can't see a road or a path.
  ♡ The indefinite article disappears.

Je ne veux ni le fromage ni le lait.
I want neither the cheese nor the milk.
  ♡ The definite articles remain when referring to specific objects

Jean_Paul ne prend ni miel ni lait avec son thé.
Jean-Paul takes neither honey nor milk with his tea.

TOPIC 94 ❖ Neither nor - *ne..ni..ni..*

Je ne peux me déplacer ni à Paris ni à Toulouse ce week-end.
I can't get to either Paris or Toulouse this weekend.
📖 **se déplacer** means 'to move about' or to get to'

Nous ne marchons ni ne courons.
We don't walk or run.

Nous ne parlons ni de politique ni de religion.
We are not talking about politics or religion.

Ce gâteau ne contient ni beurre ni huile.
This cake does not contain butter or oil.

Je n'aime ni les chiens, ni les chats, ni les poissons, ni les canards !
I don't like dogs, cats, fish or ducks!
💡 The list of **ni**'s can be as long as the listener can bare!

Elle ne mange ni pain, ni pâtes, ni riz.
She does not eat bread, pasta or rice.

Ni Pierre ni Marie ne peuvent le faire rapidement.
Neither Pierre nor Marie can do it quickly.

Je ne peux ouvrir ni celui-ci ni celui-là.
I can open neither this one or that one.
💡 a list of demonstrative pronouns

Elle ne peut mentir ni à son père ni à sa mère.
She can't lie to her father nor to her mother.
💡 a list of indirect objects

On ne peut s'asseoir ni ici ni là - rester debout est la seule option.
One can sit neither here nor there - to remain standing is the only option.
💡 a list of adverbs

Il ne mange ni ne boit.
He neither eats nor drinks.
💡 a list of conjugated verbs

Je ne veux ni chanter ni danser.
I don't want to sing or dance.
💡 a list of (second) verbs in the infinitive.

Personne ne peut entrer ni sortir.
No one can enter nor leave.
💡 a list of (second) verbs in the infinitive.

TOPIC 94 ❖ Neither nor - *ne..ni..ni..*

Je n'aime pas le sport, ni la musique.
I don't like sports or music.

💡 **pas** replacing the first **ni** is not uncommon.

Nous ne trouvons pas Gérard, ni Victor.
We can't find Gérard, nor Victor.

💡 **pas** replacing the first **ni** is not uncommon.

Bootstrap French — TOPIC 95

❖ Double negatives

Double negatives are permissible (and not uncommon) in French.

EXAMPLES:

Je ne peux plus jamais lui parler.
I can never talk to him again.

Je n'ai plus rien à te dire.
I have nothing more to say to you (familiar).
💡 OR 'I no longer have anything to say to you'

Je n'ai plus aucun argent.
I no longer have any money.

Il ne veut plus jamais être seul.
He never wants to be alone again.

Mais il ne veut plus jamais être avec elle.
But he also never wants to be with her again.

Nous ne faisons jamais rien.
We never do anything.

Il ne comprend jamais rien.
He never understands anything.

Il n'a jamais aucune idée.
He never has any idea.
💡 Not that aucune agrees with idée (f)

On ne va jamais nulle part !
We are never going anywhere!
💡 Actually 'We are never going nowhere'
📖 **nulle part** (f) means 'nowhere'

Elle n'achète jamais rien.
She never buys anything.

TOPIC 95 ❖ Double negatives

Je n'achète rien.
I am not buying nothing.

◯ CAUTION: double negatives with **pas** can be a positive

Il ne voit plus personne.
He no longer sees anyone.

Il ne fait plus rien.
He doesn't do anything anymore.

Je ne mets jamais rien dans ce tiroir.
I never put anything in that drawer.

✍ **tiroir** (m) means 'drawer'

Personne ne vient jamais ici.
No one ever comes here.

Tu ne crois jamais personne.
You (familiar) never believe anyone.

On ne parle jamais aucune langue parfaitement.
One never speaks any language perfectly.

✍ **parfaitement** means 'perfectly'

Il ne veut plus jamais le refaire.
He never wants to do it again.

✍ **refaire** (verb) means 'to do again'

Rien ne la dérange jamais - c'est une fille très calme.
Nothing ever bothers her - she is a very calm girl.

Personne n'entre jamais dans cette pièce.
No one ever comes into this room.

Il n'y a plus guère d'espoir.
There is hardly any more hope.

❖ Only - the restrictive *ne.. que*

The restrictive **ne ... que** is used to express 'only' or 'except'

Ne must always be before the (first) verb but the position of **que** can vary and that changes the meaning. The position of **que** determines what is being restricted.

- The **que** may come immediately before a second verb in which case only that verb is being 'done'.
- Or it may be before the object noun in which case the restriction 'only' applies to that noun.

The **ne.. que** restriction can apply to nouns, verbs and prepositions.

If the restriction involves an indefinite quantity (**du**, **de la** or **des**) then:

- A reduction of partitive to **de** does **not** apply if the partitive noun comes **after** the **que**.
- A reduction of the negation partitive to **de does** apply if the partitive noun comes **before** the **que**.

Of course in many cases we could just use the work **seulement** ('only') to express restriction.

EXAMPLES:

Ils n'ont qu'un fils.
They only have one son.

Nous n'avons qu'une heure environ.
We only have about an hour.
environ means 'about'

Il ne regarde que les films étrangers.
He only watches foreign films.
étranger (m) means 'foreign'

Elle n'aime que le chocolat noir.
She only likes dark chocolate.

Il ne reste qu'une seule fleur sur le buisson.
There is only one flower remaining on the bush.
buisson (m) means 'bush'

TOPIC 96 ❖ Only - the restrictive *ne.. que*

Nous n'avons qu'une solution à ce dilemme.
We only have one solution to this dilemma.

☞ **dilemme** (m) means 'dilemma'

Il ne faut que me donner l'argent pour ça.
(You) only have to give me the money for it.

Je ne veux aller qu'en Turquie pour mes vacances.
I only want to go to Turkey for my vacation.

💡 **ne..que** with the preposition **en**

Je ne veux que nager.
I just want to swim.

💡 **ne..que** with an infinitive verb **nager**

Nous ne voulons que manger de la glace.
We only want to eat ice cream.

💡 **ne..que** with an infinitive verb **manger**

Elle ne vient ici qu'en été.
She only comes here in the summer.

☞ **en été** means 'in the summer'

Il ne parle jamais que de sa fille.
He only ever talks about his daughter.

💡 Double negative with a preposition **de**

Il ne prononce guère que des banalités.
He hardly utters more than platitudes.

💡 Double negative
☞ **prononcer** (verb) means 'to utter' or 'to pronounce'
☞ **banalité** means 'banality' or 'trite remark'

Nous ne mangeons que des pâtes dans ce resto.
We only eat pasta in this restaurant.

💡 The position of **que** changes the meaning
💡 The precise meaning is 'In this restaurants the only thing we eat is pasta.'

Nous ne mangeons des pâtes que dans ce resto.
We eat pasta only in this restaurant.

💡 The position of **que** changes the meaning
💡 The precise meaning is 'The only place we eat is pasta is in this particular restaurant.'

TOPIC 96 ❖ Only - the restrictive *ne.. que*

Je ne trouve qu'une solution dans ce livre.
I can only find a solution in this book.
- 💡 The position of **que** changes the meaning
- 💡 The precise meaning here is 'In this book I did not find any more than one solution.'

Je ne trouve une solution que dans ce livre.
I can find a solution only in this book.
- 💡 The position of **que** changes the meaning
- 💡 The precise meaning here is 'Only in this book did I find a solution.'

Il ne peut lire que le français.
He can read only French.
- 💡 The position of **que** changes the meaning
- 💡 The precise meaning here is 'He can read only French.' - As opposed to English and German.

Il ne peut que lire le français.
He can only read French.
- 💡 The position of **que** changes the meaning
- 💡 The precise meaning here is 'He can only read French.' - As opposed to writing and speaking.

N'avez-vous que des pièces ?
Do you (formal) only have parts?
- 💡 Reduction of negation partitive from **de l'** to **de** does not apply if the noun comes after the **que**

Nous n'avons que de l'espoir.
We only have hope.
- 💡 Reduction of negation partitive from **de l'** to **de** does not apply if the noun comes after the **que**

Je n'ai pas d'amis suédois ; je n'ai que des amis français.
I have no Swedish friends; I only have French friends.
- 💡 Reduction of negation partitive from **des** to **de** does not apply if the noun comes after the **que**

Je n'ai de billes que vertes.
I only have marbles that are green.
- 💡 Reduction of negation partitive applies if the noun comes before the **que**

TOPIC 96 ❖ Only - the restrictive *ne.. que*

Il n'y a que des araignées sous cette roche.
There are only spiders under this rock.

- Reduction of negation partitive from **des** to **de** does not apply if the noun comes after the **que**
- **araignée** (f) means 'spider'

Il n'y a de fruits que des bananes.
There is no fruit except some bananas.

- Reduction of negation partitive (**de fruits**) applies if the noun comes before the **que**

J'ai seulement un livre.
I only have one book.

- Of course we could just use **seulement** instead of **ne..que**

Il mange seulement des pâtes dans ce resto.
He only eats pasta in this restaurant.

- Using **seulement** instead of **ne..que**

Il mange des pâtes seulement dans ce resto.
He eats pasta only in this restaurant.

- Using **seulement** instead of **ne..que**

❖ Causative construction with *faire*

The causative is a grammatical construction that is used when someone has someone else (or causes someone else) do something.

The verb **faire** followed by a second verb in its infinitive is used for this.

The 'AGENT' is who is causing the action.

The 'RECEIVER' is the object of the action being caused by the 'AGENT'.

- when the 'AGENT' or 'RECEIVER' are **alone** in the sentence then he-she-it simply follows the second verb.
- when the 'AGENT' and 'RECEIVER' are **both** present then the 'AGENT' is identified by using **par** or **à**.

The indirect (dative) pronoun can be used only if both the 'AGENT' and 'RECEIVER' are present. Often this requires context to make sense.

EXAMPLES:

Je fais sortir Pierre.
I am getting Pierre to go out.
- Agent only

Je fais sortir les valises de la voiture.
I am having the suitcases taken out of the car.
- Receiver only - the Agent is unspecified

Je fais sortir les valises par Jean_Luc.
I am having the suitcases taken out by Jean-Luc.
- Both agent & receiver so include the indirect object for the agent
- Or ... **à Jean_Luc**

Je fais tondre le gazon aujourd'hui.
I am having the lawn mowed today.
- **tondre** (verb) means 'to mow' or 'to shear'
- **gazon** (f) means 'lawn' or 'grass'

Je fais tondre le gazon à mon voisin.
I have my neighbor mow the lawn.
- Both agent & receiver so include the indirect object for the agent
- Or ... **par mon voisin**

TOPIC 97 ❖ Causative construction with *faire*

Je fais étudier ma fille chaque soir.
I make my daughter study every evening.

Il fait monter les valises. Par qui ? Par le gardien.
He is having the suitcases brought/taken up. By whom? By the caretaker.

- **par qui** means 'by who'
- **gardien** (m) means 'caretaker' (often in an apartment buidling)

Nous faisons travailler Céline ce matin.
We're having Celine work this morning.

- Céline must be the agent

Nous faisons garder les enfants.
We are having the children looked after.

- **garder** (verb) means 'to look after' or 'to keep' or 'to guard'

Nous faisons ériger un monument ici.
We are having a monument erected here.

- **ériger** (verb) means 'to erect'
- **monument** (m) means 'monument'

Tu répares ta voiture ? Non, je la fais réparer au garage par un mécanicien.
Are you (familiar) repairing your car? No, I am having it repaired at the garage by a mechanic.

- **mécanicien** (m) means 'mechanic'

Je le lui fais faire régulièrement.
I make him do it regularly.

- **lui** is the agent and is an indirect pronoun so already includes à (to him/she).

Ma famille fait construire une maison par cette entreprise.
My family is having a house built by that company.

- **construire** (verb) means 'to construct' or 'to build'

Le lave-vaisselle est en panne. Je le fais réparer.
The dishwasher is broken. I'm having it repaired.

- **lave-vaisselle** (m) means 'dishwashing machine' or 'dishwasher'

Les enfants ont faim. Je les fais manger.
The children are hungry. I am getting them to eat.

- **avoir faim** (verb) means 'to be hungry'

TOPIC 97 ❖ Causative construction with *faire*

Est-ce que tu fais laver tes chemises ?
Do you (familiar) get your shirts washed?

Tu fais faire un bouquet de fleurs ?
Are you (familiar) having a bouquet of flowers made?

Il y a beaucoup de mouches. Il les fait sortir.
There are a lot of flies. He is driving them out.
  💡 Or 'making the flies leave'
  🌿 **mouche** (f) means 'fly (insect)' or 'button'

Tu te fais faire couper les cheveux ?
Are you (familiar) getting your hair cut?

Je fais promener le chien. Je le fais promener.
I am having the dog walked. I am having it taken for a walk.
  🌿 **promener** (verb) means 'to take (someone/something) for a walk'

Le prof fait écrire un essai à ses étudiants.
The teacher makes his students write an essay.
  🌿 **essai** (m) means 'essay' or 'attempt' or 'try'

Le professeur de français fait parler en français ses étudiants.
The French teacher makes his students speak French.

❖ Getting someone to do something

A useful pattern when talking about getting or asking someone to do something is + **à quelqu'un** + **de** + .

Used in this way some verbs can change their meanings.

The following verbs have the following meanings when used in this way:

- **commander à** - 'to order (someone) (to do something)'
- **conseiller à** - 'to advise (someone) (to do something)'
- **défendre à** - 'to forbid (someone) (from doing something)'
- **demander à** - 'to ask (someone) (to do something)'
- **dire à** - 'to tell (someone) (to do something)'
- **interdire à** - 'to forbid (someone) (from doing something)'
- **ordonner à** - 'to order (someone) (to do something)'
- **permettre à** - 'to allow (someone) (to do something)'

Of course often an indirect object pronoun (such as **lui**) is used so the **à** doesn't appear.

EXAMPLES:

Elle commande à Jacques de faire le ménage.
She orders Jacques to clean up.

Ses parents conseillent à leur fils d'aller à l'université.
His parents advise their son to go to university.
  conseiller (verb) means 'to advise'

Je vous conseille de prendre le train via Avignon.
I advise you (formal) to take the train via Avignon.
  vous is the indirect object pronoun

Je dis à mon ami de faire attention.
I tell my friend to be careful.

Sa mère lui défend de revoir cette femme.
His mother forbids him to see this woman again.
  lui is the indirect object pronoun

TOPIC 98 ❖ Getting someone to do something

Je demande au serveur d'apporter un pichet de vin rouge.
I ask the waiter to bring a pitcher of red wine.
📖 **pichet** (m) means 'pitcher' or 'jug'

Le conducteur dit à ses passagers de mettre leur ceinture de sécurité.
The driver tells his passengers to put on their seat belts.

La loi vous interdit de fumer à l'intérieur.
The law prohibits you (formal) from smoking inside.

Le commandant ordonne aux soldats de le suivre.
The commander orders the soldiers to follow him.

L'école permet aux élèves de se maquiller.
The school allows students to wear makeup.

Que conseilles-tu à ta petite amie de dire à ses parents ?
What do you (familiar) advise (tell) your girlfriend to tell her parents?

Qui conseille à Jacques de prendre ce médicament ?
Who is advising (telling) Jacques to take this medicine?

Pourquoi ordonne-t-il toujours à son chien de s'asseoir ?
Why does he always order his dog to sit?

Les règles interdisent aux pilotes de survoler le centre-ville.
The rules prohibit pilots from flying over the city center.
📖 **survoler** (verb) means 'to fly over'

L'enseignant doit ordonner aux élèves de se calmer.
The teacher must order the students to calm down.
📖 **se calmer** (verb) means 'to calm (oneself) down'

❖ Past tense - *Le passé composé*

In French there are a couple of past tense forms. One of the most commonly used in everyday speech is **le passé composé**.

Le passé composé talks about specific actions that were completed in the past.

Le passé composé is constructed using an **auxiliary verb** (either **avoir** or **être**) and a **past participle** (**le participle passé**) of the verb that has been completed.

 - In this topic we will look just at using the auxiliary verb **avoir**.

The **passé composé** is formed by an auxiliary verb in its conjugated form, followed by a past participle.

The past participles of verbs follow certain patterns but can be highly irregular.

For regular **-ER** verbs the general rule is simple:

• Drop the **-er** and add **-é**.

So for example **manger** ('to eat') ⇒ **mangé**.

Rules for the other verb types and irregular verbs will be covered in the next few topics.

EXAMPLES:

J'ai mangé.
I ate.
- Auxillary verb: **avoir**⇒ **j'ai**
- Past participle: **manger** (drop **-er** and add **-é**) ⇒ **mangé**

Tu as parlé.
You (familiar) talked.
- Auxillary verb: **avoir**⇒ **tu as**
- Past participle: **parler** (drop **-er** and add **-é**) ⇒ **parlé**

Elle lui a demandé.
She asked him.
- Auxillary verb: **avoir**⇒ **elle a**
- Past participle: **demander** (drop **-er** and add **-é**) ⇒ **demandé**

Nous avons acheté des fleurs.
We brought some flowers.
- Auxillary verb: **avoir**⇒ **nous avons**
- Past participle: **acheter** (drop **-er** and add **-é**) ⇒ **acheté**

French Grammar

TOPIC 99 ❖ Past tense - *Le passé composé*

Avez-vous mangé ce matin ?
Did you (formal) eat this morning?
- Auxillary verb: **avoir** ⇒ **vous avez**
- Past participle: **manger** (drop -er and add -é) ⇒ **mangé**

Elles ont habillé la poupée.
They (females) dressed the doll.
- Auxillary verb: **avoir** ⇒ **elles ont**
- Past participle: **habiller** (drop -er and add -é) ⇒ **habillé**

Paul le lui a donné.
Paul gave it to him.
- Auxillary verb: **avoir** ⇒ **il a**
- Past participle: **donner** (drop -er and add -é) ⇒ **donné**

Qu'est-ce que Paul lui a donné ?
What did Paul give to him?
- Auxillary verb: **avoir** ⇒ **il a**
- Past participle: **donner** (drop -er and add -é) ⇒ **donné**

Qui sont ces gens qui t'ont prêté ce livre ?
Who those people who lent you (familiar) that book?
- Auxillary verb: **avoir** ⇒ **ils ont**
- Past participle: **prêter** (drop -er and add -é) ⇒ **prêté**

Nous avons passé un bon moment avec nos amis.
We had a great time with our friends.

As-tu commencé tes devoirs ?
Have you (familiar) started your homework?

Avez-vous décidé quand vous partez en vacances ?
Have you decided when you (formal) are going on vacation?

J'ai visité Paris et Bordeaux avec ma famille l'été dernier.
I visited Paris and Bordeaux with my family last summer.

Avez-vous trouvé vos clés ?
Have you (formal) found your keys?

Ils ont regardé le décollage d'avion.
They watched the plane take off.

TOPIC 99 ❖ Past tense - *Le passé composé*

Nous avons nagé dans le lac.
We did not swim in the lake.

🖉 lac (m) means 'lake'

As-tu partagé du gâteau avec ta sœur ?
Did you (familiar) share some cake with your sister?

Il m'a manqué de la farine.
I lacked flour.

Michael a rangé son bureau.
Michael tidied up his desk.

🖉 ranger (verb) means 'to tidy' or 'to put away'

Nous avons tellement rigolé !
We laughed so much!

🖉 rigoler (verb) means 'to laugh' or 'to have fun' or 'to joke around'

❖ Past participles for regular *-IR* & *-RE* verbs

So far we have seen past participles for regular **-ER** verbs.

The past participles for regular **-IR** and **-RE** verbs are also straight forward:

- For regular **-IR** verbs we drop the final **-r** to leave the **-i** ending. So for example:
 - **finir** ('to finish') ⇒ fini
 - **choisir** ('to choose') ⇒ choisi

- For regular **-RE** verbs we drop the **-re** ending and add **-u**. So for example:
 - **attendre** ('to wait') ⇒ attendu
 - **perdre** ('to loose') ⇒ perdu

The example phrases below include past participles for many more common **-IR** and **-RE** verbs.

EXAMPLES:

J'ai fini mes devoirs.
I have finished my homework.
💡 finir (to finish) ⇒ fini

Les filles, vous avez choisi des jupes ?
Girls, did you (formal) choose skirts?
💡 choisir (to choose) ⇒ choisi

Vos enfants ont beaucoup grandi.
Your (formal) children have grown a lot.
💡 grossir (to gain weight, to get fat) ⇒ grossi

Elle a guéri de la grippe.
She recovered from the flu.
💡 guérir (to cure, to heal, to recover) ⇒ guéri

Félicitations - vous avez maigri.
Congratulations - you (formal) have lost weight.
💡 maigrir (to lose weight, to get thin) ⇒ maigri
📎 félicitations (f.pl) means 'congratulations'

Quand as-tu nourri les poissons ?
When did you (familiar) feed the fish?
💡 nourrir (to feed, to nourish) ⇒ nourri

TOPIC 100 ❖ Past participles for regular -IR & -RE verbs

Le chien a obéi à mon ordre de s'asseoir.
The dog obeyed my command to sit down.
- obéir (to obey) ⇒ obéi

Il a doucement puni le chien.
He gently punished the dog.
- punir (to punish) ⇒ puni

Il a réfléchi à la question et a ensuite décidé.
He thought through the issue and then decided.
- réfléchir (to reflect, to think) ⇒ réfléchi
- ensuite means 'then' or 'next'

Le serveur a gentiment rempli cette tasse de café.
The waiter kindly refilled this cup of coffee.
- remplir (to fill) ⇒ rempli
- gentiment (adv) means 'kindly' or 'nicely'

Nous avons enfin réussi.
We succeeded at last.
- réussir (to succeed) ⇒ réussi

Elle a rougi quand tu as raconté cette blague.
She blushed when you (familiar) told that joke.
- rougir (to blush, to turn red) ⇒ rougi
- blague (f) means 'joke'
- raconter une blague (verb) means 'to tell a joke'

Et puis il a saisi la valise !
And then he grabbed the suitcase!
- saisir (to seize, to grab) ⇒ saisi

Le vin a vieilli en cave.
The wine has aged in the cellar.
- vieillir (to age, grow old) ⇒ vieilli
- cave (f) means 'cellar'
- en cave means 'in a cellar'

A-t-il attendu longtemps ?
Did he wait a long time?
- attendre (to wait (for)) ⇒ attendu
- longtemps means 'a long time'

French Grammar

TOPIC 100 ❖ Past participles for regular -IR & -RE verbs

Oh là là - j'ai encore perdu mon portable.
Oh dear - I lost my cell phone again.
- perdre (to lose) ⇒ perdu
- portable (m) means 'mobile phone' (short for téléphone portable)

J'ai entendu leur nouvelle chanson et je l'aime.
I have heard their new song and I like it.
- entendre (to hear, to understand) ⇒ entendu

Il a confondu les mots « météo » et « climat ».
He confused the words 'weather' and 'climate'.
- confondre (to confuse, to mistake, to mix up) ⇒ confondu
- climat (m) means 'climate'

La récolte a toujours dépendu de la météo.
The harvest has always depended on the weather.
- dépendre (to depend) ⇒ dépendu
- dépendre de (verb) means 'to depend on (something or someone)'
- récolte (f) means 'harvest'

Votre glace a-t-elle également complètement fondu ?
Your (formal) ice-cream - has it completely melted as well?
- fondre (to melt) ⇒ fondu
- complètement (adv) means 'completely'

La poule m'a mordu le doigt.
The hen bit my finger.
- mordre (to bite) ⇒ mordu

Oui, c'est ce qu'il a prétendu.
Yes, that's what he claimed.
- prétendre (to claim) ⇒ prétendu

J'ai rendu tous les livres à la bibliothèque.
I returned all the books to the library.
- rendre (to give back, to return) ⇒ rendu

J'ai maintenant rendu compte que vous avez raison.
I have now realized that you (formal) are correct.
- rendre (to give back, to return) ⇒ rendu

TOPIC 100 ❖ Past participles for regular -*IR* & -*RE* verbs

Enfin, il m'a répondu.
Finally he answered me.

💡 **répondre** (to answer) ⇒ **répondu**

Qu'avez-vous vendu aujourd'hui ?
What have you (formal) sold today?

💡 **vendre** (to sell) ⇒ **vendu**

Bootstrap French
TOPIC 101

❖ Irregular past participles

There are a bunch of common verbs that have highly irregular past participles. These include the following which are all covered the topic examples:

- **faire** ('to do') ⇒ **fait**
- **dire** ('to say') ⇒ **dit**
- **erire** ('to write') ⇒ **écrit**
- **conduire** ('to drive') ⇒ **conduit**
- **venir** ('to come') ⇒ **venu**
- **tenir** ('to hold') ⇒ **tenu**
- **pouvoir** ('to be able to') ⇒ **pu**
- **vouloir** ('to want') ⇒ **voulu**
- **lire** ('to read') ⇒ **lu**
- **boire** ('to drink') ⇒ **bu**
- **savoir** ('to know') ⇒ **su**
- **courir** ('to run') ⇒ **couru**
- **croire** ('to believe') ⇒ **cru**
- **voir** ('to see') ⇒ **vu**

EXAMPLES:

Qu'est-ce que tu as fait ?
What did you (familiar) do?
💡 faire (to do) ⇒ fait

J'ai fait la vaisselle.
I washed the dishes.
🍽 vaisselle (f) means 'washing up' or 'dishes'
🍽 faire la vaisselle (verb) means 'to do the dishes' or 'to wash up'

Avez-vous déjà fait le ménage ?
Have you (formal) ever cleaned?

Nous avons fait des progrès.
We have made progress.

TOPIC 101 ❖ Irregular past participles

Le professeur de français a fait parler en français ses étudiants.
The French teacher made his students speak French.

T'es-tu fait couper les cheveux ?
Did you (familiar) get your hair cut?

Qu'est-ce que tu as leur dit ?
What did you (familiar) say to them?

💡 dire (to say) ⇒ dit

Je leur ai dit : « bonjour à tous ».
I said, 'Hello everyone'.

T'ont-ils dit la vérité ?
Did they tell you (familiar) the truth?

Qu'as-tu écrit ?
What did you (familiar) write?

💡 ecrire (to write) ⇒ écrit

J'ai écrit un texto à ma mère.
I wrote a text to my mother.

D'où as-tu conduit aujourd'hui ?
Where did you (familiar) drive from today?

💡 conduire (to drive) ⇒ conduit

Avez-vous déjà conduit un van ?
Have you (formal) ever driven a van?

Je lui ai tenu la main.
I held his∆her hand.

💡 tenir (to hold, to keep) ⇒ tenu

J'ai tenu compte de ce qu'il a dit.
I took into account what he said.

✎ tenir compte de means 'to take into account', 'to take notice of'

Vous n'avez pas tenu votre parole.
You (formal) didn't keep your word.

Ils m'ont tenu pour responsable.
They held me responsible.

TOPIC 101 ❖ Irregular past participles

Enfin, j'ai pu dormir.
Finally I was able to sleep.
💡 pouvoir (to be able to) ⇒ pu

As-tu pu comprendre tout ce qu'il a dit ?
Were you (familiar) able to understand everything he said?

J'ai voulu un croissant pour le petit-déjeuner.
I wanted a croissant for breakfast.
💡 vouloir (to want) ⇒ voulu

Elle a toujours voulu visiter Paris.
She always wanted to visit Paris.

Pierre a toujours voulu être astronaute.
Pierre always wanted to be an astronaut.

J'ai lu un livre sur Napoléon.
I read a book on Napoleon.
💡 lire (to read) ⇒ lu

Vous avez lu le rapport, n'est-ce pas ?
You (formal) read the report, right?
✐ rapport (m) means 'report' or 'connection'

Il a bu trois verres de vin d'un coup.
He drank three glasses of wine (all) at once.
💡 boire (to drink) ⇒ bu

Ils ont bu toute la soirée.
They drank all evening.

J'ai couru pour arriver à l'heure.
I ran to arrive on time.
💡 courir (to run) ⇒ couru

Chloë a couru dans les bras de Laurent.
Chloë ran into the arm of Laurent.

Malheureusement, il a cru le gouvernement.
Unfortunately, he believed the government.
💡 croire (to believe) ⇒ cru

TOPIC 101 ❖ Irregular past participles

Il n'en a pas cru ses yeux.
He didn't believe his eyes.
> The pronoun **en** refers to that thing that can't be believed. This will be explained in a letter topic.

Je l'ai cru sur parole.
I took him at his word.

Hier, Léa et Manon ont vu un petit tigre au zoo.
Yesterday, Lea and Manon saw a little tiger at the zoo.
> **voir** (to see) ⇒ **vu**

Il veut voir ce qu'il a vu.
He wants to see what he saw.

Est-ce que vous avez vu le grand panneau ?
Did you (formal) see the big sign?

Nous avons déjà vu ce film.
We have already seen this film.

Finalement, tu as su la vérité.
Finally, you (familiar) knew the truth.
> **savoir** (to know) ⇒ **su**

Nous avons su quoi faire ensuite.
We knew what to do next.

De quelle manière l'avez-vous su ?
How did you (formal) find out?

Bootstrap French
TOPIC 102

❖ Must, have to - the verb *devoir*

The verb **devoir** has several meanings related to obligation, supposition, and expectation.

- It can mean 'to have to' or 'must' in the sense of 'obligation' or 'requirement'.
- For example - obligation or requirement: 'I have to go to work.'
- In the negative it means the imperative 'must not' and NOT the optional 'to not have to'.
- It can also mean 'to be due to' or 'to be bound to' in the sense of expectation of something happening.
- For example - expectation: 'A new shop is due to open.'
- It can also mean 'must' or 'to be probable' as a supposition or guess.
- For example - supposition: 'He must sleeping' or 'He must have fallen asleep.'
- With the preposition **à** the verb **devoir à** means 'to owe' (a debt for example). It therefore should take an indirect object pronoun.
- For example - obligation: 'I owe him some money'

There can in some instances be ambiguity about which of these meanings in intended. Context is required to clear this up.

- Using words like **absolument**, **tout de suite**, **à tout prix**, **impérativement**, or **vraiment** can be used to remove ambiguity.

The past participle of **devoir** is irregular ⇒ **dû**. Note the circumflex accent (**accent circonflexe**).

EXAMPLES:

Je dois manger.
I must eat.

J'ai dû manger.
I had to eat.

J'ai dû aller à l'école.
I had to go to school.

Il doit appeler sa mère.
He has to call his mother. *OR* He must be calling his mother.
  💡 There is ambiguity here

TOPIC 102 ❖ Must, have to - the verb *devoir*

Il doit appeler sa mère tout de suite.
He must call his mother right away.
💡 No ambiguity now

Il a dû appeler sa mère.
He had to call his mother. *OR* He must have called his mother.
💡 There is ambiguity here

Il a dû appeler sa mère impérativement.
He had to call his mother urgently.
💡 No ambiguity now
✍ **impérativement** means 'imperatively' or 'urgently'

Il a dû le laisser là.
He had to leave it here. *OR* He must have left it there here.
💡 There is ambiguity here

Il a dû le laisser là. Il a dû l'oublier.
He must have left it here. He must have forgotten it.
💡 No ambiguity now with context

J'ai trouvé l'écharpe d'Angela. Elle a dû l'oublier.
I found Angela's scarf. She must have forgotten it.
💡 Context makes the meaning unambiguous

Tu dois être fatigué.
You (familiar) are probably tired.
💡 Probably unambiguous

Le train doit être en retard.
The train is probably late.
💡 Probably unambiguous

Dois-tu étudier ce soir ?
Do you (familiar) have to study tonight?

Nous devons nous dépêcher, nous sommes déjà en retard.
We have to hurry; we are already late.
✍ **se dépêcher** (verb) means 'to hurry'

Ils doivent économiser de l'argent.
They have to save money.
✍ **économiser** (verb) means 'to save (money)'

TOPIC 102 ❖ Must, have to - the verb *devoir*

Elle doit être contente.
She must be (is probably) happy.

Vous devez absolument être ici à l'heure.
You (formal) absolutely must be here on time.

📖 **absolument** means 'absolutely'

Nous devons le faire tout de suite.
We have to do it right away.

Nous avons dû le faire tout de suite.
We had to do it right away.

Ils doivent le finir tôt demain matin à tout prix.
They have to finish it early tomorrow morning at all costs.

📖 **à tout prix** means 'at all costs' or 'at any price'

Elle doit être là à midi.
She has to be here at noon.

Elle ne doit pas être là à midi.
She must not be here a noon.

💡 NOT 'She does not have to be here at noon'

Tu ne dois pas faire ça !
You (familiar) must not do that!

Tu ne dois jamais faire ça !
You (familiar) must never do that!

Vous ne devez pas fermer la porte à clé.
You (formal) must not lock the door.

📖 **fermer à clé** (verb) means 'to lock'

La nouvelle salle de sport doit bientôt ouvrir.
The new gym is due to open soon.

💡 **devoir** here 'to be due to'

Nous avons dû laisser la voiture au parking.
We had to leave the car in the carpark.

Combien dois-je à Paul ?
How much do I owe Paul?

📖 **devoir à** means 'to owe (someone something)'

TOPIC 102 ❖ Must, have to - the verb *devoir*

Combien est-ce que je lui dois ?
How much do I owe him?

Tu ne lui dois rien !
You (familiar) don't owe him/her anything!

Past participles of *avoir* & *être*

Two common verbs with very irregular past participles are **avoir** and **être**.

- **avoir** ('to have') ⇒ **eu**
- The best equivalent of **avoir eu** in English is 'had' or 'to have had'.
- In the past tense **avoir eu** can also have the sense of 'to get' or 'to receive'.
- **être** ('to have') ⇒ **été**
- **avoir été** is typically used to talk about a temporary state - like 'to have been' in English.
- That said **avoir été** is most commonly used to construct the passive voice - this will be covered in detail in a later topic.

In the **passé composé** both of these words take the auxiliary verb **avoir**.

EXAMPLES:

Nous avons eu une discussion avec nos enfants.
We had a discussion with our children.

Ils ont eu un bébé.
They had a baby.

Il a eu sa fête en plein air.
He had his party outdoors.

Elle a eu une réaction allergique.
She had an allergic reaction.

J'ai eu une bonne note en mathématiques.
I got a good grade in math.
💡 Has the sense of 'to get'

Elle a eu trois cadeaux pour son anniversaire.
She got three presents for her birthday.
💡 Has the sense of 'to get'

As-tu eu son message ?
Did you (familiar) get his message?
💡 Has the sense of 'to get'

TOPIC 103 ❖ Past participles of *avoir* & *être*

Nous avons eu une très bonne idée.
We had a very good idea.

J'ai toujours été romantique.
I have always been romantic.

Elle a été une amie magnifique.
She was a wonderful friend.

Chacun d'entre vous a été très méchant aujourd'hui.
Every one of you (formal) was very naughty today.

- *chacun* means 'each'
- *entre* means 'between' or 'among'

Ils ont eu de nombreuses conversations.
They have had many conversations.

- *nombreux* (adj) means 'many' or 'numerous'

Ce repas a été fabuleux !
This meal was fabulous!

- *fabuleux* (adj) means 'fabulous'

Mon fils a eu de la fièvre, mais il n'a pas été très malade.
My son had a fever but he was not very sick.

- *fièvre* (f) means 'fever'

❖ Past tense and negation - *le passé composé* with *ne..pas*

Negation of the **passé composé** is straight forward. Simply put the auxiliary verb between **ne** and **pas**.

And any subject and object pronouns should also be inside **ne** and **pas**.

Recall also that for inverted question forms which attach a subject pronoun to the verb with a hyphen - that attached pair should stay attached and be between the **ne** and **pas** also.

EXAMPLES:

Michel n'a pas rangé son bureau.
Michel hasn't tidied up his desk.

Je n'ai pas visité Paris l'été dernier.
I did not visit Paris last summer.

Qui n'a pas mangé ses légumes ?
Who hasn't eaten their vegetables?

Elle n'a pas expliqué son problème.
She did not explain her problem.

Pourquoi n'ont-ils pas commencé leurs devoirs ?
Why didn't they start their homework?

Il ne lui a pas demandé.
He didn't ask him∆her.

Je n'ai pas acheté un seul de ces livres.
I didn't buy a single one of these books.
✍ **un(e) seul(e) de** means 'a single one of'

Ne lui as-tu pas demandé ?
Did you (familiar) not ask him?

Je ne l'ai pas fait.
I did not do it.

Je n'ai vu Mathieu nulle part.
I haven't seen Mathieu anywhere.

TOPIC 104 ❖ Past tense and negation - *le passé composé* with *ne..pas*

Je n'ai jamais rien dit !
I never said anything!

Vous n'avez rien dit à personne.
You (formal) didn't tell anyone anything.

Nous n'avions jamais vu ce film.
We had never seen this film.

Nous n'avons pas nagé dans le lac.
We did not swim in the lake.
🐟 lac (m) means 'lake'

Pourquoi n'as-tu pas partagé du gâteau avec ta sœur ?
Why didn't you (familiar) share some cake with your sister?

Nous n'avons jamais voulu vous faire de mal.
We never meant to hurt you (formal).

Ne l'avez-vous pas vu ?
Haven't you (formal) seen it?

Je n'ai jamais mangé d'escargots.
I have never eaten snails.

Pourquoi ne l'avez-vous pas cru ?
Why didn't you (formal) believe me?

Il n'a pas encore fait monter les valises.
He hasn't had the suitcases brought/taken up yet.

Je ne l'ai jamais cru.
I never believed him.

Je ne lui ai pas dit deux mots.
I didn't say two words to him.

N'as-tu jamais visité un pays étranger ?
Have you (familiar) ever visited a foreign country?

Ne l'avez-vous pas vu ?
Haven't you (formal) seen it?

Vous n'avez pas eu le temps de finir votre rapport.
You (formal) didn't have time to finish your report.

TOPIC 104 ❖ Past tense and negation - *le passé composé* with *ne..pas*

Il n'a ni parlé ni mangé.
He neither spoke nor ate.

Il n'a mangé ni le pain ni les pâtes.
He ate neither the bread nor the pasta.

Je n'ai donné que cinq euros.
I only gave five euros.

❖ *Passé composé* - agreement of the past participle

For sentences that take **avoir** in the **passé composé** the past participle should agree in gender and number if a **direct object** comes before the **avoir** + past participle pair.

This direct object can take three possible forms: ,

- A direct object pronoun (**me**, **te**, **le**, **la**, **nous**, **vous**, **les**).
- The subordinate clauses with relative pronoun **que**.
- A noun placed before the verb (usually in questions and exclamations).

This rule doesn't apply to indirect (dative) object pronouns.

For agreement, past participles change in the same way that regular adjectives change:

- Masculine singular - unchanged
- Feminine singular - add **-e**
- Masculine plural - add **-s**
- Feminine plural - add **-es**

Exceptions: There is no direct object agreement with the causative or passive.

The example comments explain all this in detail.

EXAMPLES:

Il a vu ce film et elle l'a vu aussi.
He saw this movie and she saw it too.
- The direct object pronoun **l'** comes before **a vu** so **vu** should agree with the subject **le film**
- masculine **vu** for agreement.

Il a vu la montagne et elle l'a vue aussi.
He saw the mountain and she saw it too.
- The direct object pronoun **l'** comes before **a vu** so **vu** should agree with the direct object **la montagne**
- **la montagne** (f) so feminine **vue** for agreement.

Il a vu les oiseaux et elle les a vus aussi.
He saw the birds and she saw them too.
- The direct object pronoun **les** comes before **a vu** so **vu** should agree with the direct object **les oiseaux**
- les oiseaux (m.pl) so masculine plural **vus** for agreement.

TOPIC 105 ❖ *Passé composé* - agreement of the past participle

Il a vu ses sœurs et elle les a vues aussi.
He saw his sisters and she saw them too.

- 💡 The direct object pronoun **les** comes before **a vu** so **vu** should agree with the direct object **ses sœurs**
- 💡 ses sœurs (f.pl so feminine plural **vues** for agreement.

Avez-vous regardé la nouvelle pièce de Molière ? - Oui, je l'ai regardée.
Have you (formal) seen Molière's new play? - Yes, I saw at it.

- 💡 The direct object **la pièce** of the verb **as regardé** is placed after the verb, therefore there's no agreement. But the pronoun **l'** is before the verb **ai regardee** so agreemnt required.

Je suis un homme et il m'a emmené au foot.
I am a man and he took me to football.

- 💡 Direct object **m'** before the **passé composé** verb so agreement required
- 📝 **emmener** (verb) means 'to take (someone somewhere)' or 'to transport'

Je suis une femme et il m'a emmenée au parc.
I am a woman and he took me to the park.

- 💡 Direct object **m'** before the **passé composé** verb so agreement required.

Nous sommes des hommes et il nous a emmenés au pub.
We are men and he took us to the pub.

- 💡 Direct object **nous** before the **passé composé** verb so agreement required.

Nous sommes des femmes et il nous a emmenées dans les magasins.
We are women and he took us to the shops.

- 💡 Direct object **nous** before the **passé composé** verb so agreement required.

Et la télé ? - Il l'a regardée.
And the TV? - He watched it.

- 💡 Agreement required: **la télé** (f) so **regardé** ⇒ **regardée**

Et les bonbons ? - Elle les a mangés.
And the sweets? - She ate them.

- 💡 Agreement required: **les bonbons** (m.pl) so **mangé** ⇒ **mangés**

Et les pompiers, tu les as vus ?
And the firefighters, have you (familiar) seen them?

- 💡 Agreement required: **les pompiers** (m.pl) so **vu** ⇒ **vus**

Ces statues... Tu les as faites ?
These statues... Did you (familiar) make them?

- 💡 Agreement required: **ces statues** (f.pl) so **fait** ⇒ **faites**

TOPIC 105 ❖ *Passé composé* - agreement of the past participle

A-t-il vu Marie ? Il l'a vue.
Has he seen Marie? He saw her.
- vu ⇒ vue (feminine singular)

Elle a acheté des livres. Elle les a achetés.
She bought books. She bought them.
- acheté ⇒ achetés (masculine plural)

Tu as perdu les clés. Tu les as perdues.
You (familiar) have lost the keys. You lost them.
- perdu ⇒ perdues (feminine plural)

Voici les livres qu'il m'a donnés.
Here are the books he gave me.
- The relative pronoun **que** (which repeats **les livres** (m.pl) in the subordinate clause) is before the verb **a donné** so there should be agreement.

Les fleurs que j'ai senties.
The flowers that I smelled.
- The relative pronoun **que** (which repeats **les fleurs** (f.pl) in the subordinate clause) is before the verb **ai senti** so there should be agreement.

J'aime les fraises que Maman a cueillies.
I like the strawberries Mom picked.
- The relative pronoun **que** (which repeats **les fraises** (f.pl) in the subordinate clause) is before the verb **a cueilli** so there should be agreement.

J'ai rencontré les actrices que j'ai appréciées.
I met the actresses that I liked.
- apprécié ⇒ appréciées (feminine plural)
- apprécier (verb) means 'to appreciate' or 'to admire'

Les photos que tu as prises sont toutes floues.
The pictures you (familiar) took are all blurry.
- pris ⇒ prises (feminine plural)
- flou (m) means 'blurry' or 'blurred'

As-tu lu les livres que j'ai achetés ?
Have you (familiar) read the books I bought?
- acheté ⇒ achetés (masculine plural)

Voilà la voiture qu'Amine a vendue.
This is the car that Amine sold.
- vendu ⇒ vendue (feminine singular)

TOPIC 105 ❖ *Passé composé* - agreement of the past participle

Est-ce que Jean a trouvé ses livres ? Oui, enfin il les a trouvés.
Has Jean found his books? Yes, finally he found them.

💡 **trouvé** ⇒ **trouvés** (masculine plural)

As-tu lavé les chaises ? Lesquelles ? Celles que tu as laissées dans le jardin.
Did you (familiar) wash the chairs? Which ones? The ones you left in the garden.

💡 **laissé** ⇒ **laissées** (feminine plural)

Quelle revue Muriel a-t-elle achetée ?
What magazine did Muriel buy?

💡 Noun **la revue** before the verb **a acheté** in this question so agreement required

📖 **revue** (f) means 'magazine'

Elle a emmené les enfants à l'école.
She took the children to school.

💡 Noun **les enfants** after the verb **a emmené** so no agreement required

Il les a fait travailler.
He made them work.

💡 Causative verbs like **faire travailler** (to make work) do not require past participle agreement

L'histoire que j'ai entendu lire.
The story that I heard read.

💡 The **entendre lire** is a passive contruction so not agreement

Bootstrap French
TOPIC 106

❖ *Passé composé*, negation and word order

When using the **passé composé** with any form of negation, the position of the past participle depends on which word is paired with **ne** in the negation.
- Adverb: if the **ne** is paired with an adverb (such as **pas, point, plus, guère, jamais, rien**) then the past participle is **outside** the negation.
- Noun: if the **ne** is paired with a noun (such as **personne, aucun(e), nul(le), nulle part, ni**) then the past participle is **inside** the negation.
- In the case of the restrictive **ne..que**, the **que** tends to want to stay close to the object so the past participle is typically before it.

EXAMPLES:

Je ne l'ai jamais mangé.
I never ate it.
  💡 Adverb - **jamais** so past participle is outside

N'avez-vous pas fini ?
Aren't you (formal male singular) done?
  💡 Adverb - **pas** so past participle is outside

Je ne le lui ai pas dit.
I didn't tell him.
  💡 Adverb - **pas** so past participle is outside

Je ne le lui ai jamais dit.
I never told him.
  💡 Adverb - **jamais** so past participle is outside

Je n'ai vu personne.
I saw nobody.
  💡 Noun - **personne** so past participle is inside

Nous n'avons vu que la première ébauche.
We only saw the first draft.
  💡 **que** so past participle is inside
  📖 **ébauche** (f) means 'draft' or 'sketch'

Ils n'ont fait aucun effort.
They made no effort.
  💡 Noun - **aucun** so past participle is inside

TOPIC 106 ❖ *Passé composé*, negation and word order

Je ne lui ai dit que deux mots.
I only said two words to him.

que so past participle is inside

Je ne le lui ai jamais dit.
I never told him.

Adverb - *jamais* so past participle is outside

Je ne lui ai jamais téléphoné.
I never phoned him.

Adverb - *jamais* so past participle is outside

Je ne le lui ai pas dit.
I didn't tell him.

Adverb - *pas* so past participle is outside

Je n'ai pas vendu mon camion.
I did not sell my truck.

Adverb - *pas* so past participle is outside

Elle n'a rien dit.
She didn't say anything.

Adverb *rien* so past participle is outside

Je n'ai guère fini mes devoirs.
I have hardly finished my homework.

Adverb - *guère* so past participle is outside

Tu n'as jamais entendu cette chanson.
You (familiar) have never heard this song.

Adverb - *jamais* so past participle is outside

Elle n'a commis aucune faute.
She made no mistake.

Noun - *aucun* so past participle is inside

commettre (verb) means 'to commit'

commettre faute (verb) means 'to make a mistake'

Je n'ai vu ni la lune ni les étoiles.
I saw neither the moon nor the stars.

Noun - *ni* so past participle is inside

Il n'a plus jamais voulu être seul.
He never wanted to be alone again.

Adverb - *plus* so past participle is outside

TOPIC 106 ❖ *Passé composé*, negation and word order

Elle n'a plus jamais cru personne.
She never believed anyone again.

💡 Adverb - **plus** so past participle is outside

Je n'ai jamais aimé le football ni le basket.
I never liked football, or basketball.

💡 Adverb - **jamais** so past participle is outside

Je n'ai voulu que nager.
I only wanted to swim.

💡 **que** so past participle is inside

Mon oncle n'a jamais parlé que de sa fille.
My uncle never spoke of anything but his daughter.

💡 **que** so past participle is inside

Bootstrap French
TOPIC 107

❖ *Passé composé* with *être*

Passé composé with the many **verbs of movement** (and their related forms) use **être** rather than **avoir** as the auxiliary verb.
- So we say **je suis allé** and NOT **j'ai allé**.

- The verbs of movement include **aller** ('to go'), **venir** ('to come'), **revenir** ('to come back'), **sortir** ('to go out'), **partier** ('to leave'), **monter** ('to go up') & **descendre** ('to go down').
- The verb **rester** ('to stay') is also considered a verb movement in this context.
- And the verbs **naître** ('to be born') and **mourir** ('to die') also take **être** as their **passé composé** auxiliary verb.

When a verb takes **être** as an auxiliary, the past participle always **must agree** in gender and number with the subject.

EXAMPLES:

Il est allé.
He went.
💡 **aller** (to go) ⇒ **allé** (masculine singular)

Elle est allée.
She went.
💡 **aller** (to go) ⇒ **allée** (feminine singular)

Ils sont allés.
They went.
💡 **aller** (to go) ⇒ **allés** (masculine plural)

Elles sont allées.
They (females) went.
💡 **aller** (to go) ⇒ **allées** (feminine plural)

Vous n'êtes pas allés au cinéma le week-end passé ?
Did you (formal) not go to the cinema last weekend?

Est-ce qu'elles sont allées en France ?
Did they go to France?

Oui, mais elles sont déjà revenues.
Yes, but they have already returned.

TOPIC 107 ❖ *Passé composé* with *être*

Ils ne sont jamais allés en prison pour leurs crimes.
They never went to jail for their crimes.

* crime (m) means 'crime'

Je ne suis allée ni à New York ni à Los Angeles.
I (female) have been to neither New York nor Los Angeles.

Il n'est pas revenu à son bureau.
He did not return to his office.

* revenir (to return) ⇒ revenu (masculine singular)

Elle n'est pas revenue à son bureau.
She did not return to her office.

* revenir (to return) ⇒ revenue (feminine singular)

Ils ne sont pas revenus à leurs bureaux.
They did not return to their offices.

* revenir (to return) ⇒ revenus (masculine plural)

Elles ne sont pas revenues à leurs bureaux.
They (females) did not return to their offices.

* revenir (to return) ⇒ revenues (feminine plural)

Ils sont passés par Paris en route vers Tours.
They passed through Paris en route to Tours.

* passer (to go through, to pass by, to cross) is (sometimes) a verb of motion - it has many meaning some of which are not movement-related.

Les hommes ne sont jamais arrivés.
The men never arrived.

* arriver (to arrive) is a verb of motion

Marie, à quelle heure est-ce que tu es arrivée hier ?
Marie, what time did you (familiar) arrive yesterday?

À quelle heure es-tu sortie ce matin ?
What time did you (familiar) (female) go out this morning?

Ma fille est entrée à l'université l'année dernière.
My daughter entered college last year.

* entre to enter is a verb of motion

Il n'est plus retourné en France.
He never returned to France.

French Grammar

TOPIC 107 ❖ *Passé composé* with *être*

Ils sont revenus de leurs vacances.
They (males) came back from his vacation.

Il est parti en Italie, où il a acheté une maison.
He left for Italy where he bought a house.

Élise est montée dans sa voiture.
Elise got into her car.

Je suis descendu du train.
I (male) got off the train.

- **descendre de** means 'to get off (transport)'

Qui dans la famille est resté à la maison pendant les vacances ?
Who in the family stayed home during the vacation?

- **qui** always assumes masculine singular
- **pendant** means 'during'

Geneviève est sortie mais Juliette et Emma sont restées à la maison.
Geneviève went out but Juliette and Emma stayed home.

Elle est tombée dans l'escalier.
She fell down the stairs.

- **tomber** (to fall) is a verb of motion

Anthony est devenu boulanger.
Anthony has become a baker.

- **devenir** (to become) is not a verb of motion but takes **être** in the **passé composé**

Hugo est devenu exactement ce qu'il a toujours voulu devenir.
Hugo became exactly what he always wanted to become.

Est-ce vrai que vous vous êtes rencontrés à Paris ?
Is it true that you (plural) met in Paris?

- **rencontrer** (to meet) is not a verb of motion but takes **être** in the **passé composé**

Un fantôme est soudainement apparu devant nous.
A ghost suddenly appeared in front of us.

- **apparaître** (to appear) is not a verb of motion but takes être in the **passé**
- **apparaître** ⇒ **apparu**
- **fantôme** (m) means 'ghost' o

Ma fille est née à Gosford - une petite ville d'Australie.
My daughter was born in Gosford - a small town in Australia.

- **naître** (to be born) ⇒ **né**

TOPIC 107 ❖ *Passé composé* with *être*

Elle n'est pas encore morte.
She's not dead yet.

💡 mourir (to die) ⇒ mort

Quand est-ce que ses grands-parents sont morts ?
When did his grandparents die?

Bootstrap French — TOPIC 108

❖ *Passé composé* with *être* verbs used transitively

Verbs that take **être** in the **passé composé** are **intransitive** - that is they don't need to take a direct object.
- For instance the verb **aller** ('to go') is not done **to** something - it does not take a direct object.

There are however some of these verbs of motion that can be both intransitive and transitive. For example:
- The verb **descendre** means 'to go down' so **Il est descendu** is **intransitive**.
- But he is going down **l'escalier** ('the stairs') then it becomes **transitive** - **descender** now has an object.
- Moreover **descendre** can also mean 'to take something down' and is therefore also **transitive**.

If a verb is used **transitively** in **passé composé** it must use **avoir** (and not **être**) as the auxiliary verb.

Verbs that can be both intransitive and transitive include:
- **descendre** means 'to go down' AND 'to take down'
- **monter** means 'to go up' AND 'to take up'
- **passer** means 'to go by' AND 'to pass through' or 'to pass a period of time'
- **rentrer** means 'to go back' or 'to return' AND 'to bring back'
- **retourner** means 'to go back' AND 'to take/send back'
- **sortir** means 'to go out' AND 'to take out'

EXAMPLES:

Il est descendu.
He descended.
   💡 Intransitive as here the verb **descendre** takes no direct object

Il a descendu l'escalier.
He went down the stairs.
   💡 This is transitive because **l'escalier** is a direct object

Il a descendu la valise.
He took down the suitcase.
   💡 Transitive - **la valise** is a direct object

TOPIC 108 ❖ *Passé composé* with *être* verbs used transitively

Il est monté.
He went up.
- Intransitive as here the verb **monter** takes no direct object

Il est monté au sommet d'une colline.
He climbed to the top of a hill.
- Not transitive because **au sommet** is not a direct object
- **sommet** (m) means 'summit'
- **colline** (f) means 'hill'

Il a monté les valises.
He brought up the suitcases.
- Transitive - **les valises** is a direct object

Il a monté le son très fort.
He turned up the sound very loud.
- Transitive - **le son** is a direct object

On est montés dans la voiture avant vous.
We got in the car before you (formal).
- Not transitive because **dans la voiture** is not a direct object

Elle n'a pas monté la montagne, elle est montée sur la montagne.
She didn't take up the mountain, she climbed the mountain.
- **elle est montée** is not transitive because **sur la montagne** is not a direct object

Nous sommes montés dans l'avion.
We got on the plane.
- Not transitive because **dans l'avion** is not a direct object

J'ai monté mon cheval.
I (female) rode my horse.
- Transitive
- Note that with **avoir** the past participle does not need to agree.

Je suis montée à cheval.
I (female) rode a horse.
- Not transitive because **à cheval** is not a direct object

Nous sommes passés devant le parc.
We walked past the park.
- Not transitive because **devant le parc** is not a direct object
- **devant** means 'in front of' or 'by'

TOPIC 108 ❖ *Passé composé* with *être* verbs used transitively

Nous avons passé la porte.
We walked through the door.
- Transitive - **la porte** is a direct object

Vous êtes passée devant la porte.
You (formal female singular) walked past the door.
- Not transitive because **devant la porte** is not a direct object

Vous avez passé un bon moment ?
Did you (formal) have (spend) a good time?
- Transitive - **un bon moment** is the direct object

J'ai passé un mois à Nantes.
I (male) spent a month in Nantes.
- Transitive - **un mois** is a direct object

Je suis rentré.
I (male) returned.
- Often **Je suis rentré** means 'I have returned home'

J'ai rentré les chaises.
I brought in the chairs.
- Transitive - **les chaises** is a direct object

Je suis retourné à l'école.
I (male) returned to school.
- Not transitive because **à l'école** is not a direct object

Inès est retournée en France.
Ines returned to France.
- Not transitive because **en France** is not a direct object

Inès a retourné la lettre.
Ines returned the letter.
- Transitive
- Note that with **avoir** the past participle does not need to agree.

Je suis retournée au magasin.
I (female) returned to the store.
- Not transitive because **au magasin** is not a direct object

J'ai retourné le pull au magasin.
I (male) returned the sweater to the store.
- Transitive - **le pull** is a direct object

TOPIC 108 ❖ *Passé composé* with *être* verbs used transitively

Elle est sortie avec Patrice.
She went out with Patrice.
- Not transitive because **avec Patrice** is not a direct object

Elle a sorti la voiture du parking.
She took the car out of the carpark.
- Transitive
- Note that with **avoir** the past participle does not need to agree.

Il a sorti le chien.
He took the dog out.
- Transitive
- Note that with **avoir** the past participle does not need to agree.

As-tu sorti les carottes du frigo hier soir ?
Did you (familiar, male or female) take the carrots out of the fridge last night?
- Transitive
- Note that with **avoir** the past participle does not need to agree.

❖ *Passé composé* with reflexive verbs

Reflexive verbs take **être** as their auxiliary in the **passé composé**.

The auxiliary **être** always comes immediately **after** the reflexive pronoun.

In the case of reflexive verbs, the participle generally **agrees** with the subject.

The exception is when the direct object comes after the reflexive verb. In this case, the past participle does not agree.

However for verbs like **se parler** and **se plaire** where the reflexive pronoun is in fact an indirect object ('to talk TO oneself') there is no agreement.

In a negative sentence, **ne** always comes before the reflexive pronoun, and **pas** always comes right after the auxiliary verb - always **être** in this case.

EXAMPLES:

Je me suis lavé.
I (male) washed myself.
> The auxilliary **suis** immmediately after reflexive pronoun **me**

Sarah s'est préparée.
Sarah got ready.
> **préparée** (feminine) agrees with **Sarah** (feminine)

Elle s'est lavée.
She washed herself.
> **lavée** (feminine) agrees with **elle** (feminine)

Elle s'est lavé les mains.
She washed her hands.
> Direct object **les mains** after the reflexive verb **lavé** so no agreement

Je ne me suis pas levé.
I did not get up.
> **ne** comes before the reflexive pronoun **me**, and **pas** comes right after the auxilliary verb **suis**.

Elle ne s'est pas lavé les mains.
She didn't wash her hands.
> **ne** comes before the reflexive pronoun **se**, and **pas** comes right after the auxilliary verb **suis**.

TOPIC 109 ❖ *Passé composé* with reflexive verbs

Elle s'est brossé les dents.
She brushed her teeth.

💡 The reflexive pronoun **se** is actually an indirect object so no agreement

Ils se sont acheté un nouveau chien.
They bought themselves a new dog.

💡 The reflexive pronoun **se** is actually an indirect object so no agreement

Tout le monde s'est trompé.
Everyone got it wrong.

📖 **se tromper** (verb) means 'to be mistaken' or 'to make a mistake'

Vous ne vous êtes pas trompé.
You (formal male singular) were not mistaken.

Il s'est débrouillé tout seul.
He managed on his own.

📖 **se débrouiller** (verb) means 'to manage' or 'to get by'

Elle s'est assise.
She sat down.

💡 **assis** is the past participle of **asseoir** (to sit).

Nous nous sommes assises à l'arrière.
We sat down in the back.

Ils se sont bien débrouillés en français.
They got by fine in French.

Elle s'est méfiée et nous a tout de suite appelés.
She got suspicious and called us right away.

📖 **se méfier** (verb) means 'to be wary' or 'to be suspicious'

Nous nous sommes habillés.
We got dressed.

📖 **se habiller** (verb) means 'to get dressed' or 'to dress oneself'

Elles se sont déshabillées.
They undressed.

📖 **se déshabiller** (verb) means 'to undress'

Elles se sont disputées.
They (females) argued.

📖 **se disputer** means 'to argue (with one and other)'

TOPIC 109 ❖ *Passé composé* with reflexive verbs

Suzanne s'est endormie.
Suzanne fell asleep.

📖 **s'endormir** (verb) means 'to fall asleep'

Tu t'es bien amusé hier soir ?
Did you (familiar) have fun last night?

Elles se sont blessées.
They got hurt.

Édith s'est échappée du bâtiment.
Edith escaped from the building.

Je ne me suis inquiété de rien.
I didn't worry about anything.

📖 **s'inquiéter** (verb) means 'to worry'
📖 **s'inquiéter de** (verb) means 'to worry about (something)'

Les étudiants - se sont-ils inquiétés de l'examen ?
The students - did they worry about the exam?

Est-ce que Suzanne s'est déjà endormie ?
Has Suzanne already fallen asleep?

Est-ce qu'il s'est rasé ?
Has he shaved?

Est-ce qu'il ne s'est pas rasé ?
Hasn't he shaved?

Vous êtes-vous bien débrouillé en français ?
Did you (formal male singular) get by fine in French?

Personne ne s'est demandé pourquoi.
Nobody wondered why.

💡 **pourquoi** replaces **pas** in this negation

Il n'a pas voulu se coucher trop tard.
He didn't want to go to bed too late.

💡 Dual verb sentences in passé composé - the reflexive pronoun agrees with the subject

TOPIC 109 ❖ *Passé composé* with reflexive verbs

Je n'ai pas aimé me lever tôt.
I didn't like getting up early.

Dual verb sentences in passé composé - the reflexive pronoun agrees with the subject

❖ The Reflexive Causative - *se faire*

We previous saw the causative with **faire** meaning 'to get something done' or 'to have something done'.

Recall that the 'RECEIVER' (for or to whom the action is performed) is the object of the sentence.

When the 'RECEIVER' is the subject of the sentence we can use the reflexive causative **se faire**.

- When used reflexively the causative **se faire** can indicate that the subject has done something to or for himself/herself.
- The reflexive causative can also be used (semi-passively) to indicate that something happens to the subject (as per someone else's implied action or wish).

Note that in the causative the past participle **fait** never needs to agree - it is invariant.

EXAMPLES:

Je me fais coiffer.
I'm having my hair done.

Je me suis fait coiffer.
I had my hair done.

Il se fait apporter le café chaque matin.
He has coffee brought to him every morning.

Il s'est fait apporter un café ce matin.
He had coffee brought to him this morning.

Est-ce que tu veux te faire expliquer ce problème ?
Do you (familiar) want this problem explained to you?

T'es-tu fait expliquer le problème ?
Did you (familiar) have someone explain the problem to you?

Nous nous faisons réveiller tôt chaque matin.
We get woken up early every morning.

Nous nous sommes fait réveiller ce matin.
We got woken up this morning.

TOPIC 110 ❖ The Reflexive Causative - *se faire*

Il se fait raser la barbe.
He is having his beard shaved.

Il s'est fait raser la barbe.
He had his beard shaved.

Il ne s'est pas fait raser la barbe.
He didn't have his beard shaved.

Elle s'est fait expulser de la boîte.
She got kicked out of the club.
- Something happens to the subject without requesting it
- **boîte** (f) means 'box'
- But **boîte** here is short for **la boîte de nuit** (night club).

Il s'est fait avoir.
He got had. *OR* He was conned.
- Something happens to the subject without requesting it

Pourquoi s'est-il fait virer ?
Why did he get fired?
- Something happens to the subject without requesting it

Le chien s'est fait renverser.
The dog got run over.
- Something happens to the subject without requesting it
- **renverser** (verb) means 'to be knocked down' or 'to be run over'

Nous nous sommes fait voler nos bagages.
We had our luggage stolen.
- Something happens to the subject without requesting it
- **voler** (verb) means 'to steal'

Bootstrap French
TOPIC 111

❖ To miss -*manquer*

The verb **manquer à** can mean to 'to miss' in an emotional sense.

Used this way it takes an indirect object and is therefore coupled with **à** when its object is anything other than an indirect pronoun (**me**, **te**, **lui** etc).

The fact that it takes an indirect object means that, in the mind of an English speaker, its use is inverted.

- So in French we say 'Jacques is missing to Juliette' - which means 'Juliette misses Jacques'.

Another meaning for **manquer** is 'to lack', so with the **à** we could think of this as 'Jacques is lacking to Juliette'.

Indeed **manquer** can also be used with a direct object to mean 'to lack'.

EXAMPLES:

Jacques manque à Juliette.
Juliette misses Jacques.
💡 OR 'Jacques is missing to Juliette.'

Je manque à Jean_Luc.
Jean-Luc misses me.

Elle me manque.
I miss her.

Je me demande si je lui manque.
I wonder if he misses me.

Le travail ne me manque pas.
I don't miss work.

Marianne m'a manqué pendant de nombreuses années.
I missed Marianne for many years.

Sa copine manque-t-elle à Romain ?
Does Romain miss his girlfriend?

Mes journées universitaires me manquent.
I miss my college days.

TOPIC 111 ❖ To miss -*manquer*

Hélène leur manque.
They miss Helen.

Votre pays vous manque ?
Do you (formal) miss your country?

Son chien manque à sa mère.
Her mother misses her dog.

Vous manquez de patience.
You (formal) lack patience.

👁 Without the à and with a direct object **manquer** means 'to lack'

Le café manque de sucre.
Coffee lacks sugar.

Je manque de bons outils pour le travail.
I lack the right tools for the job.

👁 **outil** (m) means 'tool'

❖ Almost - *avoir failli*

The verb **faillir** is very commonly used in the **passé composé** to express 'to almost have (done something)' or 'to nearly have (done something)'.

The passé composé **avoir failli** is followed by an infinitive.

When followed by **à** and a noun it means 'to fail at/in (something)' or 'to fail to adhere to (something)'

EXAMPLES:

J'ai failli tomber.
I almost fell.

J'ai failli avoir un accident.
I almost had an accident.

Ils ont failli me rentrer dedans.
They almost ran into me.

Nous avons failli rater le train.
We almost missed the train.

J'ai failli le faire, mais je me suis retenu.
I almost did it, but I held myself back.
   se retenir de means 'to restrain oneself (doing something)'

Nous avons failli perdre nos clés.
We almost lost our keys.

Il a failli pleurer quand elle est partie.
He almost cried when she left.

Vous avez failli renverser la vieille dame.
You (formal) almost knocked over the old lady.

Une maladie du sang rare a failli me coûter la vie.
A rare blood disease almost cost me my life.

Tu as failli y rester.
You (familiar) almost died [expression].
   Literally 'You nearly stayed there'.

TOPIC 112 ❖ Almost - *avoir failli*

J'ai failli à ma promesse.
I failed to keep my promise.

Tu as failli à ta tâche.
You (familiar) have failed in your task.

Je n'ai jamais failli à ma parole.
I have never broken my word.

Notre famille n'a pas failli à la tradition - le déjeuner de Noël sur la plage.
Our family did not break the tradition - the Christmas lunch on the beach.

Il faut ne pas faillir à sa parole.
One must not break one's word.

Bootstrap French
TOPIC 113

❖ Past participles as adjectives

Past participles can often be used as adjectives. Indeed, we have already used many such adjectives already.

When used as an adjective, the past participle needs to agree in gender and number with the word it modifies, following the normal rules of adjective agreement.

EXAMPLES:

La porte est ouverte.
The door is open.

Il a ouvert la porte. La porte reste ouverte.
He has opened the door. The door remains open.

Elle est réveillée.
She is awake.

Elle s'est fait réveiller tôt. Elle est maintenant réveillée.
She got woken up early. She is now awake.

Les devoirs sont faits.
The homework is done.

Je leur ai fait faire leurs devoirs. Les devoirs sont enfin faits.
I made them do their homework. The homework is finally done.

Leur accord commercial est rompu.
Their business agreement is broken.

✎ **rompre** (verb) means 'to break' or 'to break up'

Ils se sont disputés et l'accord est rompu.
They had an argument and the agreement is broken.

Les barrières sont rompues.
Barriers are broken/bent.

✎ **barrière** (f) means 'fence' or 'barrier'

Les bicyclettes sont cassées.
The bicycles are broken/smashed.

✎ **bicyclette** (f) means 'small bicycle'

TOPIC 113 ❖ Past participles as adjectives

La tâche est finie.
The task is finished.

Nous nous sommes vraiment appliqués et la tâche est finie.
We really applied ourselves and finally the task is finished.

- *s'appliquer* (verb) means 'to apply oneself'

Mes grands-parents sont décédés.
My grandparents are deceased.

- *décéder* (verb) means 'to pass away'

Pourquoi est-elle fâchée ?
Why is she angry?

- *fâcher* (verb) 'to anger'

Il y a une voiture arrêtée au carrefour.
There is a car stopped at the crossroads.

- *carrefour* (m) means 'crossroads' or 'intersection' or 'junction'

Fatigué, je suis rentré à minuit.
Tired, I came home at midnight.

- *fatiguer* (verb) means 'to tire' or 'to wear out'

Nous sommes épuisées.
We are exhausted.

- *épuiser* (verb) means 'to exhaust' or 'to wear out'

Le petit chien assis sur le canapé est mignon.
The little dog sitting (seated) on the sofa is cute.

Je ne peux pas voir d'homme agenouillé.
I cannot see a (any) kneeling man.

- *s'agenouiller* (verb) means 'to knell down'
- *agenouillé* from the non-reflexive form

Ces livres sont écrits en italien.
These books are written in Italian.

Ces solutions proposées ne sont pas parfaites.
These suggested solutions are not perfect.

- *proposer* (verb) means 'to suggest' or 'to propose'

Le garçon déçu a pleuré.
The disappointed boy cried.

- *pleurer* (verb) means 'to cry'

TOPIC 113 ❖ Past participles as adjectives

Déçue aussi, la fille a pleuré aussi.
Disappointed too, the girl cried too.

Il est perdu, comme d'habitude.
He is lost as usual.

✎ **comme d'habitude** means 'as usual' (often appreviated as **comme d'hab**)

Leur fils est trop gâté.
Their son is too spoiled.

✎ **gâter** (verb) means 'to spoil'

Le mois passé, il a eu la grippe.
The past month he had the flu.

Chaque seconde passée ici est dangereuse.
Every second spent here is dangerous.

Ce sont des hommes distingués.
They are distinguished men.

✎ **distinguer** (verb) means 'to distinguish'

Ils sont assis près de la scène.
They are sitting near the stage.

Bootstrap French
TOPIC 114

❖ If, so and yes - *si*

The word **si** serves as a conjunction, an adverb and a contrary exclamation.
- The conjunction **si** means 'if'
- The adverb **si** can mean 'so' or 'as much as'
  - **tellement** is commonly used in the same way.
- And **si** can also mean 'yes', in place of **oui** when responding contrarily to a question or statement.

EXAMPLES:

Si tu veux, on peut le faire.
If you (familiar) want, we can do it.

Je me demande si elle est française.
I wonder if she is French.

Si je gagne, j'achète une voiture.
If I win, I buy a car.

Si ce n'est pas indiscret, je peux vous poser une question ?
If (you) don't mind, can I ask you (formal) a question?

Vous pouvez conduire si vous voulez.
You (formal) can drive if you want.

S'il vous plaît.
Please (formal). *OR* If it is pleasing to you (formal).

S'il te plaît.
Please (familiar). *OR* If it is pleasing to you (familiar)

Je ne sais pas si elle a les yeux marron ou bleus.
I don't know if she has brown or blue eyes.
  ۪ The colors **marron**, **rose** and **orange** are invariable as adjectives

Je suis si fatigué.
I am so tired.

Ton amie Émilie - je la trouve si gentille.
Your (familiar) friend Emile - I find her so nice.

TOPIC 114 ❖ If, so and yes - *si*

Tout s'est passé si vite.
It all happened so fast.

Le garçon est si déçu.
The boy is so disappointed.

Il n'est pas si intelligent qu'il pense.
He's not as smart as he thinks.
📖 Here *si* means 'as much as'

Ce n'est pas si facile.
It is not so easy (as expected).
📖 Here *si* means 'as much as'

Tu n'as pas faim ? Si ! En fait, j'ai très faim.
You (familiar) are not hungry? Yes! In fact, I'm very hungry.

Il n'y a pas de montagnes en France. Mais si, bien sûr, il y a des montagnes.
There are no mountains in France. But yes, of course, there are mountains.

Tu n'es pas allé à l'école aujourd'hui. Si !
You (familiar) didn't go to school today. Yes (I did)!

Jeanne n'est pas prête. Si, si !
Jeanne is not ready. Yes Yes (she is)!

Non, il n'a pas dit ça, n'est-ce pas ? Je vous assure que si.
No, he didn't say that, did he? I assure you (formal) yes (he did).

❖ Passive voice

The passive voice inverts the verb so that rather than 'He did it' we can say 'It was done by him'.

Or simply 'It was done' thereby removing the subject completely.

- In the present tense this is achieved by using the verb **être** and the verb past participle - just like using the past participle as an adjective.
- In the passé composé we use **avoir été** ('has been' or 'was') and the past participle.

The AGENT who does the verb can (optionally) be specified:

- For active verbs use **par**.
- For state-of-being or emotion verbs use **de**.

Note that while the passive voice can be useful to either emphasize the subject or make the subject anonymous, it tends to be avoided. There are other ways to do this in French.

- We can emphasize the subject by using subject repetition: 'c'est..qui'.
- Use the pronoun 'on' to make the subject anonymous.
- Use reflexive verbs to make the subject anonymous.

EXAMPLES:

Le gâteau a été mangé.
The cake has been eaten.
💡 manger ⇒ (m.sing) mangé

Le gâteau a été mangé par les enfants.
The cake was eaten by the children.
💡 manger ⇒ (m.sing) mangé
💡 manger is an action verb so use **par** for agent.

Le gâteau a été mangé par qui ?
The cake was eaten by whom?
💡 manger ⇒ (m.sing) mangé

Par qui le gâteau a-t-il été mangé ?
By whom was the cake eaten?
💡 manger ⇒ (m.sing) mangé

TOPIC 115 ❖ Passive voice

Le brocoli n'a pas été mangé.
The broccoli was not eaten.
💡 manger ⇒ (m.sing) mangé

Pourquoi le brocoli n'a-t-il pas été mangé ?
Why wasn't the broccoli eaten?
💡 manger ⇒ (m.sing) mangé

Mes devoirs ont été mangés par le chien.
My homework was eaten by the dog.
💡 manger ⇒ (m.pl) mangés

Tes devoirs ont-ils vraiment été mangés par le chien ?
Was your (familiar) homework really eaten by the dog?
💡 manger ⇒ (m.pl) mangés

Il n'a pas été cru par son professeur.
He was not believed by his teacher.
💡 croire ⇒ (m.sing) cru

Le traité a été rompu par les deux parties.
The treaty was broken by both parties.
💡 rompre ⇒ (m.sing) rompu

Votre objection a été notée par le comité.
Your (formal) (female) objection has been noted by the committee.
💡 noter ⇒ (f.sing) notée

Ce film a été tourné à Montmartre par un réalisateur très connu.
This film was shot in Montmartre by a well-known director.
💡 tourner ⇒ (m.sing) tourné
✎ réalisateur (m) means 'director' (theatre or movies)

L'ambulance a été appelée par des passants.
The ambulance was called by passers-by.
💡 appeler ⇒ (f.sing) appelée

Le blessé est conduit à l'hôpital par l'ambulance.
The injured person was taken to the hospital by the ambulance.
💡 conduire ⇒ (m.sing) conduit

La voiture n'a pas pu être vendue.
The car could not be sold.
💡 vendre ⇒ (f.sing) vendue

TOPIC 115 ❖ Passive voice

Le voleur n'a pas été arrêté par le policier.
The thief was not caught by the policeman.
- attraper ⇒ (m.sing) attrapé

L'ours est suivi de ses oursons.
The bear is followed by its cubs.
- suivre ⇒ (m.sing) suivi
- suivre is an state verb so use de for agent
- suivre (verb) means 'to follow'

Ils sont admirés de tout le monde.
They are admired by everyone.
- admirer ⇒ (m.pl) admirés
- admirer is an emotion verb so use de for agent

Le patron est détesté de ses collègues.
The boss is hated by his colleagues.
- détester ⇒ (m.sing) détesté
- détester is an emotion verb so use de for agent

Elle est respectée de tous ses collègues.
She is respected by all her colleagues.
- respecter ⇒ (f.sing) respectée
- respecter is an emotion verb so use de for agent

Ces mots sont vraiment appréciés de tout le monde.
These words are really appreciated by everyone.
- apprécier ⇒ (m.pl) appréciés
- apprécier is an emotion verb so use de for agent

La voleuse a été connue de tous.
The (female) thief was known to everyone.
- connaître ⇒ (f.sing) connue
- connaître is an state verb so use de for agent

Nous avons été accompagnées de nos amis.
We (females) were accompanied by our friends.
- accompagner ⇒ (f.pl) accompagnées
- accompagner is an state verb so use de for agent

La terre a été couverte de neige.
The land was covered with snow.
- couvrir ⇒ (f.sing) couverte
- couvrir is an state verb so use de for agent

TOPIC 115 ❖ Passive voice

Je n'ai jamais été battue aux échecs.
I (female) have never been beaten at chess.
💡 battre ⇒ (f.sing) battue

La pasteurisation a été inventée par Louis Pasteur.
Pasteurization was invented by Louis Pasteur.
💡 inventer ⇒ (f.sing) inventée

Le feu a été découvert, pas inventé.
Fire was discovered, not invented.
💡 découvrir ⇒ (m.sing) découvert

❖ What is your job? - *Quel est votre travail ?*

In French when one refers to one's profession, the profession behaves like an adjective - there is no article **un** or **une**.

This topic illustrates this and some useful words and expressions used when discussing work.

EXAMPLES:

Quelle est votre profession ?
What is your (formal) profession\occupation?

✎ **profession** (m) means 'profession' or 'occupation'

Qu'est-ce que vous faites dans la vie ?
What do you (formal) do for a living?

Quel est votre travail ?
What is your (formal) job?

C'est quoi ton boulot ?
What is your (familiar) job?

✎ **boulot** (m.slang) means 'job'

Je suis plombier.
I am a plumber.

Je suis avocate.
I (female) work as a lawyer.

Il est manager.
He is a manager.

Elle est enseignante.
She is a teacher.

Elle postule cet emploi.
She is applying for that job.

✎ **postuler** (verb) means 'to apply for'

Elle postule à ce poste.
She is applying for that position.

💡 **postule à** ('to apply for (a job)') is also commonly used but is improper French

TOPIC 116 ❖ What is your job? - *Quel est votre travail ?*

Elle a eu le poste.
She got the job.

Benoît a démissionné.
Benoît has resigned.

📖 **démissionner** means 'to retire'

Philip a été renvoyé.
Philip was fired.

📖 **renvoyer** (verb) means 'to fire'

Sophie a été virée.
Sophie was sacked (female).

📖 **virer** means 'to sack' or 'to fire'

❖ Present participles as adjectives

Many verbs can become adjectives using the **present participle** form.

For instance the verb **decevoir** ('to disappoint'): Its **past** participle **déçu** means 'disappointed'.

But also its **present** participle **décevant** is an adjective meaning 'disappointing' or 'that which disappoints'

The present participle may vary considerably from the meaning of the root verb.

The masculine singular present participle is formed by dropping **-ons** from the **nous** present tense conjugation and adding **-ant**.

- So **decevoir** conjugated is **nous décevons** - drop the **-ons** and add **-ant** gives the present participle **décevant**.

There are three exceptions (**avoir**, **être** & **savoir**) but their present participles are never used as adjectives (gerunds are covered in a later topic).

Like all adjectives, these too should agree in gender and number.

EXAMPLES:

Ça le déçoit. Il est déçu. Le résultat est décevant.
That disappoints him. He is disappointed. The result is disappointing.
  ◊ décevoir (to disappoint) ⇒ (nous) décevons (drop -ons and add -ant) ⇒ décevant

Ça m'embarrasse. Je suis embarrassé. Mon nez rouge est embarrassant.
It embarrasses me. I am embarrassed. My red nose is embarrassing.
  ✎ embarrasser (verb) means 'to embarrass'
  ◊ embarrasser ⇒ (nous) embarrassons (drop -ons and add -ant) ⇒ embarrassant

Ça le dégoûte. Il est dégoûté. Il trouve les escargots dégoûtants.
That disgusts him. He is disgusted. He finds snails disgusting.
  ✎ dégoûter (verb) means 'to disgust'

Elle s'intéresse aux sciences. Elle trouve particulièrement la chimie intéressante.
She is interested in science. She particularly finds chemistry interesting.

Ça leur fait peur. Ils ont peur. Le chien qui aboie est effrayant.
They are frightened. The barking dog is frightening.
  ✎ faire peur à (verb) means 'to make (someone) frightened'
  ✎ aboyer (verb) means 'to bark'
  ✎ effrayer (verb) means 'to frighten'

TOPIC 117 ❖ Present participles as adjectives

N'es-tu pas surpris ? La nouvelle n'est-elle pas surprenante ?
Aren't you (familiar) surprised? Isn't the news surprising?

🖉 surprendre (verb) means 'to surprise'

Ils me fatiguent. Je suis fatigué. Les jeunes enfants sont si fatigants.
They tire me. I'm tired. Young children are so tiring.

🖉 fatiguer (verb) means 'to tire' or 'to wear out'

Nous sommes inquiets. Ces grosses vagues sont inquiétantes.
We are worried. These big waves are worrying.

🖉 inquiéter (verb) means 'to worry'

Nous sommes très excités. Notre petite voiture rapide est excitante.
We are very excited. Our fast little car is exciting.

🖉 exciter (verb) means 'to excite'

Qu'est-ce qui te gêne ? Les mouches sont-elles gênantes ?
What bothers you (familiar)? Are the flies annoying?

🖉 gêner (verb) means 'to bother' or 'to annoy'

J'ai été charmé. Je trouve ces filles charmantes.
I have been charmed. I find these girls charming.

🖉 charmer (verb) means 'to charme'

Les histoires nous ont amusés. Ce sont des histoires amusantes.
The stories amused us. These are fun stories.

🖉 amuser (verb) means 'to assume'

N'êtes-vous pas choqués ? Si ! Nous sommes choqués. Les prix sont choquants.
Aren't you (plural) shocked? Yes! We are shocked. The prices are shocking.

🖉 choquer (verb) means 'to shock'
🖉 prix (f) means 'price' or 'prize'

Il est confus. Le résultat est déroutant.
He is confused. The result is confusing.

🖉 confus (adj) means 'confused' (Not to be confused with the verb confonfre)
🖉 dérouter (verb) means 'to divert' or 'to disconcert'
🖉 déroutant means 'confusing' or 'disconcerting'

Le tennis est très épuisant.
Tennis is very exhausting.

🖉 épuiser (verb) means 'to exhaust' or 'to wear out'

TOPIC 117 ❖ Present participles as adjectives

Le rugby - c'est un sport extrêmement exigeant.
Rugby - it is an extremely demanding sport.

⚐ **exiger** (verb) means 'to demand' or 'to require'

J'ai lu un roman fascinant - Madame Bovary de Gustave Flaubert.
I read a fascinating novel - Madame Bovary by Gustave Flaubert.

⚐ **fasciner** (verb) means 'to fascinate'

La maison a de l'eau courante.
The house has running water.

💡 **courir** (to run) ⇒ **courons** (drop **-ons** and add **-ant**) ⇒ **courant**

Le prix d'une pizza en Norvège est exorbitant.
The price of a pizza in Norway is exorbitant.

⚐ **exorbitant** (adj) means 'exorbitant'

💡 **exorbitant** is techically not a present participle as there is no matching (modern French) verb (it derives from an unused Latin verb)

Ces grandes boîtes sont encombrantes.
These large boxes are bulky.

⚐ **encombrant** (adj) means 'cumbersome' or 'bulky'

❖ Immediate past, continuous present and immediate future

In French there are set phrases for actions that are **immediate past** (just happened), **continuous present** (happening now) and **immediate future** (about to happen).

These set phrases are:
- Immediate (or recent) past: **venir de...**
- Continuous present: **être en train de...**
- Continuous present: **être sur le point de...**

Each one of these is followed by a verb in the infinitive.

EXAMPLES:

Je viens de faire le ménage.
I just did the housework.

Il vient de quitter ma maison.
He just left my house.

Je viens de terminer cette tâche.
I just finished this task.

Louis vient de se réveiller.
Louis has just woken up.

L'eau vient de bouillir. Elle bout maintenant.
The water just boiled. It is boiling now.
  - **bouillir** (verb) means 'to boil'

La pluie vient de s'arrêter.
The rain just stopped.
  - **pluie** (f) means 'rain'
  - **s'arrêter** (verb) means 'to stop oneself'

Je viens de me faire couper les cheveux.
I just got my hair cut.

Veux-tu manger plus ? Mais tu viens de manger !
Do you want to eat more? But you (familiar) just ate!

TOPIC 118 ❖ Immediate past, continuous present and immediate future

Vous venez de rater le dernier train.
You (formal) just missed the last train.
   rater (verb) means 'to miss'

Elle vient d'être diplômée.
She just graduated.
   diplômé (adj) means 'graduated'

Sarah vient d'arriver au bureau à l'instant.
Sarah has just arrived at the office just now.
   à l'instant means 'just now' or 'at this instant'

Nous venons d'apprendre la nouvelle.
We just heard (learned) the news.
   apprendre (verb) means 'to learn' or 'to hear'

Je suis en train de faire le ménage.
I am doing housework.

Elles sont en train de préparer notre petit-déjeuner en ce moment-même.
They are preparing our breakfast right at this very moment.

Elle est toujours en train de se réveiller.
She is still waking up.

Je suis en train de parler avec ta mère.
I am talking with your (familiar) mother.

L'eau est en train de chauffer.
The water is heating up.
   chauffer (verb) means 'to heat'

Je suis en train de terminer le dernier chapitre de ce livre.
I am finishing the last chapter of this book.
   chapitre (m) means 'chapter'

Véronique est en train de faire la sieste.
Veronique is taking a nap.
   sieste (f) means 'nap' or 'siesta' or 'afternoon nap'

Elle est en train de lui parler du problème en ce moment.
She's talking to him about the problem right now.

TOPIC 118 ❖ Immediate past, continuous present and immediate future

Le bébé est sur le point de s'endormir.
The baby is about to fall asleep.

Nous sommes sur le point de manger.
We are about to eat.

Le train est sur le point de partir.
The train is about to leave.

Ils sont sur le point de déclencher une guerre.
They are about to set of a war.
- *déclencher* (verb) means 'to set off' or 'to launch'

Je suis sur le point de gagner le dernier point.
I'm about to win the last point.
- *point* (m) means 'point'

Nous sommes sur le point d'éteindre les lumières.
We're about to turn off the lights.

Le bateau est sur le point d'accoster.
The boat is about to dock.
- *accoster* (verb) means 'to dock' or 'to berth' or 'to accost'

Elle est sur le point de se faire laver les cheveux.
She is about to have her hair washed.

Ils sont sur le point de lui annoncer la nouvelle.
They are about to tell (announce to) him the news.

❖ The two ways to know - *savoir* and *connataire*

French has two common verbs - **savoir** and **connaître** - both of which can translate to 'to know' in English.

However, they have distinctly different uses:

- **savoir** means 'to know information' or 'to know how to do something' (know how).
  - It is one of those verbs that can be followed immediately (without a preposition) by an infinite verb - 'to know how to do something'. The word **comment** ('how') is not required.
  - Note however that in the passé composé (**avoir su**) means 'to have found out.
- **connaître** means 'to know' in the sense of being personally familiar with or having experienced something oneself.
  - It must **always** be followed by a noun - never a verb.

EXAMPLES:

Je sais ton nom.
I know your (familiar) name.
  💡 Je connais ton nom. is also common

Je sais les paroles de cette chanson.
I know the words of this song.
  💡 Je connais les paroles... is also accepatble

Tu sais où il habite ?
Do you (familiar) know where he lives?

Savez-vous quand ils arrivent ?
Do you (formal) know when they arrive?

Je ne sais pas pourquoi il a dit ça.
I don't know why he said that.

Je sais danser.
I know how to dance. *OR* I can dance.
  💡 comment (how) is not required

TOPIC 119 ❖ The two ways to know - *savoir* and *connataire*

Il sait très bien parler français.
He knows how to speak French very well. *OR* He can speak French very well.

💡 **comment** (how) is not required

Ma fille ne sait pas encore nager.
My daughter doesn't know how to swim yet.

💡 **comment** (how) is not required

Tu sais qu'il vient ? Oui, je sais.
Do you (familiar) know he's coming? Yes I know.

Le saviez-vous ?
Do you (formal) know that?

💡 Or colloquially 'Do you know ?'

Je l'ai su hier.
I found out yesterday.

Je connais cette chanson.
I know this song.

Tu connais mon amie Sylvie ?
Do you (familiar) know my friend Sylvie?

Est-ce que vous connaissez Paris ?
Do you (formal) know Paris?

💡 Or effectively 'Have you been to Paris?'

Connaissez-vous l'actrice française Catherine Deneuve ?
Do you (formal) know the French actress Catherine Deneuve?

Je la connais mais je ne l'ai jamais rencontrée.
I know her but I've never met her.

Est-ce que vous connaissez Carcassonne ?
Do you (formal) know Carcassonne?

Non, je ne la connais pas, mais j'ai entendu parler de cette ville.
No, I don't know it, but I've heard of this town.

💡 Here **la** perhaps refers to **la ville de Carcassonne**

Gabriel est un acteur connu de tout le monde.
Gabriel is an actor known to everyone.

💡 **être connu** has the sense of 'to be famous' or at least 'to be well know'

TOPIC 119 ❖ The two ways to know - *savoir* and *connataire*

Je connais bien les romans de Victor Hugo.
I know the novels of Victor Hugo well.

Est-ce que tu sais qui c'est ?
Do you (familiar) know who it is?

Oui je sais qui c'est, mais je ne le connais pas personnellement.
Yes I know who it is, but I don't know him personally.

Est-ce que vous savez où se trouve la poste ?
Do you (formal) know where the post office is?

Non, je ne sais pas où est la poste.
No, I don't know where the post office is.

Je connais très bien cette ville.
I know this town very well.

Oui, je sais que Berlin est la capitale de l'Allemagne mais je ne la connais pas.
Yes I know Berlin is the capital of Germany but I have not been there.

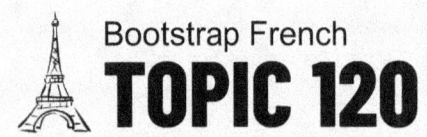 

Bootstrap French
TOPIC 120

❖ **The various uses of the verb** *arriver*

The verb **arriver** is one of the most common French verbs. It is a regular -ER verb. Besides the obvious for English speakers, it has a number of other meanings and uses.

- It can mean 'to arrive' and as a verb of motion takes **être** in the passé composé.
- It can mean 'to be coming' or 'to be on one's way'.
- It can mean 'to happen' or 'to occur'.
- This can either be with a person subject, often with an indirect pronoun - eg. 'it happened to me'.
- Or it can be impersonal using **il** - 'it happened that..' in the sense that 'there was..'.
- With the preposition **à** is means 'to reach', 'to achieve' or 'to get to' - both literally and figuratively.
- With the preposition **à** plus an infinitive means 'to manage to do (something)' or 'to succeed in doing (something)'

The reflexive verb **se passe** can also be used to convey that something happens or takes place.

EXAMPLES:

Nous arrivons bientôt à destination.
We are arriving at our destination soon.

Il est déjà arrivé.
He has already arrived.

Je suis arrivé à midi.
I arrived at noon.

Attends, j'arrive !
Wait, I am coming!

Tiens, il arrive.
Look, he is coming.

Le voici qui arrive.
Her he comes.

La voici qui arrive avec son fils.
Here she comes with her son.

TOPIC 120 ❖ The various uses of the verb *arriver*

L'eau arrive dans la maison par ces tuyaux.
The water comes into the house by these pipes.

C'est arrivé ce matin.
It happened this morning.

Les accidents arrivent à tout le monde.
Accidents happen to everyone.

Qu'est-ce qui arrive ?
What's happening?

Qu'est-ce qui est arrivé ?
What happened?

Qu'est-ce qui t'arrive ?
What's happening to you (familiar)?

Qu'est-ce qui t'est arrivé ?
What happened to you (familiar)?

Ce sont des choses qui arrivent.
These are the things that happen.

Ça m'est arrivé deux fois.
That happened to me two times.

Je t'aime quoi qu'il arrive.
I love you (familiar) whatever happens.

Il est arrivé un accident.
An accident happened.

Il arrive quelquefois que je me trompe.
It happens sometimes that I am wrong.

 Or 'Sometimes I'm wrong.'
 quelquefois means 'sometimes'

Elle est vite arrivée à la solution de l'énigme.
She quickly arrived at the solution to the riddle.

On arrive au sommet bientôt.
We are reaching the summit soon.

TOPIC 120 ❖ The various uses of the verb *arriver*

Comment êtes-vous arrivé à cette conclusion ?
How did you (formal, male, singular) reach that conclusion?

Je n'arrive pas à trouver les clés de la maison.
I can't manage to find the house keys.

Je suis enfin arrivé à lui parler.
I finally got to talk to him.

Nous sommes arrivés à le faire tout seuls.
We managed to do it on our own.

Il n'arrive pas à obtenir le permis.
He didn't manage to get the license.

Tu arrives ?
Did you (familiar) manage (to do it)?

Tu y arrives ?
Did you (familiar) manage to do it?

☿ The preposition **y** is used for 'to it'. A lot more about 'y' in in a later topic.

Bootstrap French
TOPIC 121

❖ The verb *se passer*

The reflexive verb **se passer** is another way to talk about something happening or some event occurring.

With a **de** the verb **se passer de** with a noun means 'to do without' something.

EXAMPLES:

Comment ça se passe ?
How is it going?

Tout se passe bien.
Everything is going well.

Comment se passent tes vacances ?
How are your (familiar) holidays going?

Comment se sont passées tes vacances ?
How were your (familiar) holidays?

La soirée s'est bien passée.
The evening went well.

Ça s'est mal passé.
It went wrong. *OR* I went badly.

Tout s'est bien passé.
Everything went well.

Les leçons de français se passent sur l'internet.
French lessons take place on the internet.
💡 **sur internet** is also widely used

Ça s'est passé hier.
It happened yesterday.

Cette histoire se passe en Russie.
This story takes place in Russian.

Qu'est-ce qui se passe ici ?
What is happening here?

TOPIC 121 ❖ The verb *se passer*

Que se passe-t-il ?
What's going on?
💡 Interchanable with 'Qu'est-ce qui se passe ?'

Rien ne se passe.
Nothing is happening.

Qu'est-ce qu'il s'est passé ce matin ?
What happened this morning?

Rien ne s'est passé.
Nothing happened.

Que s'est-il passé lors de la réunion d'hier ?
What happened during yesterday's meeting?
✎ **lors** means 'during' or 'at the time of'

Je ne sais pas ce qui se passe avec lui.
I don't know what's going on with him.

Je me passe de tes conseils !
I can do without your (familiar) advice!
✎ **se passer de** means 'to do without'

On peut se passer de commentaires.
We can do without the commentary.

Je peux me passer de sucre dans mon café.
I can do without sugar in my coffee.

❖ To take place - *avoir lieu*

The French equivalent of 'to take place' is **avoir lieu** where **lieu** (m) literally means 'place' or 'location'.

This expression is usually used in the context of events such as meetings etc.

Additionally **avoir lieu de** (with the **de**) + means 'to have good reason to'.

EXAMPLES:

Le marché de Noël a lieu ici.
The Christmas market takes place here.
🖉 Noël (m) means 'Christmas'

La séance n'a pas eu lieu hier ?
Did the meeting not take place yesterday?
🖉 séance (f) means 'session'

Une élection peut avoir lieu cette année.
An election may take place this year.

La fête foraine a lieu sur la place.
The funfair takes place on the square.
🖉 fête foraine (f) means 'carnival' or 'funfair'
🖉 place (f) means 'square' or place'

Pourquoi n'avez-vous pas assisté à la réunion qui a eu lieu ce matin ?
Why didn't you (formal) attend the meeting that took place this morning?

Quand est-ce que l'appel téléphonique a eu lieu ?
When did the phone call take place?

La grande ouverture a lieu la semaine prochaine.
The grand opening takes place next week.
🖉 ouverture (f) means 'openning'

Tu as lieu de te plaindre.
You (familiar) have reason to complain.
🖉 avoir lieu de (verb) means 'to have good reason to'

TOPIC 122 ❖ To take place - *avoir lieu*

Vous avez lieu d'exiger un remboursement.
You (formal) have reason to demand a refund.
📖 **remboursement** (m) means 'refund'

Nous avons lieu de croire ce qu'il a dit.
We have reason to believe what he said.

Ils ont tout lieu de le penser.
They have every reason to think that.
💡 OR '...to think so.'

Bootstrap French
TOPIC 123

❖ **Verbs + preposition *à* + infinitive**

There are many French verbs that require a preposition between itself and the second verb.

Many prepositions are used but in this topic we will look at verbs with **à**.

Examples of common verbs that take **à** include:

- **apprendre à** - 'to learn to'
- **commencer à** - 'to start to'
- **continuer à** - 'to continue to'
- **s'épuiser à** - 'to exhaust oneself (doing)'
- **s'habituer à** - 'to get used to'
- **se préparer à** - 'to prepare to'
- **réussir à** - 'to succeed at (doing)'
- **participer à** - 'to participate (doing)'

And there are several others in the examples.

EXAMPLES:

Ma fille est en train d'apprendre à nager.
My daughter is learning to swim.
apprendre à means 'to learn to (do something)'

Elle a commencé à l'apprendre la semaine dernière.
She started learning it last week.
commencer à means 'to start to (do something)'

Elle veut continuer à l'apprendre.
She wants to keep learning it.
continuer à means 'to continue to (do something)'

Elle veut vraiment continuer à apprendre à nager.
She really wants to continue learning to swim.
continuer à means 'to continue to (do something)'

aujourd'hui, elle s'est épuisée à nager.
Today she exhausted herself swimming.
s'épuiser à means 'to get tired (from doing something)'

TOPIC 123 ❖ Verbs + preposition *à* + infinitive

Elle s'habitue à nager sans aide.
She is getting used to swimming without help.

- s'habituer à means 'to get used to (doing something)'

Elle se prépare à participer à une compétition de natation.
She is preparing to participate in a swimming competition.

- préparee à means 'to prepare (to do something)'
- natation (f) means 'swimming'

Elle est presque sur le point de réussir à nager comme son frère.
She on the verge of succeeding at swimming like her brother.

- réussir à means 'to succeed (in doing something)'

Elle ne renonce jamais à apprendre.
She never gives up learning.

- renouncer à means 'to give up (doing something)'

Elle persiste à s'entraîner tous les jours.
She persists in training every day.

- persiste à means 'to persist (in doing something)'
- s'entraîner means 'to train'

On ne la pousse pas à continuer.
We are not pushing her to continue.

- pousser à means 'to push (someone) to (do something)'

Elle se plaît à réussir.
She likes to succeed.

- se plaire à means 'to take pleasure (doing something)'

Elle est en train de s'apprêter à nager en compétition.
She is getting ready to swim competitively.

- s'appreter à means 'to prepare oneself to (do something)'
- en compétition (adv) means 'competitively'

Elle est arrivée à gagner et elle est très contente.
She managed to win and she is very happy.

- arriver à means 'to manage to' or 'to succeed in (doing something);

En fait, maintenant elle arrive à gagner tout le temps.
In fact now she manages to win all the time.

- arriver à means 'to manage to' or 'to succeed in (doing something);

TOPIC 123 ❖ Verbs + preposition *à* + infinitive

Elle s'est plu à réussir.
She was happy to succeed.

- **plaire à** means 'to be pleased (to do something)'
- **plu** is the past participle of **plaire**

Ma fille s'est décidée à aller aux Jeux olympiques à l'avenir.
My daughter has made up her mind to go to the Olympics in the future.

- **s'décidé à** means 'to make up one's mind to (do something)' or 'to decide to (do something)'
- **Jeux olympiques** (m.pl) means 'Olympic Games'
- **à l'avenir** means 'in the future'

Elle est parvenue à réaliser son rêve.
She has managed to realize her dream.

- **parvenir à** means 'to manage to (do something)'. It is a verb of motion due to the **venir** root
- **réaliser** (verb) means 'to fulfil' or 'to carry out' or 'to realise (make real)'

Toute la journée, elle songe à gagner l'or.
All day she thinks about winning the gold.

- **songer à** means 'to think about (doing something)'

❖ Negating the infinitive

An infinitive verb is negated by putting the entire negating pair **ne pas** (or **ne rien** etc.) before the infinitive.

If there is a pronoun before the infinitive, **ne pas** should precede it.

EXAMPLES:

On l'a poussé à ne pas continuer.
We urged him not to continue.

    pousser à (verb) means 'to urge (someone) to do (something)'

Elle s'est décidée à ne pas aller à l'université.
She has made up her mind not to go to university.

Ils ont commencé à ne plus boire de café aussi souvent.
They have started to not drink coffee so often.

Au moins, j'ai réussi à ne plus vous embrouiller.
At least I managed not to confuse you (formal) anymore.

    au moins means 'at least'

Je me suis habitué à ne jamais la voir.
I got used to never seeing her.

    💡 The **ne pas** should precede the preposition

Il m'a appris à ne pas avoir peur.
He taught me not to be scared.

Nous avons essayé de ne pas rire.
We tried not to laugh.

J'ai peur de ne pas réussir.
I'm afraid of not succeeding.

J'espère ne pas faire d'erreurs.
I hope not to make a mistake.

L'essentiel est de ne pas perdre patience.
The main thing is not to lose patience.

    l'essentiel (m) means 'the main thing' or 'the main part'

TOPIC 124 ❖ Negating the infinitive

Peux-tu ne pas manger si vite ?
Can you (familiar) not eat so fast?

Elle a averti les enfants de ne pas jouer dans la rue.
She warned children not to play in the street.

  avertir (verb) means 'to warn'

Les policiers nous ont dit de ne pas nager ici.
The police told us not to swim here.

J'ai décidé de ne plus les manger.
I decided not to eat them anymore.

  ne pas should precede a pronoun before the verb

Il a décidé de ne pas le vendre.
He decided not to sell it.

  ne pas should precede a pronoun before the verb

J'espère m'habituer à ne pas te voir tous les jours.
I hope to get used to not seeing you (formal) every day.

Je n'arrive pas à ne pas boire quand je sors avec ces amis.
I cannot manage to stop drinking when I go out with these friends.

Il ne sait pas comment ne pas le renverser quand il boit.
He doesn't know how not to spill it when he drinks.

  ne pas should precede a pronoun before the verb

Bootstrap French
TOPIC 125

❖ **The verb infinitive as a noun**

In English we typically use the gerund in order to talk about a verb as if it were a noun.

For example: 'Playing tennis is fun' where 'playing' is the gerund ('the action of playing') and can be the subject of a sentence.

But in English we can also say 'To play tennis is fun' where the verb infinitive ('to play') is used.

French takes latter approach. That is, we use the **infinitive** when the verb is a noun.

The verb as a noun can be either the subject or object of another verb.

In this context it is common to see subject repetition (using **c'est**).

It is also possible to use the infinitive as the subject of a subordinate clause.

The 'noun' can be negated as we saw previously - by putting the entire negating pair **ne pas** (or **ne rien** etc.) before the infinitive or noun.

EXAMPLES:

Jouer au tennis est amusant.
Playing tennis is fun.
💡 Or 'To play tennis is fun.'

Jouer devant le roi fait peur.
Performing in front of the king is scary.
💡 Or 'To perform in front of the king is scary.'
💡 The verb **jouer** is also used for 'to perform' (acting, dancing, music etc.) or 'to act'.

Danser dans le noir, c'est le paradis.
Dancing in the dark - it is heaven.
💡 Or 'To dance in the dark is heaven.'
💡 With subject repetition using **c'est**
📖 **paradis** (f) means 'heaven' or 'paradise'

Voyager seul peut être dangereux.
Traveling alone can be dangerous.
💡 Or 'To traveling alone can be dangerous.'

Cuisiner, c'est un art.
Cooking - it is an art.
📖 **art** (m) means 'art'

TOPIC 125 ❖ The verb infinitive as a noun

Dire la vérité est important.
Telling the truth is important.

Le connaître, c'est l'aimer.
To know him, it is to love him.
  💡 Or in English we'd say 'To know him is to love him'

Bien manger est bon pour la santé.
Eating well is good for (your) health.

Trop boire d'alcool est mauvais pour la santé.
Drinking too much alcohol is bad for (your) health.

J'ai vu l'enfant tomber à l'eau.
I saw the child fall into the water.
  💡 Or 'I saw the child **falling** into the water.'

Il m'a regardé faire la vaisselle.
He watched me do the dishes.
  💡 Or 'He watched me **doing** the dishes.'

Être en prison n'est pas amusant.
Being in prison is not fun.
  💡 Or 'To be in prison...'

Ne pas parler de ça, c'est important.
Not talking about that is important.

Ne rien lui dire est important.
Not saying anything to him is important.

Ne plus le dire n'est pas facile.
Not saying it anymore is not easy.

Ne jamais rien lui dire est important.
Never saying anything to him is important.

Être ou ne pas être.
To be or not to be.

Voir, c'est croire.
Seeing is believing.
  💡 Or 'To see is to believe'

French Grammar

TOPIC 125 ❖ The verb infinitive as a noun

Savoir, c'est pouvoir.
Knowing (knowledge) is ability (power).
💡 Or 'Knowledge is power'

Bien manger est bon pour la santé.
Eating well is good for (your) health.

Apprendre le japonais n'est pas facile.
Learning Japanese is not easy.

Ne pas manger tous tes pois n'est pas une option.
Not eating all your (familiar) peas is not an option.

Trouver un emploi n'est pas facile.
Finding a job is not easy.
📖 **emploi** (m) means 'job' or 'employment'

Ne pas économiser de l'argent est imprudent.
To not save some money is foolish.
📖 **imprudent** (adj) means 'imprudent' or 'foolish'

Payer 100 euros pour acheter un billet ? Tu blagues !
Paying 100 euros to buy a ticket? You (familiar) are kidding!
📖 **blaguer** (verb) means 'to joke'

Sortir sans manteau en hiver : c'est fou !
Going out without a coat in winter: it's crazy!

Parler français - ce n'est pas trop difficile.
Speaking French - it is not too difficult.

Partir, c'est mourir un peu.
To leave is to die a little.

C'est toujours la même chose, travailler, travailler et encore travailler.
It's always the same thing, work, work and more work.

Travailler avec Joséphine me fait grand plaisir.
Working with Josephine gives me great pleasure.
📖 **faire plaisir** (verb) means 'to please'

❖ Verb infinitives after certain prepositions

The following prepositions are commonly used before the infinitive of a verb:
- **afin de** - 'in order to'
- **au lieu de** - 'instead of'
- **pour** - 'for' or 'in order to'
- **sans** - 'without'
- **avant de** - 'before'

BUT **apres** ('after') takes the gerund which is covered in a later topic.

EXAMPLES:

Nous devons faire une pause afin de pouvoir rassembler nos pensées.
We need to pause so that we can collect our thoughts.

Il fait de son mieux afin de réussir.
He does his best to succeed.

Ils ont ajouté un panneau d'arrêt afin de ralentir les voitures.
They added a stop sign to slow down cars.

J'ai écrit une lettre au lieu de leur téléphoner.
I wrote a letter instead of phoning them.

Ils ne font que parler au lieu de travailler.
They just talk instead of work.

Au lieu de se battre, ils ont parlé du problème.
Instead of fighting, they talked about the problem.

Nous lui prêtons de l'argent pour lui permettre de poursuivre ses études.
We lend him money to enable him to continue his studies.

Il vous fait regarder la vidéo pour mieux comprendre.
It makes you (formal) watch the video to understand better.

J'ai juste assez d'économies pour aller en vacances.
I have just enough savings to go on vacation.

Elle a vendu leur maison sans le dire à son mari.
She sold their house without telling her husband.

TOPIC 126 ❖ Verb infinitives after certain prepositions

L'enfant peut déjà marcher sans tomber.
The child can already walk without falling.

Hier après-midi, ils ont travaillé sans s'arrêter.
Yesterday afternoon, they worked without stopping.

Vous parlez trop sans savoir la vérité.
You (formal) say too much without knowing the truth.

Nous devons agir sans plus attendre.
We must act without further delay.

📖 **sans plus attendre** means 'without further ado'

Alors sans plus attendre, le marié peut embrasser la mariée.
So without further ado, the groom can kiss the bride.

Vous devez enlever vos chaussures avant d'entrer.
You (formal) must remove your shoes before entering.

Avez-vous lu le livre avant de voir le film ?
Did you (formal) read the book before seeing the film?

Il ne me faisait pas confiance avant de me connaître.
He didn't trust me before he knew me.

📖 **faire confiance** (verb) means 'to trust' or 'to have confidence in'

Pourquoi ne m'écoutes-tu pas avant de t'énerver ?
Why don't you (familiar) listen to me before you get mad?

📖 **s'énerver** means 'to get worked up'

❖ Verbs + preposition *de* + infinitive

Many French verbs take the preposition **de** before an infinitive second verb.

We have already encountered **venir de** which means 'to have just (done something)'. Other such verbs include:

- **accepter de** - 'to accept to' or 'to agree to'
- **attendre de** - 'to wait to'
- **choisir de** - 'to choose to'
- **avoir peur de** - 'to fear (doing)'
- **convenir de** - 'to agree to'
- **demander de** - 'to ask to'
- **se dépêcher de** - 'to hurry to'
- **empêcher de** - 'to prevent from (doing)'
- **finir de** - 'to finish (doing)'
- **prendre soin de** - 'to take care (doing)'
- **achever de** - 'to complete (doing)'

And there are several others in the examples.

EXAMPLES:

Mon fils vient d'obtenir son diplôme universitaire.
My son just graduated from college.

Il a accepté de commencer à travailler dès que possible.
He agreed to start work as soon as possible.

🖋 **dès que possible** means 'as soon as possible'

Nous attendons de les recevoir.
We are waiting to receive them.

Il a choisi de prendre les rouges.
He chose to take the reds.

Elle a peur de lui parler.
She is afraid to talk to him.

Nous avons convenu d'aller en Inde ensemble.
We agreed to go to India together.

TOPIC 127 ❖ Verbs + preposition *de* + infinitive

Elle m'a demandé de ne pas laver le chien.
She asked me not to wash the dog.

Nous nous sommes dépêchés de voir la reine.
We hurried to see the Queen.

La clôture empêche les animaux sauvages d'entrer.
The fence keeps wild animals out.

Nous avons enfin fini de le construire comme vous le souhaitez.
We finally finished building it the way you (formal) want.

Il a pris soin de ne pas marcher dans les trous.
He was careful not to step into the holes.

Le comité n'a pas encore achevé de préparer son rapport.
The committee has not yet completed preparing its report.

Ça ne me dérange pas d'aller acheter du pain.
It does not bother me to go buy bread.

📖 **déranger de** means 'to bother (someone) to'

Ils ont essayé de courir dix kilomètres.
They tried to run ten kilometers.

📖 **essayer de** means 'to try to (do something)'

J'ai essayé de ne pas être en retard.
I tried not to be late.

Je m'excuse d'avoir cassé le vase.
I apologize for breaking the vase.

📖 **s'excuser de** means 'to apologize for (doing)'

Jean_Luc a manqué de serrer les freins.
Jean-Luc failed to apply the brakes.

📖 **manquer de** means 'to fail to' or 'to neglect to'

Comment as-tu pu oublier de lui acheter un cadeau !
How could you (familiar) forget to buy him∆her a present!

📖 **oublier de** means 'to forget to'

Le gouvernement ne nous permet pas d'atterrir sur cette île.
The government does not allow us to land on this island.

📖 **permettre de** means 'to allow to'

TOPIC 127 ❖ Verbs + preposition *de* + infinitive

Pourquoi as-tu promis de lui donner tout ton argent ?
Why did you (familiar) promise to give him all your money?

- **promettre de** means 'to promise to'

Il a proposé d'y aller ensemble.
He offered to go there together.

- **proposer de** means 'to propose to or to suggest to'
- The **y** is a pronoun which in this case means 'to a place'

Elle a refusé de nous accompagner.
She refused to accompany us.

- **refuser de** means 'to refuse to'

Pourquoi ne vous êtes-vous pas souvenu de ne pas utiliser le four ?
Why didn't you (formal) remember not to use the oven?

- **se souvenir de** means 'to remember to'

Elle ne cesse pas de travailler ni d'étudier.
She does not stop working or studying.

- **cesser de** means 'to stop (doing)'

J'ai tâché d'être à l'heure.
I tried to be on time.

- **tâcher de** means 'to attempt to'

Nous avons tâché de faire du pain, mais nous avons échoué.
We tried to make bread but failed.

Bootstrap French
TOPIC 128

❖ **Stressed pronouns - with prepositions and conjunctions**

The French stressed pronouns are:
- je ⇒ moi
- tu ⇒ toi
- il ⇒ lui
- elle ⇒ elle
- nous ⇒ nous
- vous ⇒ vous
- ils ⇒ eux
- elles ⇒ elles

And **soi** for unspecified persons - typically used with impersonal pronouns such as **on**, **chacun**, **tout le monde** etc.

Three common uses of stressed pronouns are:
- After many prepositions such as **à, par, pour, en, vers, avec, chez, de, sans**, etc.
- With many conjunctions such as **ou, comme, et** etc.
- With the restrictives **ne..que** and **ne..ni**.

Note that the stressed pronouns (except **soi**) can refer only to people and animals.

EXAMPLES:

Je viens avec toi.
I am coming with you (familiar).
💡 With the presposition **avec**

Elle pense à moi.
She thinks of me.
💡 With the presposition **à**

Je pense aussi à elle.
I also think of her.
💡 With the presposition **à**

Les enfants sont avec leur père - ils jouent avec lui.
The children are with their father - they play with him.
💡 With the presposition **avec**

TOPIC 128 ❖ Stressed pronouns - with prepositions and conjunctions

Les gâteaux ont été faits par eux.
The cakes were made by them.
- With the presposition **par**
- **par** (prep.) means 'by' or 'via' or 'out of'

Nous remercions les Dupont - le café est fourni par eux.
We thank the Duponts - the coffee is provided by them.
- With the presposition **par**
- **remercier** (verb) means 'to thank'
- **fournir** (verb) means 'to provide' or 'to supply'

On va au Japon sans vous cette fois.
We're going to Japan without you (formal) this time.
- With the presposition **sans**

Mes filles ont du courage - j'ai confiance en elles.
My daughters have courage - I have confidence in them.
- With the presposition **en**
- **avoir confiance** (verb) means 'to have confidence (in someone)' or 'to trust'

Il a un cadeau pour elle.
He has a gift for her.
- With the presposition **pour**

Il a proposé de le faire pour eux.
He offered to do it for them.
- With the presposition **pour**

Le lion vient vers moi !
The lion is coming towards me!
- With the presposition **vers**
- **vers** (prep.) means 'towards' or 'in the direction of' or 'at about (a time)'

Un objet inconnu s'avance vers nous.
An unknown object is advancing towards us.
- With the presposition **vers**
- **s'avancer** (verb) means 'to advance' or 'to move forward'

Elle habite chez toi maintenant ?
Does she live at your (familiar) place now?
- With the presposition **chez**
- **chez** means 'to the home of' or 'at the business of'

TOPIC 128 ❖ Stressed pronouns - with prepositions and conjunctions

Nous avons dîné chez eux.
We had dinner at their home.
- With the presposition **chez**

Chez elle, il y a une piscine.
At her place, there is a swimming pool.
- With the presposition **chez**

J'adore le sport, comme vous.
I love sports, like you (formal).
- With the conjunction **comme**

Elle refuse de manger - tout comme toi.
She refuses to eat - just like you (familiar).
- With the conjunction **comme**

Elles peuvent choisir entre lui ou moi.
They can choose between me or him.
- With the conjunction **ou**
- Note that **moi** always comes last for humbleness.

Michel et moi jouons au tennis.
Michel and I play tennis.
- With the conjunction **et**

Ils ne peuvent voir ni elle ni moi.
They can't see me or her.
- With the retriction **ne..ni**
- **moi** never comes first - out of politeness

Je ne pense ni à toi ni à lui.
I don't think of you (familiar) or him.
- With the retriction **ne..ni**

Je ne connais que lui ici.
I only know him here.
- With the retriction **ne..que**

On est chez soi.
Everyone is at their home.
- Literally 'One is at home.'

Chacun pour soi.
Each for themselves.
- **chacun** (adj) means 'each'

TOPIC 128 ❖ Stressed pronouns - with prepositions and conjunctions

Il faut avoir confiance en soi.
One must have confidence in oneself.

avoir confiance (verb) means 'to have confidence'

Chacun en soi est également important.
Each in itself is equally important.

C'est assez spécial en soi.
It's quite special in of itself.

❖ Stressed pronouns - for emphasis and abbreviation

In the previous topic we saw how stressed pronouns are used after certain prepositions and conjunctions.

Stressed pronouns (also called emphatic pronouns) are also used:

- To emphasize identity in speech. Like we use 'As for me' in English. This is used in French much more than in English.
 - Often this emphasis is affected using **c'est** + + **qui**.
- To abbreviate - to act as the subject when the verb is implied - especially when answering questions.

EXAMPLES:

Moi, j'adore voyager.
Me, I like to travel.

C'est lui qui a dit ça.
It is he who said that.

Moi, je suis toujours à l'heure.
Me, I am always on time.

Moi, j'adore les cerises, mais elle, elle préfère les fraises.
Me, I love cherries, but she prefers strawberries.

Lui, il aime partir tout seul, mais moi, j'aime beaucoup voyager en groupe.
He, he likes to go alone, but me, I really like traveling in a group.

Toi et lui, vous êtes très gentils.
You (familiar) and him, you are very nice.

Je pense qu'il a raison. Moi, je pense qu'il a tort.
I think he's right. Me, I think he's wrong.

Je les ai vus - lui et elle.
I saw them - him and her.

C'est toi qui étudies l'art.
You (familiar) are the one who is studying art.

TOPIC 129 ❖ Stressed pronouns - for emphasis and abbreviation

Ce sont elles qui aiment Paris.
It is they who love Paris.

Qui a fait ça ? Moi.
Who did this? Me (I did).

Qui est là ? Moi.
Who is there? Me (it is me).

Qui va à la plage ? Lui.
Who goes to the beach? Him (he is).

J'ai faim, et toi ?
I'm hungry, and you (familiar)?

❖ Stressed pronouns - with *à* and *même*

- A stressed pronoun after **à** can be used to indicate who something belongs to.
- This is also used colloquially to indicate whose turn it is in a game.
- Stressed pronouns are also used with **même** to mean 'myself' (**moi-même**), 'yourself' (**toi-même**) etc.
- By itself **même** means 'same' or 'even'.
- Stressed pronouns are also used with certain adverbs like **aussi**, **seul**, and **surtout**.
- This is also a device for emphasis.

EXAMPLES:

La voiture est à lui.
The car is his.

Ce livre est à moi.
This book is mine.

C'est à toi.
It's yours (familiar).
💡 OR in the right context 'It is your turn.'

Je l'ai fait moi-même.
I made it myself.

Elle a fabriqué cette maquette elle-même !
She made this model herself!

Prépare-t-il le dîner lui-même ?
Does he cook dinner himself?

Nous faisons tout par nous-mêmes.
We do it all by ourselves.

Tout le monde doit le faire soi-même.
Everyone has to do it themselves.

Pouvez-vous gérer le camion vous-même ?
Can you (formal) handle the truck yourself?
📖 **gérer** (verb) means 'to manage' or 'to handle'

TOPIC 130 ❖ Stressed pronouns - with *à* and *même*

Dans la vie, il est important d'être soi-même.
In life, it is important to be yourself.

Il peut juger par lui-même.
He can judge for himself.

🍃 juger (verb) means 'to judge'

Vous devez lire le contrat par vous-même.
You (formal) must read the contract for yourself.

🍃 contrat (m) means 'contract'

Lui seul a travaillé hier.
He alone worked yesterday.

💡 Emphasises 'seul' rather than 'Il a travaillé seul hier.'

Eux aussi veulent venir.
They also want to come.

💡 Emphasises 'aussi' rather than 'Ils veulent venir aussi.'

Il ne nous aime pas - surtout moi.
He doesn't like us - especially me.

Ils ont commencé à avoir plus confiance en nous - en lui surtout.
They began to have more confidence in us - especially in him.

Stressed pronouns - agreement and disagreement

Stressed pronouns are used with certain adverbs to state (emphatic) agreement and disagreement.

Using **moi** as an example we have:

- **moi aussi** - 'me also' - agreement with a positive statement.
- **pas moi** - 'not me' - disagreement with a positive statement.
- **moi non plus** - 'me neither' - agreement with a negative statement.
- **moi si** - disagreement with a negative statement.

EXAMPLES:

J'aime prendre des photos de mes animaux de compagnie. Moi aussi.
I like to take photographs of my pets. Me too.

Je prends l'entrecôte. Moi aussi, bien cuite s'il vous plait.
I (will) take the steak. Me too, well done please.
- Ordering in the restaurant
- **entrecôte** (f) means 'rib steak'
- **cuit** (adj) means 'cooked' (from **cuire** - 'to cook')
- **bien cuit** means 'well done'

Je m'étonne du résultat. Nous aussi. C'est choquant.
I am surprised at the result. Us too. It's shocking.
- **s'étonner** (verb) means 'to be surprised'

J'adore la musique de danse électronique. Pas moi, j'aime le rap.
I adore electronic dance music. Not me, I like rap.

Il est riche. C'est-à-dire pas lui exactement, mais sa famille.
He is rich. That is to say, not him exactly but his family.

C'est elle que tu aimes ? Non, pas elle mais sa sœur.
Is it her that you (familiar) love? No, not her but her sister.
- Both **elles** are stressed pronouns
- Note that **qui t'aime** would be 'who loves you'

Je n'aime pas les araignées. Moi non plus.
I don't like spiders. Me neither.

TOPIC 131 ❖ Stressed pronouns - agreement and disagreement

Elle n'aime pas les hamburgers. Lui non plus.
She doesn't like burgers. Neither does he.

Elles non plus n'ont rien mangé.
They (female) didn't eat anything either.

Ce n'est pas bon pour moi. Et pour vous non plus, monsieur.
It's not good for me. And neither for you (formal), sir.

Je n'ai jamais visité le Louvre. Moi, si.
I have never visited the Louvre. Yes, me (I have).

Personne ne sait pourquoi. Moi, si, je sais pourquoi.
Nobody knows why. Yes, me, I know why.

❖ Using *pas* without *ne*

The negative particle **pas** can be used without **ne** to negate adjectives, adverbs, nouns, and pronouns.

But in these cases the sentence is abbreviated by dropping a verb. This **missing** verb would otherwise be bracketed with the **ne..pas**.

EXAMPLES:

Elle doit être malheureuse ! Pas malheureuse, mais pas contente, oui.
She must be unhappy! Not unhappy, but not pleased.
- Negating an adjective
- The full sentence would be **Il n'est pas malheureux...**

C'est un gars pas sympathique.
He's not a nice guy.
- Negating an adjective
- The full sentence would be **...qui n'est pas sympathique.**

Pas gentil, ça.
That's not nice.
- Negating an adjective
- The full sentence would be **Ça, ce n'est pas gentil.**

Pas possible !
That's not possible!
- Negating an adjective
- The full sentence would be **Ce n'est pas possible.**

Vas-tu boire de la bière ? Oui mais pas beaucoup.
Are you (familiar) going to drink beer? Yes, but not much.
- Negating an adjective
- The full sentence would be **Je n'en veux pas beaucoup.**

Pas bête, ça.
Not stupid, that.
- Negating an adjective
- An expression usually used in reference to a suggestion or idea
- **bête** (adj) means 'stupid'

TOPIC 132 ❖ Using *pas* without *ne*

Ça va ? Pas mal.
How are you? Not bad.

💡 Negating an adverb

Pourquoi pas ?
Why not?

💡 Negating an adverb

Pas comme ça !
Not like that!

💡 Negating an adverb

Pas si vite !
Not so fast!

💡 Negating an adverb

Pas souvent, pas encore, pas trop.
Not often; not yet; not too much.

💡 Negating an adverb

Elle va venir aujourd'hui ? Non, pas aujourd'hui. Demain, en fait.
Is she going to come today? No, not today. Tomorrow actually.

💡 Negating a noun

Elle a deux oncles, pas trois.
She has two uncles, not three.

💡 Negating a noun

Je veux deux pains au chocolat. Pas de pains au chocolat aujourd'hui.
I want two chocolate pastries. No chocolate pastries today.

💡 Negating a noun

Pas de problème !
No problem!

💡 Negating a noun

Qui peut m'aider ? Pas moi !
Who can he me? Not me!

💡 Negating a pronoun

Tu as faim ? Pas du tout !
Are you (familiar) hungry? Not at all!

💡 Negating a pronoun

French Grammar

TOPIC 132 ❖ Using *pas* without *ne*

Ah non, pas ça !
Oh no, not that!
💡 Negating a pronoun

Est-ce que ce cadeau est pour moi ? Non, pas pour toi.
Is this gift for me? No, not for you (familiar).
💡 Negating a pronoun

❖ The position of adverbs

The general rule is that French adverbs come directly after the verb that they are modifying.

There are however a few special cases:

- In complex tenses (like **passé composé**) certain adverbs come immediately after the (conjugated) auxiliary verb.
  - These include shorter adverbs (such as **bien**, **mal**, **trop**, **assez**) and certain indefinite adverbs of time (such as **souvent**, **toujours**, **trop**, **quelque fois**). The slightly longer adverbs **beaucoup**, **rarement** and **vraiment** are also included in this group.
  - In negative constructions, these adverbs are placed after the negated auxiliary construct - that is after the **pas**. The exceptions are **certainement**, **généralement**, **peut-être**, **probablement** and, **sans doute**.
- Adverbs that refer to adjectives or to other adverbs are placed before the adjective or adverb in question
- Adverbs that describe an infinitive come after the infinitive.

EXAMPLES:

Il mange rapidement.
He eats quickly.
💡 A regular adverb after the verb

Il a mangé rapidement.
He ate quickly.
💡 A regular adverb after the verb

Il ne mange pas rapidement.
He does not eat quickly.
💡 A regular adverb after the negated verb construct

Il n'a pas mangé rapidement.
He didn't eat quickly.
💡 A regular adverb after the negated verb construct

Il mange trop.
He eats too much.
💡 **trop** is a short verb

TOPIC 133 ❖ The position of adverbs

Il a trop mangé.
He ate too much.
💡 Short verbs come after the auxilliary verb

Il ne mange pas trop.
He doesn't eat too much.

Il n'a pas trop mangé.
He didn't eat too much.
💡 Short verbs come after the (negated) auxilliary verb

Il mange beaucoup.
He eats a lot.

Il a beaucoup mangé.
He ate a lot.
💡 **beaucoup** is treated like a short verb so comes after the auxilliary verb

Il ne mange pas beaucoup.
He doesn't eat much.

Il n'a pas beaucoup mangé.
He hasn't eaten much.
💡 **beaucoup** is treated like a short verb so comes after the (negated) auxilliary verb

Il est assez bon.
He is quite good.
💡 The adverb **assez** is in front of the adjective **bon** that it modifies

Le repas est délicieux.
The meal is delicious.
💡 The adverb **très** is in front of the adjective **bon** that it modifies

Il ne veut pas manger rapidement.
He does not want to eat quickly.
💡 Adverbs that describe an infinitive come after the infinitive

Ils aiment beaucoup aller au cinéma.
They really like going to the cinema.
💡 Here the adverb **beaucoup** modifies **aimer** and not **aller**

Je mange rarement au restaurant.
I rarely eat at restaurants.

TOPIC 133 ❖ The position of adverbs

Il s'est rasé rapidement.
He shaved quickly.

Elle s'est habillée élégamment.
She dressed elegantly.

💡 **élégamment** (adv) means 'elegantly'

Ils ont beaucoup aimé le film.
They really liked the movie.

💡 **beaucoup** is treated like a short verb

Quelqu'un a mal fermé la porte.
Someone has closed the door incorrectly.

💡 **mal** is a short verb

Comparison of quantities of nouns - *plus*, *moins* & *autant*

The comparative adverbs **plus** ('more'), **moins** ('less') and **autant** ('as much') are used to talk about quantities of nouns.

When used to make comparisons the relative pronoun **que** is added.

- **plus que** means 'more than'
- **moins que** means 'less than'
- **autant que** means 'as much as'

When used with noun qualities the partitive **de** is used.

When used with a noun, the comparative adverb and **que** are spilt. For example **plus de sel que** ('more salt than')

When comparing against a pronoun, a stressed pronoun (eg, **moi**, **toi** etc.) is used.

When comparing two quantities we use the partitive twice.

EXAMPLES:

J'ai plus d'argent que Jacques.
I have more money than Jacques.

   plus que means 'more than'

Il a moins de temps que son frère.
He has less time than his brother.

   moins que means 'less than'

Ils l'aiment autant que notre famille.
They love him∆her/it as much as our family does.

   autant que means 'as much as'

Est-ce-que tu veux plus de glace ?
Do you (familiar) want more ice cream?

Elle a acheté plus de fleurs qu'hier.
She bought more flowers than yesterday.

   Noun: **de fleurs** splits **plus que** ⇒ **plus de fleurs que**

Je veux plus de crème que lui.
I want more cream than him.

   stressed pronoun used after **que**

TOPIC 134 ❖ Comparison of quantities of nouns - *plus, moins* & *autant*

Sa sœur a moins de courage qu'elle.
Her sister has less courage than her.
💡 stressed pronoun used after **que**

Il veut manger moins de sel.
He wants to eat less salt.

Tu peux manger plus si tu veux.
You (familiar) can eat more if you want.

Il a cuisiné avec moins de sel cette fois.
He cooked with less salt this time.

Cet agriculteur a autant de terres que son voisin.
This farmer has as much land as his neighbor.

Joséphine a autant de chapeaux que sa mère.
Josephine has as many hats as her mother.

Mais elle a moins de chaussures qu'elle.
But she has fewer shoes than her.

En fait, elle a moins de chaussures que de chapeaux.
In fact she has fewer shoes than hats.
💡 Use the partitive twice to compare to quantities

Nous avons autant de pommes que de poires.
We have as many apples as pears.

Il y a plus de monde que de chaises - que faire ?
There are more people than chairs - what to do?

❖ Comparison of adjectives and adverbs - *plus*, *moins* & *aussi*

The comparatives **plus** ('more'), **moins** ('less') and **aussi** ('also') are used to compare adjectives and adverbs.

When used to make comparisons the particle **que** is added.

- **plus que** means 'more than'
- **moins que** means 'less than'
- **aussi que** means 'as...as'

When contrasting two adjectives we simply put them either side of the **que**.

Autant que ('as much as') can be used as an adverb in its own right.

EXAMPLES:

Marianne est plus jolie que Sophie.
Marianne is prettier than Sophie.
💡 comparing an adjective

Ils sont plus sportifs que nous.
They are more athletic as we are.

Ton sac est plus grand que ma valise !
Your (familiar) bag is bigger than my suitcase!

Mon grand-père est plus âgé que ma grand-mère.
My grandfather is older than my grandmother.

Il est aussi grand que mon frère et moi.
He is as tall as me and my brother.

Elle est déjà aussi grande que sa mère.
She is already as tall as her mother.

Ils sont aussi contents que moi.
They are as happy as me.

Joséphine est aussi timide que sa mère
Josephine is as shy as her mother
✏ **timide** (m.f.adj) means 'shy'

TOPIC 135 ❖ Comparison of adjectives and adverbs - *plus*, *moins* & *aussi*

Cet arbre est plus grand que celui-là.
This tree is bigger than that one.

Tes enfants sont moins bruyants que les miens.
Your (familiar) children are less noisy than mine.

bruyant (adj) means 'noisy'

Elle est aussi intelligente que gentille.
She is as smart as she is kind.

Contrasting two adjectives by having them either side of the **que**

Les fraises ne sont pas aussi bonnes que les framboises.
The strawberries are as good as the raspberries.

framboise (f) means 'raspberry'

La table est aussi large que longue.
The table is as wide as it is long.

large (adj) means 'wide'
long (adj) means 'long' - longue (f)

Ils marchent moins vite que nous.
They walk slower than us.

comparing an adverb

Julie parle moins vite que Marianne
Julie speaks less quickly than Marianne

Elle chante aussi bien que sa tante.
She sings as well as her aunt.

Ce train-ci est plus rapide que celui-là.
This train (here) is faster than that one.

J'étudie autant que toi.
I study as much as you (familiar).

Joanne s'est couchée plus tôt que lui.
Joanne went to bed earlier than him.

Pourquoi a-t-il fait ses devoirs beaucoup plus lentement que sa sœur ?
Why did he do his homework much more slowly than his sister?

TOPIC 135 ❖ Comparison of adjectives and adverbs - *plus*, *moins* & *aussi*

Il se comporte plus comme un Italien que comme un Français.
He behaves more like an Italian than like a Frenchman.
💡 The **comme** makes the clauses adverbs

Il peut courir plus vite que n'importe qui.
He can run faster than anyone.
📖 **n'importe qui** means 'anyone'

❖ Comparisons of 'good' - *meilleur* & *pire*

- The adjective **bon** ('good') has the irregular comparative **meilleur** ('better').
- **meilleur** changes with gender and number like a regular adjective.
- The adjective **mauvais** ('bad') has the comparative **pire** ('worse').
- **pire** is the same in the singular for both genders (**pire**) and has a common plural (**pires**).
- The inferior **moins bon** ('less good') is commonly used in French.
- The superior **plus mauvais** ('less bad') is also possible.

EXAMPLES:

Mes idées sont meilleures que tes idées.
My ideas are better than your (familiar) ideas.

Le brocoli est meilleur que le chou-fleur.
Broccoli is better than cauliflower.

Le thé, c'est bon, mais le café, c'est meilleur.
Tea is good, but coffee is better.

Son attitude est pire que la mienne.
His attitude is worse than mine.

Ethan et Julien sont les pires élèves de la classe.
Ethan and Julien are the worst students in the class.

Ce restaurant-ci est pire que celui-là.
This restaurant (here) is worse than that one.

Leurs idées sont pires.
Their ideas are worse.

Cette idée est moins bonne que la mienne.
This idea is worse than mine.

Dans cette ville, les bus sont pires que le métro.
In this city, the buses are worse than the metro.

Ces framboises sont moins bonnes que ces fraises.
These raspberries are not as good as these strawberries.

TOPIC 136 ❖ Comparisons of 'good' - *meilleur* & *pire*

Le temps en Angleterre est mauvais, mais il est pire en Écosse.
The weather in England is bad, but it is worse in Scotland.

Ton accent est mauvais, mais mon accent est plus mauvais que le tien.
Your (familiar) accent is bad, but my accent is worse than yours.

❖ Comparisons of 'well' - *meiux* & *mal*

The adverb **bien** ('well') has the irregular comparative adjective **meiux** ('better').
- **moins bien** ('less well') is also used.

The adverb **mal** ('badly') has the irregular comparative adjective **pis** ('worse').
- Also **plus mal** & **aussi mal** etc. are acceptable and in some cases preferable.

EXAMPLES:

Tu chantes bien, mais je chante mieux que toi.
You (familiar) sing well but I sing better than you.

Elle étudie mieux qu'avant.
She studies better than before.
- avant

Elle explique mieux ses idées.
She explains her ideas better.
- **expliquer** (verb) means 'to explain'

Les étudiants travaillent mieux que le professeur.
The students work better than the teacher.

C'est bien d'être beau, mais c'est mieux d'être riche.
It's good to be beautiful, but it's better to be rich.

C'est encore mieux d'être jeune.
It's even better to be young.

Son français est mauvais, mais je le parle encore moins bien que lui.
His French is bad but I speak it even less well than him.

Les singes grimpent mieux aux arbres que les humains.
Monkeys climb trees better than humans.
- **singe** (m) means 'monkey' or 'ape'
- **humain** (m) means 'human being'
- **grimper** (verb) means 'to climb'

Les humains ne peuvent pas grimper aux arbres aussi bien que les singes.
Humans can't climb trees as well as monkeys.

TOPIC 137 ❖ Comparisons of 'well' - *meiux* & *mal*

Je chante très mal. Je chante bien pire que toi.
I sing very badly. I sing much worse than you (familiar).

Ils travaillent aussi mal les une que les autres !
They work as badly as each other!

📖 **les uns que les autres** means 'as each other' or 'as one another'

Tes lunettes sont bien mais les miennes sont mieux.
Your (familiar) glasses are fine but mine are better.

💡 Using **bien** as 'fine' still contrasts with **mieux**

Vous préférez nager ou marcher ? Moi, je préfère nager, c'est meilleur pour la santé.
Do you (formal) prefer swimming or walking? Me, I prefer a swim, it's better for your health.

❖ Superlatives

Superlatives are used to express the highest quality or degree.

In French we simply add the definite article to the comparative.

For instance:

- **le meilleur** means 'the best' (masculine singular)
- **le pire** means 'the worst' (masculine singular)
- **la plus belle** means 'the most beautiful' (feminine singular)
- **les plus lentement** means 'the slowest' (plural)
- **les mons cheres** means 'the least expensive' (feminine plural)

If the superlative is an adjective, the definite articles and the comparative adjectives should agree with the noun in gender and number.

- For adjectives, the position of the superlative (before or after the noun) follows the same rules as for regular adjectives.

If the superlative is an adverb, then the definite article should always be the masculine singular **le**.

The personal pronouns can be used in place of definite articles when the superlative is attributed to someone.

EXAMPLES:

Mon école est la meilleure école de la ville.
My school is the best school in town.

C'est sans aucun doute le meilleur steak de Paris.
It is without a doubt the best steak in Paris.

Quel est le portable le moins cher d'Apple ?
What is Apple's cheapest laptop?

Ce sont les chocolats les plus savoureux du monde.
They are the tastiest chocolates in the world.

Où puis-je acheter les draps en coton les plus doux ?
Where can I buy the softest cotton sheets?

C'est la fête la plus amusante de tous les temps.
It's the funniest party ever.

TOPIC 138 ❖ Superlatives

Il n'achète que les fraises les meilleures et les plus chères.
He only buys the best and most expensive strawberries.

Ce sont les routes les plus accidentées du pays.
These are the most rugged roads in the country.

C'est sa plus mauvaise chanson.
It's his worst song.
- sa (his) in place of la

Est-ce votre meilleure tentative ?
Is this your (formal) best attempt?
- votre (his) in place of la
- tentative (f) means 'attempt'

Je viens de me réveiller du rêve le plus effrayant.
I just woke up from the scariest dream.

Ce semestre, j'ai eu mes pires notes scolaires.
This semester, I had my worst school grades.

Il est le plus grand garçon de ma classe.
He is the tallest boy in my class.

À votre avis, quel est le parfum de glace le plus populaire ?
In your (formal) opinion, which is the most popular flavor of ice cream?

À votre avis, quelle est la plus belle fleur ?
In your (formal) opinion, which is the most beautiful flower?

Il parle le mieux l'allemand parmi mes amis.
He speaks the best German among my friends.
- parmi means 'among' or 'amongst'

Mon père est le nageur le plus faible de la famille.
My father is the weakest swimmer in the family.

Mon frère nage le plus vite de la famille.
My brother swims the fastest in the family.

Le TGV est le train le plus rapide du monde.
The TGV is the fastest train in the world.

❖ The infinitive following adjectives or nouns - using *de* or *à*

In the majority of cases, an infinitive that follows (modifies) an adjective or noun is proceeded by **de**.

The **de** is also used after **que** in the second part of a comparison:

There are a few expectations where **à** is used instead:

- After **le dernier** ('the last'), **le seul** ('the only'), **le premier** ('the first'), and other numerals.
- If the infinitive conveys a passive meaning (eg. 'to be done').
- After adjectives showing tendency, appropriateness, and purpose, such as **habile** ('skillful'), **lent** ('slow'), **'prêt'** ('ready').

EXAMPLES:

Il est facile de comprendre.
It is easy to understand.

Je n'ai pas le temps de t'attendre.
I don't have time to wait for you (familiar).

Est-il capable de le faire ?
Is he able to do it?

Je suis ravi de vous revoir.
I (male) am glad to see youIn your (formal) opinion, again.

Je suis ravie de faire votre connaissance.
I (female) am delighted to make your acquaintance.

C'est mieux de prendre le bus.
It's better to take the bus.

Marguerite a peur de s'endormir.
Marguerite is afraid to fall asleep.

Elle a aussi peur de ne pas se réveiller.
She is also afraid of not waking up.

C'est étrange de ne pas demander d'aide.
It's weird not asking for help.

TOPIC 139 ❖ The infinitive following adjectives or nouns - using *de* or *à*

Je préfère lire que de regarder la télévision.
I prefer reading to watching TV.
💡 After **que** in a comparision use **de**

Il est plus relaxant de rentrer à pied que de prendre le bus.
It is more relaxing to walk home than to take the bus.
💡 After **que** in a comparision use **de**

Elle n'a pas le temps de gravir cette montagne.
She doesn't have time to climb this mountain.
📖 **gravir** (verb) means 'to climb'

Elle est la seule personne à avoir gravi cette montagne.
She is the only person to have climbed this mountain.
💡 After **la seul** use **à**

C'est le dernier train à partir d'ici aujourd'hui.
This is the last train from here today.
💡 After **le dernier** use **à**

Il a été le premier garçon à m'embrasser.
He was the first boy to kiss me.
💡 After **le premier** use **à**
📖 **embrasser à** (verb) means 'to kiss (someone)' or 'to embrasse (someone)'

Donnez moi un livre à lire.
Give me a book to read.
💡 **à lire** has a passive meaning - 'to be read' - so use **à**

J'ai un secret à te dire.
I have a secret to tell you (familiar).
💡 **à dire** has a passive meaning - 'to be told' - so use **à**

C'est le meilleur plat à commander dans ce bistrot.
This is the best dish to order in this bistro.
💡 **à commander** has a passive meaning - 'to be ordered' - so use **à**

La robe est propre et prête à porter.
The dress is clean and ready to wear.
💡 After certain adjectives use **à**

TOPIC 139 ❖ The infinitive following adjectives or nouns - using *de* or *à*

Il a tendance à se rendre tôt au travail.
He tends to come to work early.

- After certain adjectives use **à**
- **tendance** (f) means 'tendancy'
- **avoir tendance à** (verb) means 'to have a tendence to (do something)'

Bootstrap French
TOPIC 140

❖ Idiomatic expressions with *avoir..de*

There are several very common idiomatic expressions that use the verb **avoir**, the preposition **de** and an infinitive.

- **avoir l'air de** means 'to seem to'
- **avoir peur de** means 'to fear to'
- **avoir envie de** means 'to feel like (doing)'
- **avoir besoin de** means 'to have the need to'
- **avoir honte de** means 'to be ashamed to'
- **avoir tort de** means 'to be wrong to'
- **avoir raison de** means 'to be right to'

Many of these expressions can also take a noun.

EXAMPLES:

Tu as l'air d'être pressé.
You (familiar) seem to be in a hurry.
💡 With a verb

Il a l'air d'un flic.
He looks like a cop.
💡 With a noun

Ça a l'air difficile !
It looks difficult!
💡 After dropping the **de** this can taike an adjective too

Tu as l'air super fatigué.
You (familiar) look super tired.
💡 After dropping the **de** this can taike an adjective too

J'ai peur de tomber.
I'm afraid of falling.
💡 With a verb

Elles ont peur des araignées.
They are afraid of spiders.
💡 With a noun

TOPIC 140 ❖ Idiomatic expressions with *avoir..de*

Avez-vous peur du noir ?
Are you (formal) afraid of the dark?
- With a noun
- **le noir** means 'the dark'

J'ai vraiment envie d'aller aux toilettes !
I really want to go to the toilet!
- With a verb

Nous avons envie de rester à la maison toute la journée.
We want to stay home all day.
- With a verb

J'ai envie du chocolat que tu as acheté pour nous hier.
I crave the chocolate you (familiar) bought for us yesterday.
- With a noun

N'avez-vous pas envie d'aller au cinéma ?
Don't you (formal) feel like going to the cinema?
- With a verb

Je n'ai nullement envie de lui parler.
By no means do I want to talk to him.
- With a verb

J'ai besoin de repos.
I need some rest.
- With a noun

Avez-vous besoin d'aide ?
Do you (formal) need help?
- With a noun

Il n'a pas besoin de signer le document.
He does not need to sign the document.
- With a verb

Vous avez honte de continuer à fumer, n'est-ce pas ?
You (formal) are ashamed to keep smoking, aren't you?
- With a verb

N'as-tu pas honte de tes étranges habitudes ?
Aren't you (familiar) ashamed of your strange habits?
- With a noun

TOPIC 140 ❖ Idiomatic expressions with *avoir..de*

Leurs parents ont honte d'eux.
Their parents are ashamed of them.
💡 With a noun

Tu as tort de lui dire ça.
You (familiar) are wrong to tell him that.
💡 With a verb

Vous avez tort de vous sentir bouleversé.
You (formal) are wrong to feel upset.
💡 With a verb

Ils ont eu tort de se comporter ainsi.
They were wrong to behave like this.
💡 With a verb
📖 **se comporter** (verb) means 'to behave'
📖 **ainsi** means 'in this way' or 'in that way'

Tu as eu raison de lui dire la vérité.
You (familiar) were right to tell him the truth.
💡 With a verb

Nous avons raison de nous plaindre.
We are right to complain.
💡 With a verb
📖 **se plaindre** (verb) means 'to complain'

Tu as tort et j'ai raison. Bien sûr.
You (familiar) are wrong and I am right. Of course.
💡 :)

❖ The future tense - *le futur proche*

In French we can use the present tense to talk about the future especially if an adverb like **bientôt** ('soon') or **plus tard** ('later') are used.

Speech can more explicitly refer to the future by using the **futur proche** tense.

The **futur proche** expresses an immanent action in the near future.

- The equivalent in English is 'to be going to (do something)'.

The **futur proche** is formed by conjugating the verb **aller** (to go) in the present tense and adding the infinitive of the future action.

We negate the **futur proche** by surrounding the auxiliary **aller** with **ne..pas**.

EXAMPLES:

Je vais manger.
I'm going to eat.

Il va aller à l'école.
He will go to school.

Elle va lui parler demain.
She will talk to him tomorrow.

Est-ce que tu vas te rendre chez toi bientôt ?
Are you (familiar) going home soon?

Ça, c'est le train qui va partir très bientôt.
That there is the train that is going to leave very soon.

Elles vont jouer au tennis avec leurs amies.
They (female) are going to play tennis with her friends.

Nous allons manger chez nos grands-parents.
We are going to eat at our grandparents.

Allez-vous faire du vélo ce week-end ?
Are you (formal) going cycling this weekend ?

Je vais essayer d'ajouter du sel à la glace.
I am going to try adding salt to the ice cream.

🖋 **ajouter** (verb) means 'to add'

TOPIC 141 ❖ The future tense - *le futur proche*

Est-ce que tu vas partir pour les vacances ?
Are you (familiar) going on vacation?

Quand est-ce qu'elle va aller dans le Sud ?
When is she going down south?

Pourquoi est-ce-que vous allez manger sans eux ?
Why are you (formal) going to eat without them?

Avec qui vas-tu déjeuner ?
Who are you (familiar) going to have lunch with?

On va avoir besoin de faire le ménage aujourd'hui.
We are going to need to clean up today.

Il va y avoir beaucoup de bruit.
There's going to be a lot of noise.

💡 Note the preposition **y** next to the verb **avoir**

Ça va aller.
It is going (to be) OK.

💡 The future form of **ça va.**

On va faire quoi, demain ?
What are we going to do tomorrow?

Attention ! Vous allez tomber !
Attention! You (formal) will fall!

Je ne vais pas te téléphoner à midi.
I am not going to call you (familiar) at noon.

Nous n'allons pas encore manger.
We are not going to eat yet.

Je vais nager. Tu viens avec moi, Bette ?
I am going to swim. Are you (familiar) coming with me, Bette?

💡 Mixing tenses like this is fine.

❖ Verbs of perception and the infinitive

There are several very common verbs of perception that do not require a preposition between themselves and the infinitive second verb.

Some common verbs of perception are:
- **sentir** - 'to feel'
- **regarder** - 'to watch'
- **écouter** - 'to listen to'
- **apercevoir** - 'to catch a glimpse of'
- **voir** - 'to see'
- **entendre** - 'to hear'

The fact that they take the infinitive directly affects the word order.
- If the infinitive has no object then its subject can be either side of the infinitive.
- But if infinitive has both subject and object then they should be either side of the infinitive.
- If the subject of the infinitive is a pronoun and it is the only pronoun in the sentence, then the pronoun should be before all the verbs.

EXAMPLES:

Je sens souffler le vent.
I feel the wind blowing.
  ♀ The verb of preception **sentir** takes the infinitive **souffler** directly.

Je regarde courir les chevaux.
I see the horses running.
  ♀ The verb of preception **regarder** takes the infinitive **courir** directly.

J'écoute parler les enfants.
I listen to the children talk.
  ♀ The verb of preception **écouter** takes the infinitive **parler** directly.

Je regarde jouer l'équipe.
I watch the team play.
  ♀ The verb of preception **regarder** takes the infinitive **jouer** directly.

J'aperçois tomber un arbre.
I see a tree fall.
  ♀ The verb of preception **apercevoir** takes the infinitive **tomber** directly.

TOPIC 142 ❖ Verbs of perception and the infinitive

J'aperçois un arbre tomber.
I see a tree fall.

💡 No object of the infinitive **tomber** so subject **un arbre** can be either side of the infinitive

Je vois les enfants manger.
I see the children eating.

Je vois manger les enfants.
I see the children eating.

💡 No object of the infinitive **manger** so subject **les enfants** can be either side of the infinitive

Je vois les enfants manger du pain.
I see the children eating bread.

💡 The infinitive has an object **du pain** which comes after the infinitive and the subject before the infinitive.

Nous avons vu les arbres perdre leurs feuilles.
We saw the trees losing their leaves.

J'entends lire l'histoire.
I hear the story read.

💡 The infinitive has no subject so it becomes passive - 'I hear the story being read (by someone)'

J'entends un homme lire l'histoire.
I hear a man reading the story.

💡 The infinitive has an object **l'histoire** which comes after the infinitive and the subject before.

Je l'entends lire l'histoire.
I hear him reading the story.

💡 Subject of the infinitive is a pronoun so before the first verb

J'entends les hommes parler.
I hear about men.

Je les entends parler.
I hear them talking.

💡 Subject of the infinitive is a pronoun so before the first verb

Elle l'a regardé casser.
She watched it break.

TOPIC 142 ❖ Verbs of perception and the infinitive

Elle a regardé les enfants casser le jouet.
She watched the children break the toy.

Elle les a regardés casser le jouet.
She watched them break the toy.

Elle les a regardés le casser.
She watched them break it.

❖ Verbs of perception and agreement

Recall that most verbs of perception take the second verb infinitive directly.

With verbs of perception, the rules of agreement of past participles are a little different:
- If the subject of the infinitive precedes the verb of perception, there is agreement.
- There is no agreement with the direct object of the infinitive.

EXAMPLES:

J'ai vu tomber la fille.
I saw the girl fall.
> The subject of the infinitive **la file** does not precedes the verb of perception, so no agreement

La fille que j'ai vue tomber.
The girl I saw fall.
> The subject of the infinitive **la file** precedes the verb of perception, there is agreement: **vu** ⇒ **veu** (f.sing)

J'ai regardé les chevaux courir.
I watched the horses run.
> The subject of the infinitive **les chevals** does not precedes the verb of perception, so no agreement

Les chevaux que j'ai vus courir.
The horses I saw running.
> The subject of the infinitive **les chevals** precedes the verb of perception, there is agreement: **vu** ⇒ **vus** (m.pl)

Elle a aperçu la feuille tomber dans l'eau.
She saw the leaf fall into the water.

La feuille qu'elle a aperçue tomber dans l'eau.
The leaf she saw fall into the water.
> The subject of the infinitive **la feuille** precedes the verb of perception so there is agreement: **aperçu** ⇒ **aperçue** (f.sing)

L'histoire que j'ai entendu lire.
The story I heard read.
> **l'histoire** is the direct object of the infinitive so no agreement

TOPIC 143 ❖ Verbs of perception and agreement

La manifestation que j'ai vue se dérouler.
The manifestation I saw unfold.
💡 The subject of the infinitive **la manifestation** precedes the verb of perception, there is agreement

La voiture que j'ai vue heurter un lampadaire.
The car I saw hit a lamp post.

J'ai vu la fille voler cette voiture.
I saw the girl steal that car.

Je l'ai vue voler cette voiture.
I saw her steal that car.

La voiture que j'ai vu se faire voler.
The car I saw being stolen.

La fille que j'ai vue voler la voiture.
The girl I saw stealing the car.

Bootstrap French
TOPIC 144

❖ Some, any and a few - *quelques*

When the plural indefinite pronoun **quelques** is used with countable things it means 'some', 'a few' or 'a couple of'.

- The singular **quelque** is used is several fixed expressions which are covered in the next topic.

Recall that we previously introduced **un peu de** ('a little of' or 'few') which can be used for uncountable things. Or the partitive **de** itself can be used for an uncountable 'some'.

EXAMPLES:

Il a quelques amis à Paris.
He has some friends in Paris.

J'ai acheté quelques disques.
I bought a few records.

Il reste quelques bouteilles.
There are a few bottles left.

On peut finir les quelques bouteilles qui restent ?
Can we finish the few remaining bottles?

Il y a quelque temps.
Sometime ago. *OR* Once upon a time.

Je vais acheter quelques bougies pour décorer ma chambre.
I'm going to buy some candles to decorate my room.

J'ai lu ce livre quelques fois.
I have read this book a few times.

J'ai visité Madrid quelques fois, mais je ne suis jamais allé à Rome.
I have visited Madrid a few times but never been to Rome.

Je sais dire quelques mots en français.
I know how to say a few words in French.

Quelques bouteilles sont vides.
A few bottles are empty.

TOPIC 144 ❖ Some, any and a few - *quelques*

Avez-vous quelque chose à déclarer ?
Do you (formal) have anything to declare?

Bootstrap French
TOPIC 145

❖ Common uses of *quelque*

There are several fixed expressions that use the singular indefinite pronoun **quelque**.

- **quelque chose** means 'something' and **quelque chose d'autre** means 'something else'
- **quelque part** means 'somewhere'
- **quelqu'un** means 'someone'
- **quelqu'uns** means 'some' or 'a few (specific things)'
 - Must agree in gender — for example **quelqu'unes** is feminine
- **quelque temps** means 'some time' or 'a while' (a duration)
- **quelquefois** means 'sometimes'
 - Not to be confused with **quelques fois** which means 'a few times'.

And there is also **quiconque** which means 'anyone'.

EXAMPLES:

Tu veux boire quelque chose ?
You (familiar) want something to drink?

Avez-vous parlé de quelque chose avec lui ?
Did you (formal) talk about anything with him?

Ils veulent nous montrer quelque chose.
They want to show us something.

Je pense avoir vu quelque chose bouger dans les buissons.
I think I saw something moving in the bushes.

Ce film est énervant. Tu veux regarder quelque chose d'autre ?
This movie is annoying. Want to watch something else?

As-tu pensé à quelque chose d'autre ?
Did you (familiar) think of anything else?

J'ai oublié mon sac quelque part.
I forgot my bag somewhere.

Ton sac doit bien être quelque part.
Your (familiar) bag must be somewhere.

TOPIC 145 ❖ Common uses of *quelque*

Vous allez quelque part ce week-end ?
Are you (formal) going somewhere this weekend?

Quelqu'un m'a dit de prendre le bus numéro douze.
Someone told me to take bus number twelve.

Excusez-moi, je vous ai confondu avec quelqu'un d'autre !
Excuse me, I confused you (formal) with someone else!

Quelques-uns de mes amis me disent que tu es amoureuse de lui.
Some of my friends tell me that you (familiar) are in love with him.

Parmi mes copines, quelques-unes sont complètement folles de lui.
Among my girlfriends, some are completely crazy about him.

J'ai passé quelque temps avec mon oncle dans sa ferme.
I spent some time with my uncle on his farm.

Il a dû fermer la boutique quelque temps.
He had to close the shop for a while.

Vous allez devoir attendre quelque temps pour le médecin.
You (formal) are going to have to wait some time for the doctor.

Nous allons quelquefois à la campagne.
We sometimes go to the countryside.

Son frère lui a promis d'appeler quelquefois.
Her brother promised to call her sometimes.

Je comprends mieux que quiconque.
I understand better than anyone.

Il est interdit à quiconque d'entrer.
It is forbidden for anyone to enter.

Quiconque nous écoute en ce moment doit te trouver ridicule !
Anyone listening to us right now must find you (familiar) ridiculous!

❖ Indefinite pronouns with an adjective require *de*

When modifying many indefinite pronouns with an adjective we need to use **de** between the pronoun and the adjective.

- Indefinite pronouns of this type include **quelque chose**, **quelqu'un**, **quelque part**, **rien**, **certain** etc.
- The question **qu'est-ce que** can also be considerable an indefinite pronoun and thus requires **de** if modified by an adjective.

EXAMPLES:

Rien d'inhabituel ne s'est passé.
Nothing unusual happened.
- **rien** is an indefinite pronoun
- **inhabituel** means 'unusual'

Il n'y a rien d'étrange dans ce qu'il a dit.
There is nothing strange in what he said.
- **rien** is an indefinite pronoun

Il n'y a rien d'autre dans leur sac.
There isn't anything else in their bag.
- **quelque chose** is an indefinite pronoun

Quelque chose d'inattendu m'est arrivé.
Something unexpected happened to me.
- **quelque chose** is an indefinite pronoun

Elle a quelque chose d'intéressant à leur dire.
She has something interesting to tell them.
- **quelque chose** is an indefinite pronoun

Elle a vu quelqu'un d'un peu suspect.
She saw someone a little suspicious.
- **quelqu'un** is an indefinite pronoun

Il y a quelqu'un de bizarre dans votre bureau.
There's someone weird in your (formal) office.
- **quelqu'un** is an indefinite pronoun

TOPIC 146 ❖ Indefinite pronouns with an adjective require *de*

On a besoin de quelqu'un de plus compétent pour nous aider.
We need someone more competent to help us.

💡 **quelqu'un** is an indefinite pronoun

Parmi les étudiants, certains des plus âgés sont partis.
Among the students, some older ones have left.

💡 **certain** is an indefinite pronoun

Je vais t'emmener quelque part de merveilleux.
I'll take you (familiar) somewhere wonderful.

💡 **quelque part** is an indefinite pronoun

Qu'est-ce qu'il y a de bon aujourd'hui ?
What's good today?

💡 **qu'est-ce que** is indefinite

On voit beaucoup de mauvais et peu de bon.
We see a lot of bad and little good.

💡 **beaucoup** and **peu** are indefinite

Il n'y a personne de malade ici.
There's no one sick here.

💡 **personne** is indefinite

❖ Any or unspecified - *n'importe*

The adjective **n'importe** can be combined with various pronouns etc. to mean that something is unspecified.

- **n'importe qui** - 'anybody'
- **n'importe quoi** - 'anything'
- **n'importe où** - 'anywhere'
- **n'importe comment** - 'anyhow'
- **n'importe quel** (and **quelle, quels, quelles**) - 'whichever'
- **n'importe lequel** (and **laquelle, lesquels, les quelles**) - 'whichever one'
- **n'importe quand** - 'any time'
- **n'importe combien** - 'no matter how much' or 'at any amount/cost'

These can be used as both subjects and objects of sentences.

And **n'importe** can be used itself as an interjection meaning 'it doesn't matter' or 'whatever'.

N'importe should not be confused with **peu importe** which means 'doesn't matter' and is somewhat flippant.

EXAMPLES:

Vous pouvez rendre les clés à n'importe qui d'entre nous.
You (formal) can return the keys to any of us.

Ce sont des choses faciles que n'importe qui peut faire.
These are easy things anyone can do.

Je peux vous aider avec n'importe quoi.
I can help you (formal) with anything.

Il raconte n'importe quoi.
He says anything. *OR* He is talking nonsense.

S'il pense à n'importe quoi d'autre, il va me le faire savoir.
If he thinks of anything else, he'll let me know.

On peut aller n'importe où sur cette île.
We can go anywhere.

TOPIC 147 ❖ Any or unspecified - *n'importe*

L'usine peut être construite n'importe où dans le pays.
The factory can be built anywhere in the country.

Je préfère être avec toi que n'importe où ailleurs.
I'd rather be with you (familiar) than anywhere else.

ailleurs (adv) means 'somewhere else'

Comment cuire les œufs ? N'importe comment.
How to cook the eggs? Anyhow.

Les enfants peuvent jouer avec les jouets n'importe comment.
Children can play with the toys anyhow (they like).

On peut l'appeler n'importe comment.
We can call it anything.

Il chante n'importe comment ! Quelle horreur !
He sings anyhow! How awful!

C'est un chapeau pour n'importe quel temps.
This is a hat for any weather.

Tu peux acheter n'importe quel fromage. Ils sont tous délicieux !
You (familiar) can buy any cheese. They are all delicious!

Elle aime jouer n'importe quel morceau de musique pour piano.
She likes to play any piece of piano music.

Ce soir, nous allons camper sur n'importe laquelle des îles.
Tonight we will camp on whichever (one) of the islands.

Vous pouvez déposer les clés dans n'importe laquelle des boîtes aux lettres.
You (formal) can deposit the keys in any of the mailboxes.

Il peut choisir n'importe lequel des livres sur l'étagère.
He can choose any of the books on the shelf.

Quel morceau de pizza veux-tu ? N'importe lequel me convient !
What piece of pizza do you (familiar) want? Any one is fine with me!

Vous pouvez venir chez moi n'importe quand.
You (formal) can come to my house anytime.

TOPIC 147 ❖ Any or unspecified - *n'importe*

Il ne se décolore jamais, peu importe combien de fois vous le lavez.
It never fades no matter how many times you (formal) wash it.

🔖 **décolorer** (verb) means 'to fade' or 'to bleach'

Quelle glace préfères-tu ? Moi ? N'importe !
What ice cream do you (familiar) prefer? Me? Whichever!

Peu importe où vous le mettez.
It doesn't matter where you (formal) put it.

🔖 **peu importe** means 'doesn't matter'

Peu importe combien ça coûte, je le veux.
It doesn't matter how much it costs; I want it.

Quels types de pizzas voulez-vous ? Peu importe lesquelles.
What kinds of pizza do you (formal) want? It doesn't matter which.

🔖 **type** (m) means 'type' or 'kind' or 'guy'
🔖 **pizza** (f) means 'pizza'

❖ All of or every - *tout* as an adjective

The word **tout** can be used as an adjective, adverb and a noun.

As an adjective the word **tout** means 'every one of' or 'all of' and should be followed by an article or possessive pronoun.

It should agree in gender and number.

- **tout** - masculine singular
- **toute** - feminine singular
- **tous** - masculine plural
- **toutes** - feminine plural

EXAMPLES:

Tu connais tous ses amis.
You (familiar) know all his friends.

Nous avons noté toutes ces idées.
We noted all these ideas.

Il faut essayer de parler français tout le temps.
(You) have to try to speak French all the time.

Prendre tout son temps.
To take all one's time.

Leur chien aboie toute la journée.
Their dog barks all day.

J'apprends le français toute la journée.
I learn French all day.

Toute ma famille est très sportive.
My whole family is very athletic.

Il veut habiter à Paris toute sa vie.
He wants to live in Paris all his life.

Il n'arrive pas à finir tous ses devoirs.
He didn't manage to finish all his homework.

TOPIC 148 ❖ All of or every - *tout* as an adjective

En tout cas, cela vaut la peine d'attendre.
In any case, it's worth the wait.

📖 **en tout cas** means 'in any case'

📖 **valoir la peine** (verb) means 'to be worth it'

Tous mes amis sont arrivés.
All my friends have arrived.

Vous pouvez apprendre à conduire à tout moment.
You (formal) can learn to drive at any time.

Ils ont rassemblé toutes ces fleurs.
They collected all these flowers.

📖 **rassembler** (verb) means 'to collect' or 'to gather'

Tout citoyen a le droit de voter.
Every citizen has the right to vote.

📖 **citoyen** (m) means 'citizen'

❖ Everything and all of them - *tout* as a noun or pronoun

As a noun **tout** means 'everything' and is always masculine singular.

As a pronoun it means 'all (of them)' and is always plural, so it is either **tous** (masculine plural) or **toutes** (feminine plural).

- When **tous** is used as a masculine plural pronoun, it is pronounced with the 's'.
- The pronouns **tous** & **toutes** are often used in subject repetition as a device to emphasize the 'all of them'.

EXAMPLES:

Tout va bien.
Everything is fine.
noun

Tout m'ennuie.
Everything bores me.
noun

Il a raison - tout ici est ennuyeux.
He's right - everything here is boring.
noun

Il comprend tout.
He understands everything.
noun

Nous avons tout entendu.
We have heard it all.
noun

Tout ce qu'il y a d'étrange doit être mis dans cette boîte.
Everything (anything) that is strange must be put in this box.
noun

C'est tout ce que je peux dire à ce sujet.
That's all I can say about it.
noun

French Grammar

TOPIC 149 ❖ Everything and all of them - *tout* as a noun or pronoun

Malgré tout, je t'aime.
Despite everything, I love you (familiar).
💡 noun

Il n'a rien mangé du tout.
He didn't eat anything at all.
📖 du tout means 'at all'

Tout ce qui brille n'est pas or.
All that glitters is not gold.
💡 noun

Combien coûte le tout ?
How much does the lot cost?
📖 le tout means 'the whole thing'

Le tout coûte cher !
The whole thing is expensive!
📖 le tout means 'the whole thing'

Tout va bien.
Everything is going well.
💡 pronoun

Les garçons sont sortis et tous ont porté leurs chapeaux.
The boys came out and all wore their hats.
💡 pronoun
💡 masculine plural pronoun so pronounced with the 's'

Les filles sont arrivées et toutes ont dit bonjour.
The girls arrived and all said hello.
💡 pronoun

Les pommes - toutes sont mûres.
The apples - all of them are ripe.
💡 pronoun

Les chiens - tous sont mouillés.
The dogs - all of them are wet.
💡 pronoun
💡 masculine plural pronoun so pronounced with the 's'

TOPIC 149 ❖ Everything and all of them - *tout* as a noun or pronoun

Ils sont tous partis.
They all left.
- pronoun in repetition
- masculine plural pronoun so pronounced with the 's'

Les étudiants sont dans le bus ? Oui, ils sont tous déjà montés dans le bus.
Are the students on the bus? Yes, they all have already boarded the bus.
- pronoun in repetition
- masculine plural pronoun so pronounced with the 's'

Ils peuvent tous aller en enfer.
They can all go to hell.
- pronoun in repetition
- pronounced with the 's'

Vous pouvez toutes prendre quelque chose à boire.
You (females) can all have something to drink.
- pronoun in repetition

❖ Very or extremely - *tout* as an adverb

As an adverb **tout** is typically used to modify an adjective and means 'extremely', 'completely', 'entirely' or 'totally'.

- Synonyms include **entièrement**, **complètement**, and **très**.

The adjective **tout** in invariable with gender and number.

The exception is for feminine adjectives - when they begin with consonant or an aspirated 'h' there is agreement (**toute** or **toutes**).

EXAMPLES:

Il est tout seul.
He is completely alone.

Le bébé est tout petit.
The baby is very small.
💡 tout petit is a very common term

Ils sont tout étonnés.
They are quite amazed.

J'ai mangé la pizza tout entière.
I ate the whole pizza.

Je suis tout triste.
I am very sad.

C'est tout fini.
It is completely over. *OR* It is all over.

Ils sont tout heureux.
They are totally happy.

Mon chat est tout mouillé.
My cat is all wet.

Elle est tout heureuse.
She is totally happy.
💡 Feminine but before an aspirated 'h' so no agreement

TOPIC 150 ❖ Very or extremely - *tout* as an adverb

Elle est tout excitée.
She's all excited.

💡 Feminine but before vowel so no agreement

Elle est toute petite.
She is very small.

💡 Feminine before a constant so agreement

Ma mère est toute triste, mes filles sont aussi toutes tristes.
My mother is very sad, my daughters are also very sad.

💡 Feminine before a constant so agreement (in both instances)

Pourquoi le train est-il tout plein ?
Why is the train completely full?

La poste est tout loin d'ici, mais la marie est tout près.
The post office is quite far from here but the town hall is very close.

Il faut continuer tout droit.
(You) must continue straight ahead.

👉 **tout droit** means 'straight ahead'

Ils sont tout contents d'être ici.
They are very happy to be here.

Ils sont tous contents d'être ici.
They are all happy to be here.

💡 Note the difference in meaning from the previous example: **tout** ('very') verses **tous** ('extremely')

❖ Own and clean - *propre*

The adjective **propre** has two meanings:
- 'clean'
- 'own' - as in 'one's own'

Its meaning depends on its position relative to the noun it modifies.
- After the noun - like all normal adjectives - it means 'clean'.
  - The feminine remains **propre** and the plural is **propes**.
- But before the noun - and normally with a possessive - it means 'own' and is invariant.

EXAMPLES:

La table est toute propre.
The table is completely clean.
💡 After the noun so **propre** is 'clean'

Je viens de nettoyer la table, elle doit être propre.
I just cleaned the table; it must be clean.

Je veux ma propre chambre.
I want my own room.
💡 Before the nous (with a possessive pronoun) so **propre** is 'own'

Maria a fabriqué la table de ses propres mains.
Maria made the table with her own hands.

Il ne porte pas ses propres chaussures !
He doesn't wear his own shoes!

Même si elle est toute petite, elle a déjà son propre vélo.
Even though she is very small, she already has her own bike.

Il creuse sa propre tombe.
He digs his own grave.

Il ne veut pas faire son propre travail.
He doesn't want to do his own work.

TOPIC 151 ❖ Own and clean - *propre*

Ils ont leur propre culture unique.
They have their own unique culture.

Chaque État a sa propre constitution et son propre gouvernement.
Each state has its own constitution and its own government.

Il a suivi son propre chemin.
He followed his own path. *OR* He went his own way.

Chacun croit sa propre version des événements.
Everyone believes their own version of events.

Je dors dans mon propre lit.
I sleep in my own bed.

💡 Before the nous (with a possessive pronoun) so **propre** is 'own'

Je dors dans mon lit propre.
I sleep in my clean bed.

💡 After the noun so **propre** is 'clean'

❖ The past continuous - *L'imparfait*

L'imparfait (the imperfect or past continuous) is a past tense that describes states and actions that were ongoing or repeated in the past. It is also used to talk about habits.

- This contrasts with the **passé composé** which describes completed one-off or discrete events in the past.

We conjugate the **l'imparfait** by adding the endings **-ais**, **-ait**, **-ions**, **-iez** and **-aient** to the root of the present tense **nous** form of the verb.

For example the verb **habiter** ('to live') - the **nous** form is **habitons** and the root is **habit-**. We then conjugate starting from that root:

- **je** + **habit-** + **ais** ⇒ **j'habitais**
- **tu** + **habit-** + **ais** ⇒ **tu habitais**
- **il** & **on** + **habit-** + **ait** ⇒ **il** & **on habitait**
- **nous** + **habit-** + **ions** ⇒ **nous habitions**
- **vous** + **habit-** + **iez** ⇒ **vous habitiez**
- **ils** + **habit-** + **aient** ⇒ **ils habitaient**

This tense is often used to step up for an interrupted action - an ongoing action in the past (expressed in **l'imparfait**) is interrupted by second one-off action (expressed in **le passé composé**).

- For example 'While I was eating, he called' - where the 'eating' would be in **l'imparfait** and the 'called' would be in **le passé composé**.

EXAMPLES:

L'année dernière, j'habitais à Paris.
Last year, I was living in Paris. *OR* Last year, I lived in Paris.
habiter (nous habitons) ⇒ habit- + -ais ⇒ j'habitais

Et toi, où habitais-tu l'année dernière ?
And you (familiar), where did you live last year?
habiter (nous habitons) ⇒ habit- + -ais ⇒ tu habitais

Moi, j'habitais à Aix_en_Provence.
Me, I lived in Aix en Provence.
habiter (nous habitons) ⇒ habit- + -ais ⇒ j'habitais

TOPIC 152 ❖ The past continuous - *L'imparfait*

Ta petite amie, est-ce qu'elle habitait avec toi ?
Your girlfriend, did she live with you (familiar)?

💡 habiter (nous habitons) ⇒ habit- + -ait ⇒ elle habitait

Oui, nous habitions ensemble dans un petit appartement au centre-ville.
Yes, we lived together in a small apartment downtown.

💡 habiter (nous habitons) ⇒ habit- + -ions ⇒ nous habitions

Pourquoi habitiez-vous à Aix_en_Provence ?
Why did you (plural) live in Aix en Provence?

💡 habiter (nous habitons) ⇒ habit- + -iez ⇒ vous habitiez

Nous y habitions pour l'université.
We lived there for university.

💡 habiter (nous habitons) ⇒ habit- + -ions ⇒ nous habitions
💡 The proposition y is used in place of 'to there' or 'in there' when à... would be used

Et tes amis, ils y habitaient aussi ?
And your (familiar) friends, did they live there too?

💡 habiter (nous habitons) ⇒ habit- + -aient ⇒ ils habitaient

À qui parliez-vous quand je vous ai appelé ?
Who were you (formal) talking to when I called you?

💡 parler (nous parlions) ⇒ parl- + -iez ⇒ vous parliez

Je parlais à Jacques quand tu as appelé.
I was talking to Jacques when you (familiar) called.

💡 parler (nous parlions) ⇒ parl- + -ias ⇒ je parlias

Nous parlions d'aller aux Pays_Bas.
We were talking about going to the Netherlands.

💡 parler (nous parlions) ⇒ parl- + -ions ⇒ nous parlions

Nous regardions la télé quand quelqu'un a frappé à la porte.
We were watching TV when someone knocked on the door.

💡 parler (nous parlions) ⇒ parl- + -ions ⇒ nous parlions

Que regardiez-vous ?
What were you (formal) looking at?

💡 regarder (nous regardions) ⇒ regard- + -ions ⇒ nous regardions

Que faisais-tu hier matin ?
What were you (familiar) doing yesterday morning?

💡 faite (nous faisons) ⇒ fais- + -ias ⇒ tu faisias

TOPIC 152 ❖ The past continuous - *L'imparfait*

Ils faisaient le ménage toute la journée d'hier.
They were cleaning all day yesterday.
💡 faite (nous faisons) ⇒ fais- + -aient ⇒ ils faisaient

Qui chantait sous la douche hier soir ?
Who was singing in the shower last night?
💡 chanter (nous chanions) ⇒ chant- + -ait ⇒ il chantiat

Elle ne lisait pas quand je suis arrivée.
She was not reading when I arrived.
💡 lire (nous lisions) ⇒ lis- + -iat ⇒ elle lisiat

Pendant qu'elle cuisinait, j'ai reçu un coup de téléphone.
While she was cooking, I received a phone call.
💡 cuisiner (nous cuisinions) ⇒ cuisin- + -iat ⇒ elle cuisiniat
✎ un coup de téléphone (m) means 'telephone call'

Tu avais raison et j'avais tort concernant la météo.
You (familiar) were right about the time.
💡 avoir (nous avions) ⇒ av- + -ias ⇒ tu avias

En Espagne, j'avais besoin d'aide avec la langue.
In Spain, I needed help with the language.
💡 avoir (nous avions) ⇒ av- + -ias ⇒ je avias

Il y avait un problème avec la voiture.
There was a problem with the car.
💡 avoir (nous avions) ⇒ av- + -iat ⇒ il aviat

Vous n'aviez pas le droit de faire ça.
You (formal) had no right to do that.
💡 avoir (nous avions) ⇒ av- + -iez ⇒ vous aviez

❖ The irregular *imparfait* of *être*

The verb **être** is the only truely irregular verb in the **imparfait**.
- **j'étais** - 'I was'
- **tu étais** - 'you (familiar) was'
- **il était** & **elle était** - 'he was' and 'she was'
- **nous étions** - 'we were'
- **vous étiez** - 'you (pural or singular formal) was'
- **ils étaient** & **elles étaient** - 'they were' and 'they (females) were'

The verb **avoir** is regular in **l'imparfait**.

EXAMPLES:

Enfant, j'étais souvent malade.
As a child I was often sick.

Quand nous étions en Suisse, nous skiions souvent.
When we were in Switzerland, we often skied.

J'étais au supermarché toute la matinée.
I was at the supermarket all morning.

Tu n'étais pas prêt à partir avant lui.
You (familiar) weren't ready to leave before he was.

Leur réponse était décourageante.
Their response was discouraging.

Je sais que vous étiez à Montpellier l'été dernier.
I know you (formal) were in Montpellier last summer.

Les fenêtres étaient déjà ouvertes quand nous sommes arrivés.
The windows were already open when we arrived.

Il était étudiant quand il s'est marié.
He was a student when he got married.

C'était le plus beau jour de ma vie.
It was the best day of my life.

TOPIC 153 ❖ The irregular *imparfait* of *être*

Ils étaient les meilleurs amis pendant leur temps à l'armée.
They were best friends during their time in the military.

Je ne sais pas qui c'était, mais ce n'était pas moi.
I don't know who it was but it wasn't me.

TOPIC 154

❖ A few irregular *imparfait* conjugations

There are a couple of expectations to the general rule for forming **l'imparfait**:

- For verbs that end in **-cer** - for example **lancer** - the present tense for **nous** is **lançons**. The **imparfait** is therefore based on the **lanç-** root as per normal except **nous lancions** and **vous lanciez** which loose the circumflex.
- For verbs that end in **-ger** - for example **manger** - the present tense for **nous** is **mangeons**. The **imparfait** is therefore based on the **mange-** root as per normal except **nous mangions** and **vous mangiez** which loose the **e**.
- The verb **falloir** which is only used impersonally in the expression **il faut** ('it is necessary') is **fallait** in the **imparfait**.
- The verb **pleuvoir** ('to rain') which only used impersonally in the expression **il pleut** ('it rains' or 'it is raining') is **pleuvait** in the **imparfait**.

EXAMPLES:

La route était bloquée et nous avancions donc très lentement.
The road was blocked and we so were moving very slowly.
- ֍ -cer verb so for **nous** & **vous** use irregular root **avanc-** without the circumflex ⇒ nous avancions
- ✎ **avancer** means 'to advance'
- ✎ **donc** means 'so'

Les chars avançaient rapidement à travers la campagne.
The tanks were advancing rapidly through the countryside.
- ֍ -cer verb but not **nous** or **vous** so use regular root **avanç-** ⇒ ils avançaient
- ✎ **char** (m) means 'tank (military)'
- ✎ **à travers** means 'through' or 'across'

Elle menaçait de le dénoncer à la police.
She threatened to report him to the police.
- ֍ -cer verb but not **nous** or **vous** so use regular root **menaç-** ⇒ elle menaçait
- ✎ **menacer** (verb) means 'to threaten'
- ✎ **dénoncer** (verb) means 'to denounce' or 'to report to a authority'

Pourquoi menaciez-vous de le virer ?
Why were you (formal) threatening to fire him?
- ֍ -cer verb so for **nous** & **vous** use irregular root **menac-** without the circumflex ⇒ vous menaciez

TOPIC 154 ❖ A few irregular *imparfait* conjugations

Nous mangions du pain et du beurre à chaque repas.
We ate bread and butter with every meal.

💡 **-ger** verb so for **nous** & **vous** use irregular root **mang-** without the **e** ⇒ **nous mangions**

Je mangeais du pop-corn et regardais un film.
I was eating popcorn and watching a movie.

💡 **-ger** verb but not **nous** or **vous** so use regular root **mange-** ⇒ **je mangeais**

Il fallait faire un détour.
It was necessary to take a detour.

✑ **détour** (m) means 'detour'

Il nous fallait améliorer la qualité du travail.
We needed to improve the quality of work.

✑ **améliorer** (verb) means 'to improve'

Il me fallait porter un parapluie partout.
I had to carry an umbrella everywhere.

Il pleut maintenant.
It is raining now.

💡 Present tense use of **pleuvoir** - **il pleut**

Il pleuvait hier matin.
It was raining in the morning yesterday.

💡 Imparfait use of **pleuvoir** - **il pleuvait**

Il pleuvait des cordes pendant le match.
It was raining heavily during the game.

✑ **pleuvoir des cordes** (verb) means 'to rain heavily' or 'to rain cats and dogs'

✑ **corde** (f) means 'rope' or 'string'

Je savais qu'il pleuvait, alors j'ai mis un imperméable.
I knew that it was raining so I put on a raincoat.

✑ **imperméable** (m) means 'raincoat' or (adj) 'waterproof'

❖ Was going to - *aller* from the *futur proche* in the *imparfait*

As we have seen, the conjugated verb **aller** plus an infinitive forms the **futur proche** - 'to be going to (do something)'.

Putting this **aller** in the **imparfait** is used to express an interrupted or uncompleted intention.

 - English has the equivalent 'was going to (do something)'.

Technically we are expressing the **futur proche** in the **imparfait**. In French this is called **le futur proche dans le passé**.

EXAMPLES:

J'allais aller à la plage mais il a commencé à pleuvoir.
I was going to go to the beach but it started to rain.

Nous allions regarder un film mais je suis trop occupé.
We were going to watch a movie but I'm too busy.

Qu'allais-tu faire ?
What were you (familiar) going to do?

De quoi alliez-vous lui parler ?
What were you (formal) going to talk to him about?

Il allait faire les courses mais il a oublié.
He was going to go shopping but he forgot.

Tu lui as demandé ce qu'il allait faire ?
Did you (familiar) ask him what he was going to do?

Je me demandais comment il allait faire face.
I was wondering how he was going to cope.

✍ **faire face** (verb) means 'to cope'

Je croyais que vous alliez changer de cravate.
I thought that you (formal) were going to change your tie.

Ils allaient fournir une chambre pour moi.
They were going to provide a room for me.

Il s'avère qu'ils n'allaient pas me le dire.
It turns out that they were not going to tell me (it).

TOPIC 155 ❖ Was going to - *aller* from the *futur proche* in the *imparfait*

Elle a dit qu'elle allait téléphoner au plombier.
She said that she was going to call the plumber.

Tu allais manquer ton train, c'est pour ça que tu as dû te dépêcher.
You (familiar) were going to miss your train, that's why you had to hurry.

Elle allait appeler la police !
She was going to call the police!

Vous alliez nous rejoindre. Avez-vous oublié ?
You (formal) were going to join us. Did you forget?

Je ne savais pas que tu allais dormir toute la journée.
I did not know that you (familiar) were going to sleep all day.

❖ Talking about the weather

The impersonal **il fait** ('it makes') is used with an adjective to talk about the weather.
- **C'est** followed by an adjective can similarly be used.

The verbs **pleuvoir** ('to rain') and **neiger** ('to snow') also take the impersonal **il** to describe the weather.

EXAMPLES:

Quel temps fait-il ?
How is the weather?

Quel temps faisait-il ?
How was the weather?

Quel temps fera-t-il ?
How will the weather be?

Il fait beau.
The weather's nice.

Il faisait bon avant-hier.
The weather was good the day before yesterday.

Il fera mauvais après-demain.
The weather will be bad the day after tomorrow.

Il fait encore frais ici au printemps.
It is still cool here in the spring.

Il fait très froid.
It is very cold.

Il fera assez chaud pendant l'été.
It will be quite warm during the summer.

Il fait soleil en juillet.
It is sunny in July.

Il fait du vent au bord de la mer en automne.
It is windy by the sea in autumn.

TOPIC 156 ❖ Talking about the weather

Il faisait du brouillard à Londres.
It was foggy in London.

Il fait rarement orageux en hiver.
It is stormy.

C'est humide.
It is humid.

C'est gelé.
It (the weather) is freezing.

Il pleut.
It is raining.

Il a plu toute la journée d'hier.
It rained all day yesterday.

Il pleuvait pendant le match de football.
It was raining during the football match.

Il y avait un petit peu de pluie pendant le pique-nique.
There was a little bit of rain during the picnic.

Il neige.
It is snowing.

Il neigeait fort dans les montagnes.
It was snowing hard in the mountains.

❖ The pluperfect - *Le plus-que-parfait*

The pluperfect (**le plus-que-parfait**) is used to express a completed action in the past that happened before or during another past action.

- The equivalent in English is 'had (done something)'.

It is often used in a subordinate clause where the main clause is in **le passé composé** or **l'imparfait**.

Le plus-que-parfait is formed with the auxiliary in **l'imparfait** followed by the past participle of the verb.

- To put it more simply, **le plus-que-parfait** is **le passe compose** with the auxiliary in **l'imparfiat**.

Indeed, the choice of auxiliary, **être** or **avoir**, is the same as for **le passé composé**.

Le plus-que-parfait is also used to express wishes about the past - using **si seulement** ('if only...') for instance.

As always, the past participle must agree in number and gender with a preceding direct   object noun or pronoun.

EXAMPLES:

J'étais déjà sorti quand tu as téléphoné.
I had already left when you (familiar) called.

Il avait déjà commencé son travail quand son directeur a téléphoné.
He had already started his work when his manager telephoned.

Elle n'avait pas encore fini ses devoirs quand sa mère l'a appelée.
She hadn't finished her homework yet when her mother called her.

Quand je me suis réveillée, Sarah était déjà partie travailler.
When I woke up, Sarah had already left for work.

À notre arrivée, elle était déjà partie en vacances en Normandie.
When we arrived, she had already gone on vacation to Normandy.

- **arrivée** (f) means 'arrival'
- **à notre arrivée** means 'upon our arrival' (and likewise for the other possessive pronouns)

Le réveil a sonné et Valérie n'avait pas fermé l'œil.
The alarm clock rang and Valérie hadn't slept a bit.

- **ne pas fermer l'œil** (verb) means 'to not sleep a wink'

TOPIC 157 ❖ The pluperfect - *Le plus-que-parfait*

J'avais mal à l'estomac parce que j'avais mangé quelque chose de mauvais.
I had a stomachache because I had eaten something bad.

📖 **avoir mal à l'estomac** (verb) means 'to have a stomach ache'

Il marchait avec peine parce qu'il était tombé.
He walked with difficulty because he had fallen.

📖 **avec peine** (adj) means 'with difficulty'

Ce n'est pas la peine. Nous avions déjà pensé à cela.
Don't worry. We had already thought of that.

📖 **ce n'est pas la peine** means 'it is not worth the trouble' or literally 'it is not the pain**penalty**trouble'

Il n'avait pas mangé avant de faire ses devoirs.
He hadn't eaten before doing his homework.

Elles ont fait du shopping ce matin. Mais il s'est avéré que je l'avais déjà fait hier.
They (females) did the shopping this morning. But I had already done it yesterday.

Annabel a appris à aimer le chat qui l'avait mordue.
Annabel learned to love the cat that bit her.

📖 **apprendre à** (verb) means 'to learn to (do something)'

Nous avions voulu vous parler, mais il s'est avéré que nous n'avions pas le temps.
We had wanted to talk to you (formal) but it turned out that we didn't have time.

Elle ne s'était pas bien préparée avant de donner sa présentation.
She had not prepared well before giving her presentation.

Cette robe ? Elle l'avait achetée quand elle était à Paris.
This dress? She had bought it when she was in Paris.

Si seulement nous avions gagné le prix !
If only we had won the prize!

💡 Past wish or regret

Si seulement j'avais eu assez d'argent !
If only I had had enough money!

💡 Past wish or regret

❖ *Concordance des temps - le passé composé*

Sentences that have two conjugated verbs are said to have two clauses. Often the clauses are separated with words like **que**, **quand** etc.

- For example **J'ai dit qu'elle lisait** where **j'ai dit** is the main clause and **elle lisait** is the subordinate clause.
- Each clause has a conjugated verb - in this case **dire** ('to say') in **le passé composé** and **lire** ('to read') in **l'imparfait**.

When the first (main) clause is in **le passé composé** there are rules as to the tense of the second (subordinate) clause.

- If the verb in the two clauses happen **simultaneously** then the second clause should be in **'l'imparfait**.
- If the second verb happens **before** the first then the second clause should be in **le plus-que-parfait**.
- If the second verb happens **after** the first then the second clause should be in **le futur proche dans le passé**.

In French these rules are called **La Concordance des Temps**.

EXAMPLES:

J'ai dit qu'elle lisait.
I said she was reading.
💡 Simultaneous so **le passé composé** & **l'imparfiat**

J'ai dit qu'elle avait lu.
I said she had read.
💡 Before so **le passé composé** & **le plus-que-parfait**

J'ai dit qu'elle allait lire.
I said she was going to read.
💡 After so **le passé composé** & **le futur proche dans le passé**

Il dort ? Oui, j'ai dit qu'il dormait.
Is he sleeping? Yes, I said he was sleeping.
💡 Simultaneous so **le passé composé** & **l'imparfiat**

Il a dormi ? Oui, j'ai dit qu'il avait dormi.
Did he sleep? Yes, I said he had slept.
💡 Before so **le passé composé** & **le plus-que-parfait**

TOPIC 158 ❖ *Concordance des temps - le passé composé*

Il va dormir ? Oui, j'ai dit qu'il allait dormir.
Is he going to sleep? Yes, I said he was going to sleep.
💡 After so **le passé composé** & **le futur proche dans le passé**

Il m'a dit : « Nous avons raison. »
He said to me: 'We are right.'
💡 Not two clauses so **concordance** not required

Il m'a dit que nous avions raison.
He told me we were right.
💡 Simultaneous so **le passé composé** & **l'imparfiat**

Il m'a dit que tu étais chocolatier.
He told me you (familiar) were a chocolatier.
💡 Simultaneous so **le passé composé** & **l'imparfiat**

J'ai entendu dire que tu faisais du chocolat comme passe-temps.
I heard you (familiar) made chocolate as a hobby.
💡 Simultaneous so **le passé composé** & **l'imparfiat**

J'ai vu que tu avais fait ce chocolat.
I saw you (familiar) made that chocolate.
💡 After so **le passé composé** & **le futur proche dans le passé**

J'ai vu que tu mangeais le chocolat toute la journée.
I saw that you (familiar) were eating the chocolate all day.
💡 Simultaneous so **le passé composé** & **l'imparfiat**

J'ai entendu dire que tu allais faire plus de chocolat.
I heard you (familiar) were going to make more chocolate.
💡 After so **le passé composé** & **le futur proche dans le passé**

Ce matin, j'ai regardé comment Victor préparait le poulet.
This morning I watched how Victor was preparing the chicken.
💡 Simultaneous so **le passé composé** & **l'imparfiat**

Elle m'a dit qu'elle était en train de partir.
She told me she is leaving.
💡 Simultaneous so **le passé composé** & **l'imparfiat**

Je me suis souvenue que vous l'aviez acheté à Rome.
I (female) remembered that you had bought it in Rome.
💡 Before so **le passé composé** & **le plus-que-parfait**

TOPIC 158 ❖ *Concordance des temps - le passé composé*

Il m'a expliqué qu'ils déménageaient.
He explained to me that they were moving.
💡 Simultaneous so **le passé composé** & **l'imparfiat**

Il a annoncé qu'il n'allait pas venir à la réunion.
He announced that he was not going to come to the meeting.
💡 After so **le passé composé** & **le futur proche dans le passé**

C'était toi qui m'as dit qu'elle avait l'air fatiguée ?
Was it you (familiar) who told me she looked tired?
💡 Simultaneous so **le passé composé** & **l'imparfiat**

Elle a cru que vous aviez menti.
She believed that you (formal) had lied.
💡 Before so **le passé composé** & **le plus-que-parfait**

Pourquoi as-tu promis que tu allais lui donner ta veste ?
Why did you (familiar) promise that you were going to give him your jacket?
💡 After so **le passé composé** & **le futur proche dans le passé**

L'histoire que j'ai entendu lire était bizarre.
The story I heard being read was bizarre.
💡 Simultaneous so **le passé composé** & **l'imparfiat**

❖ Present participles as adverbal gerunds

We previously saw present participles used at adjectives. Present participles can also be used to form gerunds which can be used modify verbs just like adverbs.

- The idea is that we can modify 'doing this' by adding '(while or by) doing something else'. Here '(while or by) doing something else' modifies 'doing this' in much the same way that an adverb modifies a verb.

In French the (adverbal) gerund is formed by combining the preposition **en** with a verb's present participle.

The gerund can be used to modify the main verb in two ways:

- 'While' or 'upon' - to indicate that something is happening ('while') or happened ('upon') at the same time or immediately before.
- 'By' or 'because' - to indicate why or how something happens.

To emphasize the simultaneity, or to contrast the two actions, we can add the adverb **tout** in front of the gerundive clause.

EXAMPLES:

En rentrant, j'ai rencontré Paul.
While on my way home I met Paul.
💡 **en rentrant** - 'while on the way home' (simultaneous action)

En prenant le métro, il lisait le journal.
While taking the subway, he read the newspaper.
💡 **en prenant** - 'while taking' (simultaneous action)

En écoutant leur prof, les élèves ont compris.
By listening to their teacher, the students understood.
💡 **en écoutant** - 'while listening' (simultaneous action)

En entrant dans l'abri de jardin, j'ai vu une énorme araignée noire.
Upon entering the garden shed I saw a huge black spider.
💡 **en entrant** - 'upon entering' (simultaneous action)

Il pleurait en racontant l'histoire.
He wept as he told the story.
💡 **en racontant** - 'while telling' (simultaneous action)

TOPIC 159 ❖ Present participles as adverbal gerunds

Il parlait en mangeant sa glace.
He was talking while eating is ice cream.
- **en mangeant** - 'while eating' (simultaneous action)

Il est tombé en dansant.
He fell while dancing.
- **en racontant** - 'while telling' (simultaneous action)

Elle pleure tout en souriant.
She cries even while smiling.
- **en souriant** - 'while smiling' (simultaneous action)
- **tout** added for emphasis

Il s'est coupé avec le couteau en cuisinant.
He cut himself with the knife while cooking.
- **en cuisinant** - 'while cooking' (simultaneous action)

Il gagne beaucoup en travaillant dur.
He earns a lot by working hard.
- **en travaillant** - 'by working' (means)

Il commence le spectacle en chantant.
He starts the show by singing.
- **en chantant** - 'by singing' (means)

Elle est arrivée en courant.
She came (by) running.
- **en courant** - 'by running' (means)

En me réveillant à 6h, j'ai fini avant midi.
By waking up at 6 a.m., I finished before noon.
- **en se réveillant** - 'by waking up' (means)

C'est en pratiquant régulièrement que vous le faites bien.
It is by practicing regularly that you (formal) do it well.
- **en pratiquant** - 'by practicing' (means)
- note the use of 'c'est' - the gerund is in fact a noun

En m'habillant vite, je gagne 10 minutes chaque matin.
By getting dressed quickly, I save 10 minutes every morning.
- **en s'habillant** - 'by get dressed' (means)

En vous levant tôt, vous ne serez jamais en retard.
By getting up early you (formal) will never be late.
- **en se levant** - 'by getting up' (means)

TOPIC 159 ❖ Present participles as adverbal gerunds

Tout en écoutant le professeur, je faisais mes devoirs.
All while listening to the teacher, I was doing my homework.
- 💡 **en écoutant** - 'while listening' (simultaneous action)

Tout en faisant un régime, je n'ai pas perdu de poids.
Even while dieting, I did not lose weight.
- 💡 **en faisant** - 'by doing' (means)
- 💡 **tout** added for emphasis

❖ Present participles of *avoir*, *être* and *savoir*

There are three **irregular present participles** that are very widely used and should be memorized.

The three irregular gerunds are:

- avoir ⇒ **ayant**
- être ⇒ **étant**
- savoir ⇒ **sachant**

The gerunds **ayant** and **étant** can also be used as auxiliary verbs when formulating complex gerunds especially from the **passé composé**.

EXAMPLES:

Ayant fini, je suis partie.
Having finished, I (female) left.

Je le crois maintenant, ayant entendu sa version de l'histoire.
I (male) believe him now, having heard his version of the story.

Sachant le danger, je n'y suis pas allé.
Knowing the danger, I (male) did not go there.

Ayant faim, il a mangé tout le gâteau.
Being hungry, he ate all the cake.

Ayant fini mon travail, je me suis détendue.
Having finished my work, I relaxed.

se détendre (verb) means 'to relax' or 'to come loose'

Sachant ce que nous savons, nous ne sommes pas allés plus loin.
Knowing what we know, we went no further.

Les abréviations présentent l'avantage de ne pas toujours avoir besoin de prononcer un long mot tout en sachant de quoi il s'agit.
Abbreviations have the advantage of not always having to pronounce a long word while knowing what it is.

Ayant déjà mangé, nous n'avons rien commandé.
Having already eaten, we didn't order anything.

TOPIC 160 ❖ Present participles of *avoir*, *être* and *savoir*

Étant parti de bonne heure, il est arrivé à l'heure.
Having left early, he arrived on time.

En étant motivé, on peut apprendre le français en quelques mois.
By being motivated, one can learn French in a few months.

Ayant bien observé, Jacques est maintenant capable de faire le travail lui-même.
Having observed well, Jacques is now able to do the work himself.

Ayant dit ce que je viens de dire, moi-même, je n'irai jamais seul.
Having said what I have just said, myself, I will never go alone.

Sachant qui sera là, nous avons décidé de ne pas y aller.
Knowing who will be there, we decided not to go.

Ayant parlé au voisin, ils ont déménagé en Dordogne il y a deux mois.
Having spoken to the neighbor, they moved to the Dordogne two month ago.

Étant allées à la piscine hier, les filles n'ont pas envie d'y retourner aujourd'hui.
Having gone to the pool yesterday, the girls don't want to go back today.

Ayant trop bu, je ne pouvais pas conduire.
Having drunk too much, I could not drive.

Elle est partie, oubliant ses clefs.
She left, forgetting her keys.

Nous étant levés de bonne heure, nous avons profité du temps libre.
(We) having gotten up early, we took advantage of the free time.

❖ Present participles as adjectives - modifying a noun

In addition to present participles modifying verbs like adverbs, present participles in French can also modify nouns, like adjectives.

In this mode the present participle effectively replaces the relative clause that begins with **que** ('that') or **qui** ('who').

EXAMPLES:

Je vois des gens portant des sacs.
I see people carrying bags.

Les chiens aboyant doivent rester dehors.
Barking dogs should stay outside.

Les étudiants venant de l'Afrique peuvent s'inscrire ici.
Students from Africa can register here.

Il y a une pénurie de médecins parlant français.
There is a shortage of French-speaking doctors.

Les membres voulant partir peuvent sortir par la porte arrière.
Members wishing to leave may exit through the back door.

Les voyageurs venant de l'Europe n'ont pas besoin de visa.
Travelers from Europe do not need a visa.

Dans les jours suivants, ils ont réussi à méditer tous les jours.
In the following days, they managed to meditate every day.

Une étudiante portant un chemisier jaune cherche le professeur.
A female student wearing a yellow blouse is searching for the professor.

Nos nouvelles passionnantes seront révélées ce soir.
Our exciting news will be revealed tonight.

La femme dansante, c'est la sœur de mon ami Jacques.
The dancing woman, she is the sister of my friend Jacques.

The days of the week - *Quel jour est-ce ?*

Talking about days of the week in French has some nuances.
- Asking about the day of the week we can say 'Which day are we?' - **Quel jour sommes-nous ?**
- To say 'on' a particular day no preposition is needed.
- NOT **sur samedi**, NOT **en samedi**, NOT **à samedi**, NOT **au samedi** - just **samedi**.
- To say 'every' some-day-of-the-week, we add the definite article.
- All the days of the week are masculine.
- The days of the week are not capitalized in French.
- The French week starts on Monday.
- **les jours de la semaine** means 'the days of the week' - all seven days.
- **les jours de semaine** means 'weekdays' - Monday to Friday.
- **en semaine** also means 'during the (work) week'
- **le week-end** means 'the week-end'. With the article **le** it means 'every weekend'.

EXAMPLES:

Quel jour est-ce ? C'est lundi.
What day is it? It's Monday.

Quel jour sommes-nous ? Nous sommes mardi.
What day is it? It is Tuesday.

Quel jour est-on aujourd'hui ? aujourd'hui, on est mercredi.
What day is it today? Today is Wednesday.

Tu arrives quel jour ?
What day are you (familiar) arriving?
💡 NOT 'à quel jour'

J'arrive jeudi.
I arrive on Thursday.
💡 NOT 'à jeudi' NOR 'au jeudi'

La réunion est vendredi.
The meeting is Friday.

TOPIC 162 ❖ The days of the week - *Quel jour est-ce ?*

Quels jours de la semaine travaillez-vous ?
What days of the week do you (formal) work?

Je ne travaille pas mercredi.
I don't work this Wednesday.
💡 NOT 'ce lundi'

Normalement, je ne travaille pas le mercredi.
Normally I don't work on Wednesdays.
✎ With the article **le** it means 'every Wednesday'

Je déteste le lundi.
I hate Mondays.

Le vendredi est mon jour de la semaine préféré.
Fridays are my favorite day of the week.

Nous mangeons des bagels au petit-déjeuner le samedi.
We eat bagels for breakfast on Saturdays.

Nous mangeons des bagels au petit-déjeuner tous les samedis.
We eat bagels for breakfast every Saturday.
💡 Using 'tous les' rather than just 'le' for emphasis

Vous entraînez-vous tous les jours de la semaine ?
Do you (formal) train every day of the week?

La boulangerie est ouverte tous les jours de la semaine sauf le dimanche.
The bakery is open every day of the week except Sundays.

On cuisine uniquement en semaine - le week-end, nous mangeons à l'extérieur.
We only cook on weekdays - on weekends we ate out.

Ce week-end, nous sommes allés à la plage.
This weekend we went to the beach.

Le week-end, nous nous reposons à la maison.
On weekends we rest at home.

Noël tombe quel jour cette année ?
On what day does Christmas fall this year?

Bootstrap French
TOPIC 163

❖ Telling the time - *Quelle heure est-il ?*

Telling the time in French uses the impersonal **il** with the verb **etre**.

When talking about the time of day we use **l'heure** ('hour'), not **le temps** - **le temps** refers to periods or durations of time.

The word **heure** is feminine so we use **quelle** when asking the time.

In French you always have to say **heure** when telling the time, except when saying **midi** ('noon') and **minuit** ('midnight').

While it is usual to tell the time by saying **X heures et Y (minutes)** we also have:

- **et le quart** for 'quarter past'
- **et demie** for 'half past'
- **moins le quart** for 'quarter to'

The French, like most Europeans, use the 24 hour clock. So 3 p.m. is 15h and 2:15 a.m. is 2h15.

Note that you should avoid using **demie**, **le quart** and **moins le quart** when using the 24 hour clock.

It is not uncommon to use the 12 hour clock and **du matin** for a.m. and **de l'après-midi** or **du soir** for p.m.

EXAMPLES:

Quelle heure est-il ?
What time is it?
  💡 Literally 'which hour is it?'

Il est une heure.
It is one o'clock.

Il est deux heures.
It is two o'clock.

Il est trois heures et quart.
It is a quarter past three.

Il est quatre heures et demie.
It is four thirty.
  ✏ **demi** (adj) means 'half'
  💡 The feminine **demie** is used because **l'heure** is feminine

TOPIC 163 ❖ Telling the time - *Quelle heure est-il ?*

Il est cinq heures moins le quart.
It is quarter to five.

👁 **quart** (m) means 'quarter'

Il est quatre heures quarante-cinq.
It is four forty-five.

Il est cinq heures dix.
It is ten past five.

Il est sept heures moins dix.
It is ten to seven.

Il est six heures cinquante.
It is six fifty.

Il est sept heures vingt.
It is seven twenty.

Il est neuf heures moins vingt.
It is twenty to nine.

Il est huit heures quarante.
It is eight forty.

Il est huit heures du matin.
It is eight in the morning (8 a.m.).

👁 **matin** is masculine so **du**

Il est cinq heures de l'après-midi.
It is five in the afternoon (5 p.m.).

👁 the gender of **après-midi** is undefined but **de l'** because it begins with a vowel

Il est dix-sept heures.
It is seventeen hours (17h).

Il est huit heures du soir.
It is eight in the evening (8 p.m.).

Il est vingt heures.
It is twenty hours (8 p.m.).

Il est midi.
It is noon.

TOPIC 163 ❖ Telling the time - *Quelle heure est-il ?*

Il est minuit.
It is midnight.

Avez-vous le temps ?
Do you (formal) have the time?
💡 Asking someone the time.

Est-ce que vous avez l'heure, s'il vous plaît ?
Do you (formal) have the time, please?

À quelle heure est le concert ?
What time is the concert?

Le concert est à huit heures du soir.
The concert is at eight o'clock in the evening.

À quelle heure a lieu la réunion ?
What time does the meeting take place?

À quelle heure vous êtes-vous réveillé ?
What time did you (formal) wake up?

Quelle heure était-il quand nous avons mangé ?
What time was it when we ate?

Cinq heures et demie, c'est trop tôt pour le dîner.
Five thirty is too early for dinner.

Le train arrive vers 21h.
The train arrives around 9 p.m.
✏️ **vers** means 'about' or 'towards'

Bootstrap French
TOPIC 164

❖ For how long? - durations with *pendant*, *depuis* & *pour*

Firstly we can use **combien de temps?** to ask about durations of time - 'how long?' or 'how much time?'

To answer this question the prepositions **depuis**, **pendant** and **pour** can be used to specify the duration of an event.

- Use **pendent** ('during') to talk about durations that started in the past. The event may either have ended or be ongoing.
- Use **depuis** ('since') in a context that emphasizes a duration that continues up to the present.
- **depuis** can also be used to talk about actions in the past that were interrupted.
- And **depuis** can also be used to talk about a duration since a particular date to the present.
- Use **pour** ('for') to talk about durations in the future with a concrete start and end.
- Note that **pendant** can also be used in place of **pour** in these situations.

EXAMPLES:

Pendant combien de temps avez-vous vécu à Paris ?
How long did you (formal) live in Paris?
- completed in the past so **pendant**
- **combien de temps** means 'how long' or 'how much time'
- **vécu** is the past participle of **vivre**
- **vivre** (verb) means 'to live'

J'ai vécu à Paris pendant dix ans.
I lived in Paris for ten years.
- completed in the past so **pendant**

Pendant combien de temps avez-vous étudié le français ?
How long have you (formal) studied French?
- completed in the past so **pendant**

J'ai étudié le français pendant trois ans.
I studied French for three years.
- completed in the past so **pendant**

French Grammar

TOPIC 164 ❖ For how long? - durations with *pendant*, *depuis* & *pour*

J'ai joué au foot pendant trois heures aujourd'hui.
I played soccer for three hours today.
- 💡 completed in the past so **pendant**

Je joue au foot pendant trois heures tous les mercredis.
I play football for three hours every Wednesday.
- 💡 ongoing so **pendant**

La classe a été suspendue pendant un an.
The class was suspended for a year.
- 💡 ongoing so **pendant**
- 💡 Assumes that the suspension will continue into the future.

Depuis combien de temps vivez-vous à Bordeaux ?
How long have you (formal) lived in Bordeaux?
- 💡 up to the present so **depuis**

Je vis à Bordeaux depuis dix ans.
I have lived in Bordeaux for ten years.
- 💡 up to the present so **depuis**

Mon enfant joue du piano depuis cinq mois.
My child has been playing the piano for five months.
- 💡 up to the present so **depuis**

Leur fille et mon fils se fréquentent depuis trois ans.
Their daughter and I have been dating for three years.
- 💡 up to the present so **depuis**
- 📖 **se fréquenter** means 'to date' or 'to go out together'

Depuis quand étudiez-vous le français ?
Since when do you (formal) study French?
- 💡 **depuis** for a duration from a particular date to the present

J'étudie le français depuis 2020.
I have been studying French since 2020.
- 💡 **depuis** for a duration from a particular date to the present

Ça veut dire que j'étudie le français depuis trois ans.
That means I've been studying French for three years.
- 💡 up to the present so **depuis**

TOPIC 164 ❖ For how long? - durations with *pendant*, *depuis* & *pour*

Depuis combien de temps dormais-tu quand je suis arrivé ?
How long had you (familiar) been asleep when I arrived?

💡 **depuis** for an interupted action in the past

Il vivait en France depuis deux ans quand je l'ai vu.
He had been living in France for two years when I saw him.

💡 **depuis** for an interupted action in the past

Elle dormait depuis trois heures quand le chien a aboyé.
She had been sleeping for three hours when the dog barked.

💡 **depuis** for an interupted action in the past

Pendant combien de temps allez-vous vivre à Lille ?
How long are you (formal) going to live in Lille?

💡 ongoing with start in the future so **pendant**

Je vais vivre à Lille pendant dix ans.
I am going to live in Lille for ten years.

💡 ongoing with start in the future so **pendant**

Je vais y habiter pour seulement deux mois.
I will live there for only two months.

💡 start and end in the future so **pour**

Il va me rendre visite pour dix jours.
He is going to visit me for ten days.

💡 start and end in the future so **pour**

On dit qu'il va pleuvoir pendant deux semaines.
They say it will rain for two weeks.

💡 start and end in the future so with **pendant** used in place of **pour**

Bootstrap French
TOPIC 165

❖ How long does it take?

In the previous topic we used **combien de temps** to ask about durations of time. This expression can be augmented with several verbs.

- **prendre** ('to take') - for example **ça prend combien de temps ?**
- **mettre** ('to put') - for example **vous mettez combien de temps ?**
- **mettre à** + is used to say 'to take (time) to do (something)'.
- **il faut** ('it is necessary') is also used - for example **combien de temps faut-il ?**
- **il faut** can also be used with the verbs **prendre** and **mettre**.
- **il faut** can also be used with the verb **compter** ('to count') in which case the sense is 'to have to allow' or 'to have to reckon on' a period of time.
- **durer** ('to last') can also be used to state duration - for example **ça dur combien de temps ?**

EXAMPLES:

Ça prend combien de temps ?
How long does it take?

Ça prend deux heures pour aller de Madrid à Paris en avion.
It takes two hours to go from Madrid to Paris by plane.

Combien de temps cela prend-il ?
How long does that take?

Il a pris combien de temps pour lire ce livre ?
How long did it take him to read this book?

Il a pris une semaine pour le finir.
It took a week to finish it.

Combien de temps faut-il prendre pour y aller à pied ?
How long does it take to walk there?

Il nous a fallu trois heures et demie pour aller de Marseille à Paris en TGV.
It took us three and a half hours to go from Marseille to Paris by TGV.

Combien de temps avez-vous pris pour remplir le questionnaire ?
How long did you (formal) take to complete the questionnaire?

TOPIC 165 ❖ How long does it take?

J'ai mis trente minutes à le faire.
It took me thirty minutes to do it.
 mettre à le faire - 'to take time do it'

Combien de temps mettez-vous pour aller au travail en métro ?
How long do you (formal) take to get to work by metro?

Habituellement, je mets vingt minutes pour aller travailler en métro.
Usually, I take twenty minutes to go to work by metro.

Et il vous faut combien de temps pour y aller en bus ?
And how long does it take you (formal) to get there by bus?

En bus, il faut compter au moins cinquante minutes.
By bus it takes at least fifty minutes.

Il faut compter environ treize heures.
One has to allow about thirteen hours.

Il faut compter environ deux heures pour y aller.
It takes about two hours to get there.

Combien de temps dure la sauvegarde des données ?
How long does data backup take?

Quel est le temps nécessaire à la préparation du rapport ?
How long does it take to prepare the report?

Combien de temps vous a-t-il fallu pour être certifié ?
How long did it take you (formal) to get certified?

Il y a mis le temps !
He took his sweet time!
 A colloquialism

Bootstrap French
TOPIC 166

❖ Time ago - *il y a*

To say 'ago' in French, we use the expression **il y a** followed by the time duration. This should not be confused with using the same **il y a** to mean 'there is'.

EXAMPLES:

J'ai mangé il y a une heure.
I ate an hour ago.

Elle est venue à Avignon il y a trois ans.
She came to Avignon three years ago.

Ils sont arrivés chez nous il y a presque une semaine.
They arrived at our house almost one week ago.

La bataille de Waterloo a eu lieu il y a plus de deux cents ans.
The Battle of Waterloo took place more than two hundred years ago.

J'y suis allée il y a sept ans.
I (female) went there seven years ago.

Il a vécu en France il y a vingt ans.
He lived in France twenty years ago.

Vous êtes venus la deuxième fois il y a trois mois.
You (formal) came the second time three months ago.

Elle a commencé ses études en langues étrangères il y a dix ans.
She began her studies in foreign languages ten years ago.

How long since? - *ça fait combien de temps?*

To talk about how long since some event or since something happened we can use **ça fait...**.

- When a noun follows the question is **ça fait combien de temps depuis...** .
- When a clause follows the question is **ça fait combien de temps que...** .

To answer we can repeat **ça fait** + .

- It is also common to reply using **voilà** + .
- Or, as we saw previously, **il y a** + .

Of course we could ask the question 'since when?' by using **depuis quand..?** but **ça fait combien de temps** is asking explicitly for a duration.

EXAMPLES:

Ça fait combien de temps depuis votre dernier rendez-vous ?
How long has it been since your (formal) last meeting?

💡 **votre dernier rendez-vous** is an noun so we use **depuis**

Ça fait combien de temps que vous souffrez ?
How long has you (formal) been suffering?

💡 **vous souffrez** is a verbal clause so we use **que**

Ça fait une semaine que je souffre.
I've been suffering for a week.

Ça fait très longtemps que je ne t'ai pas vu.
It's been a long time since I saw you (familiar).

💡 Note the negative construction

Oui, voilà deux ans que je ne t'ai pas vu.
Yes, it has been two years that I haven't seen you (familiar).

Ça ne fait pas très longtemps depuis la dernière pluie.
It has not been long since the last rain.

Ça fait très longtemps que nous avons fini l'école.
It's been a long time since we have finished school.

TOPIC 167 ❖ How long since? - *ça fait combien de temps?*

Vingt-quatre ans, ça fait un bail !
Twenty-four years old, it's been ages!

📖 **ça fait un bail** means ' it has been ages' - literally 'it has been a lease'
📖 **bail** (m) means 'lease'

Ça fait un bail que je suis venue te voir.
It's been ages that I came to see you (familiar).

Ça fait combien de temps que vous portez des lunettes ?
How long since you (formal) (started) wearing glasses?

Depuis quand avez-vous commencé à porter des lunettes ?
Since when did you (formal) start wearing glasses?

❖ Dates

To state a date we use the definite article **le** + + .

But when we include a day of the week we drop the **le** and say + + .

- Recall that adding **le** to a day of the week means 'every' that day.

When we state the date without the number of the day (just the month and/or year) we begin with **en**.

We can say **le premier** for the first day of the month but NOT **le deuxième** or **le troisième** etc.

- **Le premier** is frequently abbreviated as **1er**.

Note that in French years are usually referred to by stating the complete number.

- So 2021 is **deux-mille-vingt-et-un** and NOT **vingt vingt-et-un**.

When we talk about 'in' or 'during' a month or year we use **en**. We NEVER use **dans**.

EXAMPLES:

Quelle date est-ce aujourd'hui ?
What date is it today?

C'est le vingt-sept janvier aujourd'hui.
Today is the twenty-seventh of January.
   The definite article **le** before the number

C'est mardi vingt-sept janvier aujourd'hui.
It's Tuesday January twenty-seventh today.
   drop the **le** when the day of week is included

C'est le dix-huit.
It's the eighteenth.

On est le combien aujourd'hui ?
What date is it today?
   le combien - another common way to ask the date
   from the antiquated word **combientième which** means 'which (ordinal) number'

C'est le premier février.
It's the first of February.
   Also written **C'est le 1er février.**

TOPIC 168 ❖ Dates

On était le combien hier ?
How many were we yesterday?

Hier était le 31 juin.
Yesterday was June 31.

Ton anniversaire est le combien ?
How much is your (familiar) birthday?

Quelle est la date de ton anniversaire ?
What is the date of your (familiar) birthday?

Mon anniversaire est le 11.
My birthday is the 11th.

Nous avons acheté notre voiture le 2 avril 2020.
We bought our car on April 2, 2020.

J'ai un rendez-vous chez le dentiste le 3 octobre.
I have a dentist appointment on October 3rd.

Le 1er mai est un jour férié.
May 1 is a public holiday.

📖 **jour férié** (m) means 'public holiday'

J'ai un rendez-vous chez le médecin en mars.
I have a doctor's appointment in March.

Quel mois est-ce ?
What month is it?

En quel mois est Pâques ?
What month is Easter?

📖 **Pâques** (m) means 'Easter'

Pâques est en mars cette année.
Easter is in March this year.

L'année dernière, Pâques était en avril.
Last year Easter was in April.

En quelle année sommes-nous ?
What year is it?

En quelle année vous ont-ils rencontrés ?
In what year did you (formal) meet them?

TOPIC 168 ❖ Dates

En 2025, je vais aller en Nouvelle_Zélande.
In 2025, I will go to New Zealand.

En quelle année la Seconde Guerre mondiale a-t-elle commencé ?
In what year did World War Il begin?

En quel mois les Russes ont-ils fêté la révolution ?
In which month did the Russians celebrate the revolution?

Ma fille est née en décembre.
My daughter was born in December.

Cette année, en janvier, il y a deux pleines lunes.
This year during January there are two full moons.

❖ Intervals of time - *du..au* & *de..à*

To state an interval between two times or date dates is straight forward:
- When there is no **le** present in stating the time or date, then we use **de** and **à**.
- And if the time or date requires an **le** then we use **du** and **au**.

We can also use **entre** ('between') two times or dates with **le** included if required.

EXAMPLES:

Cette semaine, la boucherie est ouverte de lundi à jeudi uniquement.
This week the butcher is open from Monday to Thursday only.
- 💡 Only this week, so **le** not required
- ✏ **uniquement** means 'only' or 'one off'

Habituellement, il est ouvert du lundi au samedi.
Usually it is open from Monday to Saturday.
- 💡 Every week so **le** required
- ✏ **habituellement** means 'usually' or 'normally'

Le boxeur s'entraîne du lundi au samedi, toute l'année.
The boxer trains from Monday to Saturday, all year round.
- 💡 Every week so **le** required so use **du..au**

Cette année, le festival durait du 21 juillet au 3 août.
This year, the festival lasted from July 21 to August 3.
- 💡 Dates only always take **le** so use **du..au**

Je suis restée là de huit heures et demie à onze heures moins le quart.
I stayed there from half past eight until a quarter to eleven.
- 💡 Time does not require an article so we use **de..à**

Tous les jours, je travaille de neuf heures à dix-huit heures.
Every day I work from nine o'clock to six o'clock.

Chaque soir, elle regarde la télé de dix-neuf heures trente à vingt-et-une heure.
Every evening, she watches TV from 7:30 to 9:00 p.m.

Entre juin et septembre, il pleut beaucoup en Inde.
Between June and September, it rains a lot in India.

TOPIC 169 ❖ Intervals of time - *du..au* & *de..à*

Quels jours le coiffeur est-il ouvert ?
What days is the hairdresser open?

Le coiffeur est ouvert du lundi au jeudi.
The hairdresser is open Mondays to Thursdays.

💡 Every week so **le** required so use **du..au**

Le coiffeur est ouvert entre le lundi et le jeudi.
The hairdresser is open between Monday and Thursday.

Time with *dans* and *en*

- **dans** indicates a period of time until something WILL happen.
- **en** expresses the length of time something TAKES to be done.
- The question 'how long something takes' can be posed using **en combien de temps ?**

EXAMPLES:

Nous allons manger dans une heure.
We are going to eat in an hour.

Votre colis va arriver dans cinq jours ouvrés.
Your (formal) package will arrive in five working days.

Je vais finir dans 10 minutes.
I an going to finish in 10 minutes.

Je termine normalement en 10 minutes.
I normally finish in 10 minutes.
💡 OR 'Normally it takes me 10 minutes to finish.'

Nous avons mangé en 40 minutes.
We ate in 40 minutes.
💡 OR 'It took us 10 minutes to eat.'

Le pont a été construit en six mois.
The bridge was built in six months.

Tu as lu Guerre et Paix en combien de temps ?
How long did it take you (familiar) to read War and Peace?

Je ne sais pas en combien de temps le tout doit se faire.
I don't know how long it takes for it all to be done.

❖ *Matin* & *matinée*, *soir* & *soirée*, *jour* & *journée* and *an* & *année*

In French there are two words for 'morning', 'evening', 'day' and 'year' - a masculine form and a feminine form.

We use the masculine forms **matin**, **jour**, **soir** or **an** when counting or referring to them generically.

- We already saw the use of the masculine forms to count for durations of time.
- Additionally with an article **le matin**, **le jour** and **le soir** the masculine forms refer reoccurring or repetitive instances. Likewise with **tous les**.
- With adverbs of time like **hier soir** or **demain matin** we use the masculine form.

We use the feminine forms **matinée**, **journée**, **soirée** and **année** to refer one distinct instance or distinct duration.

- Note that **une année** is often used in place of **un an** probably because it is easier to say and hear.
- The feminine **-née** forms are sometimes used to emphasize long periods of time.

To say 'every' we use **tous les** with the masculine form. And to say the complete durations we use **toute la** with the feminine form.

Often the exact meaning has to be taken from context - especially the tense being used.

Having said all this, there are many set expressions that use these words that just need to be memorized.

EXAMPLES:

L'été dernier, j'ai passé trois jours en Italie.
Last summer I spent three days in Italy.
> Counting for durations

Je nage chaque matin.
I swim every morning.
> Counting or defining instances or durations

Nous avons passé tous les soirs à la terrasse du café.
We spent every evening at the café terrace.
> Counting or defining instances or durations

J'ai eu plein de cadeaux le jour de mon anniversaire.
I got lots of presents on my birthday.
> With **passé composé** (implying a one-off event), **le jour** means a 'the day of my birthday'

TOPIC 171 ❖ *Matin* & *matinée*, *soir* & *soirée*, *jour* & *journée* and *an* & *année*

Je me couche à onze heures le soir.
I go to bed at eleven o'clock at night.

> With **le present** (implying an on-going action) and the article **le soir** means 'every evening'

Je prends le train le matin.
I take the train in the morning.

> With **le present tense and the article le matin** means 'every morning'

Hier, nous avons passé toute la soirée à la terrasse du café.
Yesterday we spent the whole evening at the café terrace.

> A complete duration of a particular evening

Le soir, je bois un verre avec mes amies.
In the evening, I have a drink with my (female) friends.

> With **le present tense and the article le soir** means 'every evening'

La semaine dernière, j'ai passé une matinée à la bibliothèque.
Last week, I spent a morning at the library.

> With **passé composé**, **matinée** refers to the duration of a particular morning

J'ai étudié le passé-composé toute l'année.
I studied the past tense all year.

> With **passé composé**, **année** refers to the duration of a particular year

J'ai travaillé toute la matinée.
I worked all morning.

> With **passé composé**, **matinée** refers to the duration of a morning

Cette soirée s'est très bien passée.
This evening went very well.

> With **passé composé** and the allusion to **soirée** meaning 'evening party' it refers to a particular evening

Les chauves-souris dorment pendant la journée.
Bats sleep during the day.

> With **pendant**, **la journée** refers to a span of time

Pendant son année sabbatique, il a appris à jouer au piano.
During his sabbatical year, he learned to play the piano.

> With **pendant**, **son année** refers to a span of time

Le billet est valable pour une année.
The ticket is valid for one year.

> With **pour**, **une année** refers to a span of time

TOPIC 171 ❖ *Matin* & *matinée*, *soir* & *soirée*, *jour* & *journée* and *an* & *année*

Pendant la première journée, j'étais en formation.
During the first day, I was in training.
💡 With **pour**, **la journée** refers to a span of time

Tout était nouveau lors de la première journée de travail.
Everything was new on the first day of work.
💡 With **lors de**, **la journée** refers to a span of time

Tout est toujours nouveau le premier jour.
Everything is always new on the first day.
💡 With **le present** tense **le premier jour** refers generally to all first days.

Ils sont fiancés depuis quinze ans. Oui, quinze années - incroyable !
They have been engaged for fifteen years. Yes, fifteen years - unbelievable!
💡 **-née** form for emphasis

Bootstrap French
TOPIC 172

❖ **How old are you? - talking about age**

In French one 'has' an age - we use the verb **avoir**.
- We never drop the word **an(s)** when talking about age.
And when talking about age in the past we use **l'imparfait** of **avoir**.
Plus âgé is used to say 'older' and **moins âgé** to say 'younger'.

EXAMPLES:

Quel âge as-tu ?
How old are you (familiar)?

J'ai vingt-et-un an.
I am twenty-one years old.

Quel âge a-t-elle ?
How old is she?

Ma mère a quarante-six ans.
My mother is forty-six.

Vous me demandez quel âge j'ai ?
You (formal) ask me how old am I?

Oui, puis-je vous demander votre âge ?
Yes, can I ask your (formal) age?

> ○ **puis** is an archaic **je** conjugation of **pouvoir**. Nowdays it is only really used in the inversion when asking a question. It has the sense of 'may I'. One would NEVER say 'peux-je'

Savez-vous quel âge a Stéphanie ?
Do you (formal) know how old Stephanie is?

En 2005, il avait 13 ans.
In 2005, he was 13 years old.

Ma mère avait vingt-cinq ans quand je suis né.
My mother was twenty-five when I was born.

Vous devez avoir plus de 18 ans pour conduire une voiture.
You (formal) must be over 18 to drive a car.

TOPIC 172 ❖ How old are you? - talking about age

J'ai encore moins de 18 ans.
I'm still under 18.

Mon grand-père vient d'avoir 65 ans.
My grandfather just turned 65.

Combien de semaines ont les bébés ?
How many weeks old are the babies?

Ma mère est un peu plus âgée que mon père.
My mother is a little older than my father.

Je suis beaucoup plus jeune que ma sœur.
I am much younger than my sister.

Les enfants grandissent vite - quel âge ont-ils maintenant ?
The children are growing up fast - how old are they now?

🖋 **grandir** (verb) means 'to grow'

Malheureusement, nous vieillissons en même temps.
Unfortunately, we age at the same time.

🖋 **vieillir** (verb) means 'to age'

Bootstrap French TOPIC 173

❖ Le futur simple

Le futur simple is used to talk about future plans or intentions, as well as to make predictions.

Le futur simple is more formal then **le futur proche** and can refer to events more distant into the future.

The **le futur simple** has no auxiliary. It conjugates with regular endings which are attached to a verb root.

- The **je** ending is **-ai**
- The **tu** ending is **-as**
- The **il** & **elle** ending is **-a**
- The **nous** ending is **-ons**
- The **vous** ending is **-ez**
- The **ils** & **elles** ending is **-ont**

For regular **-ER** and **-IR** verbs the **futur simple** root is the infinitive.

For regular **-RE** verbs the **futur simple** root is formed by removing the final **-e** from the infinitive.

While the **futur simple** endings are regular, many common verbs have irregular **futur simple** root which must be memorized.

EXAMPLES:

je mangerai
I will eat
 manger is an -er verb so for je add -ai to the infinitive ⇒ je mangerai

tu finiras
you (familiar) will finish
 finir is an -ir verb so for tu add -as to the infinitive ⇒ tu finiras

il regardera
he will watch
 regarder is an -er verb so for il add -a to the infinitive ⇒ il regardera

nous vendrons
we will sell
 vendre is an -re verb so drop the final -e from the infinitive and for nous add -ons ⇒ nous vendrons

TOPIC 173 ❖ *Le futur simple*

vous boirez
you (formal) will drink
💡 **boire** is an **-re** verb so drop the final **-e** from the infinitive and for **vous** add **-ez** ⇒ **vous boirez**

ils partiront
they will leave
💡 **partir** is an **-ir** verb so for **ils** add **-ont** to the infinitive ⇒ **il partiront**

Vous ne finirez jamais en une journée.
You (formal) will never finish in a day.
💡 **finir** ⇒ **finir-** + **-ez** ⇒ **vous finirez**

Demain, je rangerai les dossiers.
Tomorrow I will put the files away.
💡 **ranger** ⇒ **rangerai-** + **-ai** ⇒ **je rangerai**

Ça prendra combien de temps ?
How long will it take?
💡 **prendre** ⇒ **prendr-** + **-a** ⇒ **il prendra**

Si on fait les courses à deux, on les finira plus vite.
If we go shopping together, we will finish them faster.
💡 **finir** ⇒ **finir-** + **-a** ⇒ **on finira**

Quand prenez-vous votre retraite ?
When will you (formal) retire?
💡 **prendre** ⇒ **prendr-** + **-ez** ⇒ **vous prendrez**

Pas de soucis, je conduirai le camion.
No worries, I'll drive the truck.
💡 **condiure** ⇒ **condiur-** + **-ai** ⇒ **je conduirai**

Rentrez-vous chez vous dans le noir ?
Do you (formal) come home in the dark?
💡 **rentre** ⇒ **rentr-** + **-ez** ⇒ **vous rentrez**

Il se couchera dès qu'il finira son travail.
He will go to bed as soon as he finishes his work.
💡 **se coucher** ⇒ **se coucher-** + **-a** ⇒ **il se couchera**

Je partirai en vacances quand il fera beau.
I will go on vacation when the weather is nice.
💡 **partirai** ⇒ **partir-** + **-ai** ⇒ **je partirai**

TOPIC 173 ❖ Le futur simple

Nous vendrons la maison avant d'aller à l'étranger.
We will sell the house before going abroad.
💡 vendre ⇒ vendr- + -ons ⇒ nous vendrons

Je réfléchirai si cela vaut la peine d'y aller.
I'll think about whether it's worth going.
💡 se réfléchira ⇒ se réfléchir- + -ai ⇒ je me réfléchirai

Perdront-ils le match ?
Will they lose the match?
💡 perdre => perdr- + -ont ⇒ ils perdront

Qui me dira ce qui s'est passé ?
Who will tell me what happened?
💡 dire ⇒ dir- + -a ⇒ il dira

Tu me manqueras probablement quand tu partiras.
I will probably miss you when you (familiar) leave.
💡 manquer ⇒ manquer- + -as ⇒ tu manqueras

Eh bien, tu ne me manqueras certainement pas.
Well, I certainly won't miss you (familiar).
💡 manquer ⇒ manquer- + -as ⇒ tu manqueras

M'attendras-tu ? Non, je ne t'attendrai pas.
Will you (familiar) wait for me? No, I won't wait for you.
💡 manquer ⇒ manquer- + -as ⇒ tu manqueras

La neige fondra en un ou deux jours.
The snow will melt in a day or two.
💡 fondre ⇒ fondr- + -a ⇒ elle fondra

Ils ne répondront à aucune de nos questions.
They won't answer any of our questions.
💡 répondre ⇒ répondr- + -ont ⇒ ils répondront

Je ne prétendrai jamais être un expert.
I will never claim to be an expert.
💡 prétendre ⇒ prétendr- + -ai ⇒ je prétendrai

❖ *Le futur simple - avoir* and *être*

Le futur simple verb root for the verb **avoir** is **aur-**.
And the root for **être** it is **ser-**.
The endings remain regular. So we have:
- **je** ⇒ **j'aurai** ('I will have') & **je serai** ('I will be')
- **tu** ⇒ **tu auras** ('you will have) & **tu seras** ('you will be')
- **il** & **elle** ⇒ **il aura** ('he will have) & **il sera** ('he will have)
- **nous** ⇒ **nous aurons** ('we will have) & **nous serons** ('we will have)
- **vous** ⇒ **vous aurez** ('you will have) & **vous serez** ('you will have)
- **ils** & **elle** ⇒ **ils auront** ('they will have) & **ils seront** ('they will have)

EXAMPLES:

Il y aura trop de personnes sur le bateau.
There will be too many people on the boat.
- avoir ⇒ au- + -a ⇒ il aura

J'aurai besoin de me faire opérer.
I will need to have an operation.
- avoir ⇒ au- + -ai ⇒ j'aurai
- opérer means 'to operate (medically)'

Je crois que les enfants seront très heureux.
I believe the children will be very happy.
- être ⇒ ser- + -ont ⇒ ils seront

Bientôt, tu auras un jeune chaton à soigner.
Soon you (familiar) will have a kitten to look after.
- avoir ⇒ au- + -as ⇒ tu auras
- chaton (f) means 'kitten'
- soigner (verb) means 'to look after' or 'to take care of' or 'to nurse'

La semaine prochaine, nous serons en vacances.
Next week we will be on vacation.
- être ⇒ ser- + -ons ⇒ nous serons

TOPIC 174 ❖ *Le futur simple - avoir and être*

Vous aurez sans doute soif après cette longue promenade.
You (formal) will no doubt be thirsty after this long walk.
💡 être ⇒ ser- + -ez ⇒ vous serez

Je serai plus prudent la prochaine fois.
I will be more careful next time.
💡 être ⇒ ser- + -ai ⇒ je serai

J'aurai dix-huit ans le mois prochain.
I will be eighteen next month.
💡 avoir ⇒ au- + -ai ⇒ j'aurai

Demain, à cette heure-ci, nous serons dans l'avion pour le Maroc.
Tomorrow, at this time, we will be on the plane for Morocco.
💡 être ⇒ ser- + -ons ⇒ nous serons

Quand vous serez libres, nous parlerons d'aller à la patinoire.
When you (formal) are free, we'll talk about going to the ice rink.
💡 être ⇒ ser- + -ez ⇒ vous serez
📖 patinoire (f) means 'ice rink'

Le mois prochain, auras-tu l'occasion de nous rencontrer ?
Next month, will you (familiar) have the opportunity to meet us?
💡 avoir ⇒ au- + -as ⇒ tu auras

Papa aura besoin de ton aide pour déplacer les meubles.
Dad will need your (familiar) help moving the furniture.
💡 avoir ⇒ au- + -a ⇒ il aura
📖 meuble (m) means 'piece of furniture'

Les candidats seront pressés de connaître leurs résultats.
Candidates will be eager to know their results.
💡 être ⇒ ser- + -ont ⇒ ils seront

Après mes études, je serai enfin indépendant.
After my studies I will finally be independent.
💡 être ⇒ ser- + -ai ⇒ je serai

Ta sœur aura ses cadeaux au plus tard demain.
Your (familiar) sister will have her presents by tomorrow at the latest.
💡 avoir ⇒ au- + -a ⇒ elle aura
📖 au plus tard means 'at the latest'

TOPIC 174 ❖ *Le futur simple - avoir* and *être*

Je te l'ai déjà dit : je serai toujours là pour toi !
I told you (familiar) before: I will always be there for you!

💡 être ⇒ ser- + -ai ⇒ je serai

Ne vous inquiétez pas, je m'occupe de tout et tout sera parfait.
Don't you (formal) worry, I'll take care of everything and everything will be perfect.

💡 être ⇒ ser- + -a ⇒ tout sera
✏ s'occuper de means 'to take care of' or 'to deal with'

N'apportez rien de chez vous, il y aura tout ce qu'il faut ici.
Do not bring (formal) anything from home, there will be everything (you) need here.

💡 avoir ⇒ au- + -a ⇒ il aura

Ils arriveront avant nous et seront déjà installés.
They will arrive before us and will already be installed.

💡 être ⇒ ser- + -ont ⇒ ils seront
✏ être installé means 'to be settled in' or 'to have moved in (to accomadation'

Quand tu seras installé près de Paris, nous dinerons ensemble souvent.
When you (familiar) are settled near Paris, we'll dine together often.

💡 être ⇒ ser- + -as ⇒ tu seras

Le passeport sera à votre disposition dès demain.
The passport will be available to you (formal) tomorrow.

💡 être ⇒ ser- + -a ⇒ il sera

Bootstrap French
TOPIC 175

❖ *Le futur simple* - other irregulars

There are many verbs with irregular **futur simple** roots.
Here are several of the more common ones:

- aller ⇒ ir-
- faire ⇒ fer-
- vouloir ⇒ voudr-
- voir ⇒ verr-
- savoir ⇒ saur-
- pouvoir ⇒ pourr-
- devoir ⇒ devr-
- pleuvoir ⇒ pleuvr-
- lever ⇒ lèver-
- envoyer ⇒ enverr-
- tenir ⇒ tiendr-
- venir ⇒ viendr-

EXAMPLES:

J'irai en ville cet après midi.
I will go to town this afternoon.
💡 aller ⇒ ir- + -ai ⇒ j'irai

L'année prochaine, nous irons en Italie.
Next year we will go to Italy.
💡 aller ⇒ ir- + -ons ⇒ nous irons

N'y iront elles pas ?
Won't they (females) go (there)?
💡 aller ⇒ ir- + -ont ⇒ elles iront

Qui fera le ménage avant leur arrivée ?
Who will do the cleaning before their arrival?
💡 faire ⇒ fer- + -a ⇒ qui fera

TOPIC 175 ❖ *Le futur simple* - other irregulars

Elles feront leurs devoirs demain.
They (females) will do their homework tomorrow.

💡 faire ⇒ fer- + -ont ⇒ elles feront

Il ne fera rien demain.
He won't do anything tomorrow.

💡 faire ⇒ fer- + -a ⇒ il fera

Savez-vous s'il voudra manger à son arrivée ?
Do you (formal) know if he will want to eat when he arrives?

💡 vouloir ⇒ voudr- + -a ⇒ il voudra

Nous ne verrons pas la lune car il y aura des nuages.
We will not see the moon because there will be clouds.

💡 voir ⇒ verr- + -ons ⇒ nous verrons

Sauront-ils ouvrir la porte sans la clé ?
Will they know how to open the door without the key?

💡 savoir ⇒ saur- + -ont ⇒ ils sauront

Nous pourrons venir chez toi.
We will be able to come to your (familiar) house.

💡 pouvoir ⇒ pourr- + -ons ⇒ nous pourrons

Tu auras vingt-six ans dans quatre jours. Tu ne pourras plus bénéficier des réductions pour les jeunes.
You (familiar) will be twenty-six in four days. You will no longer be able to benefit from the youth discounts.

💡 pouvoir ⇒ pourr- + -as ⇒ tu pourras

Ils devront entrer par la fenêtre.
They will have to enter through the window.

💡 devoir ⇒ devr- + -ont ⇒ ils devront

Vous devrez répondre par courrier recommandé avec accusé de réception.
You (formal) must respond by registered mail with acknowledgment of receipt.

💡 devoir ⇒ devr- + -ez ⇒ vous devrez

Ils disent qu'il pleuvra toute la semaine.
They say it will rain all week.

💡 pleuvoir ⇒ pleuvr- + -a ⇒ il pleuvra

TOPIC 175 ❖ *Le futur simple* - other irregulars

Je pense qu'il pleuvra demain.
I think it will rain tomorrow.
💡 pleuvoir ⇒ pleuvr- + -a ⇒ il pleuvra

Je lèverai le doigt pour te faire savoir si je veux un autre café.
I'll raise my finger to let you (familiar) know if I want another coffee.
💡 lever ⇒ lèver- + -ai ⇒ je lèverai

Il se lèvera dans quelques heures.
He will be up in a few hours.
💡 se lever ⇒ se lèver- + -a ⇒ il se lèvera

Elle ne t'enverra pas le paquet avant mercredi.
She won't send you (familiar) the package until Wednesday.
💡 envoyer ⇒ enverr- + -a ⇒ elle enverra

Nous tiendrons également compte de vos antécédents professionnels.
We will also consider your (formal) work history.
💡 tenir ⇒ tiendr- + -ons ⇒ nous tiendrons

Le vice-président tiendra une conférence de presse cet après-midi.
The vice-president will hold a press conference this afternoon.
💡 tenir ⇒ tiendr- + -a ⇒ il tiendra

J'espère qu'elle viendra demain.
I hope she comes tomorrow.
💡 venir ⇒ viendr- + -a ⇒ elle viendra

Les chiens reviendront-ils par eux-mêmes ?
Will the dogs come back by themselves?
💡 revenir ⇒ reviendr- + -ont ⇒ ils reviendront

Qui nettoiera sa chambre avant son arrivée ?
Who will clean their room before they arrive?
💡 nettoyer ⇒ nettoie- + -a ⇒ qui nettoiera

L'année prochaine, nous déménageons à la campagne.
Next year we are moving to the countryside.
💡 déménager => déménage- + -ons ⇒ nous déménageons

❖ *Si* with *le futur simple*

Using **si** ('if') to express some conditional future action is common.

The patterns is **le present> + si + le futur simple>**

- The condition clause (before the **si**) should NOT be in **le futur simple**.

The conditional clause can also be in **le passe compose** with the outcome remaining in **le futur simple**.

EXAMPLES:

Si j'ai soif, je boirai de l'eau.
If I'm thirsty, I will drink water.

S'ils peuvent, ils mangeront dans l'avion.
If they can, they will eat on the plane.

Si j'ai l'argent, j'achèterai la voiture.
If I have the money, I will buy the car.

S'il ne veut pas lire, il regardera la télé.
If he doesn't want to read, he will watch TV.

Je le ferai si j'ai le temps.
I will (do it) if I have time.

Si tu étudies, tu réussiras à l'examen.
If you (familiar) study, you will pass the exam.

Si vous me dites la vérité, je vous croirai.
If you (plural) tell me the truth, I'll believe you.

Il m'aidera si j'ai des problèmes.
He will help me if I have any problems.

S'il ne commence pas immédiatement, il n'aura pas fini avant minuit.
If it doesn't start immediately, he won't be finished before midnight.

S'il n'a pas fini à 17 heures, il me le dira.
If he has not finished by 5pm he will tell me.

💡 With **le passé composé**

TOPIC 176 ❖ Si with le futur simple

S'il a cessé de neiger d'ici demain, l'aéroport rouvrira.
If it has stopped snowing by tomorrow the airport will reopen.
💡 With **le passé composé**

S'ils ont déjà commencé les réparations du toit, ils m'appelleront.
If they have already started the roof repairs, they will call me.
💡 With **le passé composé**

❖ When *où* means 'when'

The word **où** means 'where' but it can also mean 'when'.

In French when we need a relative pronoun that refers to a time or period of time, we use **où**.

- In English we say 'the day **that** something happened' but in French we say **le jour** où **quelque chose s'est passé**.

EXAMPLES:

Lundi, c'est le jour où nous faisons les courses.
Monday is the day we go shopping.

2017, c'est l'année où j'ai déménagé à Sydney.
2017 is the year I moved to Sydney.

Elle est arrivée le jour où il est parti.
She arrived the day he left.

Je n'oublierai jamais le jour où nous avons gagné le match.
I'll never forget the day we won the game.

On ne l'a plus vue depuis le jour où elle est partie.
We haven't seen her since the day she left.

Le jeudi est le jour où il rend visite à ses grands-parents.
Thursday is the day he visits his grandparents.

Nous nous baignons dans le lac pendant les mois où il fait chaud.
We bathe in the lake during the warmer months.

Les jours où nous étions à l'hôtel étaient superbes.
The days we were at the hotel were great.

L'époque où nous vivons est paisible.
The time in which we live is peaceful.

C'était l'année où ils ont gagné la coupe du monde.
It was the year they won the world cup.

J'ai mis la table au moment où ma mère a sorti le rôti du four.
I set the table when my mother took the roast out of the oven.

TOPIC 177 ❖ When *où* means 'when'

Au moment où nous sommes arrivés à la maison, le téléphone a sonné.
The moment we got home, the phone rang.

❖ More time-related prepositions

In this topic we cover a bunch more common time-related prepositions and expressions:

- **dès** means 'as soon as' or 'as of' a particular date or event.
- **à partir de** also means 'from' or 'starting from' a particular time or event.
- **jusqu'à** means 'up to' or 'until'
- **d'ici** means 'from now'
- **jusqu'ici** means 'up till now' or 'so far'
- **avant** means 'before'
- **après** means 'after'
- **d'ici demain** means 'by tomorrow'; **d'ici la semaine prochaine** etc.
- **lors de** means '(at some point) during'.
- Note that **lors de** does not mean during the **entire** duration. We use **pendant** for that.

EXAMPLES:

Il vous appellera dès son retour.
He will call you (formal) as soon as he returns.

Les jeux commencent dès demain.
The games start as soon as tomorrow.
💡 OR '...as early as tomorrow'

Je l'ai acheté, et dès le lendemain, il était cassé.
I bought it and already the next day it was broken.
📚 **lendemain** (m) means 'the next day'

Dès le début, je ne lui ai pas fait confiance.
Since the start I didn't trust him.

Les transports en commun seront gratuits dès 2028.
Public transport will be free from 2028.
📚 **transports en commun** (m.pl) means 'public transport'

On dit qu'il cessera de pleuvoir à partir de demain.
They say it will stop raining from tomorrow.

TOPIC 178 ❖ More time-related prepositions

L'hélicoptère sera disponible à partir de lundi prochain.
The helicopter will be available from next Monday.

Je serai ici jusqu'à mardi à peu près.
I will be here until about Tuesday.

📖 *à peu près* means 'about' or 'approximately'.

Il fait généralement chaud jusqu'à la mi-août.
It is generally warm until mid-August.

📖 *mi-mois* means 'mid-month' (can also be used with individual month names)

Jusqu'ici, nous n'avons eu aucun problème.
So far we haven't had any problems.

Il est arrivé avant toi.
He arrived before you (familiar).

Je préfère finir mes devoirs avant de manger.
I prefer to finish my homework before I eat.

Je me suis couché après son départ.
I went to bed after he left.

Je préfère manger après avoir fini mes devoirs.
I prefer to eat after finishing my homework.

J'espère le recevoir d'ici demain.
I hope I will receive it by tomorrow.

Il cessera de neiger d'ici la semaine prochaine.
It will stop snowing by next week.

D'ici la fin de l'année, nous devons avoir rédigé la proposition de travail.
By the end of the year, we must have drafted the working proposal.

Je l'ai rencontré lors de mon stage au bureau.
I met him during my internship at the office.

La police était présente lors de ces événements.
The police were present during these events.

Elle était nerveuse lors de sa présentation.
She was nervous (at some point) during her presentation.

❖ As soon as and since - *dès que* and *depuis que*

We previously saw that **dès** and **depuis** can be used with times or periods of time.
- **dès** means 'as soon as' and **depuis** means 'since'.
When combined with **que** then **dès que** and **depuis que** serve as conjunctions.
We also have the common phrase **dès que possible** - 'as soon as possible'.

EXAMPLES:

Je me suis levée dès que le réveil a sonné.
I got up as soon as the alarm clock rang.

Dès que j'aurai une minute, je le ferai.
As soon as I have a minute, I will do it.

Je me coucherai dès qu'ils seront partis.
I'll go to bed as soon as they have left.

L'air devient plus pur dès que le vent chasse les nuages de fumée.
The air becomes cleaner as soon as the wind blows away the clouds of smoke.

Dès que je t'ai rencontrée, je suis tombé amoureux.
As soon as I met you (familiar), I fell in love.

Dès que je l'ai vue, j'ai compris que c'était elle, la femme de ma vie.
As soon as I saw her, I understood that it was she - the woman of my life.

Elle s'est arrêtée de fumer dès qu'elle a su qu'elle était enceinte.
She quit smoking as soon as she found out she was pregnant.

Je mettrai la table et je vous servirai dès que le dîner sera prêt.
I'll set the table and serve you (formal) as soon as dinner is ready.

👉 **prévenir** (verb) means 'to let (someone) know'

Il me préviendra dès que possible.
He will notify me as soon as possible.

👉 **dès que possible** means 'as soon as possible'

Il faut prendre rendez-vous dès que possible.
(You) should schedule an appointment as soon as possible.

👉 **prendre rendez-vous** (verb) means 'to make an appointment'

TOPIC 179 ❖ As soon as and since - *dès que* and *depuis que*

Il n'a plus beaucoup de temps libre depuis qu'il a commencé son nouveau travail.
He hasn't had much free time since he started his new job.

Depuis que je te connais, je ne suis plus le même.
Since I have known you (familiar), I am no longer the same.

Depuis qu'il habite ici, il n'a pas cessé de se plaindre.
Since he's been living here, he hasn't stopped complaining.

Depuis qu'elle est ministre, elle ne nous parle plus.
Since she became a minister, she no longer speaks to us.

Depuis qu'il fait du sport, il ne fume plus.
Since he started playing sports, he no longer smokes.

Depuis qu'elle s'est arrêtée de fumer, elle se sent mieux.
Since quitting smoking, she feels better.

Depuis que mon chien est parti de la maison, nous le cherchons partout.
Ever since my dog left home, we've been looking for him everywhere.

Depuis qu'il a compris comment on doit effectuer ce travail, il ne fait plus d'erreurs.
Since he understood how to carry out this work, he no longer makes mistakes.

✐ **effectuer** (verb) means 'to carry out' or 'to do'

Bootstrap French
TOPIC 180

❖ The pronoun *y*

The pronoun 'y' is used to replace position or direction, or the object of verbs that take \à\ or \par\.

It can also replace static locations like 'in here' or 'at there' where **dans** or other such prepositions are implied.

The **y** should always come before the verb of which it is the object.

- And when that verb couples with an auxiliary (as in **le passé composé**) the **y** should come before the auxiliary.

EXAMPLES:

Nous restons à l'hôtel. Nous y restons trois jours.
We stay at the hotel. We stay there for three days.
💡 à l'hôtel is replaced by y

Dans le jardin il y a cinq poires. J'y vois aussi douze pommes.
In the garden there are five pears. I also see twelve apples there.
💡 dans le jardin is replaced by y

Vous allez au restaurant ? Non, je n'y vais pas aujourd'hui.
You (formal) are going to the restaurant? No, I'm not going today.
💡 au restaurant is replaced by y

Le restaurant, est-il dans la gare ? Oui, il y est.
The restaurant, is it in the station? Yes, it is there.
💡 dans la gare is replaced by y

Est-il déjà allé en France ? Bien sûr, il y est allé plusieurs fois.
Has he ever been to France? Of course, he had been (to) there several times.
💡 en France is replaced with y

As-tu déjà dormi à la belle étoile ? Oui, j'y ai dormi une fois.
Have you (familiar) ever slept under the stars? I slept there once.
💡 à la belle étoiles is replaced with y
📝 à la belle étoiles means 'under the stars'

Il y était au tout début.
He was there at the very beginning.
📝 au tout début means 'from the very beginning'

TOPIC 180 ❖ The pronoun *y*

Il répond au téléphone. Il y répond.
He answers the phone. He answers it.
💡 The verb is **repondre à** so we can use **y**

Pensez-vous à la situation ? Oui, nous y pensons.
Do you (formal) think about the situation? Yes, we are thinking about it.
💡 The verb is **penser à** so we can use **y**

Répondez-vous au courrier ? Non, je ne veux pas y répondre.
Do you (formal) answer mail? No, I don't want to answer it.
💡 The verb is **repondre à** so we can use **y**

Pensez-vous à votre avenir ? Oui, j'y pense constamment.
Are you (formal) thinking about your future? Yes, I constantly think about it.
💡 The verb is **penser à** so we can use **y**

Avez-vous assisté à la réunion ? Oui, j'y ai assisté.
Did you (formal) attend the meeting? Yes, I attended.
💡 The verb is **assister à** so we can use **y**

Vous ne vous attendiez pas à cette réponse, n'est-ce pas ? Mais si ! Je m'y attendais pleinement.
You (formal) weren't expecting this answer, were you? But yes, I fully expected it.
💡 The verb is **attendre à** so we can use **y**

Je crois aux régimes mais ma mère n'y croit pas.
I believe in diets but my mother doesn't.
💡 The verb is **croire à** so we can use **y**

Vous devriez faire attention au signal. Oui, j'y fais attention.
You (formal) should pay attention to the signal. Yes, I pay attention to it.
💡 The verb is **faire attention à** so we can use **y**

Vous êtes-vous habitué à vivre seul ? Non, je n'y suis pas encore habitué.
Have you (formal) gotten used to living alone? No, I'm not used to it yet.
💡 The verb is **habituer à** so we can use **y**

Vous devez essayer de ne pas trop y penser.
You (formal) must try not to think too much about it.
💡 The verb is **penser à** so we can use **y**

Êtes-vous intéressé par le jardinage ? Oui, je m'y intéresse beaucoup.
Are you (formal) interested in gardening? Yes, I'm very interested in it.
💡 The verb is **intéresser par** so we can use **y**
📖 **intéresser par** (verb) means 'to be interested in'

TOPIC 180 ❖ The pronoun *y*

Nous nous opposons à la guerre. Tout le monde s'y oppose.
We oppose war. Everyone opposes it.
 💡 The verb is **s'opposer à** so we can use **y**

Je ne suis pas sûr. J'y penserai.
I am not sure. I will think about it.
 💡 The verb is **penser à** so we can use **y**

Nous devons résister au fascisme. Bien sûr, nous devons y résister.
We must resist fascism. Of course, we must resist it.
 💡 The verb is **resiter à** so we can use **y**

Il y songe tous les jours et toute la journée.
He thinks about it every day and all day.
 💡 The verb is **songer à** so we can use **y**

J'irai à la fashion week de Paris. J'y participerai un jour.
I'm going to Paris fashion week. I will participate one day.
 💡 The verb is **aller à** so we can use **y**

Vous devez essayer de ne pas trop y penser.
You (formal) must try not to think too much about it.
 💡 The verb is **penser à** so we can use **y**

J'irai à Paris. J'irai bientôt.
I will go to Paris. I will go soon.
 💡 In this case we would like to say **J'y irai bientôt** but because of the continuous vowels **y** and **i** this should be avoided.

J'irai à Paris. J'y serai bientôt.
I will go to Paris. I will be there soon.
 💡 Here using **y** is fine before **serai** given its first letters is a consonant

Bootstrap French
TOPIC 181

❖ Expressions using *y*

There are many common colloquial expressions that use the pronoun **y**. Some of these are listed as this topic's example phrases.

EXAMPLES:

Ça y est.
It's done.
💡 Literally 'that there is'

Ça y est, j'ai fini ma rédaction !
That's it, I finished my essay!
📖 **rédaction** (f) means 'essay'

Il fallait s'y attendre.
It was to be expected.
💡 The verb is **attendre à** meaning 'to expect (something)'

Je n'y peux rien.
I can't do anything about it.

Je n'y suis pour rien.
It has nothing to do with me.

Nous sommes prêts. Allons-y.
We are ready. Let's go.

On y va !
Let's go!

Il s'y connaît.
He is an expert on that.

La comète était visible dans toute l'Europe, y compris en Ukraine.
The comet was visible in all Europe, including in Ukraine.
📖 **y compris** means 'including' or 'there included'

Bootstrap French
TOPIC 182

❖ The pronoun *en*

The pronoun **en** is used to replace either a quantity or the object of a verb that takes the preposition **de**.

- The best equivalent in English is 'of it' or 'of them'.

The quality can one referred to using partitive like **de**, **du**, **de la**, **des**. Or a number. Or a fraction like **un quart**. Or an adverb of quantity like **beaucoup de** or **un peu de**. Or a measurement of quantity like **un kilo de**, **duex litres de** or **une boîte de**.

In French we do NOT say **j'ai acheté 5 litres** - the **5 litres** is considered an adjective and it needs a noun/pronoun. We can use **en** for this. So we say **j'en ai acheté 5 litres** ('I bought 5 litres of it').

- Likewise we do NOT ask **avez-vous un ?** - we need a noun or pronoun. So instead we say **en avez-vous un ?** meaning 'have you got one (of them)'

The pronoun **en** can also be used to replace the object of verbs that take the preposition **de**.

- When that verb couples with an auxiliary (as in **le passé composé**) the **en** should come before the auxiliary.

But when the **de** refers to a person **en** can't be used - instead a stressed pronoun (**moi**, **toi**...) must be used.

EXAMPLES:

Voulez-vous de l'eau ? Oui, s'il vous plaît, j'en veux.
Do you (formal) want some water? Yes please, I want some.
💡 de l'eau ⇒ en

Voulez-vous de la salade ? Oui, j'en veux, merci.
Do you (formal) want some salad? Yes, I do want some, thanks.
💡 de la salade ⇒ en

Vous voulez six pommes, n'est-ce pas ? Oui, j'en veux six.
You (formal) want six apples, right? Yes, I want six (of them).
💡 trois unités de pommes ⇒ en
💡 Can NOT say Oui, je veux six.'

En voulez-vous un ?
Do you (formal) want one (of them)?
💡 un de (quelque chose) ⇒ en

TOPIC 182 ❖ The pronoun *en*

Avez-vous bu de la bière ? Non, je n'en ai pas bu.
Did you (formal) drink some beer? No, I did not drink any.
💡 de la bière ⇒ en

Y a-t-il des éléphants dans le zoo ? Oui, il y en a.
Are there elephants in the zoo? Yes, there are some (of them).
💡 des éléphants ⇒ en

Combien de chiens avez-vous ? J'en ai trois.
How many dogs do you (formal) have? I have three (of them).
💡 de chiens ⇒ en

Est-ce qu'il y des éléphants au zoo ? En fait, il y en a sept.
Are there any elephants in the zoo? If fact, there are seven (of them).
💡 des éléphants ⇒ en

Mais des tigres - il n'y en a pas.
But tigers - there are none (of them).
💡 des tigres ⇒ en

Ils ont des enfants, non ? Oui, c'est vrai. Ils en ont trois.
They have kids, right? Yes, that's right. They have three (of them).
💡 des enfants ⇒ en

Avez-vous des idées ? Oui, j'en ai une.
Do you (formal) have any ideas? Yes, I have one (of them).
💡 des idées ⇒ en

Elle en a beaucoup bu !
She drank a lot (of it)!
💡 beaucoup de so we can use en

Je pense qu'elle n'en a bu qu'un peu.
I think she only drank a little (of it).
💡 un peu de so we can use en

Oui, j'en veux si possible.
Yes, I want some (of it) if possible.
💡 un de (quelque chose) ⇒ en

Parlez-vous de la météo ? Oui, on en parle.
Are you (formal) talking about the weather? Yes, we are talking about it.
💡 The verb is parler de so we can use en

TOPIC 182 ❖ The pronoun *en*

Quand reviens-tu de Madrid ? J'en reviendrai dans une semaine.
When do you (familiar) come back from Madrid? I will come back from there in a week.

💡 The verb is **revenir de** so we can use **en**

Avez-vous besoin d'essence ? Oui, j'en ai besoin.
Do you (formal) need petrol? Yes, I need some.

💡 The verb is **avoir besion de** so we can use **en**

Es-tu certaine qu'elle est enceinte ? Oui, j'en suis certain.
Are you (familiar) certain she is pregnant? Yes, I am certain of it.

💡 The verb is **être certain de** so we can use **en**

Il est portugais ; J'en suis certain.
He is Portuguese; I am certain of it.

💡 The verb is **être certain de** so we can use **en**

Elle n'en parle jamais.
She never talks about it.

💡 The verb is **parler de** so we can use **en**

J'ai peur de la mort. Tu en as peur aussi ?
I have a fear of death. Are you (familiar) afraid of it too?

💡 The verb is **avoir peur de** so we can use **en**

Va-t-il bientôt sortir du bureau ? Il en est déjà sorti.
Will he go out from the office soon? He has already left (from it).

💡 The verb is **sortir de** so we can use **en**

Je rêve d'aller au Japon. J'en rêve souvent.
I dream of going to Japan. I dream of it often.

💡 The verb is **rêver de** so we can use **en**

Ella a-t-elle acheté des cahiers ce matin ? Oui, elle en a acheté.
Did Ella buy notepads this morning? Yes, she brought (some of them).

💡 **en** is before the aixillary verb **avoir**

Mais moi, je n'en ai acheté aucun encore.
But me, I didn't buy any (of them) yet.

💡 **en** is before the aixillary verb **avoir**

Avez-vous assez d'essence ? Oui, j'en ai acheté cinq litres.
Do you (formal) have enough petrol? Yes, I bought five liters (of it).

💡 **cinq litres de** so we can use **en**

💡 **ne** is before the aixillary verb **avoir**

French Grammar

TOPIC 182 ❖ The pronoun *en*

Y a-t-il un restaurant dans la gare ? Oui, il y en a un.
Is there a restaurant in the station? Yes, there is one (of them).
- The answer is 'there is one (of them)'

Avez-vous mangé tous les biscuits ? Je n'en ai mangé qu'un.
Did you (formal) eat all of the biscuits? I only ate one of them.
- **ne.. qu'un de** so we can use **en**
- **ne** is before the aixillary verb **avoir**

Bootstrap French
TOPIC 183

❖ Expressions using *en*

There are many common colloquial expressions that use the pronoun **en**. Some of these are listed as this topic's example phrases.

EXAMPLES:

J'en ai marre.
I'm fed up.

J'en ai assez.
I've had enough.

J'en ai ras-le-bol.
I've had it.
> The literal meaning of 'ras-de-bol' is 'full bowl' in the sense of 'full to the brim'

Je lui en veux.
I'm mad at him∆her. *OR* I resent him∆her.
> Literally 'I want some of for him'. What exactly the 'something' is, it's hard to say...

Il lui en veut toujours, mais la donne va bientôt changer.
He is still angry at him∆her, but that will soon change.

Je m'en veux.
I feel guilty.

Je m'en veux vraiment de ne pas t'avoir cru.
I'm really guilty for not having believed you (familiar).

Je m'en vais.
I'm leaving.

Je m'en sors.
I'm dealing with it.

Je m'en suis sorti.
I dealt with it. *OR* I figured it out.

Ne t'en fais pas.
Don't worry.

TOPIC 183 ❖ Expressions using *en*

Je t'en prie.
You (familiar) are welcome. *OR* You are welcome. *OR* Go ahead, please do.

Je vous en prie.
You (formal) are welcome. *OR* You are welcome. *OR* Go ahead, please do.

Je n'en sais rien.
I do not know (about it).

Je m'en fiche.
I do not care. *OR* I don't give a damn.

> *se ficher de* means 'to not care about (something)'

Je n'en peux plus.
I cannotstand it anymore.

J'en pince pour lui.
I have a crush on him.

Pour en revenir à cette question.
To come back to this question.

On va en rester là.
We'll stop there.

Qu'est-ce que vous en pensez ?
What do you (formal) think (about it)?

Je n'en croyais pas mes yeux.
I could not believe my eyes (about that).

Je t'en supplie !
I beg you (familiar)!

Tu en es sûr ? Oui, j'en suis sûr et certain.
Are you (familiar) sure (about that)? Yes, I'm sure and certain (of it).

Il est malade, mais il va s'en sortir.
He's sick but he'll come through.

> *s'en sortir* means 'to come through' or 'to manage' or 'to get out of (a difficult situation)'

Il en veut vraiment. C'est quelqu'un qui en veut vraiment.
He really wants it. He's someone who really tries hard.

> Implying that he tries hard (to win for example)

❖ Of which, about which - the relative pronoun *dont*

The relative pronoun **dont** is used to refer back to a clause which is the object of the verb in the second clause and that second verb takes the pronoun **de**.

- Given that **de** can denote possession, so too can **dont**.
- Member of a group can also be identified using **dont** - **un groupe dont certains sont particuliers** - 'a group **of which** certain (members) are special.'

It is common to form the first clause using the indefinite relative pronoun **ce dont** meaning 'the thing(s) that...'.

When used in reference to possession or a relationship, the object in the second clause requires an article.

Note that **dont** cannot be used alongside compound prepositions like **à cote de** etc. that include **de**. In such case in place of the preposition's **de** we use **duquel** or **d'où** etc.

EXAMPLES:

C'est l'homme dont je parle.
That is the man about who I speak.
- Or **C'est l'homme (de qui) je parle.**
- The verb Is **parler de**
- Transposed we have **Je parle de cet homme.**

C'est celui dont tout le monde parle.
This is the one that everyone is talking about.
- Or **C'est celui (de qui) tout le monde parle.**
- The verb Is **parler de**
- Transposed we have **Tout le monde parle de celui.**

C'est la ville dont je suis revenue.
This is the city I came back from.
- Or **C'est la ville (d'où) je suis revenue.**
- The verb Is **revenir de**
- Transposed we have **Je suis revenue de cette ville.**

Voici le livre dont j'ai besoin.
This is the book that I need.
- Or **Voici le livre (duquel) j'ai besoin.**
- The verb Is **avoir besion de**
- Transposed we have **J'ai besoin de ce livre-ci.**

French Grammar

TOPIC 184 ❖ Of which, about which - the relative pronoun *dont*

Les serpents sont la seule chose dont j'ai peur.
Snakes are the only thing that I am afraid of.
- Or **Le serpent est la seule chose duquel j'ai peur.**
- The verb Is **avoir peur de de**
- Transposed we have **J'ai peur d'une seule chose - c'est le serpent.**

Le livre dont nous parlons est Les Misérables.
The book we are talking about is Les Misérables.
- The verb is **parler de**

Le garçon dont je m'occupe le matin est très méchant.
The boy I take care of in the morning is very naughty.
- The verb is **s'occuper de**

Je ne sais pas ce dont j'ai besoin.
I don't know what I need.
- The verb is **avoir besion de**

Voilà ce dont j'ai besoin !
This is what I need!
- The verb is **avoir besion de**

Nous avons tout ce dont nous avons besoin.
We have everything we need.
- The verb is **avoir besion de**

Ce dont tu rêves est impossible à réaliser.
What you (familiar) dream of is impossible to achieve.
- The verb is **rêves de**
- Here **ce** serves as the first clause.

C'est la voiture dont je rêvais depuis que je suis enfant.
It's the car I've dreamed of since I was a kid.
- The verb is **rêves de**

Tout ce dont je me souviens de cet instant, c'est que je suis tombée.
All I remember from that moment is that I fell.
- The verb is **se souvenir de**
- Here **tout ce** serves as the first clause.

Comment savoir si l'article dont j'ai envie est encore disponible ?
How do I know if the item I want is still available?
- The verb is **avoir envie de**

TOPIC 184 ❖ Of which, about which - the relative pronoun *dont*

Je connais la femme dont la voiture est en panne.
I know the woman whose car broke down.
💡 The lady who possesses the car - **la voiture de la femme est en panne**

Je cherche une maison dont le toit est rouge.
I'm looking for a house whose a red roof.
💡 The house that possesses a red roof - **le toit de la maison est rouge**

C'est la fille dont je connais le père.
This is the girl whose father I know.
💡 **dont** refers to possession (the girl's father) so article is required ⇒ **le pere**

J'ai rencontré une femme dont le mari est policier.
I met a woman whose husband is a policeman.
💡 **dont** refers to possession (the lady's husband) so article is required ⇒ **le mari**

Romain, dont la sœur est journaliste, vit en Algérie.
Romain, whose sister is a journalist, lives in Algeria.
💡 **dont** refers to possession (Romain's sister) so article is required ⇒ **la sœur**

J'ai plusieurs amis, dont deux français.
I have several friends, two of whom are French.
💡 There are 'deux francais' who are members of the group of 'mes amis'

Dans le sac, il y a deux livres, dont l'un est en anglais.
In the bag there are two books, one of which is in English.
💡 There are 'un livre en anglais' that is member of the group 'les livres dans le sac'

Il y avait plusieurs personnes, dont l'une était Bénédicte.
There were several people, one of whom is Bénédicte.
💡 It is Bénédicte who is member of the group 'plusieurs personnes'

C'est la fille à côté de qui je me suis assis.
She's the girl I sat next to.
💡 Can NOT use **à côté dont**

C'est le café en face duquel se trouve le théâtre.
This is the café across from which the theater is located.
💡 Can NOT use **en face dont**

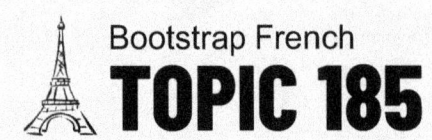

❖ What - *quoi*

We have seen that the indefinite relative pronoun **ce dont** references the object of a verb that takes the preposition **de**.

When a verb takes a preposition other than **de** then **quoi** is used as the indefinite relative pronoun.

 - Used in this way the verb's preposition is placed before **quoi**.

Having said that, colloquially **quoi** can simply mean 'what'.

EXAMPLES:

Je sais ce à quoi tu penses.
I know what you (familiar) are thinking.
 The verb is **penser à** so we use **à quoi**

À quoi penses-tu ?
What are you (familiar) thinking about?
 The verb is **penser à** so we use **à quoi**

Nous ne savons jamais à quoi il pense.
We never know what he is thinking.
 The verb is **penser à** so we use **à quoi**

Maintenant, vous savez dans quoi j'étais coincé.
Now you (formal) know what I was stuck in.
 The verb is **coincer dans** so we use **dans quoi**

J'ai trouvé avec quoi laver le chien.
I found something to wash the dog with.
 The verb is **laver avec** so we use **avec quoi**

Avec quoi écrit-il ?
What does he write with?
 The verb is **ecrire avec** so we use **avec quoi**

Ce à quoi je m'attends - votre invitation.
That is what I am expecting - your (formal) invitation.
 The verb is **attendre à** so we use **à quoi**

TOPIC 185 ❖ What - *quoi*

Je me demandais derrière quoi il se cachait.
I was wondering what he was hiding behind.
> The verb is **se cacher derrière** so we use **derrière quoi**

Il n'y a pas de quoi.
You are welcome. *OR* There is nothing (to mention).
> Literally 'There is not anything (what) (to say thanks for)'

Pas de quoi.
Welcome.
> **il n'y a** is dropped colloquially

Quoi ?
What?
> Colloquial. Rather rude. 'Pardon?' is better.

Pourquoi ?
Why?
> **pour** + **quoi** = **pourquoi** (for what = why)

Tu fais quoi ce weekend ?
What are you (familiar) doing this weekend?
> Rather than (for instance) 'Que fais-tu ce weekend ?'

Quoi de neuf ?
What's new?

Relative pronouns after propositions with *de* - *duquel*, *de laquelle*, *desquels* & *desquelles*

When the relative pronoun follows a preposition the ends with **de** then we need to use one of the following: **duquel, de laquelle, desquels & desquelles**.

These kinds of prepositions include **près de, loin de, à côté de, à l'intérieur de**.

And can also include other expressions with **de** such as **au sujet de** and **à partir de**.

These relative pronouns need to agree in gender and number with the noun they refer to.

- Recall that even if the verb takes **de**, the relative pronoun **dont** cannot be used if it follows a preposition that ends with **de**. In this case we need to use one of the above relative pronouns.

EXAMPLES:

L'arbre près duquel tu es assis est un chêne.
The tree near which you (familiar) are sitting is an oak tree.

près de means 'close to'

Voici les amis au sujet desquels nous sommes inquiets.
Here are the friends about whom we are worried.

au sujet de means 'about'

Demain est le jour à partir duquel la loi entre en vigueur.
Here is the date from which the law comes into force.

entrer en vigueur (verb) means 'to come into force'

Merci à vos amies, sans l'aide desquelles rien n'aurait été possible.
Thanks to you (female) friends, without whose help nothing would have been possible.

L'homme à côté duquel nous étions assis est un acteur très connu.
The man we were sitting next to is a very well-known actor.

à côté de means 'next to'

Voici le petit bateau à bord duquel j'ai traversé le fleuve.
This is the small boat onboard which I crossed the river.

à bord means 'onboard'

Prends la chaise au-dessous de laquelle il y a un sac.
Take the chair under which there is a bag.

au-dessous means 'under'

TOPIC 186 ❖ Relative pronouns after propositions with *de*

La boîte à l'intérieur de laquelle se trouvent les clés est rouge.
The box inside which the keys are located is red.
- Note that feminine singular **de quelle** does NOT exist - instead **de laquelle** is used
- **à l'intérieur** means 'inside'

C'est un roman à la fin duquel tout a bien fini.
This is a novel at the end of which everything ends well.

La classe près de laquelle nous nous trouvons est très grande.
The class near which we find ourselves is very large.
- Note that feminine singular **de quelle** does NOT exist - instead **de laquelle** is used

Les personnes en face desquelles nous étions - elles parlaient finnois.
The people (females) we are opposite of - they were speaking Finnish.
- **en face** means 'in front' or 'opposite'

C'est un parc au centre duquel se trouvent de belles fontaines.
It is a park in the center of which there are old trees.

Il y a eu des élections à la suite desquelles le gouvernement n'a pas changé.
There were elections following which the government did not change.
- **à la suite de** means 'after (something)'

Je vous ai donné un chèque au bas duquel j'ai signé.
I gave you (formal) a check at the bottom of which I signed.

Ce sont des sujets à propos desquels nous nous disputons régulièrement.
These are the topics we argue about regularly.
- **à propos de** means 'about' or 'concerning'

Ces personnes loin desquelles je me trouvais parlaient fort.
These people I was far from spoke loudly.
- **loin de** means 'far from'

L'homme à côté duquel Mme Dupont est assise est son mari.
The man Mrs. Dupont is sitting next to is her husband.

Le parc près duquel je travaille est très grand.
The park near where I work is very big.

Les filles à côté desquelles je me suis assis n'étaient pas contentes.
The girls I sat next to were not happy.

TOPIC 186 ❖ Relative pronouns after propositions with *de*

La date à partir de laquelle nous devrons porter un masque a été reportée.
The date from which we will have to wear a mask has been postponed.

C'est un film à la fin duquel tout le monde rit.
It's a film at the end of which everyone laughs.

Beaucoup de maisons près desquelles coule la rivière sont un peu humides.
Many of the houses near which the river runs are a little damp.

La cheminée, au-dessus de laquelle est posée la statuette, est très ancienne.
The fireplace, above which the statuette is placed, is very old.

C'est un très beau chemin au bout duquel on peut voir toute la côte.
It is a very beautiful path at the end of which one can see the whole coast.

La colline, au sommet de laquelle il est monté, offre un joli point de vue.
The hill, to the top of which he climbed, offers a nice view.

Nous n'avons pas de nouvelles du bateau à bord duquel il est parti.
We have no news of the ship on which he left.

J'ai revu la pièce à propos de laquelle nous avions longuement discuté.
I saw the play about which we had discussed at length.

C'est l'escalier en bas duquel il t'attendra.
It's the stairs at the bottom of which he'll be waiting for you (familiar).

Nice est la ville pas loin de laquelle je suis né.
Nice is the city not far from which I was born.

C'est le jardin au travers duquel je passe souvent.
It is the garden through which I often pass.

Voici le quai au bord duquel se trouve le fameux Hôtel du Nord.
Here is the quay on the edge of which is the famous Hôtel du Nord.

Les séances lors desquelles nous parlerons d'économie auront lieu demain.
The sessions in which we will talk about economics will take place tomorrow.

Relative pronouns after prepositions without *de* - *lequel*, *laquelle*, *lesquels* & *lesquelles*

When the relative pronoun follows a preposition that does NOT end with **de** then we need to use one of the following: **lequel**, **laquelle**, **lesquels** & **lesquelles**

These kinds of prepositions include **dans**, **sous**, **sur**, **chez**, **pour**, **parmi** etc.. But NOT **à**.

The relative pronoun needs to agree in gender and number with the noun they refer to.

EXAMPLES:

Les raisons pour lesquelles nous sommes parties sont confidentielles.
The reasons why we left are confidential.

la raison pour means 'the reason why'

Elle a un sac à main dans lequel elle garde son portable.
She has a purse in which she keeps her cell phone.

Les deux personnes entre lesquelles je me trouvais ne me parlaient pas.
The two people I was between didn't speak to me.

entre means 'between'

La chaise sur laquelle je suis assise est inconfortable.
The chair I'm sitting on is uncomfortable.

Les outils avec lesquels je travaille sont tous cassés.
The tools I work with are all broken.

Je ne trouve plus le bout de papier sur lequel j'avais écrit son adresse.
I can no longer find the piece of paper on which I had written his addresses.

Les poupées avec lesquelles elle joue sont très vieilles.
The dolls she plays with are very old.

Je repeins le mur sur lequel il avait écrit.
I repaint the wall on which he had written.

Les filles parmi lesquelles je me suis retrouvé avaient beaucoup voyagé.
The girls I found myself among had traveled a lot.

parmi means 'among'

TOPIC 187 ❖ Relative pronouns after prepositions without *de*

Ces dernières semaines pendant lesquelles j'ai voyagé étaient agréables
These last few weeks that I have been traveling have been pleasant

Les amis chez lesquels j'habiterai sont très riches.
The friends I will be staying with are very wealthy.

Le livre dans lequel j'ai écrit mon nom.
The book in which I wrote my name.

Les charges dépendent du pays depuis lequel vous appelez.
Charges depend on from which country you (formal) are calling.

C'est la fille avec laquelle j'avais envie de me marier.
She's the girl to whom I wanted to get married.

📖 **se marier avec** means 'to get married to'

La ville vers laquelle nous nous dirigeons est très peuplée.
The city to which we are heading very crowded.

📖 **se diriger** (verb) means 'to head to' or 'to make one's way to'

Où est le coffre dans lequel j'avais mis mes souvenirs ?
Where is the chest in which I put my souvenirs?

📖 **coffre** (m) means 'chest' or 'car boot'

Voici le pinceau avec lequel tu pourras peindre le mur.
Here is the brush with which you (familiar) can paint the wall.

📖 **pinceau** (m) means 'brush'

Les étagères sur lesquelles j'ai mis des livres sont remplies.
The shelves I put books on are full.

Cette route mène à un village au bout duquel on trouve une église.
This road leads to a village at the end of which there is a church.

📖 **mener** (verb) means 'to lead'

Voici les plantes et les animaux parmi lesquels je vis.
Here are the plants and animals among which I live.

La salle dans laquelle je fais de la danse est très froide.
The room where I dance is very cold.

Il allait nettoyer la table sur laquelle on voit de multiples marques.
He was going to clean the table on which we see multiple marks.

Le film pendant lequel j'ai dormi était vraiment ennuyeux.
The movie I slept through was really boring.

TOPIC 187 ❖ Relative pronouns after prepositions without *de*

Les gens avec lesquels je parle sont très intéressants.
The people I talk to are very interesting.

Bootstrap French
TOPIC 188

❖ Relative pronouns *auquel, auxquels & auxquelles*

When the verb takes the preposition **à** then we use the relative pronouns **à quel**, **auxquels** & **auxquelles**.

Note that feminine singular **à quelle** does NOT exist - instead **à laquelle** is used.

EXAMPLES:

Le parti politique auquel nous avions adhéré est sur le point de se scinder.
The political party that we joined is about to split.

adhérer à (verb) means 'to join' or 'to follow' or 'to adhere to'

Les passe-temps auxquels je m'intéresse sont des activités solitaires.
The hobbies that I am interested in are solitary pursuits.

s'intéresser à (verb) means 'to be interested in'

Le petit chien, auquel tu as fait peur, s'est caché sous la table.
The little dog, of which you (familiar) scared, hid under the table.

faire peur à (verb) means 'to be fearful of' or 'to fear (something)'

Les activités sportives auxquelles il s'adonne sont très dangereuses.
The sports activities that he engages in are very dangerous.

s'adonner à (verb) means 'to engage in'

Les tâches auxquelles elle a consacré sa vie sont futiles.
The tasks to which she devoted her life are futile.

consacrer à (verb) means 'to devote (something) to'

Cette ambiance à laquelle je ne pouvais m'habituer n'existe plus.
This atmosphere that I could not get used to no longer exists.

s'habituer à (verb) means 'to get used to'
Note that feminine singular **à quelle** does NOT exist - instead **à laquelle** is used

La discipline à laquelle elle s'intéresse est exigeante.
The discipline in which she is interested is demanding.

s'intéresser à (verb) means 'to be interested in'
Note that feminine singular **à quelle** does NOT exist - instead **à laquelle** is used

Ce problème, auquel je réfléchis, me rend fou !
This problem, which I am thinking about, is driving me crazy!

réfléchir à (verb) means 'to think about' or 'to reflect on'

TOPIC 188 ❖ Relative pronouns *auquel*, *auxquels* & *auxquelles*

Toutes les filles, auxquelles tu mentais, sont furieuses.
All the girls who you (familiar) lied to are furious.

* *mentir à* (verb) means 'to lie to'

Mes amis, auxquels j'écris régulièrement, ne répondent plus.
My friends, to whom I write regularly, don't respond anymore.

* *ecrire à* (verb) means 'to write to'

Le prix auquel vous souhaitez vendre votre maison est trop élevé.
The price at which you (formal) want to sell your house is too high.

* *vendre à un prix* (verb) 'to sell at a price'

C'est un projet auquel tous les ouvriers doivent participer.
It is a project in which all workers must participate.

* *participer à* (verb) means 'to participate in'

L'actrice à laquelle elle ressemble est canadienne.
The actress who she resembles is Canadian.

* *ressemble à* (verb) means 'to look like' or 'to resemble'

La réunion à laquelle j'avais besoin d'assister a été reportée.
The meeting that I needed to attend has been postponed.

* *assister à* (verb) means 'to attend (a meeting)'
* *reporter* means 'to reschedule'

La voiture à laquelle je songe.
The car that I am considering.

* *songe à* (verb) means 'to consider' or 'to think about'

La réunion à laquelle nous nous étions préparés a été annulée.
The meeting that we had been preparing for was cancelled.

* *preparer à* (verb) means 'to prepare for'

La décision à laquelle il s'est plié le rend malheureux.
The decision that he has submitted to makes him unhappy.

* *se plier à* means 'to submit to'

C'est une situation à laquelle il faut s'habituer.
It's a situation that (you) have to get used to.

* *s'habituer à* (verb) means 'to get used to'

Le roi auquel le prince a succédé ne voulait pas qu'il devienne roi.
The king who the prince succeeded did not want him to become king.

* *succéder à* (verb) means 'to succeed (someome)'

TOPIC 188 ❖ Relative pronouns *auquel, auxquels* & *auxquelles*

Je ne me souviens plus du nom du livre auquel ton histoire me fait penser.

I can't remember the name of the book that your (familiar) story reminds me of.

faire penser à (verb) means 'to be reminded of'

❖ In what way? - *de quelle manière* & *de quelle façon*

When asking or talking about how or in what way something is done we can ask using the adverbal phrases:

- **de quelle façon ?**
- **de quelle manière ?**

And answer using

- **d'une manière...** or **de manière...**
- **d'une façon...** or **de façon...**

And the answer to these questions will often (but not necessarily) echo the instrumental **de**.

Note that **de quelle..?** can also be used to ask more general questions about the way in which something is done.

EXAMPLES:

De quelle manière dois-je commencer ?
How should I start?

De quelle manière comptes-tu le faire ? Je vais le faire de mon mieux.
How do you (familiar) intend to do it? I will do my best.
compter faire (verb) means 'to intend to' or 'to plan to'

De quelle manière pouvons-nous résoudre la dispute ?
How can we resolve the dispute?
résoudre (verb) means 'to solve' or 'to resolve'

De quelle manière a-t-il été construit ? Il a été construit à la main.
How was it built? It was built by hand.

De quelle façon marche-t-il ? Il marche de façon étrange.
How does it work? It works strangely.

De quelle façon votre vie est-elle différente maintenant ?
How is your (formal) life different now?

De quelle façon cet objectif peut-il être atteint ?
How can this goal be achieved?

TOPIC 189 ❖ In what way? - *de quelle manière* & *de quelle façon*

De quelle façon avez-vous appris le français si rapidement ?
How did you (formal) learn French so quickly?

Je suis arrivé à la solution d'une manière étrange.
I arrived at the solution in a strange way.

Il parle d'une manière bizarre.
He speaks in a weird way.

Les adolescents s'habillent d'une façon très particulière.
Teenagers dress in a very particular way.

De quelle main écris-tu ? J'écris de la main gauche.
What hand do you (familiar) write with? I write with my left hand.

❖ In the style of or in the manner of - *à la*

The term **à la** is used to describe something that is 'in the style of' or 'in the manner of' something else.

It is an abbreviation of **à la mode de** ('in the fashion of') or **à la manière de** ('in the manner of').

While there are many fixed expressions that use **à la** in this way, it can be used with any feminine singular adjective or a proper noun (someone's or something's name).

EXAMPLES:

J'aime flâner dans les jardins à la française de Paris.
I love to stroll through the French-style gardens of Paris.

✎ **flâner** (verb) means 'to stroll'

C'est une manifestation du socialisme à la française !
It is a manifestation of French-style socialism!

Ce restaurant à l'espagnole sert les meilleurs vins espagnols.
This Spanish restaurant serves the best Spanish wines.

Ils vendent de la haute couture avec une touche de chic à la parisienne.
They sell haute couture with a touch of Parisian chic.

💡 haute couture (f) means 'high fashion'

Il ne préfère que le thé à la russe.
He only prefers Russian tea.

Les œufs à la diable sont un favori de la famille.
Deviled Eggs are a family favorite.

✎ **diable** (m) means 'devil'

C'est sa première sculpture à la cubiste.
This is his first cubist sculpture.

Il y a beaucoup d'auteurs qui ont essayé d'écrire à la manière de Jean_Paul Sartre.
There are many authors who have tried to write in the manner of Jean-Paul Sartre.

TOPIC 190 ❖ In the style of or in the manner of - *à la*

La réunion avait été organisée par lui et il l'a fait à la hussarde.
The meeting had been organized by him and he did it like a hussar.

- à la hussarde means 'in a rough manner'
- hussarde (m) means 'a soldier in a light cavalry regiment'

Les petits-déjeuners sont tous fraîchement préparés à la commande.
Breakfasts are all freshly made to order.

- à la commande means 'as per ordered'

Nous avons adoré le poulet à la broche.
We loved a spit-roasted chicken.

- broche (f) means 'spit'
- un poulet à la broche (means) 'spit-roasted chicken'

Pendant toutes les vacances, nous avons dormi toutes les nuits à la belle étoile.
During the whole vacation, we slept every night under the stars.

- à la belle étoile means 'under the stars'

Quel dommage - ils ont vendu toutes les tartes à la crème.
What a pity - they have all of the cream pies.

Apprendre le français à la « Bootstrap French Grammar » est la voie à suivre.
Learning French à la 'Bootstrap French Grammar' is the way to go.

- voie (f) means 'way' or 'track' or 'lane'
- suivre

❖ Because of - *grâce à* & *à cause de*

In French we make a distinction between causing something good and causing something bad.
- If the outcome is unequivocally good we use **grâce à** - 'thanks to'
- If the outcome is bad or neutral we use **à cause de** - 'due to'

We can also use **en raison de** which is more neutral.

We can preface all these with an impersonal **c'est** to form a clause that can be connected to the next clause using **que** - 'it is due to (something) that...'.

EXAMPLES:

Grâce à l'aide de mon ami, j'ai réussi à l'examen.
Thanks to the help of my friend, I passed the exam.

Grâce à eux, nous avons pu mieux atteindre nos objectifs.
Thanks to them, we were able to better achieve our goals.
atteindre (verbs) means 'to achieve' or 'to reach'

Je me sens beaucoup mieux, grâce à vos remèdes.
I feel much better, thanks to your (formal) remedies.
remède (f) means 'medicine' or 'cure'

J'ai réussi uniquement grâce à l'avis de ton ami.
I succeeded only thanks to the opinion of your (familiar) friend.

Le pique-nique a été reporté à cause de la pluie.
The picnic was postponed due to rain.

Je devrais mettre un manteau à cause du froid.
I should put on a coat because of the cold.

Ma grand-mère ne peut pas conduire à cause de sa vue.
My grandmother can't drive because of her eyesight.
vue (f) means 'eyesight' or 'view'

J'ai perdu le dossier à cause de mon récent déménagement.
I lost the file due to my recent move.

TOPIC 191 ❖ Because of - *grâce à* & *à cause de*

C'est à cause de la tempête que la rivière est en crue.
It is because of the storm that the river is in flood.
- tempête (f) means 'storm'
- rivière (f) means 'river'
- en crue means 'rising' or 'flooding'

Il a finalement dû démissionner en raison de sa mauvaise santé.
He eventually had to resign due to his poor health.
- démissionner (verb) means 'to resign'

En raison de la grève, le métro est fermé.
Due to the strike, the metro is closed.
- grève (f) means 'strike (industrial action)'

C'est grâce à toi que j'ai réussi à résoudre le problème.
It is thanks to you (familiar) that I managed to resolve the problem.

Si tu rates ton examen, c'est à cause d'un manque d'effort.
If you (familiar) fail your exam, it's because of a lack of effort.
- manque de (m) means 'lack of'

Nous avons résolu le problème grâce à tous nos efforts.
We have solved the problem thanks to all our efforts.
- résolu is the past participle of résoudre ('to solve')

Grâce au système politique, on peut choisir notre président.
Thanks to the political system we can choose our president.

Je m'en suis sorti grâce à l'aide de ma famille.
I got out thanks to the help of my family.

Ils ont résolu le crime grâce aux témoins.
They solved the crime thanks to the witnesses.
- témoin (m) means 'witness'

Le médicament grâce auquel j'ai récupéré était par ailleurs toxique.
The drug on which I recovered was also toxic.
- drogue (f) means 'drug'
- récupérer (verb) 'to recover' or 'to get back (something)'
- par ailleurs (adv) means 'otherwise'

TOPIC 191 ❖ Because of - *grâce à* & *à cause de*

Ils ont apporté des modifications grâce auxquelles la durée du trajet a été réduite de moitié.

They have made changes due to which the travel time has been cut in half.

- **durée** (f) means 'duration' or 'length (of time)'
- **réduire** (verb) means 'to reduce' or 'to lower'
- **de moitié** (adv) means 'by a half'

On ne peut prendre qu'un sac chacun à cause du manque d'espace.

We can only take one bag each because of the lack of space.

- **espace** (m) means 'space'

Il y avait plusieurs raisons à cause desquelles on ne pouvait pas réserver de billet en ligne.

There were several reasons due to which one could not book a ticket online.

Ils ont corrigé le bug à cause duquel nous ne pouvions pas réserver de billet en ligne.

They fixed the bug due to which we couldn't book ticket online.

- **corriger** (verb) means 'to correct' or 'to mark (an exam)'

Bootstrap French TOPIC 192

❖ **It is about -** *il s'agit de*

The construction **il s'agit de...** is a fixed expression that introduces the subject of a work (book, film, etc.) or of a situation.

It is only ever used impersonally - with **il**.

- When used with a noun is means 'it is about**...**'.
- It is often used to talk about the topic of a book or film etc. In this the pattern is **dans ce livre, il s'agit de...** .
- When used with a verb is means 'it is a matter of**...**' in the sense of 'one should'.

EXAMPLES:

Dans ce film, de quoi s'agit-il ?
That film - what is it about?

Dans ce film, il s'agit d'un crime.
In this film, it is about a crime.

Dans ce roman, il s'agit d'une princesse.
In this novel, it is about a princess.

Il s'agissait bien d'un ours.
It was indeed about a bear.

Il ne s'agit pas d'une vraie stratégie.
This is not a real strategy.

Il s'agissait d'un grand événement dans notre vie.
It was a big event in our life.

Il ne s'agit pas seulement de l'appartement.
It's not just about the apartment.

Il s'agissait de la première baisse en cinq ans.
It was the first decline in five years.

🔖 **laïcité** (f) means 'secularism (the separation of religon and state)'. In France this is a constitutional principle which is strictlly abided by.

Quand vous parlez de la laïcité, de quoi s'agit-il exactement ?
When you (formal) speak of secularism, what exactly is it?

TOPIC 192 ❖ It is about - *il s'agit de*

Il ne s'agissait pas de nous. Il s'agissait de la société en général.
It wasn't about us. It was about society in general.

Il s'agira de partir à l'heure.
You should leave on time.

💡 Used with a verb the sense is 'one should...'

Il s'agit de faire son travail maintenant.
It's about doing one's job now.

Il s'agit de ne pas se faire attraper.
It's about not getting caught.

Il faut bien réussir tes exams - il s'agit de ton avenir.
(You) have to do well in your (familiar) exams - it's about your future.

Il ne s'agit pas de plaisanter.
It is not a joking matter.

✏️ **au plus vite** means 'as fast as possible'

Il s'agit de le faire au plus vite.
It is a matter of doing it as fast as possible.

Il ne s'agit pas d'argent. Il s'agit de tenir ses promesses.
It's not about money. It is a matter of keeping one's promises.

Ce dont il s'agit, c'est de fierté.
What it's about is pride.

Il s'agit maintenant de faire attention.
Now we should take care.

Il s'agit maintenant d'expliquer les nuances subtiles de la langue française.
It is now a question of explaining the subtle nuances of the French language.

❖ The Imperative

An imperative is a command or request. The imperative mood in French sounds really harsh and really should be avoided.

There are three forms of the imperative: **tu**, **nous** and **vous**.

- The **nous** form is used to give an order that involves oneself as well as others so often expresses a suggestion ('Let's**...**').

The imperative is formed according to these rules:

- **tu** (familiar) - use the present tense **tu** form but drop the final **-s** for **-ER** verbs.
- **nous** - use the present tense **nous** form unchanged.
- **vous** (formal or plural) - use the present tense **vous** form unchanged.

The rules for using imperatives with pronouns are complicated. They depend on whether it is an affirmative or negative imperative. And whether we use one or more than one pronoun.

For an affirmative imperative with one pronoun (including **y** and **en**):

- Use stressed pronouns (**moi, toi** etc.) for the indirect object and reflexive pronouns.
- The pronoun should come immediately after the imperative verb.
- The pronoun should be connected to the imperative with a hyphen.

If the adverbial pronouns **y** or **en** come after an imperative that ends with a vowel, we add an **-s** to the imperative verb to make pronunciation easier. So for example **vas-y !** '(Go there!') and **not va-y**.

For an affirmative imperative with more than one pronoun the order is:

- **le**, **la**, **les** + **moi** then **nous, vous, lui, leur** then **m'**, **t'** then **y, en**

If an object pronoun comes between the verb and an indirect pronoun then all three words should be connected with hyphens.

EXAMPLES:

Arrête !

Stop (familiar)!

> **tu** imperative: start with present tense **arrêtes** - it is an **-ER** verb so drop the final **-s** ⇒ **arrête**

Donne-moi ça.

Give (familiar) me that.

> **tu** imperative: start with present tense **donnes** - it is an **-ER** verb so drop the final **-s** ⇒ **donne**

TOPIC 193 ❖ The Imperative

Viens chez moi, il y une chambre d'amis.
Come (familiar) to my house, there's a guest room.
💡 tu imperative: start with present tense **viens** - it is NOT an **-ER** ⇒ **viens**

Dis merci à la dame !
Say (familiar) thank you to the lady!
💡 tu imperative: start with present tense **dis** - it is NOT an **-ER** ⇒ **dis**

Mettez votre ceinture !
Put on (formal) your belt!

Faites attention !
Take care (formal)! *OR* Be careful!

Allez chercher les enfants à l'école.
Go (formal) get the children from school.

Passez me prendre à 6 heures.
Come by (formal) and pick me up at 6 o'clock.

Faites passer le sel.
Pass (formal) the salt.
💡 Rather than **Passez le sel.**

Nettoie ta chambre dès que possible.
Clean (familiar) your room as soon as possible.

Dites-moi ce que vous voulez.
Tell (formal) me what you want.
💡 Indirect pronoun should be stressed, come after the imperative and connected with a hypen

Aidez-moi ! Je n'arrive pas à me relever.
Help (formal) me! I can't get up.

Dites-leur d'arrêter immédiatement.
Tell (formal) them to stop immediately.

Voici le document. Prends-le avec toi.
Here is the document. Take it with you (familiar).

Laissez-moi tranquille.
Leave (formal) me in peace.
💡 OR 'Leave me alone.'

TOPIC 193 ❖ The Imperative

Charlotte, va au supermarché ! Vas-y !
Charlotte, go (familiar) to the supermarket! Go ahead!
💡 y an imperative that ends with a vowel, add an -s to the imperative

J'ai besoin de stylos. Achètes-en trois pour moi !
I need pens. Buy (familiar) three for me!
💡 en an imperative that ends with a vowel, add an -s to the imperative

J'ai trop de bananes. Prenez-en si vous voulez.
I have too many bananas. Take some if you (formal) want.

Souviens-toi de moi quand nous serons séparés.
Remember (familiar) me when we are apart.
💡 Reflexive pronoun should be the stressed form

Dépêche-toi - le train est sur le point de partir.
Hurry up (formal) - the train is about to leave.

Les enfants, levez-vous. Vous serez en retard à l'école.
Children - get up (plural). You will be late for school.

Assurez-vous d'être là à cinq heures précises.
Be sure (formal) to be there promptly at five.

Rendez-le-lui !
Give (formal) it to him!
💡 More than one pronoun : object pronoun before the indirect pronoun

Vendons-les-leur !
Let's sell them to them!
💡 More than one pronoun : object pronoun before the indirect pronoun

Elle veut lire ton livre. Donne-le-lui !
She wants to read your (familiar) book. Give it to her!
💡 More than one pronoun : object pronoun before the indirect pronoun

Achète-m'en.
Buy (familiar) me some.
💡 More than one pronoun : adverbial pronoun comes last

TOPIC 193 ❖ The Imperative

Va-t'en !
Go away (familiar)!
💡 More than one pronoun : adverbial pronoun (**en**) comes last

Réfléchissez-y et faites-le-moi savoir.
Think about (formal) it and let me know.
💡 More than one pronoun : adverbial pronoun (**y**) comes last

❖ The Negative Imperative

For a negative imperative place **ne...pas** around the imperative verb.

For the negative imperative all pronouns should come before the imperative verb.

For the negative imperative the reflexive pronoun should NOT be the stressed form. And should come before the verb.

For a negative imperative with more than one pronoun the order is:

- **me**, **nous**, **vous** then **le**, **la**, **les** then **m'**, **t'**, **lui**, **leur** then **y**, **en**

EXAMPLES:

Ne bougez pas.
Do not move (formal).
💡 Negative imperative - place **ne...pas** around the imperative verb.

Ne parlez à personne !
Don't tell (formal) anyone!

N'oublions rien !
Let's not forget anything!

N'oubliez pas de m'acheter des stylos.
Do not forget (formal) to buy some pens for me.

Ne touchez jamais à mon téléphone.
Don't ever touch (formal) my phone.

N'oubliez pas de prendre tous vos sacs avec vous.
Don't forget (formal) to take all your bags with you.

N'oublie jamais la personne qui t'aime.
Never forget (familiar) the person who loves you.

Ne leur parlons pas.
Let's not talk to them.
💡 All pronouns before the verb in negative imperatives

Doucement. Ne le faites pas trop vite !
Gently. Don't do (formal) it too fast!

TOPIC 194 ❖ The Negative Imperative

Ne le lui rends pas !
Don't give it back (familiar)!
  💡 More than one pronoun : direct before indirect pronouns

Ne les leur vendez pas !
Don't sell (formal) them!

Ne t'en va pas !
Do not go (familiar)!
  💡 More than one pronoun : adverbial pronoun (**en** or **y**) comes last

Ne m'en achète pas.
Don't buy (familiar) it from me.

N'y va pas sans moi.
Don't go (familiar) without me.

Ne t'inquiète pas.
Don't worry (familiar).
  💡 Reflexive pronoun should be the normal form (NOT the stressed form)

Ne te moque pas de moi !
Do not make fun (familiar) of me!

Ne vous asseyez pas encore.
Don't sit (formal) down yet.

Ne nous moquons pas d'Emmanuelle !
Let's not make fun of Emmanuelle!

Ne te lève pas. Tu sembles être malade.
Do not get up (familiar). You seem to be sick.

❖ Irregular Imperatives - *avoir*, *être* & *savoir*

The verbs **avoir**, **être** & **savoir** have irregular imperative forms:
- avoir: **tu aie, nous ayons, vous ayez**
- être: **tu sois, nous soyons, vous soyez**
- savoir: **tu sache, nous sachons, vous sachez**

The verb **vouloir** also has an irregular imperative. It is used as in the sense of 'would (you) please...' - **veuillez....** Or in the expression **Ne m'en veux pas !**

EXAMPLES:

S'il vous plaît, soyez prudent !
Please be careful!

Sachez que le prof a raison !
Know that the teacher is right!

Veuillez parler en français, s'il vous plaît.
Please speak in French.

Aie un peu de patience !
Have a little patience!

Ne m'en veux pas !
Don't blame me!

Mathieu, ne sois pas méchant avec ton frère !
Mathieu, don't be mean to your (familiar) brother!

Soyons réalistes un instant.
Let's be real for a moment.

Les filles, soyez gentilles avec votre grand-mère !
Girls, be nice to your (plural) grandma!

Petit écureuil, n'aie pas peur !
Little squirrel, don't be afraid!

📖 **écureuil** (m) means 'squirrel'

Ayons foi en notre force !
Let's have faith in our strength!

TOPIC 195 ❖ Irregular Imperatives - *avoir*, *être* & *savoir*

Mes amis, ayez confiance en moi !
My friends, have confidence in me!

Mon amour, sache que je pense toujours à toi.
My love, know that I always think of you (familiar).

Sachons tirer les leçons du passé.
Let's learn the lessons of the past.

Chers collègues, sachez combien votre aide a été appréciée.
Dear colleagues, know how much your (formal) help has been appreciated.

Ne soyez pas excitée par tout sans raison.
Don't be excited(female) about everything without reason.

Ayez de bons résultats.
Have good results.
💡 Wishing someone the best for their exams

Aie du courage.
Have courage.

Sois gentil avec le chien !
Be nice to the dog!

Soyez tranquille, je m'occupe de tout !
Don't worry, I'll take care of everything!

❖ The future perfect - *Le futur antérieur*

The **le futur antérieur** (the future perfect) is used to describe an action or event that will have been completed in the future - normally before some other future event or action.

The subsequent action is conjugated in **le futur simple**.

- The English equivalent is 'will have happened'.

This tense may seem awkward for English speakers but keep in mind that it emphasizes a completed action in the future - something (**le futur simple**) will happen when something else (**le futur antérieur**) will have been completed.

The **futur antérieur** is formed with the **futur simple** of an auxiliary verb (**avoir** or **être**) plus a past participle.

- The **futur antérieur** is often used after **quand**, **lorsque**, **dès que**, **aussitôt que**, **tant que** etc.
- And it can also be used to express probability or supposition in the past.

- This is the equivalent of 'must have' in English.

EXAMPLES:

J'aurai mangé à midi.
I will have eaten by noon.
OR 'will have finished eating by noon'

Quand tu arriveras, il l'aura déjà fait.
When you (familiar) arrive, he will already have done it.

Nous sortirons dès qu'il aura ouvert la porte.
We will leave as soon as he opens the door.
OR 'as soon as he will have opened the door' - when the future action is completed

Je t'enverrai les photos que j'aurai prises pendant le voyage.
I will send you (familiar) the photos that I will take during the trip.
OR 'photos that I will have taken' - when the future action is completed

En quelques heures, nous aurons cueilli au moins cinq kilos de framboises.
In a couple of hours, we will have picked at least five kilos of raspberries.

TOPIC 196 ❖ The future perfect - *Le futur antérieur*

Nous partirons dès qu'ils auront mangé.
We will leave as soon as they have eaten.

💡 OR 'as soon as they have finshed eating' - when the future action is completed

Il me fera savoir aussitôt qu'il aura terminé la tâche.
He will let me know as soon as he has completed the task.

✎ **aussitôt que** means 'as soon as'

Je travaillerai lorsque j'aurai fini mes études.
I will work when I (will) have finished my studies.

J'espère qu'Émilie aura réussi cette entrevue.
I hope that Émilie will succeed in this interview.

✎ **entrevue** (f) means 'interview'

Dès que je t'aurai présenté Jacques, bien sûr tu l'adoreras.
As soon as I introduce you (familiar) to Jacques, you will adore him.

Elle révisera les documents que nous aurons préparés.
She will review the documents we prepare.

💡 OR 'that we will have prepared' - - when the future preparing is completed

Ils auront eu leurs résultats avant midi.
They will have had their results before noon.

Je sortirai quand j'aurai retrouvé mes clés.
I'll go out when I have found my keys.

💡 OR 'will have found my keys' - when the future finding succeeds

Après que tu auras vu tes cadeaux, tu pourras te plaindre.
After you (familiar) have seen your gifts, you can complain.

Je comprendrai mieux dès que je me serai aperçue de mes erreurs.
I will understand better as soon as I (female) realize my mistakes.

💡 OR 'when I will have realized' - when the future realising is done

Pendant notre vie, nous aurons vécu au Canada et en France.
During our lifetime, we will have lived in Canada and France.

💡 When we die the living will be complete

Elle excusera mon comportement une fois que je lui aurai offert des fleurs.
She'll excuse my behavior once I get her flowers.

✎ **une fois que** means 'once' or 'as soon as'

TOPIC 196 ❖ The future perfect - *Le futur antérieur*

Il aura fini le travail avant la fin de la journée.
He will have finished the work before the end of the day.

Je ne veux plus te parler tant que tu ne te seras pas excusée.
I don't want to talk to you again until you (female) have apologized.

tant que means 'until'

Vous pourrez voter aussitôt que vous vous serez inscrite.
You (formal, female) can vote as soon as you register.

Il sera arrivé quelque chose.
Something must have happened.

Expressing express probability or supposition

Il n'a pas téléphoné. Il aura perdu mon numéro de téléphone.
He didn't call. He must have lost my phone number.

Expressing express probability or supposition

Pierre n'est pas ici ; il aura oublié.
Pierre is not here; he must have forgotten.

Expressing express probability or supposition

Brigitte est heureuse ; elle sera tombée amoureuse.
Brigitte is happy; she must have falling in love.

Expressing express probability or supposition

❖ If… then - *Le conditionnel présent*

In French, we use the conditional mood to express conditionality or possibility.

The present tense form of the conditional, **le conditionnel présent**, can be used to express a possible action in the present or future - often used with an 'if..then' (**si**) condition.

When a sentence is used to express a condition in the present that has an unlikely subsequent outcome then the conditional **si** clause should in **l'imparfait** and the (unlikely) outcome in **le conditionnel présent**.

The **conditionnel présent** conjugation is straight forward - add the **imparfait** ending to the stem of **le futur simple**.

- **je** + **aimer-** + **-ias** ⇒ **j'aimerais** - 'I would like'
- **tu** + **finir-** + **-ias** ⇒ **tu finirais** - 'you (familiar) would finish'
- **il** + **vendr** + **-ait** ⇒ **il vendrait** - 'he would sell'
- **elle** + **voudr** + **-ait** ⇒ **elle voudrait** - 'she would want to'
- **nous** + **aur-** + **-ions** ⇒ **nous aurions** - 'we would have'
- **vous** + **ser-** + **-iez** ⇒ **vous seriez** - 'you (formal or plural) would be'
- **ils** + **pourr-** + **-aient** ⇒ **ils pourraient** - 'they would be able to'
- **elles** + **ir-** + **-aient** ⇒ **elles iraient** - 'they (females) would go'

EXAMPLES:

Si j'avais le temps, j'aimerais aller en Guadeloupe.
If I had time I would like to go to Guadeloupe.

Si tu avais le temps, finirais-tu de construire ton bateau ?
If you (familiar) had time, would you finish building your boat?

S'il avait le temps, il vendrait son vélo et en achèterait un nouveau.
If he had time, he would sell his bike and buy a new one.

Si elle avait le temps, voudrait-elle retourner à l'université ?
If she had time, would she want to go back to college?

Si nous avions le temps, nous aurions plus d'enfants.
If we had time, we would have more children.

Si vous aviez le temps, seriez-vous plus heureux ?
If you (formal) had time, would you be happier?

TOPIC 197 ❖ If... then - *Le conditionnel présent*

S'ils avaient plus de temps, ils pourraient aussi peindre l'arrière de la maison.
If they had more time, they could also paint the back of the house.

S'ils avaient plus de temps, ils iraient rendre visite à leurs grands-parents.
If they had more time, they would go visit their grandparents.

S'il partait pour les Caraïbes, il pourrait aller à la plage tous les jours.
If he went to the Caribbean, he could go to the beach every day.

Je t'appellerais si j'entendais des nouvelles.
I'll call you (formal) if I hear any news.

Tu réussirais à l'examen si tu étudiais.
You (formal) would pass the exam if you studied.

S'il était fatigué, il irait se coucher.
If he were tired he would go to bed.

S'il faisait beau, nous irions nous promener.
If the weather was nice, we would go for a walk.

Je l'achèterais si ce n'était pas si cher.
I would buy it if it wasn't so expensive.

Si j'avais le temps, je ferais mes devoirs.
If I had time, I would do my homework.

Si ce n'était pas si bruyant, je ferais mes devoirs.
If it wasn't so loud, I'd be doing my homework.

❖ Polite requests and wishes - *Le conditionnel présent* of *vouloir* & *aimer*

In French, we use the conditional mood to make polite requests and to express wishes.

- The verb **vouloir** can be softened and made more indirect by using it in the conditional mood - so rather than **je veux** ('I want') we can use **je voudrais** ('I would like').
- The verb **aimer** in the conditional can be used to express a wish or desire - **j'aimerais** ('I would like').

Both of these are in effect 'if...then' conditionals but with the 'if possible...' omitted.

EXAMPLES:

Demain, j'aimerais aller au restaurant.
Tomorrow I would like to go to a restaurant.

Il ne voudrait pas m'aider à préparer le dîner par hasard ?
He wouldn't want to help me cook dinner by any chance?

On pourrait peut-être aller au cinéma ?
Maybe we could go to the cinema?

Voudrais-tu de l'eau ?
Would you (familiar) like some water?

Jacques aimerait être en vacances.
Jacques would like to be on vacation.

J'aimerais partir à midi.
I would like to leave at noon.

Aimeriez-vous manger avec nous ?
Would you (formal) like to eat with us?

Voudriez-vous venir chez nous demain ?
Would you (formal) like to come to us tomorrow?

Aimeriez-vous commander un apéritif pour commencer ?
Would you (formal) like to order an aperitif to start?

Je voudrais une salade verte, s'il vous plaît.
I would like a green salad, please.

TOPIC 198 ❖ Polite requests and wishes

J'aimerais acheter une nouvelle maison.
I would like to buy a new house.

Elle voudrait commencer son nouveau travail demain.
She would like to start her new job tomorrow.

Vous auriez du feu, s'il vous plaît ?
Do you (formal) have a light, please?

💡 The verb **avoir** used in the conditional **conditionnel présent** for politeness

Bootstrap French
TOPIC 199

❖ Could - the conditional *pouvoir*

The verbs **pouvoir** ('to be able to') can be used in the conditional mood make a request sound less like an order and instead sound like a suggestion.

So the condition with **pouvoir** can be used to politely ask 'could (you)'.

EXAMPLES:

Je pourrais vous aider ?
Could I help you (formal)?

Pourrais-tu me passer l'eau ?
Could you (familiar) pass me the water?

Est-ce que tu pourrais m'aider ?
Could you (familiar) help me?

Pourrais-tu m'expliquer ce mot ?
Could you (familiar) explain this word to me?

Pourriez-vous fermer la porte s'il vous plaît ?
Could you (formal) close the door please?

S'il vous plaît, est-ce que je pourrais téléphoner ?
Please (formal) could I call?

Tu pourrais me prêter de l'argent ?
Could you (familiar) lend me some money?

Je pourrais t'y emmener si tu voulais.
I could take you (familiar) there if you want.

Pourriez-vous épeler « écureuil » pour moi, s'il vous plaît ?
Could you (formal) spell "squirrel" for me, please?

   ✎ épeler (verb) means 'to spell'

Pourriez-vous m'indiquer où se trouve la poste, s'il vous plaît ?
Could you (formal) point out for me where the post office is please?

   ✎ indiquer (verb) means 'to point out'

TOPIC 199 ❖ Could - the conditional *pouvoir*

Pourrions-nous avoir un Ricard et un Perrier ?
Could we have a Ricard and a Perrier?

Pourriez-vous me dire où se trouve le métro ?
Could you (formal) tell me where the metro is?

Excusez-moi, pourriez-vous préciser votre réponse ?
Excuse me, could you (formal) clarify on your answer?

📖 **préciser** (verb) means 'to clarify' or 'to be more specific'

❖ Would have - *Le conditionnel passé*

The **conditionnel passé** is used to express what would have taken place in the past had some other action, event, or situation happened.

For past hypotheticals the pattern is **si** + <**plus-que-parfait**> & <**conditionnel passé**>.

 - An English example is something like 'I would have gone out had it not rained.'

The **conditionnel passé** is also used to report unconfirmed or hypothetical news.

 - This usage sounds affected, and it only really used by reporters and journalists.

The **conditionnel passé** is formed by using the conditional of auxiliary verb (**avoir** or **être**) + a past participle.

Le conditionnel passé follows the same rules of agreement as all complex tenses that use the past participle, such as **le passé composé**.

EXAMPLES:

Je serais sorti s'il n'avait pas plu.
I would have gone out if it hadn't been raining.

Si j'avais su qu'il allait pleuvoir, j'aurais pris mon parapluie.
If I had known it was going to rain, I would have taken my umbrella.

J'aurais fini mes devoirs s'ils m'avaient laissé tranquille.
I would have finished my homework if they had left me alone.

Si j'avais su l'heure de son arrivée, je serais allé le chercher.
If I had known the time of his arrival, I would have gone to look for him.

Il l'aurait salué, mais il ne l'a pas vu.
He would have greeted him, but he didn't see him.

Si tu n'avais pas suivi notre conseil, qu'est-ce qui serait arrivé ?
If you (familiar) hadn't taken our advice, what would have happened?

Ils seraient restés en France s'ils avaient pu.
They would have stayed in France if they could.

Si tu n'avais pas réveillé les filles, elles auraient dormi jusqu'à midi.
If you (familiar) hadn't woken the girls, they would have slept until noon.

TOPIC 200 ❖ Would have - *Le conditionnel passé*

Juliette serait arrivée à l'heure, mais sa voiture était en panne.
Juliette would have arrived on time, but her car had broken down.

Elle se serait réveillée tôt, mais son réveil n'a pas marché.
She would have woken up early, but her alarm clock didn't work.

Même avec plus de temps, il n'aurait jamais fini la tâche.
Even with more time, he would never have finished the task.

Je n'aurais plus dansé parce que j'avais mal à tête.
I wouldn't have danced anymore because I had a headache.

J'aurais tellement aimé aller en Argentine !
I would have loved to go to Argentina so much!

Jacques aurait pu être un grand artiste.
Jacques could have been a great artist.

❖ Should, should have - the conditional *devoir*

The condition with **devoir** means 'should' or 'ought to'.

And in the **conditionnel passé** - using the past participle **dû** - means 'should have' or 'ought to have'.

EXAMPLES:

Nous devrions faire les courses le plus tôt possible.
We should go shopping as soon as possible.

Tu devrais travailler un peu plus.
You (familiar) should work a little more.

Ils devraient arriver avant nous.
They should arrive before us.

Vous devriez apprendre le français !
You (formal) should learn French!

Tu devrais arrêter de boire du café. Tu n'arrives plus à dormir.
You (familiar) should stop drinking coffee. You won't be able to sleep anymore.

Les enfants, vous devriez être plus polis avec vos parents !
Kids, you (formal) should be more polite to your parents!

Tu devrais mettre un manteau.
You (familiar) should put on a coat.

Je ne devrais pas fumer, c'est mauvais pour la santé.
I shouldn't smoke, it's bad for (my) health.

Je pense que tu ne devrais pas faire ça.
I don't think you (familiar) should do that.

S'il fait beau aujourd'hui, nous devrions aller au parc et profiter du temps.
If the weather is nice today, we should go to the park and enjoy the weather.

Tu n'aurais pas dû écouter Jean_Luc.
You (familiar) shouldn't have listened to Jean-Luc.

TOPIC 201 ❖ Should, should have - the conditional *devoir*

Vous auriez dû me prévenir de votre arrivée !
You (formal) should have told me you were coming!

Vous auriez dû nous prévenir.
You (formal) should have told us.

Elle aurait dû me le dire !
She should have told me!

Tu n'aurais pas dû mettre une robe blanche, la mariée à l'air fâché.
You (familiar) shouldn't have put on a white dress; the bride looks angry.

Les filles auraient dû faire leurs devoirs avant de regarder la télé.
The girls should have done their homework before watching TV.

📖 **télé** (f) means 'telly' (abbreviation of **télévision**)

Vous auriez dû les amener à l'aéroport, les taxis coûtent si cher.
You (formal) should have brought them to the airport, taxis are so expensive.

S'il avait faim, il aurait dû manger plus à midi au lieu de se gaver de bonbons.
If he was hungry, he should have eaten more at noon instead of stuffing himself with sweets.

Ils n'auraient pas dû manger tant de chocolat.
They shouldn't have eaten so much chocolate.

Quand nous étions en France, nous aurions dû aller au Mont St Michel.
When we were in France, we should have gone to Mont St Michel.

Il me semble qu'elle aurait dû tomber amoureuse de la vie française.
It seems to me that she should have fallen in love with the French life (style).

Bootstrap French
TOPIC 202

❖ The verb *tenir* and it's many uses

The verb **tenir** means 'to hold' or 'to keep' but it has many and varied uses. Likewise the reflexive form **se tenir**.

EXAMPLES:

Tu peux tenir la lampe, s'il te plaît ?
Can you (familiar) hold the lamp, please?
- 💡 tenir - 'to hold'

Il tenait ses fils par la main.
He held his sons by the hand.
- 💡 tenir - 'to hold'

Qu'est-ce qu'il tient à la main ?
What is he holding in his hand?
- 💡 tenir - 'to hold'

Pourquoi se tient-il la jambe ?
Why is he holding his leg?
- 💡 se tenir - 'to hold (himself)'

Il est poli de tenir la porte aux autres.
It is polite to hold the door for others.
- 💡 tenir - 'to hold'

Pouvez-vous, s'il vous plaît, tenir cette vis en place ?
Can you (formal) please hold this screw in place?
- 💡 tenir - 'to hold'

Cela dit, Jacques n'a jamais pu tenir sa langue.
That said, Jacques could never hold his tongue.
- 💡 tenir - 'to hold'

Le café me tient éveillé jusqu'à minuit.
Coffee keeps me up until midnight.
- 💡 tenir - 'to keep'
- ✏️ éveillé (adj) means 'awake'

French Grammar

TOPIC 202 ❖ The verb *tenir* and it's many uses

Elle tient toujours ses promesses.
She always keeps her promises.
- *tenir* - 'to keep'

Notre prof ne sait jamais tenir notre classe.
Our teacher never knows how to get control of our class.
- *tenir* - 'to keep under control'

Qui tient ce magasin-là ?
Who runs that store there?
- *tenir* - 'to run (a business)'

Il tient un café au Quartier Latin depuis longtemps.
He's been running a cafe in the Latin Quarter for a long time.
- *tenir* - 'to run (a business)'

Il tient à la fois de son père et de sa mère.
He takes after both his father and his mother.
- *tenir de quelqu'un* - 'to take after somebody'
- *à la fois* means 'at once' or 'both'

Je ne tiens pas à son opinion.
I don't care about his opinion.
- *tenir à quelque chose* - 'to care about something'

Je tiens à vous remercier.
I want to thank you (formal).
- *tenir à +* - 'to be eager to' or 'to be determined to'

Elle tient à y aller.
She wants to go there.
- *tenir à +* - 'to be eager to' or 'to be determined to'

Il tient à ce que tu sois à l'aise.
He wants you (familiar) to be comfortable.
- *tenir à ce que +* - 'to be eager that'

Nous tenons à ce que vous assistiez à la réunion.
We want you (formal) to attend the meeting.
- *tenir à ce que +* - 'to be eager that'

À quoi tient votre grand succès ?
What accounts for your (formal) great success?
- *à quoi tient..?* - 'what accounts for...?'

TOPIC 202 ❖ The verb *tenir* and it's many uses

Nous tenons compte de vos opinions.
We take your (formal) opinions into account.
💡 **tenir compte de** - 'to take into account'

Tiens, voilà un stylo.
Here's a pen.
💡 **tiens** - a command or request

Tiens, je t'ai acheté des fleurs.
Here, I bought you (familiar) flowers.
💡 **tiens** - a command or request

Tu peux me prêter ton portable ? Alors, tiens.
Can I borrow your (familiar) mobile phone? Here you go.
💡 **tiens** - a command or request

Tiens, c'est Corentin là-bas !
Hold on, it's Corentin over there!
💡 **tiens** - an exclamation

Tiens, je viens de trouver 10 euros !
Hey, I just found 10 euros!
💡 **tiens** - an exclamation

Tiens, tiens, tu es enfin arrivé.
Well well, you (familiar) have finally arrived.
💡 **tiens tiens** - 'well well'

Il se tenait près de la porte.
He was standing near the door.
💡 **se tenir** - 'to stand' or 'to sit'

Tiens-toi droit !
Stand up straight!
💡 **se tenir** - 'to stand' or 'to sit'

Arrête de manger le nez dans ton assiette, tiens-toi droit.
Stop eating (with) your nose in your (familiar) plate, sit up straight.
💡 **se tenir** - 'to stand' or 'to sit'

La foire va se tenir place du marché.
The fair will be held in the marketplace.
💡 **se tenir** - 'to take place'

❖ The subjunctive mood - *Le subjonctif*

The subjunctive mood is used in dependent clauses to indicate subjectivity or uncertainty in the mind of the speaker.

There are many conjunctions (that connect clauses) which use the relative pronouns **que** or **qui** that require the subjunctive mood in the dependent clause.

But only sentences where the verb in the dependent clause (after **que** or **qui**) has a subject requires the subjunctive.
- This usually means that sentences with the same subject in both clauses should not use subjunctive conjunctions.

This topic's examples will use one of the following three common subjunctive conjunctions (there are many others):

- **vouloir que** - 'to want that' (a request so there is doubt in the mind of the speaker it will done).
- **il faut que** - 'it is required that' (it is a requirement so doubt that it will be obeyed).
- **il vaut mieux que** - 'it is better that' (it is an opinion so the veracity is in doubt).

To conjugate the subjunctive, start with the present **ils** conjugation and drop –**ent** ending. And then add endings as follows:

- **je** + **mang-** + -e ending ⇒ **je mange** - '(that) I eat'
- **tu** + **finiss-** + -es ending ⇒ **tu finisses** - '(that) you (familiar) finish'
- **il** + **vend-** + -e ending ⇒ **il vende** - '(that) he sells'
- **elle** + **mett-** + -e ending ⇒ **elle mette** - '(that) she put'
- **nous** + **part-** + -ions ending ⇒ **nous partions** - '(that) we leave'
- **vous** + **couvr-** + -iez ending ⇒ **vous couvriez** - '(that) you (formal or plural) cover'
- **ils** + **tienn-** + -ent ending ⇒ **ils tiennent** - '(that) they hold'
- **elles** + **diss-** + -ent ending ⇒ **elles dissent** - '(that) they (females) say'

There are many important exceptions which will be covered in the following topics.

EXAMPLES:

Il veut que je mange tout.
He wants me to eat everything.
　💡 manger ⇒ ils mangent ⇒ mang- + -e ⇒ (que je) mange

TOPIC 203 ❖ The subjunctive mood - *Le subjonctif*

Ils veulent que tu finisses le travail.
They want you (familiar) to finish the job.
💡 finer ⇒ ils finessent ⇒ finiss- + -es ⇒ (que tu) finisses

Elle veut qu'il vende la voiture.
She wants him to sell the car.
💡 vendre ⇒ ils vendent ⇒ vend- + -e ⇒ (que il) vende

Je veux qu'elle mette le livre sur la table.
I want her to put the book on the table.
💡 mettre ⇒ ils mettent ⇒ mett- + -e ⇒ (que elle) mette

Il veut que nous partions.
He wants us to go.
💡 partir ⇒ ils partent ⇒ part- + -ions ⇒ (que nous) partions

Nous voulons que vous couvriez la nourriture.
We want you (formal) to cover the food.
💡 couvrir ⇒ ils couvrent ⇒ couvr- + -iez ⇒ (que vous) couvriez

Elle veut que les enfants tiennent le parapluie.
She wants the children to hold the umbrella.
💡 tenir ⇒ ils tiennent ⇒ tienn- + -ent ⇒ (que ils) tiennent

Je veux que les filles me disent la vérité.
I want girls to tell me the truth.
💡 dire ⇒ ils disent ⇒ dis- + -ent ⇒ (que elles) disent

Il faut que je le lise.
I must read it.
💡 lire ⇒ ils lisent ⇒ lis- + -e ⇒ (que je) lise

Il faut que tu te couches maintenant.
You (familiar) must go to bed now.
💡 se coucher ⇒ ils se couchent ⇒ se couch- + -es ⇒ (que tu te) couches

Il faut qu'il ne conduise pas la voiture.
He must not drive the car.
💡 conduire ⇒ ils conduisent ⇒ conduis- + -e ⇒ (que il) conduise

Il faut qu'elle commence à cuisiner tout de suite.
She needs to start cooking right away.
💡 commencer ⇒ ils commencent ⇒ commenc- + -e ⇒ (que elle) commence

TOPIC 203 ❖ The subjunctive mood - *Le subjonctif*

Il faut que nous demandions le chemin à quelqu'un.
We have to ask someone the way.

💡 demander ⇒ ils demandent ⇒ demand- + -ions ⇒ (que nous) demandions

Il faut que vous montriez votre blessure à un médecin.
You (formal) need to show your injury to a doctor.

💡 montre ⇒ ils montrent ⇒ montr- + -iez ⇒ (que vous) montriez

Il faut qu'ils réfléchissent avant de se lancer.
They have to think before they start.

💡 réfléchir ⇒ ils réfléchissent ⇒ réfléchiss- + -ent ⇒ (que ils) réfléchissent

Il faut qu'elles apprennent à le faire correctement.
They need to learn how to do it properly.

💡 apprendre ⇒ ils apprennent ⇒ apprenn- + -ent ⇒ (que elles) apprennent

Il vaut mieux que j'étudie pendant que je suis jeune.
It is better that I study while I am young.

💡 étudier ⇒ ils étudieent ⇒ étudi- + -e ⇒ (que je) étudie

Il vaut mieux que tu te couches tôt et te lèves tôt.
It is better that you (familiar) go to bed early and get up early.

💡 se lever ⇒ ils se levent ⇒ te lev- + -es ⇒ (que tu te) leves

Il vaut mieux qu'il prenne le bus plutôt que son vélo.
It is better that he takes the bus rather than his bicycle.

💡 prendre ⇒ ils prennent ⇒ prenn- + -e ⇒ (que il) prenne

Il vaut mieux qu'elle passe son temps à lire.
She better spend her time reading.

💡 passeer ⇒ ils passent ⇒ pass- + -e ⇒ (que elle) passe

Il vaut mieux que nous louions une maison au centre de la ville.
It is better that we rent a house in the center of the city.

💡 louer ⇒ ils louent ⇒ lou- + -ions ⇒ (que nous) louions

Il vaut mieux que vous posiez la question vous-même.
You (formal) better ask the question yourself.

💡 poser ⇒ ils posent ⇒ pos- + -iez ⇒ (que vous) posiez

Il vaut mieux qu'ils ne dépensent pas tout leur argent.
It is better that they do not spend all their money.

💡 dépenser ⇒ ils dépensent ⇒ dépens- + -ent ⇒ (que ils) dépensent

TOPIC 203 ❖ The subjunctive mood - *Le subjonctif*

Dans cette situation, il vaut mieux qu'ils ne se marient jamais.
In this situation, it is better that they never marry.

💡 se marier ⇒ ils se marient ⇒ se mari- + -ent ⇒ (que elles se) marient

❖ Irregular subjunctives - *être* & *avoir*

There are nine common verbs that have irregular subjunctive conjugations.

In this topic we cover the first two: **être** & **avoir**.

The verb **être** ('to be'):

- **je sois**
- **tu sois**
- **il soit** & **elle soit**
- **nous soyons**
- **vous soyez**
- **ils soient** & **ells soient**

The verb **avoir** ('to have').

- **j'aie**
- **tu aies**
- **il ait** & **elle ait**
- **nous ayons**
- **vous ayez**
- **ils aient** & **ells aient**

This topic's examples introduce more conjunctions that require the subjunctive. These all relate to expressing an opinion.

EXAMPLES:

C'est dommage que je ne sois que deuxième.
It's a shame that I'm only second.
    être dommage que means 'to be a shame that' (an opinion so takes the subjunctive)

C'est incroyable que tu sois astronaute.
It's amazing that you (familiar) are an astronaut.
    être incroyable que means 'to be incredible that' (an opinion so takes the subjunctive)

Elle est triste qu'il soit malade.
She is sad that he is sick.
    être triste que means 'to be sad that' (an opinion so takes the subjunctive)

TOPIC 204 ❖ Irregular subjunctives - *être* & *avoir*

Mes parents adorent que nous ne soyons pas loin d'eux.
My parents love that we are not far from them.

    🖉 **adorer que** means 'to love that' (an opinion so takes the subjunctive)

Il est surprenant que vous ne soyez pas français.
It is surprising that you (formal) are not French.

    🖉 **il est surprenant que** means 'it is surprising that' (an opinion so takes the subjunctive)

J'ai aimé que mes frères soient dans l'équipe.
I liked that my brothers were in the team.

    🖉 **aimer que** means 'to like that' (an opinion so takes the subjunctive)

Mes amis sont heureux que j'aie une petite amie.
My friends are happy that I have a girlfriend.

    🖉 **être heureux que** means 'to be happy that' (an opinion so takes the subjunctive)

Il est convenable que tu aies le trophée - tu étais la meilleure.
It's fitting that you (familiar) have the trophy - you were the best.

    🖉 **il est convenable que** means 'it is proper/fitting that' (an opinion so takes the subjunctive)

Je suis surpris que l'écureuil ait autant de noix dans la bouche.
I am surprised that the squirrel has so many nuts in his mouth.

    🖉 **être surpris que** means 'to be surprised that' (an opinion so takes the subjunctive)

C'est très bon que nous ayons maintenant les bonnes informations.
It's very good that we now have the right information.

    🖉 **il est bon que** means 'it is good that' (an opinion so takes the subjunctive)

Est-ce normal que vous ayez un verre dans chaque main ?
Is it normal for you (formal) to have a drink in each hand?

    🖉 **il est normal que** means 'it is normal that' (an opinion so takes the subjunctive)

Nous apprécions vraiment que vous soyez ici avec nous.
We really appreciate you (formal) being here with us.

    🖉 **apprécier que** means 'to appreciate that' (an opinion so takes the subjunctive)

Il est regrettable que Jacques n'ait pas le temps d'être ici.
It is unfortunate that Jacques does not have time to be here.

    🖉 **être regrettable que** means 'to be regrettable that' (an opinion so takes the subjunctive)

Je suis surpris que Béatrice ne soit pas encore une actrice célèbre.
I'm surprised that Beatrice isn't a famous actress yet.

    🖉 **être surpris que** means 'to be surprised that' (an opinion so takes the subjunctive)

TOPIC 204 ❖ Irregular subjunctives - *être* & *avoir*

Nous trouvons étrange que vous ayez un tel succès avec un livre sur les femmes d'Henri IV.

We find it strange that you (formal) have such success with a book on the wives of Henri IV.

il est etrange que means 'it is strange that' (an opinion so takes the subjunctive)

❖ The past subjunctive - *Le passé du subjonctif*

The subjunctive forms of both **être** and **avoir** can be used as auxiliary verbs to form a **passé composé** form of the subjunctive called **le passé du subjonctif**.

Whether the initial clause is in the present or past tense, the subordinate (subjunctive) clause can remain in the **passé du subjonctif**.

This topic's examples introduce more conjunctions that connote uncertainty including judgement, perceptions or feelings.

EXAMPLES:

Je suis surpris qu'il ait dit une telle bêtise.
I'm surprised he said such nonsense.
- être surpris que means 'to be surprised that'

Nous sommes contents qu'ils se soient réunis.
We're glad they got together.
- être content que means 'to be happy that'

Il est regrettable que le gouvernement n'ait pas baissé les impôts.
It is unfortunate that the government has not reduced taxes.
- il est regrettable que means 'it is regrettable that'

J'ai honte que mon fils ait dit ça.
I'm ashamed my son said that.
- avoir honte que means 'to be ashamed that'

Il est faux que des extraterrestres aient kidnappé le président.
It is not true that aliens kidnapped the president.
- il est faux que means 'it is false that'

C'est bizarre que les kangourous aient une poche.
It's weird that kangaroos have a pouch.
- il est bizarre que means 'it is odd that'

Nous sommes contents qu'ils se soient réunis.
We're glad they got together.
- être content que means 'to be happy that'
- Uses the past subjunctive

French Grammar

TOPIC 205 ❖ The past subjunctive - *Le passé du subjonctif*

Nous détestions que nous ayons dû aller à l'école le week-end.
We hated that we had to go to school on weekends.

📖 *détester que* means 'to hate that'

Nous regrettons que nous ne soyons pas allés à Paris cet été.
We regret that we did not go to Paris this summer.

📖 *regretter que* means 'to regret that'

Ce n'est pas juste que tu y sois allée sans ta sœur.
It's not fair that you (familiar) went without your sister.

📖 *il est juste que* means 'it is right/fair that'

Je doute qu'elle ait fini ses devoirs.
I doubt she's finished her homework.

📖 *douter que* means 'to doubt that'

J'apprécie qu'elle ait pu venir.
I appreciate that she could come.

📖 *apprécier que* means 'to appreciate that'

Nous nous sommes réjouis que tu sois venu à la fête.
We were delighted that you (familiar) came to the party.

📖 *se réjouir que* means 'to be delighted that'

Il était regrettable qu'il n'ait pas réussi.
It was unfortunate that he did not succeed.

📖 *être regrettable que* means 'to be regrettable that'

J'avais peur qu'ils soient tombés.
I was afraid they had fallen.

📖 *avoir peur que* means 'to be afraid that'

Il était utile que vous veniez avec quelques outils.
It was helpful that you (formal) came with some tools.

📖 *il est utile que* means 'it is useful that'

Il était inutile que vous veniez sans aucun outil.
There was no need for you (formal) to come without any tools.

📖 *il est inutile que* means 'it is useless that'

C'était honteux qu'il n'ait pas payé ses impôts.
It was shameful that he didn't pay his taxes.

📖 *il est honteux que* means 'it is shameful that'

TOPIC 205 ❖ The past subjunctive - *Le passé du subjonctif*

Ayant parlé au voisin, il semble qu'ils aient déménagé en Dordogne.
Having spoken to the neighbor, it seems they have moved to the Dordogne.

il semble que means 'it seems that'

Bootstrap French TOPIC 206

❖ More irregular subjunctives - *faire*, *aller* & *pouvoir*

In this topic we cover three more irregular verbs with irregular subjunctives: **faire**, **aller** and **pouvoir**.

- **faire**: je fasse, tu fasses, il fasse, nous fassions, vous fassiez, ils fassent
- **aller**: j'aille, tu ailles, il aille, nous allions, vous alliez, ils aillent
- **pouvoir**: je puisse, tu puisses, il puisse, nous puissions, vous puissiez, ils puissent

Notice that once you know the subjunctive 'verb stems' then all the conjugations take the same endings.

This topic's examples introduce conjunctions that convey possibilities, opinions, doubt and suppositions that require the subjective.

EXAMPLES:

Mes parents s'attendaient à ce que je fasse mes devoirs avant le dîner.
My parents expected me to do my homework before dinner.

🖉 **s'attendre à ce que** means 'to expect' (requires the subjunctive)

Même si je lui ai demandé, je doute que mon fils fasse le ménage.
Even though I asked him, I doubt my son is doing the house cleaning.

🖉 **douter que** means 'to doubt that' (requires the subjunctive)

Il semble qu'ils fassent la tête.
It seems that they are sulking.

🖉 **il semble que** means 'it seems that' (requires the subjunctive)

Il se peut que nous fassions des économies d'argent en achetant une voiture diesel.
It may be that we save money by buying a diesel car.

🖉 **il se peut que** means 'it may be that' (requires the subjunctive)

Il est peu probable que le tigre fasse exactement la même chose deux fois.
It is improbable that the tiger does the exact same thing twice.

🖉 **il n'est pas probable que** means 'it is improbable that' (requires the subjunctive)

Le fait que l'éléphant aille à la rivière signifie qu'il a soif.
The fact that the elephant goes to the river means that it is thirsty.

🖉 **le fait que** means 'the fact that' (requires the subjunctive)

TOPIC 206 ❖ More irregular subjunctives - *faire, aller & pouvoir*

À cause de la grève, il n'est pas certain que vous alliez en Grèce lundi.
Because of the strike, it is not certain that you (formal) will go to Greece on Monday.

> *il n'est pas certain que* means 'it is not certain that' (requires the subjunctive)

Il est peu probable que quelqu'un aille en prison pour un crime aussi mineur.
It is unlikely that anyone will go to jail for such a minor crime.

> *il est improbable que* means 'it is improbable that' (requires the subjunctive)

On m'a dit qu'il était impossible que nous puissions nous rendre en Grèce lundi.
I was told it is impossible that we can go to Greece on Monday.

> *il est impossible que* means 'it is impossible that' (requires the subjunctive)

Il est peu probable qu'il puisse grimper sur le toit sans échelle.
It is doubtful that he can climb onto the roof without a ladder.

> *il est douteux que* means 'it is doubtful that' (requires the subjunctive)

Je ne pense pas qu'il soit possible que vous puissiez parler huit langues.
I don't think it's possible that you (formal) can speak eight languages.

> *il est possible que* means 'it is possible that' (requires the subjunctive)

Il n'est pas sûr que nous puissions y prendre un taxi.
It is not sure that we can get a taxi there.

> *il n'est pas sûr que* means 'it is not certain that' (requires the subjunctive)

Le bébé pleure de crainte que le docteur ne lui fasse mal.
The baby is crying for fear that the doctor will hurt him.

> *de crainte que* means 'for fear of' (requires the subjunctive)

❖ Two more irregular subjunctives - *savoir* & *vouloir*

Two more verb with irregular subjunctive forms are **savoir** & **vouloir**.

- **savoir**: je sache, tu saches, il sache, nous sachions, vous sachiez, ils sachent
- **vouloir**: je veuille, tu veuilles, il veuille, nous voulions, vous vouliez, ils veuillent

Notice that once you know the subjunctive 'verb stem' then the conjugations take the same endings.

This topic's examples introduce subjunctive conjunctions that convey preferences, advice, needs, desires and orders.

EXAMPLES:

Il est essentiel que vous sachiez le mot de passe par cœur.
It is essential that you (formal) know the password by heart.
  il est essentiel que means 'it is essential that'

Il est temps qu'ils sachent ce qu'on attend d'eux.
It is time for them to know what is expected of them.
  il est temps que means 'it is time that'

Il est à souhaiter qu'elle sache quoi faire une fois là-bas.
Hopefully she knows what to do once there.
  il est à souhaiter que means 'it is to be hoped that'

Il suffit que vous et moi le sachions sans le dire au monde entier.
It is enough that you (formal) and I know it without telling the whole world.
  il suffit que means 'it is enough that'

Leurs parents ont tenu à ce que leurs enfants sachent parler chinois.
Their parents wanted their children to know how to speak Chinese.
  tenir à ce que means 'to insist that'

Il est nécessaire que tu saches que j'étais sérieuse.
You (familiar) need to know that I was serious.
  il est nécessaire que means 'it is necessary that'

TOPIC 207 ❖ Two more irregular subjunctives - *savoir* & *vouloir*

Il est préférable qu'ils veuillent tous la même chose pour le déjeuner.
It is preferable that they all want the same thing for lunch.

☞ **préférer que** means 'to prefer that'

❖ So that - the subjunctive conjunctions *pour que* & *afin que*

The common conjunctions **pour que** and **afin que** are used to express purpose.

They essentially mean the same thing: 'so that', 'in order that' or 'for the purpose that'.

And both take the subjunctive.

Note that if the subject of both clauses is the same, we do not use these subjunctive conjunctions.

- Just use the subject first and then **pour** + .

EXAMPLES:

Je le lui ai dit pour qu'il sache à l'avance.
I told him so he knew in advance.

Je vais répéter afin que tout soit clair.
I will repeat so that everything is clear.

Je vous le dis maintenant pour que vous ne soyez pas surpris.
I tell you (formal) now so that you are not surprised.

J'ai ouvert les fenêtres afin que le vent puisse souffler.
I opened the windows so the wind could blow.

Je lui ai prêté mon pull pour qu'elle n'ait pas froid.
I lent her my sweater so she wouldn't be cold.

Louis donne 10 euros à ses enfants pour qu'ils achètent des fournitures.
Louis gives his children 10 euros to buy supplies.

Louis apporte des pommes à sa mère afin qu'elle prépare une tarte.
Louis brings apples to his mother to bake a pie.

Transmettez cet article à Marc pour qu'il le revoie.
Forward this article to Mark for review.

Je ferais tout pour que tu m'aimes.
I would do anything so that you (familiar) love me.

Elle travaille dur afin qu'il ne manque de rien.
She works hard so that he doesn't lack anything.

TOPIC 208 ❖ So that - the subjunctive conjunctions *pour que* & *afin que*

J'y vais afin que ma femme soit contente.
I go there to make my wife happy.

Il faudra que je porte mes lunettes pour que je puisse voir l'écran.
I will have to wear my glasses so that I can see the screen.

Je devrai parler en anglais pour que tu ne ries pas de moi.
I will have to speak in English so that you (familiar) don't laugh at me.

Nous sommes allés au magasin pour que tu puisses acheter du papier à lettres.
We went to the store so you (familiar) could buy stationery.

Elle va nous conduire à la banque afin que nous la cambriolions.
She will drive us to the bank so that we (can) rob it.

Il vous a donné ses clés afin que vous puissiez entrer par vous-même.
He gave you (formal) his keys so you could enter on your own.

　💡 **vous-même** and NOT **vous-mêmes** because it is second person singular

J'ai acheté ce chapeau pour que tu aies bien chaud cet hiver.
I bought this hat to keep you (familiar) warm this winter.

Je suis allée au magasin pour acheter des fruits.
I went to the store in order to buy fruit.

　💡 NOTE: The subject of both clauses is the same, so do not use the subjunctive construction.

Il est à la bibliothèque afin de pouvoir étudier en paix.
He is at the library so that he can study in peace.

　💡 NOTE: The subject of both clauses is the same, so do not use the subjunctive construction.

❖ Although - the subjunctive conjunction *bien que* & *quoique*

The very common conjunctions **bien que** and **quoique** are used to express contradiction.

Both mean 'although' or 'even though'.

And both take the subjunctive.

The term **meme si** also means 'even if' or 'even though' but it takes the indicative - not the subjunctive.

EXAMPLES:

Elle ne le fait pas, bien qu'elle le puisse sans aucun doute.
She doesn't, although she undoubtedly can.

Je sais conduire, bien que je n'aie pas le permis depuis longtemps.
I know how to drive, although I haven't had a license for a long time.

Il assume des fonctions de directeur financier, bien qu'il n'en ait pas le titre.
He serves as chief financial officer, although he does not have the title.

Elle est partie, bien que je lui aie dit de rester ici.
She left even though I told her to stay here.

Bien qu'elles soient intelligentes, nous ne leur avons pas donné le travail.
Although they are smart, we didn't give them the job.

Bien que je sache les réponses, je ne veux pas passer l'examen.
Although I know the answers, I do not want to take the exam.

Je viendrai, bien que je sois très fatigué.
I will come even though I am very tired.

Jacques a échoué à son examen, bien qu'il ait travaillé dur.
Jacques failed his exam despite studying/working hard.

Bien que Pierre soit venu, je suis sortie.
Although Pierre came, I left.

Bien qu'elle soit très grande, elle n'aime pas jouer au basket.
Although she is very tall, she does not like to play basketball.

TOPIC 209 ❖ Although - the subjunctive conjunction *bien que* & *quoique*

Il m'a brisé le cœur, bien que ce ne soit pas la première fois.
He broke my heart, although this is not the first time.

Je viens chez toi quoiqu'il soit assez tard.
I'm coming to your (familiar) house although it's quite late.

Il ne le fait plus, quoiqu'il le puisse.
He doesn't do it anymore, although he can.

Quoique je veuille faire, ma copine n'est jamais d'accord.
Whatever I want to do, my girlfriend never agrees.

Quoique le prix ait baissé, ça ne vaut quand même pas la peine de l'acheter.
Although the price has dropped, it is still not worth buying.

Il semble que vous puissiez le faire facilement, quoique cela me paraisse difficile.
It seems that you (formal) can do it easily, although it seems difficult to me.

Quoiqu'il pleuve de temps en temps sur les collines, on y va !
Though it rains once in a while on the hills, let's go!

Je ne te crois pas même si tu me l'affirmes.
I don't believe you (familiar) even though you tell me.

💡 *meme si* does not require the subjunctive

Je lui rendrai visite même si cela me coûte.
I will visit him even if it costs me.

💡 *meme si* does not require the subjunctive

Tu ne serais pas parti en voyage même si je t'avais accompagné.
You (familiar) wouldn't have gone on a trip even if I had accompanied you.

💡 *meme si* does not require the subjunctive

Bootstrap French
TOPIC 210

❖ **Until - the subjunctive conjunction** *jusqu'à ce que*

A very common time-related related subjunctive conjunction is **jusqu'à ce que**. It means 'until (some action)' and requires a relative clause.

EXAMPLES:

J'attendrai jusqu'à ce qu'il ait terminé.
I'll wait until he's finished.

Je le chatouille jusqu'à ce qu'il rie aux éclats.
I tickle him until he laughs out loud.

Jusqu'à ce que la mort nous sépare.
Until death do us part.

Laissez la glace au congélateur jusqu'à ce qu'elle soit prise
Leave the ice cream in the freezer until set

Je ferai la vaisselle avant que je parte.
I'll do the dishes before I leave.

On peut rester ici jusqu'à ce qu'il cesse de pleuvoir.
We can stay here until it stops raining.

Il faut le remuer jusqu'à ce que la sauce soit bien épaisse.
(You) have to stir it until the sauce is thick.

Il a secoué la branche jusqu'à ce qu'elle casse.
He shook the branch until it broke.

Nous continuerons jusqu'à ce qu'ils veuillent bien négocier.
We will continue until they are willing to negotiate.

Je reste ici jusqu'à ce que tu sois bien installée.
I'll stay here until you (familiar) (female) are settled.

Le petit garçon était anxieux jusqu'à ce que sa mère revienne de voyage.
The little boy was anxious until his mother returned from a trip.

Il l'appellera jusqu'à ce qu'elle réponde.
He will call her until she answers.

TOPIC 210 ❖ Until - the subjunctive conjunction *jusqu'à ce que*

Nous sommes restés à l'intérieur du café jusqu'à ce que la pluie s'arrête.
We stayed inside the cafe until the rain stopped.

Bootstrap French
TOPIC 211

❖ The subjunctive with negated verbs expressing doubt or uncertainty

The subjunctive is used after the negative form of verbs that express doubt or uncertainty.

This includes subjunctive conjunctions like (but not limited to):

- **ne pas penser que** - 'to not think that'
- **ne pas croire que** - 'to not believe that'
- **ne pas être sûr que** - 'to not believe that'
- **ne pas être convaincu que** - 'to not be convinced that'
- **ne pas être persuadé que** - 'to not be persuaded that'
- **ne pas prétendre que** - 'to not claim that'

It is however possible (especially in written French) to use the indicative mood in these types of phrases if the speaker wants to emphasize that he/she is certain about some action or outcome.

EXAMPLES:

Je ne pense pas qu'il revienne.
I don't think he's coming back.

Je ne pense pas qu'ils soient encore prêts.
I don't think they are ready yet.

Je pense qu'il viendra, mais je ne pense pas qu'elle vienne.
I think he will come but I don't think she will.

Il était malade donc je ne pense pas qu'il soit allé à l'opéra hier soir.
He was sick so I don't think he went to the opera last night.

Elle ne croit pas qu'il veuille nous inviter.
She doesn't think he wants to invite us.

Je ne suis pas sûr qu'ils viennent.
I'm not sure they're coming.

Je ne suis pas sûr que tout le monde comprenne que les avalanches sont dangereuses.
I'm not sure everyone understands that avalanches are dangerous.

TOPIC 211 ❖ The subjunctive with negated verbs expressing doubt or uncertainty

Nous ne sommes pas convaincus qu'il ait la bonne solution.
We are not convinced that he has the right solution.

Je ne suis pas convaincu que le gouvernement puisse réduire le chômage.
I am not convinced that the government can reduce unemployment.

Je ne suis pas convaincu que ce ne soit pas possible.
I'm not convinced it's not possible.

Je ne suis pas persuadé que ce soit le cas.
I am not convinced that is the case.

Je ne prétends pas que ce soit comme ça partout en France.
I do not claim that it is like that everywhere in France.

Je ne prétends pas que cette option soit parfaite.
I don't claim that this option is perfect.

❖ Subjunctive with Negative Pronouns and Indefinite Pronouns

The negative pronouns **ne..personne** and **ne..rien** take the subjunctive in their subordinate clause.

Likewise, **quelqu'un qui** and **quelque chose qui** require the subjunctive when there is doubt as to whether the person or thing being referenced actually exists.

EXAMPLES:

Il n'y a personne ici que nous connaissons.
There is no one here that we know.

Il n'y a personne ici qui nous connaisse.
There is no one here who knows us.

Je ne connais personne qui sache parler le portugais.
I don't know anyone who can speak Portuguese.

Il n'y a rien qu'il puisse dire qui puisse m'empêcher.
There's nothing he can say that can prevent me (from doing something).
　📖 empêcher (verb) means 'to prevent'

Nous ne voulons rien qui se vende dans ce magasin.
We don't want anything being sold in this store.

Il n'y a rien du tout dans cette situation qui soit compréhensible.
There is nothing at all in this situation that is understandable.

Ils n'ont rien dit de nouveau ou qui m'ait surpris.
They didn't say anything new or that surprised me.

Dites-moi s'il y a quelqu'un qui se souvienne de l'adresse.
Tell me if anyone remembers the address.
　💡 Doubt whether such a person exists

Je veux quelque chose qui puisse simplifier la vie.
I want something that can make life easier.
　💡 Doubt whether such a thing exists

Nous cherchons quelqu'un qui puisse travailler indépendamment.
We are looking for someone who can work independently.
　💡 Doubt whether such a person exists

TOPIC 212 ❖ Subjunctive with Negative Pronouns and Indefinite Pronouns

Il ne connaît personne qui veuille venir à la fête.
He doesn't know anyone who wants to come to the party.
💡 Doubt whether such a person exists

C'est quelque chose qui me restera pour toujours.
It's something that will stay with me forever.
💡 No doubt thing exists so use indicative form

Bootstrap French
TOPIC 213

❖ To see to it that - the subjunctive with *faire en sorte que*

The conjunction **faire en sorte que** means 'to make sure that (something happens)'. It takes the subjunctive in the relative clause.

EXAMPLES:

Il faut faire en sorte que des profils en ligne soient protégés.
We must ensure that online profiles are protected.

Faites en sorte que vous arriviez avant moi.
Make sure you (formal) get there before me.

Pourriez-vous faire en sorte qu'il revienne avant 10 h ?
Could you (formal) arrange for him to return before 10:00 a.m.?

Nous ferons en sorte que vous soyez logés convenablement.
We will make sure that you (formal) are properly accommodated.

Elle a fait en sorte que personne ne l'ait reconnue.
She made sure no one recognized her.

Sophie fait en sorte que tous ses invités ne manquent de rien.
Sophie makes sure that all her guests lack for nothing.

Faites en sorte de ne pas arriver en retard !
Make sure (formal) not to arrive late!

Elle fait en sorte que son avis soit entendu lors du débat.
She makes sure that her opinion is heard during the debate.

Il voulait faire en sorte que cette date limite soit respectée.
He wanted to make sure that deadline was met.

    date limite (f) means 'deadline'

Pour faire en sorte que personne n'ait faim, nous en avons commandé assez pour une petite armée.
To make sure no one goes hungry, we've ordered enough for a small army.

❖ Impersonal subjunctives - *falloir*, *pleuvoir* & *valoir*

There are three common verbs that are used impersonally and that have irregular subjunctives:
- **falloir** in its present tense is **il faut** ('it is necessary') and its subjunctive is **il faille**.
- **pleuvoir** in its present tense is **il pleut** ('it rains') and its subjunctive is **il pleuve**.
- **valoir** in its present tense is **il vaut** ('it is worth') and its subjunctive is **il vaille**.

EXAMPLES:

Il est probable qu'il faille faire plus.
It is likely that more needs to be done.

Pas étonnant qu'il faille six ou sept ans pour le construire.
Not surprising that it takes six or seven years to build.

Il se peut qu'il faille demander au patron si ce serait possible.
It could be that (we) need to ask the boss if that would be possible.

Je crains qu'il faille être d'accord avant de continuer.
I'm afraid it is necessary to agree before continuing.

Je ne pense pas qu'il faille venir ce soir.
I don't think (you) need to come tonight.

Au cas où il pleuve, n'oubliez pas de fermer les fenêtres.
In case it rains, remember to close the windows.

Il est important qu'il pleuve bientôt - sinon, nous devrions arroser le jardin nous-mêmes.
It is important that it rains soon - otherwise we would have to water the garden ourselves.

Je n'ai pas l'impression qu'il vaille la peine.
I don't feel like it's worth it.

Bootstrap French
TOPIC 215

❖ **Whatever, whoever, whenever - the subjunctive with *quoi que*, *qui que* & *où que***

The subjunctive is used with concessive conjunctions like:
- **quoi que** means 'whatever'
- **qui que** means 'whoever'
- **où que** means 'wherever'

Note that **quoi que ce soit** ('whatever (thing)') and **qui que ce soit** ('whichever person') are frequently used as indefinite pronouns in their own right.

The common pattern **si** + + **que** meaning 'however' or 'no matter how' something (is)' also takes a subjunctive subordinate clause.
- For example 'No matter how big it (is)...' or 'However strange it (is)**...**'.

EXAMPLES:

Quoi que je fasse, il semble que j'ai des problèmes.
Whatever I do, it seems that I have problems.

Où que je sois, je pense à toi.
Wherever I am, I think of you (familiar).

Qui que vous soyez, je vous demande de partir.
Whoever you are, I'm asking you (formal) to leave.

Quoi que vous fassiez, vous devez arrêter tout de suite !
Whatever you do, you (formal) must stop immediately!

Il leur donne quoi qu'ils veuillent.
He gives them whatever they want.

Si tu as besoin de quoi que ce soit, fais-le-nous savoir.
If you (familiar) need anything, let us know.

J'ai toujours mon mobile avec moi, où que j'aille.
I always have my mobile with me, wherever I go.

Vous devez vous adresser à qui que soit de responsable.
You (formal) should contact whoever is responsible.

Quoi que tu fasses, ne dis rien à mon petit ami !
Whatever you (familiar) do, don't tell my boyfriend!

TOPIC 215 ❖ Whatever, whoever, whenever

Où que j'aille dans la vie, je me souviendrai de votre gentillesse.
Wherever I go in life, I will remember your (formal) kindness.

Toute personne, d'où qu'elle vienne, doit obéir à la loi du pays.
Everyone, no matter not matter where they come from, must obey the law of the land.

Quoi qu'il te dise, je ne lui fais pas confiance.
Whatever his arguments, I don't trust him.

Si tu veux changer quoi que ce soit dans ton appartement, il faut demander au propriétaire.
If you (familiar) want to change anything in your apartment, you have to ask the landlord.

💡 **quoi que ce soit** here is used as a noun
✎ **quoi que ce soit** (m) means 'whatever'

Ne laissez pas l'enfant toucher quoi que ce soit.
Do not let the child touch anything.

💡 **quoi que ce soit** here is used as a noun

Si difficile que ce soit, rends-moi ce petit service.
As difficult as it is, do me that little favor.

❖ Whichever - the subjunctive and indefinite pronoun *quel que*

The indefinite pronoun **quel que** ('whichever' or 'whatever') takes the verb in the subjunctive mood directly.

And of course, this pronoun should agree in gender and number by using **quel que**, **quelle que**, **quels que** or **quelles que** as appropriate.

EXAMPLES:

Quelle que soit l'heure, n'hésitez pas à me téléphoner.
Whatever time it is, don't hesitate to telephone me.

Quel que soit le problème, je m'en occuperai.
Whatever the problem, I'll take care of it.

Quel que soit le moment où tu décides, fais-moi savoir ce que tu voudrais faire.
Whenever you (familiar) decide, let me know what you would like to do.

Quelle que soit la manière dont tu choisis, je suis sûr que cela marchera bien.
Whichever way you (familiar) choose, I'm sure it will work out well.

Quelles que soient les dimensions de la pièce, on a le tapis pour vous.
Whatever the size of the room, we have the rug for you (formal).

Quelle que soit la manière dont tu le vois, c'est toujours injuste.
Whichever way you (familiar) see it, it's still unfair.

Quelle que soit la manière dont il s'y est pris, ça n'a pas fonctionné.
Whichever way he went about it, it didn't work.

Quelles que soient ses raisons, il ne devrait pas se comporter ainsi en public !
Whatever his reasons, he shouldn't behave like that in public!

Quelles qu'aient pu être ses excuses, je ne le lui pardonnerai jamais !
Whatever his excuses may have been, I will never forgive him!

❖ Inverted subjunctive conjunctions

Sentences that include a subjunctive conjunction can be inverted so that the subordinate clause becomes the subject of the sentence.

EXAMPLES:

Qu'il vienne est très important.
That he comes is very important.

Qu'il ne puisse pas venir est regrettable.
That he can't come is unfortunate.

Qu'il ait dit ça m'a choqué.
That he said that shocked me.

Qu'il ne puisse pas venir s'explique très facilement.
That he cannot come is very easily explained.

Que la fusée explose est peu probable.
That the rocket explodes is unlikely.

Qu'elle puisse venir, c'est certain.
That she can come, is certain.

Bootstrap French
TOPIC 218

❖ Superlative and the subjunctive

When a superlative is used as a conjunction (with **que**) the subordinate clause can be in the subjunctive mood.

Only when the speaker is not certain that the fact is actually 'the best' or 'the last' etc. (when the word 'probably' can be injected) then the subjunctive should be used.

And if the speaker is certain of the fact then the indicative mood should be used.

The superlatives conjunctions include **le meilleur que** ('the best that'), **le pire que** ('the worst that'), **le plus...que** ('the most..that'), etc.

Also limiting adjectives like **le premier que** ('the first that'); **le dernier que** ('the last that'); **le seul que** ('the only that'); **l'unique que** ('the only that') etc.

EXAMPLES:

Ce garçon est le plus grand que j'aie vu.
This boy is (probably) the tallest I have seen.

Ce livre est le pire que j'aie lu.
This book is (probably) the worst I have read.

C'est la meilleure idée que tu aies jamais eue !
It's the best idea you (familiar, female) have ever had!

Julie est la seule femme que je connaisse ici.
Julie is (probably) the only woman I know here.

C'est probablement la dernière lettre d'amour que je lui aie écrite.
This is probably the last love letter I wrote to her.

C'est l'homme le plus intelligent que je connaisse.
He's (probably) the smartest man I know.

Elle est la seule personne qui vienne qui est célibataire.
She is (probably) the only person who comes who is single.

C'est le meilleur livre français que j'aie jamais lu.
This is (probably) the best French book I have ever read.

C'est le meilleur casse-croûte qui se vende sur le marché.
It is (probably) the best snack that is sold in the market.

TOPIC 218 ❖ Superlative and the subjunctive

C'est le dernier bus que tu puisses prendre à la gare.
This is (probably) the last bus you (familiar) can take from the station.

Pierre est le meilleur joueur que j'aie jamais vu.
Pierre is (probably) the best player I have ever seen.

Ce sont les enfants les plus bruyants que je connaisse.
They are (probably) the loudest kids I know.

Nous avons acheté le vélo le moins cher que nous ayons pu trouver.
We bought the cheapest bike we could find.

C'est le livre le plus intéressant sur ce sujet que j'aie pu trouver.
This is the most interesting book on this subject that I have been able to find.

C'est le dernier conseil qu'il m'ait donné.
This is (probably) the last piece of advice he gave me.

C'est le seul bateau qui soit arrivé.
It is (probably) the only boat that has arrived.

Elle est la seule personne qui puisse nous aider maintenant.
She's (probably) the only person who can help us now.

The subjunctive and the *ne explétif*

There are certain subjective conjunctions that require the subordinate clause to be expressed in the negative. This is done by inserting the particle **ne**.

These subjective conjunctions usually involve verbs with a negative connotation such as 'to fear', 'to doubt' etc.

Examples include:
- **craindre que** or **avoir craint que** = 'to fear that'
- **avoir peur que** - 'to be afraid that'
- **de peur que** - 'for fear that' or 'lest (that)'
- **douter que** or **redouter que** - 'to doubt that'
  - **douter** only takes the **ne explétif** if the main clause is negated.
  - The reflexive **se douter** ('to suspect') does not take require the **ne explétif** in any circumstance.

The **ne explétif** in the subordinate clause serves to emphasize the negative aspect of the conjunction.

Note that the inclusion of **pas** in addition to the **explétif ne** is likely to completely change the meaning of the sentence.

EXAMPLES:

Je crains qu'il n'arrive pas à l'heure.
I fear that he won't arrive on time.

Je crains que tu ne deviennes un peu snob.
I'm afraid you (familiar) are becoming a bit of a snob.

Je crains que son souhait ne se réalise.
I fear his wish will come true.

Il a vraiment craint que je sois sérieux.
He really feared that I was serious.

définitif (adj) means 'permanent' or 'final'

On a craint que cette mesure temporaire ne devienne définitive.
It is feared that this temporary measure will become permanent.

J'ai peur qu'il ne soit trop tard.
I'm afraid it's too late.

TOPIC 219 ❖ The subjunctive and the *ne explétif*

N'as-tu pas peur que ta famille le sache ?
Aren't you (familiar) afraid that your family will find out (know)?

Il a bien peur que son père soit malade.
He is afraid that his father is sick.

Il ne voulait pas te le dire de peur que tu n'aies raison.
He didn't want to tell you (familiar) for fear that you were right.

Je lui ai fait une liste de peur qu'il n'oublie quelque chose.
I made him a list lest he forget something.

- **admettre** (verb) means 'to admit' ot 'to allow'
- **infliger** (verb) means 'to impose' or 'to inflict'

Nous ne voulions pas l'admettre de peur que le juge ne nous inflige une amende.
We didn't want to admit it lest the judge impose a fine on us.

Il était à craindre que cette mesure temporaire ne devienne définitive.
It was feared that this temporary measure would become permanent.

Il ne doute pas qu'elle ne dise la vérité.
He does not doubt that she is telling the truth.

Nous ne doutons pas que nos voisins ne soient riches.
We have no doubt that our neighbors are rich.

Nous redoutons qu'il amène sa nouvelle petite amie à dîner.
We're dreading he's bringing his new girlfriend to dinner.

On a peur qu'ils ne le fassent.
We are afraid that they will do it.

On a peur qu'ils ne le fassent pas.
We're afraid they won't do it.

- Note that complete change in meaning with **pas**

Elle craint que je ne vienne.
She is afraid that I will come.

Elle craint que je ne vienne pas.
She is afraid that I will not come.

- Note that complete change in meaning with **pas**

❖ Subjunctive conjunctions with and without the *ne explétif*

This topic introduces four more conjunctions that may or may not require the **ne explétif**.

These first three all requires the **ne explétif**:

- **à moins que** - 'unless'
- **éviter que** - 'avoid that'
- **empêcher que** - 'prevent that'

And **sans que** ('without (doing)') typically does not take the **ne explétif** unless the main verb is negated and then still only optional.

EXAMPLES:

Je n'irai pas, à moins que vous ne veniez.
I won't go unless you (formal) come.

Quitte-la, à moins que tu l'aimes toujours.
Leave her, unless you (familiar) still love her.

Je te fais confiance, à moins que tu ne me mentes.
I trust you unless you (familiar) lie to me.

Évitons que la situation ne dégénère !
Let's prevent the situation from degenerating!

Évitez qu'il ne vous voie.
Avoid that he sees you (formal).

Elle empêche que la porte ne se ferme.
She prevents the door from closing.

Il veut éviter que cela n'arrive.
He wants to prevent that from happening.

Il porte un masque afin d'empêcher qu'il soit reconnu.
He wears a mask to prevent him from being recognized.

Notre priorité est d'empêcher que la rivière ne déborde.
Our priority is to prevent the river flooding.

📖 **déborder(verb)** means 'to flood' or 'to overflow'

TOPIC 220 ❖ Subjunctive conjunctions with and without the *ne explétif*

J'ai réussi sans qu'ils le veuillent.
I succeeded without them wanting it.

Ça fait une journée sans qu'il ait mangé.
It has been one day without him having eaten.

Il est venu sans que nous le sachions.
He came without us knowing (it).

Elle ne viendra pas sans qu'on ne l'invite.
She won't come unless we invite her.
   💡 The **ne explétif** can optionally be included since the **venir** in the main clause is negated

❖ Before and after - *avant que* & *après que*

When used as simple adverbs **avant** and **après** both take a noun or an infinitive verb.
- Note however that it is **avant de** before a verb.

When used as conjunctions **avant que** and **après que** are treated differently:
- **avant que** ('before doing') takes the subjunctive with the **ne explétif**.
- **après que** ('after doing') takes indicative.

EXAMPLES:

Il nous faudra aller chercher Jacques après le déjeuner.
We'll have to pick up Jacques after lunch.
💡 **après** taking a noun

Après son départ, j'ai pleuré pendant des jours.
After he left, I cried for days.
💡 **après** taking a noun

Je déballerai les sacs après notre retour du magasin.
I will unpack the bags after we return from the store.
💡 **après** taking a noun

Nous viendrons après avoir fait la vaisselle.
We'll come after we've done the dishes.
💡 **après** taking an infinitive verb

Quelques semaines après être tombé malade, il est décédé.
A few weeks after falling ill, he died.
💡 **après** taking an infinitive verb

Avant les vacances, j'ai beaucoup de choses à faire.
Before the holidays, I have a lot of things to do.
💡 **avant** taking a noun

J'ai pris les clés avant d'aller au magasin.
I took the keys before going to the store.
💡 **avant** taking a noun

TOPIC 221 ❖ Before and after - *avant que* & *après que*

N'oubliez pas de me prévenir avant de partir.
Don't forget (formal) to let me know before you leave.

💡 *avant de* taking a infinitive verb

Je voulais tout maîtriser avant de tenter de le faire seul.
I wanted to master everything before trying to do it alone.

💡 *avant de* taking a infinitive verb

✏ *tenter* (verb) means 'to try' or 'to attempt' or 'yo tempt'

Tu partiras avant que je puisse te dire « au revoir ».
You (familiar) will leave before I can say 'goodbye' to you.

💡 *avant que* takes the subjunctive

Avant que vous ne preniez une décision, n'oubliez pas de parler à Jacques.
Before you (formal) make a decision don't forget to talk to Jacques.

💡 *avant que* takes the subjunctive

Nous sommes arrivés avant qu'il ne soit trop tard !
We arrived before it was too late!

💡 *avant que* takes the subjunctive

Je veux lire ta lettre avant que tu ne le lui envoies.
I want to read your (familiar) letter before you send it to him.

💡 *avant que* takes the subjunctive

Avant de n'en prendre qu'un, pensez à en prendre un autre également.
Before taking just one, consider (formal) taking another one as well.

💡 *avant que* takes the subjunctive

Avant que nous ne commencions, je voudrais vous remercier.
Before we begin, I would like to thank you (formal).

💡 *avant que* takes the subjunctive

Il viendra te voir avant que tu ne partes.
He will come to see you (familiar) before you leave.

💡 *avant que* takes the subjunctive

Avant que je n'aille chez ma mère, je dois acheter des fleurs.
Before I go to my mother, I have to buy flowers.

💡 *avant que* takes the subjunctive

Mes amis sont arrivés avant que je n'aie fini mes devoirs.
My friends arrived before I finished my homework.

💡 *avant que* takes the subjunctive

TOPIC 221 ❖ Before and after - *avant que* & *après que*

Je ferai la vaisselle après que tu auras regardé la télé.
I'll do the dishes after you (familiar) watch TV.
💡 **après que** takes the indicative

Après que j'ai parlé avec lui, j'étais bouleversé.
After I spoke with him, I was upset.
💡 **après que** takes the indicative
📖 **bouleverser** (verb) means 'to be moved deeply' or 'to over turn'

Après que nous avons visité la France, nous avons commencé à apprendre le français.
After we visited France, we started to learn French.
💡 **après que** takes the indicative

Nous dînerons après que le film sera terminé.
We'll have dinner after the movie is over.
💡 **après que** takes the indicative

Bootstrap French
TOPIC 222

❖ To have to - *avoir à*

Another example of a preposition changing the meaning of a verb is **avoir à**. When used as an auxiliary verb **avoir à** means 'to have to' (do something). **Avoir à** is similar to the verb **devoir**.

EXAMPLES:

Nous avons à parler français à l'école.
We have to speak French at school.

J'ai à vous remercier.
I have you (formal) to thank.

J'ai à vous parler, c'est urgent.
I have to talk to you (formal), it's urgent.

Il a à choisir.
He has to choose.

Tu n'as pas à t'excuser.
You (familiar) do not have to apologize.

Vous n'avez qu'à lui demander.
You (formal) just have to ask him.

Tu n'as pas à me poser des questions.
You (familiar) do not have to ask me questions.
💡 The sense here is 'you should not be asking me...'

Tu n'as pas à avoir honte.
You (familiar) don't have to be ashamed.

Je vais le dire dans sa langue pour qu'il n'ait pas à écouter l'interprétation.
I'll say it in his language so he doesn't have to listen to the interpretation.

Faites en sorte qu'il n'ait pas à regretter sa bonté.
Make sure he doesn't have to regret his kindness.

❖ Direct and indirect speech - *il dit que...*

Indirect (or reported) speech is when someone reports what has been said.

Like in English we can simply put the verbatim phrase in inverted commas (called **les guillemets** in French). This is referred to a 'direct speech'.

Alternatively, we can report the speech as a subordinate clause using **dire que** etc.

If the 'reporting' verb (eg. **Il dit: « »**) is in **le present**, the tense in the subordinate clause in indirect speech remains unchanged.

However for any other tenses there need to be agreement. The rules are as follows:

- (direct) present tense ⇒ (indirect) present tense
- (direct) **passé composé** ⇒ (indirect) **plus que parfait**
- (direct) **futur simple** ⇒ (indirect) **conditionnel present**

This very similar to what is done in English.

Additionally, regardless of the reporting tense:

- (direct) imperative ⇒ (indirect) infinitive

EXAMPLES:

Patrice dit : « J'ai faim. »
Patrice says, 'I'm hungry.'
💡 present & present

Patrice dit qu'il a faim.
Patrice says he's hungry.
💡 present reporting so no change to the subordinate clause tense

Patrice dit : « J'ai eu faim toute la journée d'hier. »
Patrice says, 'I was hungry all day yesterday.'
💡 present & passé composé

Patrice dit qu'il a eu faim toute la journée d'hier.
Patrice says he was hungry all day yesterday.
💡 present reporting so no change to the subordinate clause tense

Patrice dit : « J'aurai bientôt encore faim. »
Patrice says, 'I'll soon be hungry again.'
💡 present & futur simple

TOPIC 223 ❖ Direct and indirect speech - *il dit que...*

Patrice dit qu'il aura bientôt encore faim.
Patrice says he will soon be hungry again.
 💡 **present** reporting so no change to the subordinate clause tense

Patrice dit : « J'aurais bientôt de nouveau faim si je n'avais pas mangé le matin. »
Patrice says, 'I would soon be hungry again if I hadn't eaten in the morning.'
 💡 **present** & **conditionel**

Patrice dit qu'il aurait bientôt de nouveau faim s'il n'avait pas mangé le matin. »
Patrice says he would soon be hungry again if he hadn't eaten in the morning.'
 💡 **present** reporting so no change to the subordinate clause tense

Patrice a dit : « J'ai faim. »
Patrice said, 'I'm hungry.'
 💡 **Passé composé** & **present**

Patrice a dit qu'il avait faim.
Patrice said he was hungry.
 💡 **Passé composé** reporting so **present** ⇒ **imparfait** in the subordinate clause

Patrice a dit « J'ai eu faim toute la journée d'hier. »
Patrice said, 'I was hungry all day yesterday.'
 💡 **Passé composé** & **passé composé**

Patrice a dit qu'il avait eu faim toute la journée d'hier.
Patrice said he was hungry all day yesterday.
 💡 **Passé composé** reporting so **passé composé** ⇒ **plus que parfait** in the subordinate clause

Patrice a dit « J'aurai bientôt encore faim. »
Patrice said, 'I will soon be hungry again.'
 💡 **Passé composé** & **futur simple**

Patrice a dit qu'il aurait bientôt de nouveau faim.
Patrice said he would soon be hungry again.
 💡 **Passé composé** reporting so **futur simple** ⇒ **conditionel** in the subordinate clause

Les touristes m'ont demandé : « Où sont les toilettes ? »
Tourists asked me, 'Where are the toilets?'

Les touristes me demandent où sont les toilettes.
Tourists ask me where the toilets are.

TOPIC 223 ❖ Direct and indirect speech - *il dit que...*

Marie dit : « Mes amis sont en retard et ils me rendront visite demain. »
Marie said, 'My friends are late and they will visit me tomorrow.'

Marie dit que ses amis sont en retard et qu'ils lui rendront visite demain.
Marie says her friends are late and they will visit her tomorrow.

Il raconte : « Je pense à elle depuis hier. »
He says, 'I have been thinking about her since yesterday.'

Il raconte qu'il pense à elle depuis hier.
He says he has been thinking about her since yesterday.

Il a dit : « J'ai vu une animatrice de télé. »
He said, 'I saw a TV host. '

Il a dit qu'il avait vu une animatrice de télé.
He said he had seen a TV host.

Il a remarqué : « Elle a été très aimable avec moi. »
He remarked, 'She was very kind to me. '

Il a remarqué qu'elle avait été très aimable avec lui.
He noticed that she had been very kind to him.

J'ai demandé : « T'a-t-elle donné un pourboire ? »
I asked, 'Did she tip you (familiar)?'

J'ai demandé si elle lui avait donné un pourboire.
I asked if she had given him a tip.

Il a affirmé : « Un jour, je serai animateur de télé. »
He claimed: 'One day I will be a TV host.'

Il a affirmé qu'un jour, il serait animateur de télé.
He said that one day he would be a TV host.

J'ai demandé : « Arrêtez de vous plaindre ! »
I asked, 'Stop complaining!'

  ♀ passé composé & imperative

Je lui ai demandé d'arrêter de se plaindre.
I asked him to stop complaining.

  ♀ passé composé reporting so imperative ⇒ infinitive in the subordinate clause

❖ Common French Idioms

A collection of common French idioms. Each example's note gives the literal translation.

EXAMPLES:

Balayer devant sa porte.
Practice what you preach. *OR* Put our own house in order first.
💡 Literally 'Sweep in front of one's door.'

Chercher midi à 14h.
Complicate the issue.
💡 Literally 'To look for noon to 2 p.m.'

Avoir un compte à régler avec quelqu'un.
Have a bone to pick with someone.
💡 Literally 'To have a score to settle with someone.'

Monter sur ses grands chevaux.
Get on one's high horse.
💡 Literally 'Get on his big horse.'

Marcher sur des œufs.
Walk on eggshells.
💡 Literally 'Walk on eggs.'

Trembler comme une feuille.
To shake like a leaf. *OR* To be quaking in one's shoes.
💡 Literally 'Shake like a leaf.'

Être comme un poisson dans l'eau.
Like a duck to water.
💡 Literally 'To be like a fish in water.'

Reculer pour mieux sauter.
To make a strategic withdrawal. *OR* To delay the inevitable.
💡 Literally 'Back up to jump better.'

Être fait comme un rat.
Be trapped like a rat.
💡 Literally 'To be done like a rat.'

TOPIC 224 ❖ Common French Idioms

Mieux vaut être seul que mal accompagné.
Better be alone than in bad company.
- Literally 'Better alone than in a bad comapny.'

On n'est jamais mieux servi que par soi-même.
If you want a thing done well, do it yourself.
- Literally 'You are never better served than by yourself.'

Chacun pour soi, et Dieu pour tous.
Every man for himself and the devil take the hindmost.
- Literally 'Each for himself, and God for all.'

L'habit ne fait pas le moine.
You can't judge a book by its cover.
- Literally 'The clothing doesn't make the monk.'

Être comme chien et chat.
Fight like cat and dog.
- Literally 'To be like dog and cat.'

Qui vole un œuf vole un bœuf.
Once a thief, always a thief.
- Literally 'Whoever steals an egg steals an ox.'

On ne mélange pas les torchons avec les serviettes.
Don't apples and oranges.
- Literally 'Do not mix tea towels with towels.'

À quelque chose malheur est bon.
Every cloud has a silver lining.
- Literally 'A misfortune is good for something.'

Être aux abonnés absents
To be absent
- Literally 'To be absent subscribers.'
- Harks back to the now-defunct French internet service

Se mettre le doigt dans l'œil.
Be entirely mistaken.
- Literally 'To put one's finger in one's eye.'

C'est la fin des haricots !
Game over! *OR* The goose is cooked!
- Literally 'It is the end of beans !'

TOPIC 224 ❖ Common French Idioms

Faut pas pousser mémé dans les orties.
Don't push it. *OR* To go too far.

💡 Literally 'Shouldn't push even in the nettles.'

En faire tout un plat.
Make a big deal out of something.

💡 Literally 'To do it all on a plate.'

Ne pas casser trois pattes à un canard.
Nothing to write home about. *OR* To make a big deal out of nothing.

💡 Literally 'Don't break the three feet of a duck.'

Qui sème le vent récolte la tempête.
As you sow so shall you reap.

💡 Literally 'Who sows the wind reaps the whirlwind.'

L'argent ne fait pas le bonheur, mais il y contribue.
Money can't buy happiness.

💡 Literally 'Money does not buy happiness, but it contributes.'

Donner, c'est donner ; reprendre, c'est voler.
One can't take back what one has given.

💡 Literally 'To give is to give
💡 to take back is to steal.'

Tourner sept fois sa langue dans sa bouche avant de parler.
Think twice before you speak.

💡 Literally 'Turn your tongue seven times in your mouth before speaking.'

Other French learning mobile apps

Declan Software also offers two more mobile French language learning apps:

Words: Language FlashCards

Learn 4400 of the most useful and common French words. Words are organised by topic with high quality native speaker audio. Start by reviewing the words and then jump into the exercises - multiple choice, spelling, listening and more.

Phrases: Language Immersion

Immerse yourself in French using repetition, reinforcement, and memorization to develop an intuitive feel for the language. The app features over 1500 common colloquial French phrases organised into topics and all with native speaker audio pronunciation. Language acquisition is re-enforced with exercises that emphasise reiterative exposure to each phrase, and most especially repeated exposure to the phrase's pronunciation.

www.ingramcontent.com/pod-product-compliance
Lightning Source LLC
Chambersburg PA
CBHW081142290426
44108CB00018B/2417